References for the Rest of Us

COMPUTER BOOK SERIES FROM IDG

Are you intimidated and confused by computers? Do you find that traditional manuals are overloaded with technical details you'll never use? Do your friends and family always call you to fix simple problems on their PCs? Then the *"... For Dummies"™* computer book series from IDG is for you.

"... For Dummies" books are written for those frustrated computer users who know they aren't really dumb but find that PC hardware, software, and indeed the unique vocabulary of computing make them feel helpless. *"... For Dummies"* books use a lighthearted approach, a down-to-earth style, and even cartoons and humorous icons to diffuse computer novices' fears and build their confidence. Lighthearted but not lightweight, these books are a perfect survival guide to anyone forced to use a computer.

"I like my copy so much I told friends; now they bought copies."

Irene C., Orwell, Ohio

"Quick, concise, nontechnical, and humorous."

Jay A., Elburn, IL

"Thanks, I needed this book. Now I can sleep at night."

Robin F., British Columbia, Canada

Already, hundreds of thousands of satisfied readers agree. They have made *"... For Dummies"* books the #1 introductory level computer book series and have written asking for more. So if you're looking for the most fun and easy way to learn about computers look to *"... For Dummies"* books to give you a helping hand.

IDG BOOKS

MORE WORDPERFECT 6 FOR DOS FOR DUMMIES™

MORE WORDPERFECT 6 FOR DOS FOR DUMMIES™

by Wallace Wang

Edited by Dan Gookin

IDG BOOKS

IDG Books Worldwide, Inc.
An International Data Group Company

San Mateo, California ♦ Indianapolis, Indiana ♦ Boston, Massachusetts

MORE WordPerfect 6 For DOS For Dummies

Published by
IDG Books Worldwide, Inc.
An International Data Group Company
155 Bovet Road, Suite 310
San Mateo, CA 94402

Library of Congress Catalog Card No.: 93-81200

ISBN: 1-56884-047-0

Printed in the United States of America

10 9 8 7 6 5 4 3 2 1

1D/QV/SV/ZU

Distributed in the United States by IDG Books Worldwide, Inc.

Distributed in Canada by Macmillan of Canada, a Division of Canada Publishing Corporation; by Computer and Technical Books in Miami, Florida, for South America and the Caribbean; by Longman Singapore in Singapore, Malaysia, Thailand, and Korea; by Toppan Co. Ltd. in Japan; by Asia Computerworld in Hong Kong; by Woodslane Pty. Ltd. in Australia and New Zealand; and by Transword Publishers Ltd. in the U.K. and Europe.

For general information on IDG Books in the U.S., including information on discounts and premiums, contact IDG Books at 800-762-2974 or 415-312-0650.

For information on where to purchase IDG Books outside the U.S., contact Christina Turner at 415-312-0633.

For information on translations, contact Marc Jeffrey Mikulich, Foreign Rights Manager, at IDG Books Worldwide; FAX NUMBER 415-358-1260.

For sales inquiries and special prices for bulk quantities, write to the address above or call IDG Books Worldwide at 415-312-0650.

About the Author

Wallace Wang

Wallace Wang, author of *Visual Basic 3 For Dummies* and coauthor of *The Illustrated Dictionary For Dummies,* both published by IDG Books, writes a bi-weekly column for programmers in Computer Edge Magazine and writes software reviews for stand-up comedians and comedy writers in a monthly comedy newsletter. He also performs stand-up comedy at night, teaches computer classes during the day, and once taught at the University of Zimbabwe, where he slept in a hut and wild monkeys stole his breakfast. When he's not busy writing computer books and magazine articles, Wallace is busy running a BBS, writing jokes, and infecting an old 386 with computer viruses just to see what'll happen next.

About IDG Books Worldwide

Welcome to the world of IDG Books Worldwide.

IDG Books Worldwide, Inc., is a subsidiary of International Data Group, the world's largest publisher of computer-related information and the leading global provider of information services on information technology. International Data Group publishes over 200 computer publications in 63 countries. Forty million people read one or more International Data Group publications each month.

If you use personal computers, IDG Books is committed to publishing quality books that meet your needs. We rely on our extensive network of publications, including such leading periodicals as *Macworld*, *InfoWorld*, *PC World*, *Computerworld*, *Publish*, *Network World*, and *SunWorld*, to help us make informed and timely decisions in creating useful computer books that meet your needs.

Every IDG book strives to bring extra value and skill-building instructions to the reader. Our books are written by experts, with the backing of IDG periodicals, and with careful thought devoted to issues such as audience, interior design, use of icons, and illustrations. Our editorial staff is a careful mix of high-tech journalists and experienced book people. Our close contact with the makers of computer products helps ensure accuracy and thorough coverage. Our heavy use of personal computers at every step in production means we can deliver books in the most timely manner.

We are delivering books of high quality at competitive prices on topics customers want. At IDG, we believe in quality, and we have been delivering quality for over 25 years. You'll find no better book on a subject than an IDG book.

John Kilcullen
President and CEO
IDG Books Worldwide, Inc.

IDG Books Worldwide, Inc. is a subsidiary of International Data Group. The officers are Patrick J. McGovern, Founder and Board Chairman; Walter Boyd, President. International Data Group's publications include: **ARGENTINA'S** Computerworld Argentina, Infoworld Argentina; **AUSTRALIA'S** Computerworld Australia, Australian PC World, Australian Macworld, Network World, Mobile Business Australia, Reseller, IDG Sources; **AUSTRIA'S** Computerwelt Oesterreich, PC Test; **BRAZIL'S** Computerworld, Gamepro, Game Power, Mundo IBM, Mundo Unix, PC World, Super Game; **BELGIUM'S** Data News (CW) **BULGARIA'S** Computerworld Bulgaria, Ediworld, PC & Mac World Bulgaria, Network World Bulgaria; **CANADA'S** CIO Canada, Computerworld Canada, Graduate Computerworld, InfoCanada, Network World Canada; **CHILE'S** Computerworld Chile, Informatica; **COLOMBIA'S** Computerworld Colombia, PC World; **CZECH REPUBLIC'S** Computerworld, Elektronika, PC World; **DENMARK'S** Communications World, Computerworld Danmark, Macintosh Produktkatalog, Macworld Danmark, PC World Danmark, PC World Produktguide, Tech World, Windows World; **ECUADOR'S** PC World Ecuador; **EGYPT'S** Computerworld (CW) Middle East, PC World Middle East; **FINLAND'S** MikroPC, Tietoviikko, Tietoverkko; **FRANCE'S** Distributique, GOLDEN MAC, InfoPC, Languages & Systems, Le Guide du Monde Informatique, Le Monde Informatique, Telecoms & Reseaux; **GERMANY'S** Computerwoche, Computerwoche Focus, Computerwoche Extra, Computerwoche Karriere, Information Management, Macwelt, Netzwelt, PC Welt, PC Woche, Publish, Unit; **GREECE'S** Infoworld, PC Games; **HUNGARY'S** Computerworld SZT, PC World; **HONG KONG'S** Computerworld Hong Kong, PC World Hong Kong; **INDIA'S** Computers & Communications; **IRELAND'S** ComputerScope; **ISRAEL'S** Computerworld Israel, PC World Israel; **ITALY'S** Computerworld Italia, Lotus Magazine, Macworld Italia, Networking Italia, PC Shopping, PC World Italia; **JAPAN'S** Computerworld Today, Information Systems World, Macworld Japan, Nikkei Personal Computing, SunWorld Japan, Windows World; **KENYA'S** East African Computer News; **KOREA'S** Computerworld Korea, Macworld Korea, PC World Korea; **MEXICO'S** Compu Edicion, Compu Manufactura, Computacion/Punto de Venta, Computerworld Mexico, MacWorld, Mundo Unix, PC World, Windows; **THE NETHERLANDS'** Computer! Totaal, Computable (CW), LAN Magazine, MacWorld, Totaal "Windows"; **NEW ZEALAND'S** Computer Listings, Computerworld New Zealand, New Zealand PC World, Network World; **NIGERIA'S** PC World Africa; **NORWAY'S** Computerworld Norge, C/World, Lotusworld Norge, Macworld Norge, Networld, PC World Ekspress, PC World Norge, PC World's Produktguide, Publish& Multimedia World, Student Data, Unix World, Windowsworld; IDG Direct Response; **PAKISTAN'S** PC World Pakistan; **PANAMA'S** PC World Panama; **PERU'S** Computerworld Peru, PC World; **PEOPLE'S REPUBLIC OF CHINA'S** China Computerworld, China Infoworld, Electronics Today/Multimedia World, Electronics International, Electronic Product World, China Network World, PC and Communications Magazine, PC World China, Software World Magazine, Telecom Product World; IDG HIGH TECH BEIJING'S New Product World; IDG SHENZHEN'S Computer News Digest; **PHILIPPINES'** Computerworld Philippines, PC Digest (PCW); **POLAND'S** Computerworld Poland, PC World/Komputer; **PORTUGAL'S** Cerebro/PC World, Correio Informatico/Computerworld, Informatica & Comunicacoes Catalogo, MacIn, Nacional de Produtos; **ROMANIA'S** Computerworld, PC World; **RUSSIA'S** Computerworld-Moscow, Mir - PC, Sety; **SINGAPORE'S** Computerworld Southeast Asia, PC World Singapore; **SLOVENIA'S** Monitor Magazine; **SOUTH AFRICA'S** Computer Mail (CIO),Computing S.A.,Network World S.A., Software World; **SPAIN'S** Advanced Systems, Amiga World, Computerworld Espana, Communicaciones World, Macworld Espana, NeXTWORLD, Super Juegos Magazine (GamePro), PC World Espana, Publish; **SWEDEN'S** Attack, ComputerSweden, Corporate Computing, Natverk & Kommunikation, Macworld, Mikrodatorn, PC World, Publishing & Design (CAP), DataIngenjoren, Maxi Data,Windows World; **SWITZERLAND'S** Computerworld Schweiz, Macworld Schweiz, PC Tip; **TAIWAN'S** Computerworld Taiwan, PC World Taiwan; **THAILAND'S** Thai Computerworld; **TURKEY'S** Computerworld Monitor, Macworld Turkiye, PC World Turkiye; **UKRAINE'S** Computerworld; **UNITED KINGDOM'S** Computing /Computerworld, Connexion/Network World, Lotus Magazine, Macworld, Open Computing/Sunworld; **UNITED STATES'** Advanced Systems, AmigaWorld, Cable in the Classroom, CD Review, CIO, Computerworld, Digital Video, DOS Resource Guide, Electronic Entertainment Magazine, Federal Computer Week, Federal Integrator, GamePro, IDG Books, Infoworld, Infoworld Direct, Laser Event, Macworld, Multimedia World, Network World, PC Letter, PC World, PlayRight, Power PC World, Publish, SWATPro, Video Event; **VENEZUELA'S** Computerworld Venezuela, PC World; **VIETNAM'S** PC World Vietnam

Acknowledgments

This book actually had a top-secret, WordPerfect-approved advisor working on the project. I can't mention his name because he'd get into serious trouble if I did. But he knows who he is, and I'd definitely like to thank him for his marvelous and insightful contributions.

I'd also like to thank Lauren Straub, who is now working as a fully corrupted member of the media at a large Los Angeles newspaper, for her wondrous contributions to this text. Resume Speed will miss her input.

Thanks to Bo the cat. Purr on.

Thanks to Matt Wagner at Waterside Productions for eventually realizing the magnitude of this project and for his mildly toned words of advice.

Thanks to Dan Gookin, and at IDG Books, thanks to Kezia Endsley, Barbara Potter, Corbin Collins, Mary Corder, Erik Dafforn, Leigh Davis, Shawn MacLaren, Bill Barton, and others who contributed to this undertaking.

(The publisher would like to give special thanks to Patrick McGovern, without whom this book would not have been possible.)

Credits

Publisher
David Solomon

Managing Editor
Mary Bednarek

Acquisitions Editor
Janna Custer

Production Director
Beth Jenkins

Senior Editors
Sandra Blackthorn
Diane Graves Steele
Tracy L. Barr

Production Coordinator
Cindy L. Phipps

Associate Acquisitions Editor
Megg Bonar

Editorial Assistant
Jodi Thorn

Project Editors
Kezia Endsley
Corbin Collins

Editor
Barbara L. Potter

Technical Reviewer
Michael Partington, Partington Design

Production Staff
Tony Augsburger
Valery Bourke
Mary Breidenbach
Chris Collins
Sherry Gomoll
Drew Moore
Kathie Schnorr

Proofreader
Chuck Hutchinson

Indexer
Sherry Massey

Book Design
University Graphics

Cover Design
Kavish + Kavish

Contents at a Glance

Cartoons at a Glance

By Rich Tennant

page 376

page 377

page 49

page 7

page 391

page 281

page 250

page 225

page 123

page xxvi

Table of Contents

Part III: WordPerfect Macro Land....................................225

The 5th Wave
By Rich Tennant
Rumors that there won't be another upgrade to
WordPerfect for DOS are traced to Larry.

Introduction

Welcome to *MORE WordPerfect 6 For DOS For Dummies*, a book that's not afraid to say, "There's even more to WordPerfect and here's the best way to understand it without frying your brain."

This book is the product of a dilemma. Obviously there's a lot to WordPerfect — even more than could be fit into this book. So, as a follow-on to the successful *WordPerfect 6 for Dummies*, I had to do a lot of picking and choosing between what was vital, what was fun, and what wasn't at all even necessary. You'll find the results in this book, which contains a lot of interesting and occasionally obtuse (but always useful) stuff you can do with WordPerfect.

Like all the Dummies books, this book informs and entertains. Please keep in mind that the topic here isn't "Let's all *love* WordPerfect." That's sick. Instead, be prepared to encounter some informative, down-to-earth explanations — in English — of how to do more with the program that you already use as a word processor. And please don't take WordPerfect too seriously.

About This Book

This book is a reference. Please don't read everything here cover to cover. Instead, think of a topic that piques your interest, look it up in the Table of Contents or Index, turn to that page, and start reading.

This book is organized into various sections or modules. The chapters cover general topics, and the sections go into detail on various subjects related to those topics. Sample sections in *MORE WordPerfect 6 for Dummies* include:

- Rolling Your Own Keyboard
- How to Draw a Line
- Recording Macros (the Easy Method)
- Jumping from Here to There with Hypertext

Each section contains useful examples and descriptions of how to carry out some of the more complex tasks. Tips and such are offered throughout the book (especially in Chapter 27). Technical information, where necessary or appropriate, has been shoved off into gray boxes which you don't have to read if you don't want to.

How to Use This Book

WordPerfect uses *key combinations,* several keys you may press together or in sequence to get the job done. This book shows you those key combinations in the following manner:

Shift-F7, C, Enter

This means you should press and hold both the Shift key and the F7 key. Release both keys. Then press the C key. Then press the Enter key. ***Note:*** Don't type the commas or any period that ends a sentence.

Any details about what you type or what happens after you type it are explained in the text.

This book never refers you to the WordPerfect manual or — yech! — to the DOS manual. It *does* refer you to a companion book in this series, *WordPerfect 6 for Dummies*, published by IDG Books Worldwide. A lot of the basic word-processing concepts are addressed in that book and are not repeated here because, well, I thought I'd be original here. (You *may* also need *DOS for Dummies*, also published by IDG Books Worldwide, as a reference.)

Foolish Assumptions

Here are my assumptions about you:

- You use a computer and you use WordPerfect, specifically version 6.0, the DOS version.
- You have this book's progenitor, *WordPerfect 6 For Dummies*. This book builds upon the concepts presented in that book, but there's really little overlap. (Actually, I *could* do a third book on WordPerfect's macros and maybe even a few other key topics, but I really don't want to.)
- You use WordPerfect 6 in the Page or Graphics mode. This is vital. Most of the good stuff can only be seen in that mode. If you're using WordPerfect 6 in Text mode, you're missing a lot.
- Although this book does work as advertised without a mouse, I heartily suggest you get and use one in order to benefit from the features WordPerfect 6.0 attempts to offer.

How This Book Is Organized

This book contains five major Parts, each of which is divided into three or more chapters. The chapters themselves have been crafted into smaller, modular sections. You can pick up the book and read any section without necessarily knowing what has already been covered in the rest of the book. Start anywhere.

Here is a breakdown of the parts and what you find in them:

Part I: More on Stuff

This part contains chapters that offer information readers of the first book wanted "more" of: the document, interface, printing, lists, and on and on. There is much depth to even the basics of WordPerfect. This part rounds out that coverage.

Part II: Formatting for Fun and Profit

Formatting is the heart that beats in WordPerfect's massive chest. This part of the book goes into deep detail on how you can format your text, including such trivia as the Style command, DTP (desktop publishing) tricks, columns, math (yes, *math*), and graphics.

Part III: WordPerfect Macro Land

Run for the hills! It's macro time! Actually, this part of the book provides insight and a brief wade into the waters of WordPerfect's macros. Quite a few examples are presented here, though if you *really* want to go nuts with macros, I recommend that you obtain a book specific to that subject. Using macros is almost like programming the PC, which you'll see an example of in Chapter 17.

Part IV: Advanced, Ugly Tasks Carefully Explained

Advanced Ugly Tasks describes about 80 percent of what WordPerfect is up to. Word processing? That's easy. Try outlining, or the equation editor, envelopes, hypertext, or any of a number of features which you know are in there but which a paralyzing fear has prevented you from attempting. Until now.

Part V: Shortcuts and Tips Galore

This book ends with a bunch of interesting suggestions, tips, and a few trick-or-treats. It's a bonus section! Awarded to all the loyal *WordPerfect 6 for Dummies* readers who appreciated that book and wanted *MORE WordPerfect 6 for Dummies*.

Icons Used in This Book

This icon alerts you to overly nerdy information and technical discussions of the topic at hand.

This icon flags useful, helpful tips, or shortcuts.

This icon marks a friendly reminder to do something.

This icon marks a friendly reminder not to do something.

This icon flags information about using WordPerfect with a mouse.

This icon flags a command you can access from the menu.

This icon marks the occasional WordPerfect command that can be accessed from the standard Button Bar.

Where to Go from Here

My advice: Scour the Table of Contents for what you wanted *more* of in *WordPerfect 6 for Dummies*. It's in here, most likely. Otherwise, use the Index, or just pick a page and start reading. You're bound to find something that interest you.

- Don't forget to browse the checkmarks that end just about every section. They contain useful information that shouldn't be overlooked.
- I apologize in advance for the haphazard nature of this book. It was a real job trying to organize all the various and sundry things WordPerfect does and still not repeat what's already been said in *WordPerfect 6 for Dummies*. My only words to offer after *really* diving into this program are — to quote from Charlton Heston's masterful acting in just about any film he did in the 70s — *"Oh my God!"*
- Contrary to popular rumor, this guy was *not* drawn to resemble John Kilcullen, IDG Books Worldwide's president.

Part I
More on Stuff

The 5th Wave By Rich Tennant

In this part . . .

WordPerfect is a heck of a complex computer program that also doubles as a word processor. Indeed, *word processor* is to car as WordPerfect is to the entire area of transportation. Most people use it to process words, which is techno-talk for the art of writing. Oh, but that's just basic stuff. WordPerfect can do more than write. More! More! More! That is the gist of this part of the book; it covers all that *more stuff* that you knew was in there and terrified you. Well, now it's time to take a peek.

Chapter 1

More on the Pretty Interface

In This Chapter

- Creating the ideal WordPerfect setup (is it possible?)
- Changing the screen colors
- Making the perfect Button Bar
- Understanding the Ribbon
- Adding scroll bars
- Taking the bus tour of the Screen Setup dialog box

WordPerfect is like an ugly blind date who instantly takes to you. It gets right into the car and sits up close, touching you. You're a sport about it, but you're very careful not to get caught in a tunnel behind a wobbly hydrogen truck lest it explode and you have to spend tedious hours in there, trapped and alone, trying to convince your date that you're not the last two living people on earth. Yeah, WordPerfect works something like that. A tenuous beauty at best, but getting better thanks to its changeable face, its *interface.*

An interface is the way a program presents itself to you — and it's supposed to be useful. All the pretty buttons, bars, ribbons, and gee-gaws WordPerfect lets you blithely slap on the screen are nothing more than obtrusive decorations if they don't make it easier to get your work done. If the interface stands between you and getting your work done, you can change it (which is like your date looking better after the hydrogen explosion). This chapter is about making WordPerfect's interface as functional as possible — not just pretty.

Creating the Ideal WordPerfect Setup

No, there isn't any ideal WordPerfect setup. The perfect setup is different for each person. Even your own idea of the perfect setup may change as you spend more time with WordPerfect. Fortunately, it's all controllable from a central place, the Setup dialog box (see Figure 1-1).

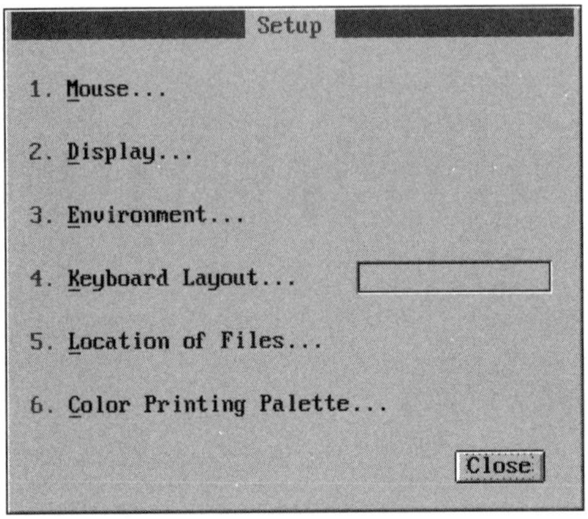

Figure 1-1: The Setup dialog box.

Of course, the Setup dialog box by itself is merely a road map. It's a menu that lists several salad bars where you can whip up your own WordPerfect salmagundi, exactly to your own tastes. It's a launch pad that detonates several other, complex dialog boxes that explode on-screen, complete with lists of WordPerfect's customizable options. Here is where you make your own WordPerfect perfect setup.

- Each of the options in this dialog box leads you to another dialog box, where you actually do something.
- Other setup dialog boxes are covered in the appropriate places. For example, the Print Setup dialog box is covered in Chapter 8. The Font Setup dialog box is covered in Chapter 9. The Screen Setup dialog box is covered later in this chapter.
- Fingers too short? Try Alt-F, T to see the Setup submenu, which contains the same options as in the Setup dialog box.
- Use setup options to make permanent or semipermanent changes to WordPerfect. You normally visit setup dialog boxes only once, and visit them again only if you want to change a setting. These settings aren't made for just the current document, but for all future documents.

Setting up video display nonsense

You may not remember, but when you bought your computer you paid a wee bit extra for some fancy graphics. The salesman smiled, patted you on the back, and remarked how clever you were because your PC would have better graphics than your neighbor Vern's did. Maybe you forgot that, but anyway now comes the time to prove it.

Everything you see on-screen is made up of a bunch of dots. The more dots, the better your text and graphics look. Your PC's video probably has the ability to put a better face on WordPerfect than you're seeing right now. To test this theory, follow these steps:

1. **Press Shift-F1, D.**

   The Display dialog box appears.

2. **Press G.**

   The Graphics Mode Screen Type/Colors dialog box pops up.

3. **Press S (Screen Type).**

   The Setup Graphics Screen Type dialog box appears.

4. **Use the up- and down-arrow keys to highlight the name of your PC's video thing.**

   For most of us, it will probably be IBM VGA or some other type of VGA card.

5. **Press Enter.**

   The Setup Graphics Screen Type dialog box displays a list of options, as shown in Figure 1-2.

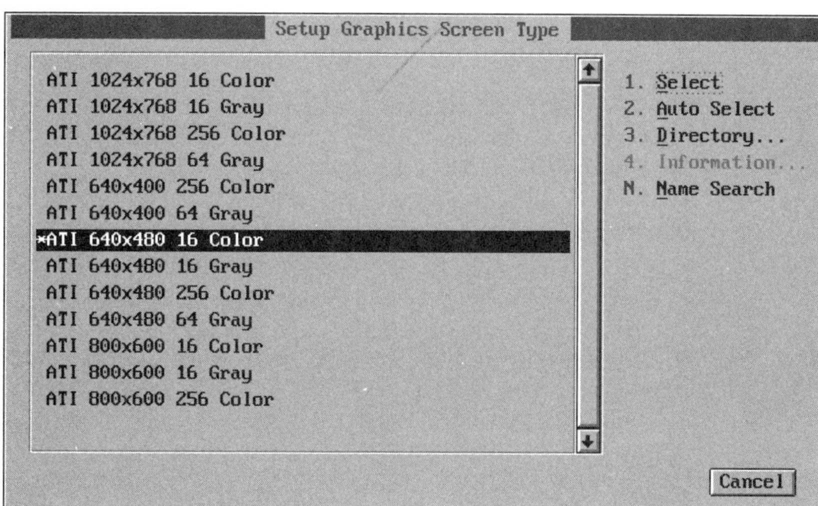

Figure 1-2: The Setup Graphics Screen Type dialog box.

6. **Use the up- and down-arrow keys to highlight the video quality (the number of dots) you want to use and press the Enter key.**

   You may be blessed and discover that a "higher resolution" is available. For example, you may see an 800 × 600 graphics mode where you only had 640 × 480 available before. If so, highlight that mode and press Enter. WordPerfect will respond by displaying more dots on-screen. The same goes with colors. If you see a 64 or 256 color mode, select it and you'll get a more colorful screen.

   If you don't know what monitor type or video circuitry you have, STOP! You can really mess things up by selecting a video setup you don't have. Get your PC guru to investigate your equipment and its capabilities for you.

7. **Press Home, F7.**

   Thwoop! Your choice is accepted, and the screen may go blank for a moment while WordPerfect resets the display. Eventually, you'll be back at your document, ready for work in a new graphics mode.

- Your list of options may be more limited than the one in Figure 1-2. The standard graphical resolution used by WordPerfect is 640 × 480. For higher resolutions you need to pay much more money for your PC's video system.
- The resolution and number of colors you choose have no effect on the way your documents print, only how they appear on-screen. Unfortunately, all the other screen elements — menus, buttons, scroll bars, and so on — do get smaller as your resolution gets higher. That's the breaks.
- Okay, wise guy, so you do have high-resolution graphics. One setback you may witness firsthand is that WordPerfect slows down a lot when you have higher resolution graphics. If performance suffers too much after selecting a higher resolution, back down to a lower resolution and learn to live with it.
- *Coaches* are some of the most helpful of the WordPerfect help features. Unfortunately, they don't work in any other resolution than 640 × 480. If you're using any other resolution, you need to follow the steps outlined in the preceding list to switch to 640 × 480 to use Coaches.

Boring information on other WordPerfect drivers you may have

Often when you buy a computer, you get a disk labeled Video Drivers or something technical. What that disk contains is a bunch of helper files for programs like WordPerfect. For example, my most recent PC came with a Video Drivers disk that came with a lot of fun stuff for WordPerfect, including special high-resolution graphics drivers.

Most of the time (hopefully) the Video Drivers disk will come with some sort of installation program. If not, you'll need to copy the WordPerfect files to WordPerfect's directory on your hard drive. (See *DOS 6 For Dummies* for help with copying files.) To get at the driver files, press Shift-F1, D, G, S, D. That complex sequence brings up a Directory for Graphics Files dialog box. It will display WordPerfect's directory; press Enter and select your drivers from the list.

Yeah, this is technical stuff and it may take you a few pokes before you get it right, but the results can be very nice.

Color your WordPerfect world

The concept of *color scheme* in WordPerfect used to imply whether or not your underline color was blue on white or orange on puce. Things change, and with version 6 of WordPerfect, you can really spruce up the display with lots of interesting colors. For example, you can be stuck with WordPerfect's basic color scheme, obviously inspired by the Navy, with gray, blue, and white. Or you can be bizarre and select another color scheme or dream up your own. This may not be central to using the program, but it's a heck of a time burner.

To change screen colors to one of the included color schemes, press Shift-F1, D, G, C. Use the up- and down-arrow keys to highlight the color scheme name you want to try. Just for kicks, check out Clown Town, which I think should be renamed Herman Munster. Press the Enter key and then press Home, F7 when you're done.

To create your own screen colors, press Shift-F1, D, G, C and then C again. Type a name for your color scheme — something like *Barforama* — and press Enter. You'll see a huge dialog box that shows you a list of things to color and a sample of how it will look (see Figure 1-3).

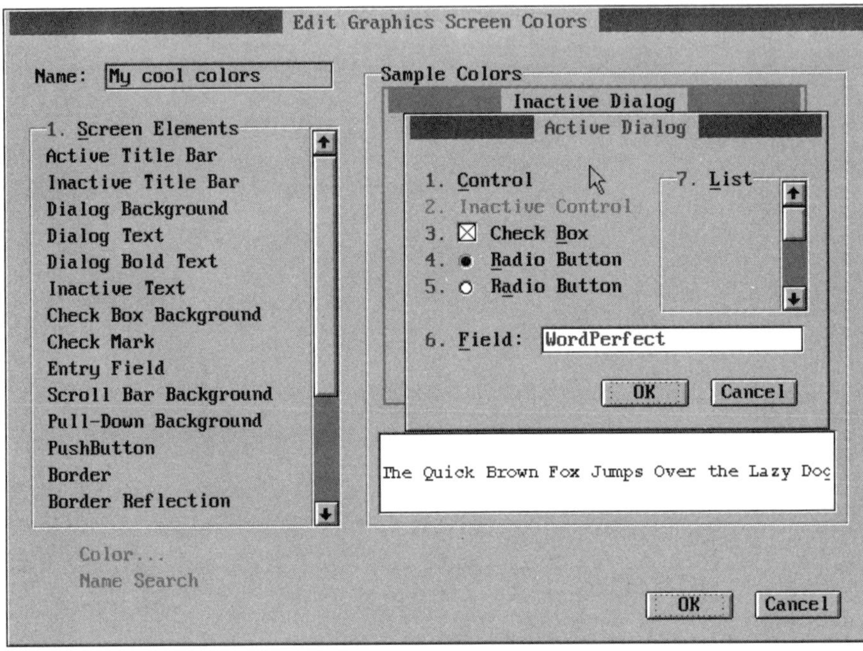

Figure 1-3: The Edit Graphics Screen Colors dialog box.

Press S to select the Screen Element dialog box and use the up- and down-arrow keys to select a screen element; then press C to set its color. The Colors dialog box appears, as shown in Figure 1-4.

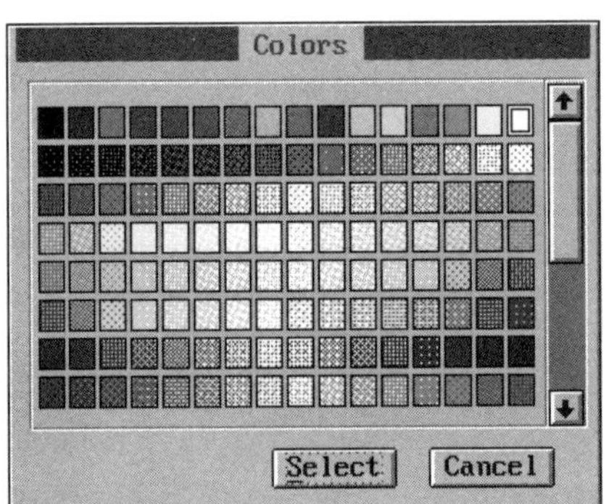

Figure 1-4: The Colors dialog box.

Remember that black light will not work on a computer screen. Press Home, F7 when your van Gogh is through.

- You can't tell from the color scheme names what god-awful color combinations they'll give you. You'll just have to try them out. Brace yourself.
- If you pick a color scheme that is truly awful and want things back the way they were, repeat the preceding steps and choose the WP Default color scheme.
- If you create your own color scheme, sleep well with the knowledge that the colors you choose don't affect the way your documents print, only how they look on-screen.

Taming your mouse

How many times have you pounded your mouse relentlessly into its fuzzy little mouse pad? Do your double clicks go like this: click-click, clickclickclick? Does the mouse pointer slip across the screen so quickly you can't keep up, or does it dawdle over each tiny pixel? Whatever the mouse woe, the Mouse setup will fix your rodent's behavior.

To open the Mouse setup dialog box, press Shift-F1, M — where the *M* means *Mouse*. See Figure 1-5.

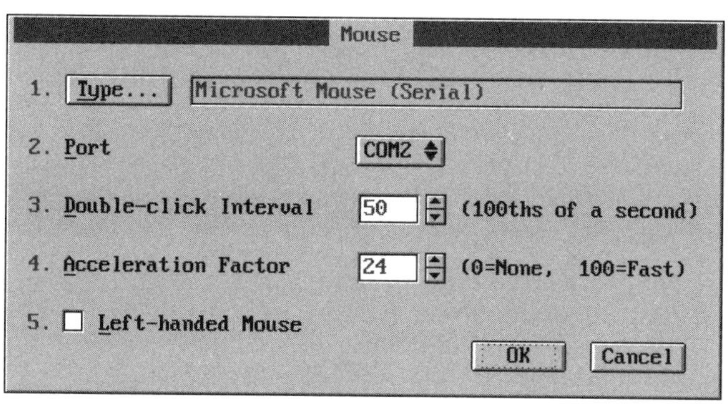

Figure 1-5: The Mouse setup dialog box.

Nod your head and stroke your beard as you ponder the Mouse dialog box. Then press the Enter key (or click the OK button) to accept any changes or press Escape (or click the Cancel button) if you were just fooling around. Mouse dialog box go away.

- If you don't have a mouse, get one. Mice make working with WordPerfect easier and — dare I say it — more fun.
- If you don't know all your mouse's details (and who would?), artfully persuade your PC guru to make any necessary changes for you.
- Press T to display a list of mouse types. Use the up- and down-arrow keys to highlight your mouse type and press the Enter key. Most of us are using Microsoft mouses (mice, meeses?). If you're unsure, press A for Auto Select, and WordPerfect psychically guesses your mouse type.
- If you have a serial mouse (meaning it's plugged into your PC's COM or serial port instead of a specific mouse port), press 2 and use the up- and down-arrow keys to specify the COM port where your mouse lives. As a suggestion, try to keep your mouse on COM1 or COM2. Most mice live on COM2.
- The Double-click Interval tells WordPerfect how long to wait for a click-click. Use a higher number, say 75 or 100, if you have trouble double-clicking. Later, you can reduce the number when your fingers heal, or the sedatives wear off. Press D, type a number (50 = 1/2 second allowed between clicks), and then press the Enter key.
- The Acceleration Factor controls the speed of the mouse, where 100 is zippy fast and 0 means the mouse is on Quaaludes. Press A to change the speed of the on-screen mouse pointer, and type a number (50 seems about right to me), and then press the Enter key.
- The Left-handed Mouse box is intended to make life easier for southpaws, who often hold the mouse in their left hand (gauche, but acceptable). Primarily, an X in the box there means you click the right mouse button instead of the left mouse button to get things done in WordPerfect.
- Get rid of the mouse driver (probably MOUSE.SYS or MOUSE.COM) in your PC's CONFIG.SYS or AUTOEXEC.BAT unless you need it there for other programs. WordPerfect doesn't need it. Getting rid of it and using one of WordPerfect's internal mouse drivers saves memory that WordPerfect can use for better performance. However . . .
- Don't get rid of the mouse driver in your PC's CONFIG.SYS or AUTOEXEC.BAT if you run WordPerfect within Windows. WordPerfect gets confused if it doesn't find an external mouse driver.

Environmental cleanup

When you can't think of anywhere to put something, you stuff it into a closet. With WordPerfect, the closet for various uncategorized setup options is called the Environment. It's a nice, wholesome name, but not truly appropriate because its dialog box is full of junk.

To open the Environment setup dialog box, press Shift-F1, E. The Environment dialog box muscles its way on-screen, as shown in Figure 1-6. Don't try to organize it in your brain. Don't try to make sense of it. The Environment dialog box, like a crowded closet, just is.

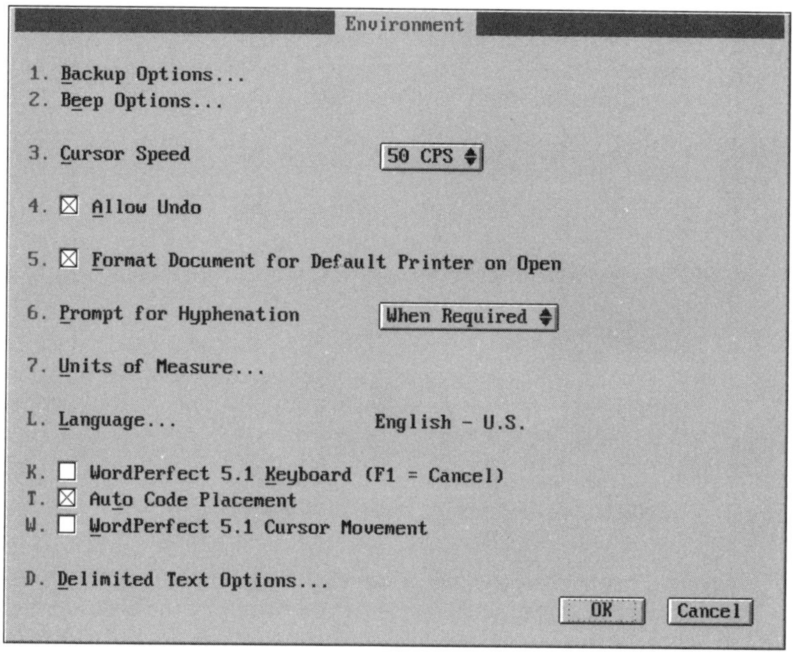

Figure 1-6: The Environment dialog box.

The following hoard of check mark items discusses various items you can set in the Environment dialog box. After you change the options you want to change, press Home, F7 to return to your document.

- Backup Options are the most important options in this dialog box. Setting them right can really be a blessing from beyond. See Chapter 2 for information on these not-to-be-missed features.
- Beep options are the least important options. Hey, right after the most important item in the dialog box comes the least important. Leave this one alone unless you want WordPerfect beeping at you all the time. Because you're usually awake and looking at the screen while using WordPerfect, forget the beeps.
- The Cursor Speed option lets you speed up or slow down how fast the cursor slips around your text when you hold down one of the arrow keys. The preset speed is 50. That's the fastest it'll go, but it's not so fast you'll lose control.

TIP

- Screens on some laptop computers have a nasty habit of losing the cursor as it zips across the screen. If you have one of those machines, slowing down the cursor may help. Press C to display a pop-up list of speed options and use the up arrow to highlight a lower number and press Enter.
- Allow Undo? YES! This is another of WordPerfect's lifesaving features. If Undo is turned off, there's no X in the box. Press A to put an X in the box to turn it on. (It may be off because you're using a particularly slow or memory-starved PC. If so, leave it off to save your precious memory — but check with your guru first to ensure that's the case.)
- Leave the X in the box in front of Format Document for Default Printer on Open. This option causes WordPerfect to correctly format documents you receive from other people using other printers. If there isn't an X in the box, press F.
- You can have WordPerfect prompt you before it inserts hyphens during its automatic hyphenation process. For more about the Prompt for Hyphenation option, see Chapter 4.
- Unless you're more comfortable working in centimeters or points than inches, leave the Units of Measure option alone. Inches is the way it's set and that's how it should stay, by gum.
- Language? If you think you need to change this option, you're reading the wrong translation of this book, *n'est pas*?
- The WordPerfect 5.1 Keyboard option causes a couple of the function keys and the Esc key to operate the way they did in the previous version of the program. *Don't use this option!* Even if the way the keys worked in 5.1 is burned into your brain, it's time to get over it. It's the 6.0 generation now.
- Auto Code Placement helps put WordPerfect's mysterious formatting codes where they belong. This is another of the new features in 6.0 that can drive 5.1 old-timers crazy. Leave it on anyway. For more information about codes and Auto Code Placement, see Chapter 4.
- WordPerfect 5.1 Cursor Movement. NO! The new method is better. It says so right in the WordPerfect 6.0 brochure. Better get used to the new way.
- Delimited Text Options? Huh? This has to do with getting WordPerfect to use information created in other programs for merging. Leave it alone until you need to send form letters to everyone on the corporate database. For more merge information, see Chapter 24.

Making the Perfect Button Bar

BUTTONS

WordPerfect's Button Bar can be a handy tool — but only if the buttons that live on the bar are useful to you. Otherwise, it's all flash and dazzle and, heck, if we wanted that, we'd be rolling the dice in Vegas right now and not word processing.

Good news: You don't need the Button Bar to write. Nope. Not at all. Press Alt-V, B to turn it off (or on — same command does it all).

Better news: You're not stuck with the buttons that appear on the standard Button Bar, which is called the WPMAIN Button Bar in case you didn't know. If you're interested, WordPerfect lets you select from a list of six other predefined and equally unimaginative Button Bars. Or, if you're feeling lucky, you can create your own Button Bar.

- Use Button Bar? Need mouse.
- Scroll buttons, on the left and right ends of the Button Bar, appear only if there are more buttons than can be viewed.
- Change the location of your Button Bar to make room for more buttons. Press Alt-V, S, O to display the Button Bar Options dialog box. Click Left Side or Right Side to display the Button Bar vertically. Then click Text Only if you desire to banish the cryptic pictures. Finally, click the OK button.
- Special Button Bars appear automatically when you're working in Print Preview or the Image Editor. Both of these special Button Bars can be edited just like any other Button Bar. To learn more about Print Preview, see Chapter 8. For information about graphics and the Image Editor, see Chapter 13.

Hoping for a better Button Bar

To select one of WordPerfect's other, predefined Button Bars — which is almost as risky as ordering the chef's surprise in a Chinese smorgasbord — choose Alt-V, S, S. This summons the Select Button Bar dialog box, which lists a few of the ones that come with WordPerfect. Double-click the new Button Bar you want to test drive. All of them are equally awful, so I'm not making any recommendations here.

Stop hoping and just create your own Button Bar

To create your own Button Bar with just the buttons you want, follow these steps:

1. **Go directly to the Select Button Bar dialog box.**

   Press Alt-V, S, S. The Select Button Bar dialog box appears.

2. **Click Create.**
3. **Type a name for your new Button Bar in the Button Bar Name text box.**

Keep the name to no more than eight characters because it's the first part of a filename. For example, WAYCOOL tells me all I need to know about this Button Bar.

4. **Click the OK button or press the Enter key.**

   The Edit Button Bar dialog box appears, as shown in Figure 1-7.

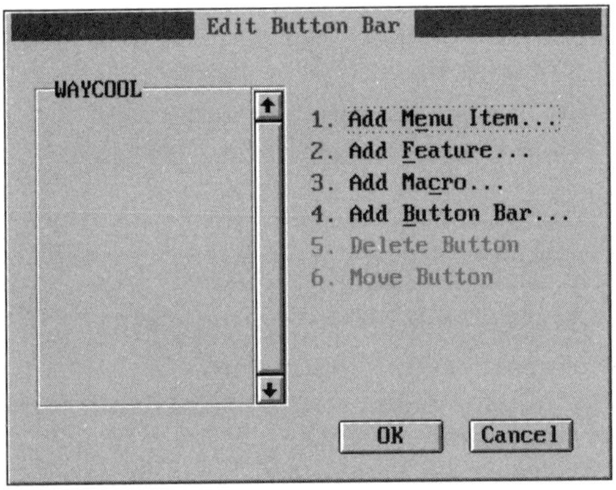

Figure 1-7: The Edit Button Bar dialog box.

   Until you add some buttons, the Delete Button and Move Button options are dimmed because there are no buttons to delete or move. Duh. Notice that the Button Bar you were using politely disappeared to make room for your new buttons.

5. **Click one of the four options — Add Menu Item, Add Feature, Add Macro, or Add Button Bar — to add a button.**

   For example, to add a quick-save button, click Add Menu Item and then select the Save command from the File menu. A Save button appears on your new Button Bar, complete with title and picture.

6. **Continue to select menu items to add as buttons.**

   Repeat Step 5 until your Button Bar is full, or until you've added the buttons you need. (The Button Bar doesn't need to be full.)

7. **Click the OK button when you're done.**

   - Click Add Feature to add a button for a feature that isn't a menu command. WordPerfect displays a long list of every feature, including menu items.
   - Click Add Macro to add a button for a macro. See Part III of this book for more information about macros.

- The Add Button Bar option lets you add a button to your new Button Bar that lets you switch to another Button Bar. This allows you to use two or more Button Bars at a time. Click Add Button Bar and double-click the name of the Button Bar you want a button for. For example, double-click on WPMAIN to add a button for instantly switching back to the standard Button Bar.
- After adding buttons, you can rearrange their order. Click the button title in the dialog box and then click Move Button. In the dialog box, click the button name you want to place the button ahead of and then click Paste Button.
- Delete any buttons you don't want by clicking the button name in the dialog box and then clicking the Delete Button. Then click Yes to confirm the deletion.

8. **When you're done, click the OK button or press Enter.**

   You return to the Select Button Bar dialog box.

9. **Click Select to button down your Button Bar as your choice.**

- There's no point to having more buttons than you can see on-screen at one time. Most buttons save you only one or two mouse clicks or keystrokes, so why waste keystrokes clicking a scroll button?
- The number of buttons you can see at one time depends on how your Button Bar is arranged on-screen and whether it displays text, pictures, or both. Also, the higher your screen resolution, the smaller the buttons and the more buttons you can see at once.

Using the Ribbon

The Ribbon is the strip of drop-down lists under the menu bar. It's basically a shortcut feature, which you may or may not use; all the Ribbon's formatting options are also available from the menus. The Ribbon just makes them more convenient.

To make the Ribbon visible or invisible, press Alt-V, R. This selects the Ribbon item from the View menu, which hides or shows the Ribbon depending on your mood.

To use one of the Ribbon's drop-down lists, click the little down arrow next to the list you want to use. A list of choices drops down. Double-click your choice to select it. The following list describes the six items on the Ribbon from the left:

1. **The Zoom drop-down list.**

   This lets you choose how big your document looks. It doesn't change your text size; instead, it works like a magnifying glass. The standard setting is Marg, so you see your page from margin to margin. Use a small percentage to get a bird's-eye view or a large percentage to zoom in for a close-up of your text.

2. **The Paragraph Style drop-down list.**

   This lets you apply styles to your paragraphs. Don't mess with them until you read Chapter 11. Chapter 20 will also help you understand what's going on here.

3. **The Column drop-down list.**

   This lets you quickly change text into multiple newspaper-style columns. For more column info, see Chapter 14.

4. **The Justification drop-down list.**

   This lets you change the justification of your text, *justification* being typesetter slang for how your text lines up against the left and right margins. See Chapter 10 for more information on justification.

5. **The Font drop-down list.**

   This lets you change to a different font by double-clicking the font name from the list, or you can type a font name after clicking the box (which goes against the mousy nature of the Ribbon). Personally, I don't think this is a time-saver, but be your own best judge. Also, refer to Chapter 9.

6. **The Point Size drop-down list.**

   This lets you change the size of your text. See Chapter 9 to get the point about sizes.

- Want to use Ribbon? Must have mouse.
- It's a good idea to keep the Ribbon visible even if you don't use a mouse. Whether you use the Ribbon or menu commands to apply your formatting, the Ribbon lets you know at a glance which of its options are currently in effect. Without it, you can go goofy trying to eyeball everything.

Adding Scroll Bars

WordPerfect seems to have more bars than Bourbon Street: Button Bars, menu bars, and scroll bars. But don't pick out a designated driver just yet. Most of these bars are for your mouse. So as long as you're doing the driving, everything should be okay.

Scroll bars allow you to view different parts of your document on-screen, as well as quickly move from one part of a document to the next. If you have a mouse, it's often easier to use a scroll bar than to repeatedly jab the PgDn key to find something.

If the vertical scroll bar isn't visible, press Alt-V, V. This selects the Vertical Scroll Bar command from the View menu.

- Don't use the horizontal scroll bar (Alt-V, H). Just keep your Zoom setting at Margin Width and you won't need it. If your Zoom setting isn't at Margin Width, press Alt-V, Z, M.
- Click the scroll bar's up arrow to move up one line.
- Click the scroll bar's down arrow to move down one line.
- Drag the scroll box (the thingy in the middle of the scroll bar) to reposition the cursor over large distances.
- Click above the scroll box to move up one screen.
- Click below the scroll box to move down one screen.
- The scroll box's position reflects the cursor position in the document. If the scroll box is in the middle of the scroll bar, the cursor is roughly in the middle of the document. For example, if the document is ten pages and the scroll box is in the middle of the scroll bar, the cursor is somewhere around page five or six.

The Overwhelming Screen Setup Dialog Box

A lot of doojabbies on-screen are controlled from one central place. This follows the airline motif, where the pilot can fly the plane from one cockpit. And, as you would expect, the central screen control place in WordPerfect is just about as complex as an airplane cockpit. Fortunately, there's very little possibility of a mid-air collision here. But bring your seat backs up and your tray tables to their upright and locked positions before continuing.

Press Alt-V, N to open the Screen Setup dialog box. It gets plastered all over your screen, as shown in Figure 1-8.

To work this dialog box, first press the area number (1 through 6) and then the number next to the item you want to change. When you're finished making changes, press the Enter key to lock them in.

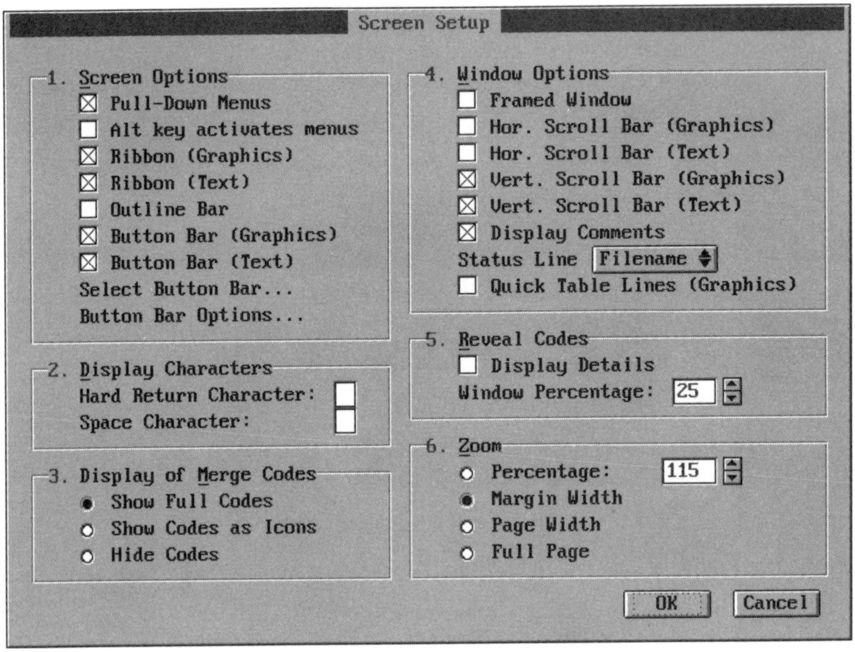

Figure 1-8: The Screen Setup dialog box.

- An X in a box means that item is "on." Select the item to switch it off, which removes the X from the box.
- Most of the options in the Screen Setup dialog box can also be controlled from the View menu and other places in WordPerfect.

- Use the mouse to click any check box or option button (the round ones) to toggle choices on or off.

- In the Screen Options area, don't switch on the Alt key activates menus option. This causes the Alt key to operate in a nonstandard (weird) way, one that will frustrate you to no end.
- Several options let you make separate choices for Graphics mode and Text mode (see area 4, Window Options). If you turn off the Ribbon while you're in Graphics mode, but you don't turn it off while you're in Text mode, the Ribbon will be staring you in the face if you ever switch to Text mode.
- In the Display of Merge Codes area, make sure that the Show Full Codes option is selected. You won't regret it. To learn more about decoding WordPerfect codes, see Chapter 4.
- In the Reveal Codes portion of the dialog box, leave the Display Details option off (unchecked) and keep the Window percentage set to 25.

- If you accidentally turn off the Pull-Down Menus option and close the Screen Setup dialog box, you can get the menu bar back by pressing Alt-=.

Chapter 2

More on the Document

In This Chapter

- S.O.S. (Save Obsessively and then Save again)
- Fast Save?
- Using a Document Summary
- More on backup options
- Saving blocks to disk
- Comparing documents

Documents are what you create in WordPerfect. Spreadsheets are for spreadsheets. Paper? Ha! Get a pencil and live in the dark ages. Only by using sleek software, such as WordPerfect, can you electronically compose your thoughts in a *document*. It's so professional sounding. So . . . legal. Paper? Paper is for shopping bags (or plastic, if you prefer). People line bird cages with paper. Dogs get trained on paper. Give me WordPerfect and its documents any day of the week.

This chapter opens the door a bit wider and sheds some "more" light on WordPerfect's documents. Keep in mind that a document is anything you create in WordPerfect — anything from a small note, to a memo, to a letter, to a very thick chapter in a plodding novel. Everything's a document. This chapter shows you how to treat 'em right.

S.O.S. (Save Obsessively and then Save again)

I've found more ways to lose my work than I care to count. Unfortunately, "the dog ate it" doesn't pass muster with big league publishers. Instead, I should be more careful — and so should you. The idea is to save your work and save it often. Save! Save! Save! That way, if the dog trips over the computer's power cord, you won't lose too much of your work.

When you're typing away and editing up a storm, just remember to press Ctrl-F12 to save every few minutes. (Refer to the section "So, how often should I save my work?") Or . . .

- You can also click on the Save button on WordPerfect's Button Bar. Refer to Chapter 1 for information on adding such a button if it isn't there already.
- The first time you save a document, a Save Document dialog box appears. Type a filename (up to eight characters — letters and numbers only, please) that relates to the contents of the file. Press the Enter key and your document is tucked safely away on your computer's disk.
- Refer to Chapter 14 in the original *WordPerfect 6 For Dummies* for more information on general saving.
- If a scary-looking Document Summary dialog box pops up the first time you save your document, press the Esc key twice to banish it from your screen and get to the much friendlier Save Document dialog box. To learn how to keep that pesky Document Summary dialog box from ever bothering you again (or for some information about how and why you may actually want to use it), see the "Using the Hated Document Summary" section later in this chapter.

"So, how often should I save my work?"

Save your work often enough that your heart won't stop for long after you discover that the computer has flaked out on you again. For me, that's about every five or ten minutes. My computer may be reliable, but saving that often makes me feel better.

- Another suggestion: Save any time you get up from the computer to do something else. I always save whenever the phone rings or when someone comes by my office to bug me.
- Give yourself extra security by using WordPerfect's automatic save feature. See the section called "The Timed Backup option" later in this chapter for more information about using this extra bit of insurance.
- For real security, you need to make redundant copies, called *backups*, of your important files and place them on separate disks. For details on copying files, see Chapter 7.

How "fast" is a Fast Save?

There's a fast way to save and a slow way to save. Which one should you choose? (Think about it.)

If you said the fast way, you may be right. Then again, you may be wrong. It all depends. (I can never imagine Alex Trebek saying that on *Jeopardy!*)

When you save your document, WordPerfect automatically sends it to your disk as fast as it can. Zip-zip-zip. You can slow down the process if you like. This may sound like a dumb thing to do, but "slow saving" makes your document print faster. Sounds odd, but it's true.

If fast printing is more important to you than fast saving, you can shut off WordPerfect's Fast Save feature. Here's how:

1. **Press F10 (the Save As key) and then press Shift-F1.**

   The Save Setup dialog box appears, as shown in Figure 2-1.

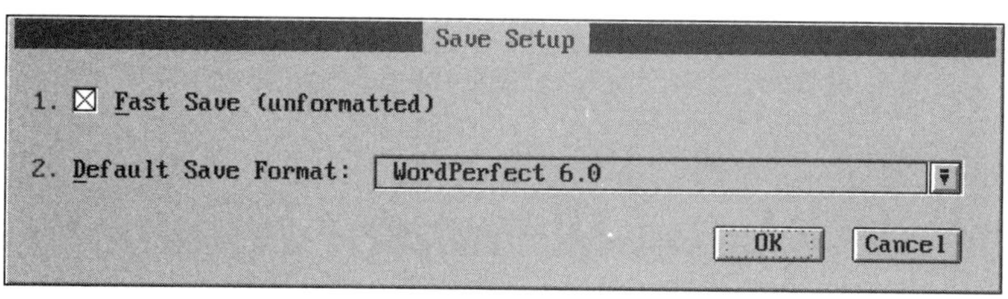

Figure 2-1: The Save Setup dialog box.

2. **Look at the box next to Fast Save (unformatted).**
3. **If there's an X in the box, press the 1 key.**

   This removes the X from the box and switches off the Fast Save, which allows you to print faster.

4. **Press Enter and then Esc twice to return to your document, and you can be assured that Fast Save is turned off.**

- You can always change your mind and turn Fast Save back on by repeating the preceding steps and sticking an X in the box.
- Fast Save stores your document on disk without the special formatting information required by your printer to put your masterpiece on paper. When you tell WordPerfect to print the document, it must take the time to format the document for printing. In other words, Fast Save = slow print.

- Fast Save also means slow retrieve. WordPerfect has to, once again, format your document for the printer when you load it.
- Most of the time, Fast Save is a good trade-off because you usually save more often than you print. If it doesn't sound like a good trade-off to you, turn it off.
- Try saving some documents with Fast Save on and then again with Fast Save off. If you don't notice much difference, keep Fast Save turned off to speed printing.

Saving and exiting

Don't leave too fast! When you press the F7 key to exit WordPerfect, a dialog box opens and asks whether you want to save the document.

- If you made any changes to the document before pressing F7, the message *Document has been modified* appears in the middle of the dialog box to tell you that you'll lose any edits you made since the last time you saved.
- If you see the message that the document has been modified (as if you wouldn't have already known), press Y to save it. Then press Y again to exit WordPerfect or N to clear the screen and stay in WordPerfect.

Using the Hated Document Summary

You can put all sorts of boring information into a document summary, such as who the author is (I am), who typed it (I did), and what the subject or type of document is (who cares?).

You can use the document summary information to locate documents that meet certain criteria. For example, you can search for all the documents typed by Sam, whose author is Elaine, whose type is REPORT, and discover whether Sam and Elaine do more than carpool together.

- I don't use document summaries. Law firms, the government, and big bureaucracies with too many levels of management use document summaries. Of course, if you're stuck in such a place, you already knew that.
- If you aren't sure whether you need document summaries, you probably don't.
- A description of what's what in the Document Summary dialog box appears in the following section.
- You can choose which fields appear in the Document Summary dialog box. See the "Customizing the Document Summary" section later in this chapter.

A quick tour of the Document Summary dialog box

To see the Document Summary dialog box, choose File ⇨ Summary or press Alt-F, U. What it may look like appears in Figure 2-2.

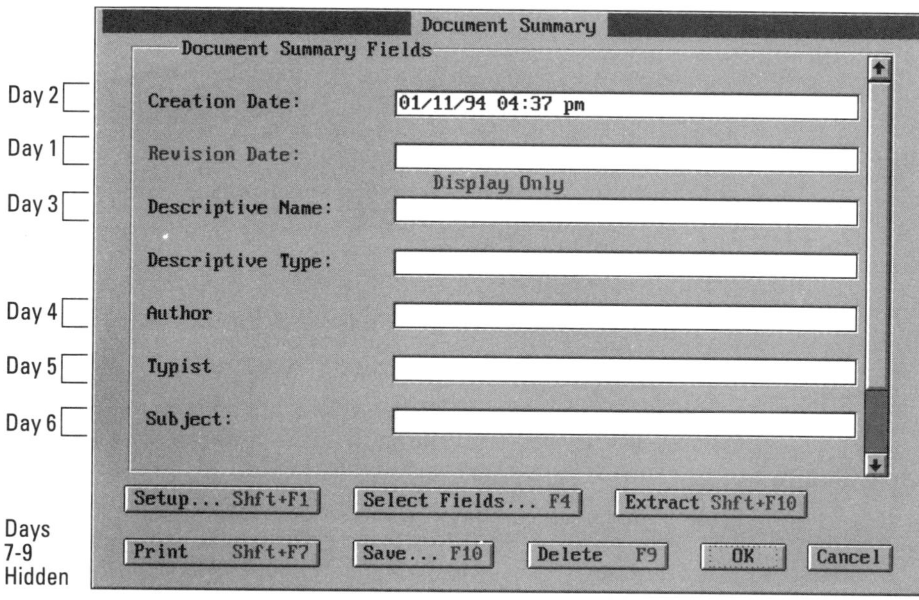

Figure 2-2: The Document Summary dialog box.

The Document Summary Fields portion of the dialog box provides the spaces for you to enter the information you want to track. It's a scrolling list (see the scroll bar to the right?), so there's more information described in today's tour than you may see on-screen (or in the figure) at the same time.

Day 1. Revision Date. This is usually today, although if you're crossing the international date line it could also be tomorrow.

Day 2. Creation Date. The date the file was first worked on — something you can't change, not even by crossing the international date line.

Day 3. Descriptive Name/Type. These two fields are for your own pleasure. Descriptive Name may be REPORT or MEMO; Descriptive Type could be ROUGH DRAFT or INTEROFFICE. WordPerfect is pretty flexible here.

Day 4. Author. Well, who wrote it? Not typed it. But whose ideas are these? For example, if you were a plagiarist, you'd put the original author's name here.

Day 5. Typist. The grunt work person. The *Encyclopaedia Britannica* may have written it (Author), but seventh grader Davey Wilson is typing in the report as his own.

Day 6. Subject. "How romantic music affects milk production in dairy cattle."

Day 7. Account. If you're in this for the money, this field contains the guy who's paying for it. So if you work for the government, the Account field always contains *Mr. and Ms. Taxpayer.*

Day 8. Keywords. Sometimes it's nice to put down a few descriptive words that relate to the subject at hand: MEMO, COWS, MILK, etc. These can be used to quickly find this and related documents later.

Day 9. Abstract. A brief description of the document written so that only an abstract artist would comprehend it.

- Click the OK button when you're done entering the information.
- The Print button (or Shift-F7) prints only the Document Summary information.
- Not all fields require information in them.
- You can automatically fill the Abstract and Subject fields. This secret is divulged in the section properly titled "Automatically filling fields in the Document Summary" later in this chapter.
- The Document Summary information is really used for searching through various documents. Chances are, if you're the only one in your office using WordPerfect, you're just wasting time filling in all this information.

Customizing the Document Summary

Don't let WordPerfect push you around. I mean, Document Type/Name. Who needs to know? You can tailor the Document Summary dialog box to display just the fields you want to use. To change the fields, follow these steps:

1. **Choose File⇨Summary, or press Alt-F, U.**

   The Document Summary dialog box appears on-screen.

2. **Press F4, Select Fields.**

   The Select Summary Fields dialog box pops on-screen over the Document Summary dialog box. Figure 2-3 depicts it nicely.

3. **Use the up- and down-arrow keys to highlight a field you want to remove.**

4. **Press R to Remove the field.**

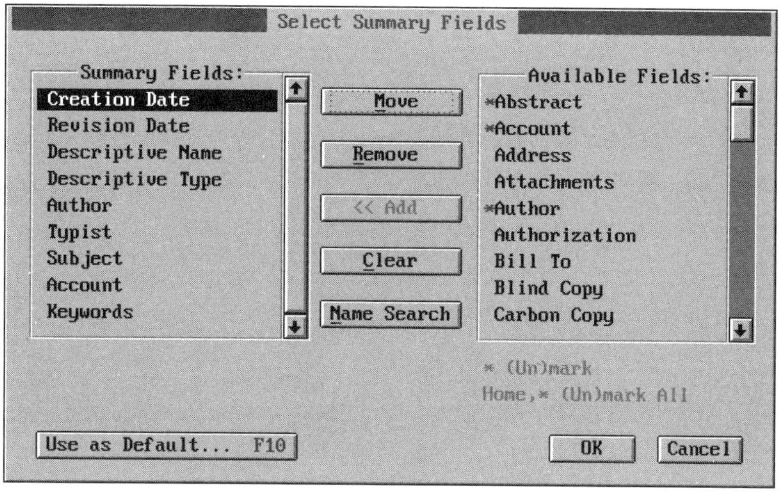

Figure 2-3: The Select Summary Fields dialog box.

5. **Repeat Steps 3 and 4 until just the fields you want remain.**
6. **To add fields, press the Tab key.**
7. **Highlight a field you want to add and press A (for Add).**
8. **Repeat Step 7 to add as many fields as you like.**

   The fields preceded by an asterisk are already on the Summary Fields list. No need to add them twice.

9. **When you're through adding and removing fields, press F10 and then Y to make your changes permanent.**

   If you don't follow this step, the changes affect only the Document Summary for the current document.

10. **Press Home, F7 to return to your document.**

- The Document Summary doesn't print when you print your document unless you tell WordPerfect to do so. To print the Document Summary with the document, press Shift-F7, 4, 6. Refer to Chapter 8 for more information about printing.
- If only having eight characters to name your document is too limiting, use the Descriptive Name field in the Document Summary dialog box to enter a long name for your document. Refer to Chapter 7 to learn how to display long filenames in File Manager.

Getting rid of the Document Summary prompt that bothers you every time you save a new document

WordPerfect may spring the Document Summary dialog box on you every time you save a document for the first time. If you want to be sure that this appears, or if you want to turn the blasted thing off, follow these steps:

1. **Press Shift-F8, 4, 4.**

   The Document Summary dialog box opens for the document on-screen.

2. **Press Shift-F1.**

   This gets you to the Document Summary Setup dialog box, as shown in Figure 2-4.

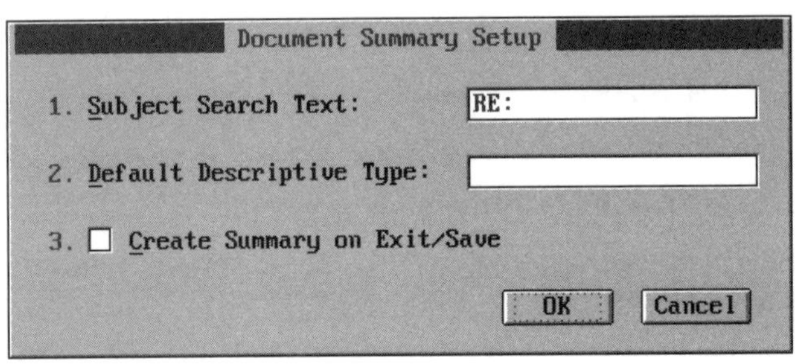

Figure 2-4: The Document Summary Setup dialog box.

3. **Press 3.**

   Put an X in the box next to **C**reate Summary on Exit/Save if you think it's a good idea to enter information in the Document Summary, or remove the X if you don't.

4. **Press Home, F7.**

   This lands you safely back in your document.

- If you turned on the Create Document Summary on Exit/Save, you'll get a Document Summary dialog box every time you save a document for the first time or start to exit WordPerfect, if you haven't saved the document that's on-screen.
- Refer to Chapter 7 for information on using Document Summary information to locate files and viewing the Document Summary information.
- TIP: Pressing Home, F7 (see Step 4) is a quick way to get back to your document from several layers of dialog boxes. If you press F7 without first pressing Home, you need to press F7 four times to get back to the document. You could wear out your finger doing that.

Automatically filling fields in the Document Summary

One of the most useful Document Summary fields is the Abstract field, in which you can enter some text from your document to help you find the document you're looking for later. Unfortunately, making something up or typing in a chunk of text from your document into the Abstract field is really more trouble than it's worth. Fortunately, there is a shortcut.

To have WordPerfect automatically fill in some Document Summary information, follow these steps:

1. **Press Shift-F8, D (Document), S (Summary)**

   The Document Summary dialog box appears.

2. **Press Shift-F10 to extract the information.**

   A dialog box opens and asks whether you really want to extract the Document Summary information.

3. **Press Y.**

   The first 400 characters of your document are entered into the Abstract field. Cool.

If your document is in a memo format, WordPerfect can also fill in the Subject field. If you have a subject line beginning with RE:, such as *RE: Obligatory meeting,* the Subject field is automatically filled in if you follow the preceding steps.

More on Backup Options

I don't work without a net. In fact, I usually wear a parachute when I'm playing Microsoft Flight Simulator. Seriously, I don't want to lose any of the information I type. If it weren't important to me, I wouldn't type it in the first place.

With that in mind, a couple of the best safety nets you can use in WordPerfect are the Timed Document Backup and Back Up Original Document options. They're easy to use, painless, no uncomfortable bindings, and there's no need to fear the word "impact" because of them.

The Timed Document Backup option

The Timed Document Backup feature saves your document at specified intervals, even if you forget to. However, it doesn't save the document with the name you've assigned to the document. It is a secret temporary backup file you use only if you accidentally turn off the computer or the power goes out before you save your document. Secret stuff. Shhh!

These secret backup files disappear if you exit WordPerfect properly, so having them is no excuse for not saving properly. Save, save, save as you normally do. Just be happy knowing the secret backup files exist.

To turn on the **T**imed Document Backup feature, press Shift-F1, 3, 1. You'll see the Backup dialog box, looking a lot like Figure 2-5.

Figure 2-5: The Backup dialog box.

- Look at the Timed Document Backup box. Is there an X there? If not, press 1 to activate the feature.
- Enter a backup interval by pressing 2 and typing the number of minutes you want between the times WordPerfect automatically saves your document. For example, I want WordPerfect to save my document every five minutes, so I enter **5** in the box.
- Press Home, F7 to get back to your document.
- Suppose that the computer crashes! BOOM! There goes your document. When you start WordPerfect again (because, after all, life does go on), you'll see an ominous dialog box telling you that WordPerfect stopped without exiting properly. Oooo! Press O to open it and see how much was saved.

The Back Up Original option

Have you ever made a bunch of major edits to a document, dutifully saved it, and then realized that it was better the way it was before the edits? The Back Up Original Document feature saves you from this potential tragedy by always keeping the next-to-last version you saved as well as the last version you saved.

To turn on the Back Up **O**riginal Document feature, press Shift-F1, 3, 1. This opens the Backup dialog box (see Figure 2-5). If there isn't an X in the Back Up **O**riginal Document box, press 3 and then press Home, F7.

- If, after saving a document, you want to get the previous version back, press Shift-F10 and type the name of the document, but followed by a BK! extension. For example, if you want to get back the previous version of a document called FORGERY.DOC, you would press Shift-F10 and enter **FORGERY.BK!** in the Filename text box of the Open Document dialog box.
- If you had more than one document open at the time WordPerfect was terminated, you need to open each of them (*terminated* is the proper verb).
- If you exit WordPerfect properly, the temporary backup files created by the timed backup option are erased. Moral: Save your documents. Ctrl-F12.
- The files created by the Original Document Backup feature are not automatically erased and can end up eating up a lot of disk space if you leave them on your computer forever. Get in the habit of erasing unneeded files — especially backup files — regularly. Regularly means more often than every spring. Refer to Chapter 7 for information on using the File Manager to erase files.
- If your computer completely malfunctions or, heaven forbid, is stolen, the WordPerfect backup options won't help you a bit. The fact that your documents are saved on the computer's disk doesn't matter if you can't use the disk. It's crucial that you back up your documents on separate disks (or tape if you're lucky enough to have a tape backup system). Chapter 7 explains how to copy files to a disk by using WordPerfect's File Manager. If you need more information about backing up documents, refer to *DOS For Dummies*, 2nd Edition, published by IDG Books Worldwide.

Saving Blocks to Disk

One of the many things you can do with a block is to save it to disk. This is better than just copying the block; you can only copy one block of text at a time. You can save hundreds of blocks to disk and then retrieve them later. Yeah, it's a bit advanced for cut-and-paste, but it works very nicely.

To save a block to disk, follow these steps:

1. **Position the cursor at the beginning of the text you want to block.**
2. **Press F12.**

   The words `Block on` appear on the left side of the status bar. You're ready to start marking your block.
3. **Use the cursor keys to mark your block.**

   As you move the cursor around, text becomes selected and highlighted on-screen. That text becomes your block.
4. **Press F10.**

   The Save Block dialog box appears.

5. **Type a name for the block and press the Enter key.**

   Chugga-chugga. It's saved to disk for instant re-use at any time.

- Detailed information on marking blocks can be found in Chapter 6 of the original *WordPerfect 6 For Dummies*.
- The rules for naming a block are the same as for any other document: Up to eight characters, letters and numbers only please.
- A saved block is just a normal, separate document, just like any other document you create and save. In fact, you can save a block to disk and then open it by using WordPerfect's File⇨Open command. It becomes another document in WordPerfect. (Such promotion! From block to document in one fell swoop. If only becoming a saint were as easy.)

Retrieving a saved block

Retrieve saved blocks just as you would any other document. Press Shift-F10, WordPerfect's **O**pen command. In the Open dialog box, enter the name you assigned to the block. Press the Enter key, and the block becomes its own document.

To stick a saved-to-disk block into the middle of another document, you need to use the File⇨Retrieve command. Move the cursor to the spot in your document where you want the block, and then choose File⇨Retrieve or press Alt-F, R. Type the name of the block into the Retrieve Document dialog box, and press Enter to stick it into your other document.

Appending a block to another document on disk

You can append a block to the end of an existing document on disk. This actually assembles a document on disk — kinda like gluing pieces of paper together. The block is just stuck on to the end of a WordPerfect document. Tacky, but effective.

The technical word for this is *appending*. To append a block to a WordPerfect document on disk, first highlight the block and then press Ctrl-F4, 4. In the Append To dialog box, enter the name of the file you want the block attached to.

If you try to append a block to a file that doesn't exist, a new document file with that name is created and contains just the block.

Comparing Documents with Revision Markings

Editing is the *raison d'etre* for word processing, where *raison d'etre* means "reason of dirt." You edit and revise until your document is just right. The hard part is keeping up with the changes. Moving your head back and forth between two versions of a document can give you a headache. There are two solutions.

- Take plenty of little Doan's pills before comparing two versions of a document.
- Use WordPerfect's Compare Documents feature to show what's been changed.

The second method is faster-acting and recommended over the first.

Making the comparison

Suppose that you wrote a nasty letter to the IRS to justify your deductions for every time you visited McDonalds — deductions they capriciously and arbitrarily disallowed. You named the letter HEYIRS. Your spouse understands that it's wiser to make nice to the tax folk and edited your nasty gram to soften the blow, and saved it with the filename WESORRY.

To see exactly what changes were made to your version, follow these steps to compare HEYIRS with WESORRY:

1. **Open the new version of the document you want to compare.**

   In this example, WESORRY is the new version.

2. **Press Alt-F5, K (Add Markings).**

   The Compare Documents dialog box appears, as shown in Figure 2-6.

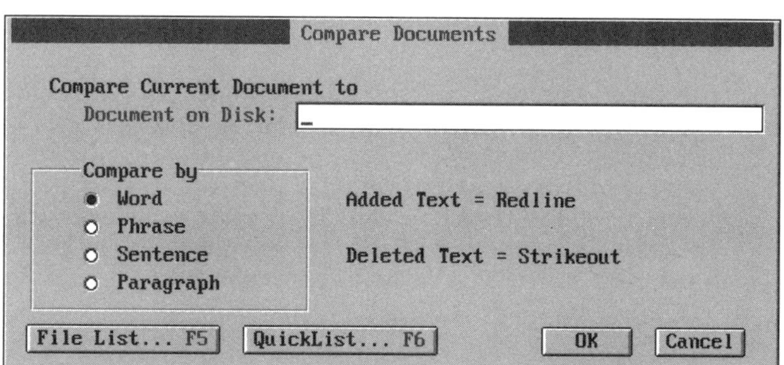

Figure 2-6: The Compare Documents dialog box.

3. **Press D (Document on Disk).**
4. **Type the name of the previous version of the document in the Document on Disk text box.**

   In this example, the old version is HEYIRS.
5. **Press the Enter key.**
6. **Press C (Compare by).**
7. **Press the underlined letter of the comparison method you want to use.**

   For example, press W to compare word by word.
8. **Press the Enter key to begin the comparison.**

   Any deleted text magically reappears on-screen but with a line through it (called *strikeout*) that tells you it is text that was in the previous version but not in the new version. Text that has been added to the new version appears in red (called *redline*), if you have a color monitor. You may see redline text as another shade if you have a black-and-white monitor.

Text that was moved appears unchanged in its new location with the words *THE FOLLOWING TEXT WAS MOVED* before the moved text and *THE PRECEDING TEXT WAS MOVED* after the moved text.

TIP

- It's a good idea to save the new version of your document with a different name before performing the comparison. For example, if the old file is called MYTEXT, you might name the new one MYTEXT2. This way, if anything goes wrong during the comparison, both the old and new versions are safely stored on disk.
- It may make it easier to spot the added and deleted text if you print the marked-up document. If you need more information on printing your document, see Chapter 8.
- The redline and strikeout text is actually just regular text with special redline and strikeout font attribute codes surrounding it. You can add these attributes manually as you edit, but it's easier to let WordPerfect do the work for you. See Chapter 9 to learn more about fonts and font attribute codes.

TECHNICAL STUFF

- You can change the appearance of the redline text. Press Shift-F8, D (Document), R (Redline Method). Use the up- or down-arrow keys to highlight the method you want to use, and then press the Enter key. If you want the added text marked with a character other than a vertical bar, press L (Redline Character), and then press the character you want to use. The default Redline Method (Printer Dependent) usually gives the best results, especially if you have a laser printer.

Removing the marks

After WordPerfect has run the comparison, you need to get rid of all those nasty redline markings and the strikeout text. To have WordPerfect perform this feat for you automatically, have the marked-up version on-screen and follow these steps:

1. **Press Alt-F5, R (Remove Markings).**

   The Remove Markings dialog box appears.

2. **Press Enter.**

   Zap! All the added text remains, but without the redline attributes. All the text with strikeout markings disappears.

- If you save the new version of the document with a different filename than the original version, just clear the screen and then open the new version of the document.
- There's no need to save the marked-up version of the document because you can always recompare the old and new versions.
- If you added any redline or strikeout attributes to your text for appearance, it will be treated just as the other redline and strikeout text. Saving the new and old versions with different filenames alleviates this problem because you can just clear the screen and open the new version of the document.

Chapter 3

More on Multiple Documents

In This Chapter

- One program — many documents
- The big switch
- Window framing
- Minimizing and maximizing windows
- Tiling windows
- Cascading windows
- Moving and sizing windows

Information overload is a disease of the '90s, and WordPerfect is certainly infected. If you're one of those types who reads the newspaper while watching television and listening to the radio, this chapter is for you. WordPerfect lets you juggle enough documents to keep even the most hyperactive among us buzzing along. You may even find that WordPerfect's ability to work with multiple documents can actually bring you a sense of power and control formerly only experienced by U.S. Senators and comic book superheroes.

One Program — Many Documents

You don't have to have a bank of computers sitting on your desk to work with multiple documents. Thank goodness! Just open all the documents you want to work with — but no more than nine documents at once. (If you want to open more than nine documents at a time, you need more help than I can give you.)

Why in the world would an otherwise rational person want to juggle that many documents at once? Beats me. Actually, there are good, legitimate, and socially acceptable reasons for having three or four documents available. One of the best reasons is so that you can edit, copy, and move among them without all the open-and-closing required otherwise.

- You don't have to save and close one document before opening the next. Right there, you can save yourself loads of time. You may want to have several documents relating to one project open — say, chapters of a book.
- Another excuse for this: Perhaps you're working on a long document. Instead of scrolling back and forth to the beginning and end of the document, you can have the document open two or more times with the cursor positioned differently.
- If you have more than one copy of the same document open, make all your editing changes to the first copy. For example, if DOC 1 and DOC 2 are different views of the same document, move text from DOC 2 to DOC 1.

Opening more than one document

To open another existing document, use the Open command on the File menu or use Shift-F10. Pick a document to work on from those listed. WordPerfect opens that document in its own document window right there on-screen.

Another way to work on more than one document is to start a new document. To do that, choose File⇨New or press Alt-F, N. WordPerfect opens a fresh, blank document window so that you can start typing away madly — because you're never bothered by writer's block, right?

- Each open document uses memory — WordPerfect's lifeblood. To keep WordPerfect humming along as rapidly as possible, don't open any more documents than you really need.
- When you open another copy of a document that is already open — say, to look at two different parts of a long document — WordPerfect lets you know. And you won't be able to save the second copy unless you save it with a different name. This is just a safety feature, but don't let it bother you.
- The status bar tells you which document you're working on. If you see *DOC 1* in the lower-right corner of the screen, you're working on document 1. *DOC 2* means the current document is document 2.
- What you do with one document doesn't affect the other documents you have open. For example, you can print only one document of all the ones you have open. The other documents just sit and wait until you decide to work on them. (There is a way to print multiple documents by using the File Manager. See Chapter 7 for the lowdown on the File Manager.)
- When you have several documents open, pressing the F7 key to exit closes only the current document — just as if you used the File⇨Close command. To quit WordPerfect and close all your documents, refer to the next section.
- After editing your current document, always save it before switching to another document. Remember, save often and save again!

Using the Big Exit command

To quit WordPerfect when you have many documents open, you need the Big Exit command. Press Home, F7 to close all open documents and exit WordPerfect.

When you press Home, F7, an Exit WordPerfect dialog box appears listing all the open documents (see Figure 3-1). An X appears in front of each document that was changed since the last time it was saved. Save those documents!

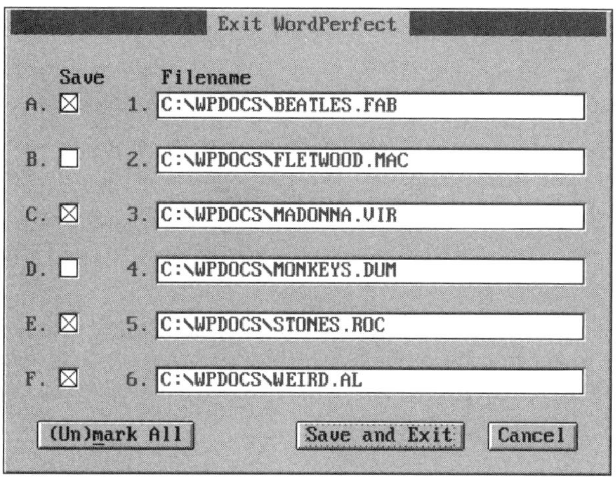

Figure 3-1: The Exit WordPerfect dialog box with multiple documents.

The Big Switch

Normally, WordPerfect doesn't give you a clue that you have more than one document open. This is a problem for first-time users, which is why working on multiple documents is only mentioned briefly in *WordPerfect 6 For Dummies*. In this big-league *MORE* book, you get the full treatment.

You can switch to any other open document in WordPerfect by using the Switch To command (F3). This summons the Switch to Document dialog box, which lists all open documents. Press the number next to the document you want and poof, you are there.

TIP

- I usually work on multiple documents and keep my index or outline in DOC 1. To switch there, I press F3, 1.

- The Switch To command is found in the Window menu.
- If a document has been saved to disk (and it certainly should have been), then its cryptic DOS pathname appears by its document number in the Switch to Document dialog box. Otherwise, you see `(Untitled)` listed.
- You can copy a block from one document to another. After you highlight the block and press Ctrl-C to copy it, press F3 and zip to the other document and press Ctrl-V to paste the block in its new location. You can't use the drag-and-drop method to copy or move blocks between documents.
- To flip back and forth between the current document and the preceding document, use the Switch command, Shift-F3.
- To cycle through the open documents, press Ctrl-Y. Each time you press Ctrl-Y, you move to the next document. Ctrl-Y? I dunno.
- Use the Previous command from the Window menu to move to the preceding open document.
- If you know the number of the document you want, press Home and then the number (1 through 9). For example, if you want to switch to document 4, press Home, 4.
- If you are finished working with a document, save and close it before switching to another document. WordPerfect then has one less document to keep track of, and you have one less thing to worry about when you exit WordPerfect.

Window Framing

If you find there isn't enough clutter on-screen, help is on the way. You can put a frame around your document so there's even *less* space for its contents. Imagine how busy you can look without getting that much more work done!

Window framing does give you some information about and control over the document window that you don't have without it. A title bar across the top of the document displays the document number followed by the document name. This leaves the left side of the status bar free to display the current font.

Use the Frame command from the Window menu to have WordPerfect put a frame around the current document, as shown in Figure 3-2.

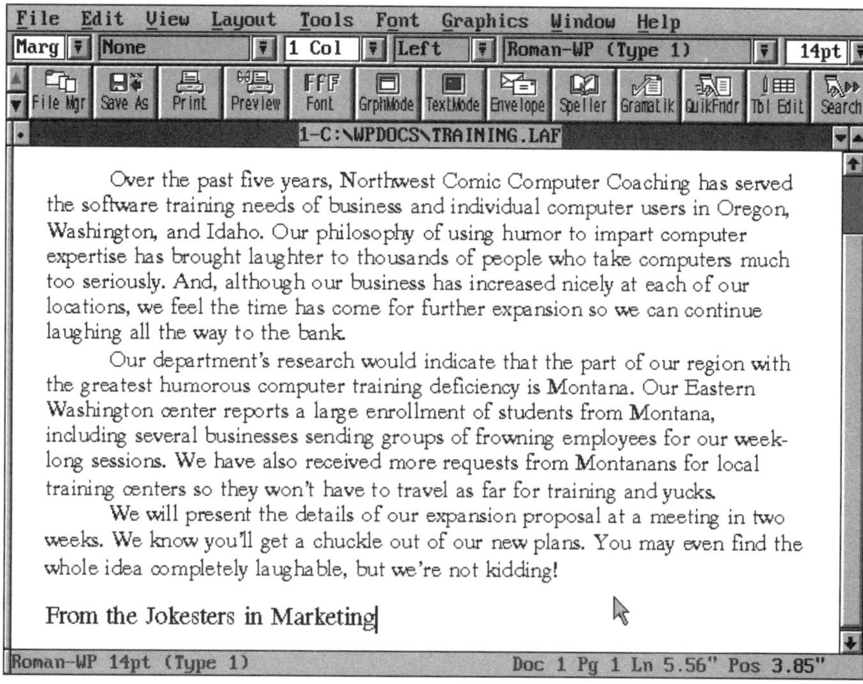

Figure 3-2: A framed window.

- On the left side of the title bar is a little circle thingy called a close box. Just click the close box to close the document.
- If you want all your documents to open in framed windows, press Alt-V, N, 4, 1. Repeat these steps to unframe these windows after you realize that was a terrible mistake.
- Don't confuse document windows, whether framed or unframed, with the Microsoft Windows program. One has nothing to do with the other. There is a version of WordPerfect that requires the Windows program, but that's not the version this book is about.

Minimizing and Maximizing Framed Windows

On the right end of the title bar are up- and down-pointing arrows for expanding the document to maximum size or for shrinking it to itty-bitty size.

- Click the up arrow (called the *maximize arrow*) to remove the frame and make the document fill the screen.
- Click the down arrow (called the *minimize arrow*) to shrink the window to its smallest size, as shown in Figure 3-3. Is there any good reason to minimize a window? Nope, none that I can think of.

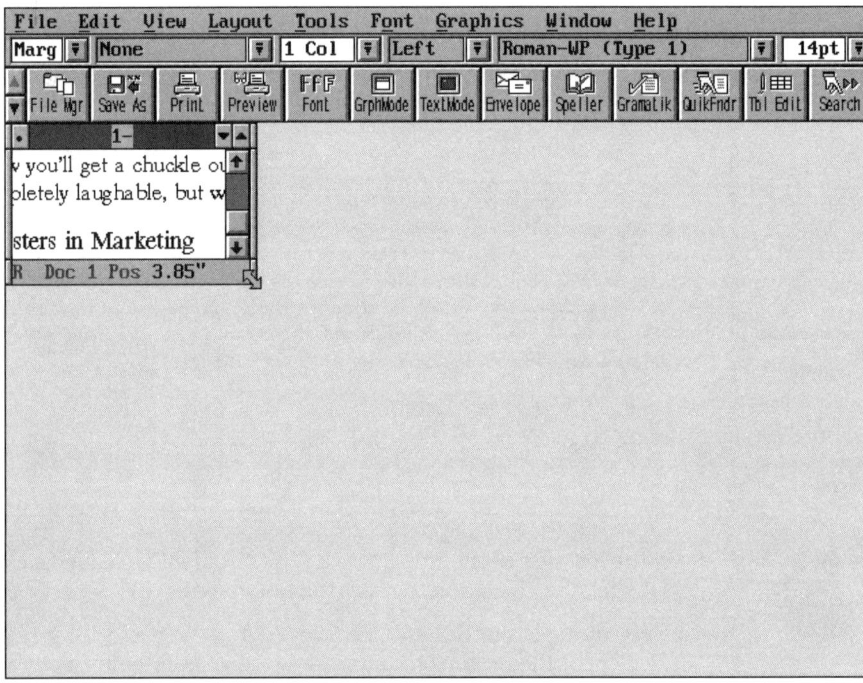

Figure 3-3: A practically useless minimized document window.

- Refer to the preceding section on window framing, and this sizing stuff may make sense to you if it doesn't already.
- So little of a minimized document is visible that it makes little sense to minimize a document.
- Use the Maximize command from the Window menu to remove a window frame and maximize its size.

Tiling Document Windows

One way to work with multiple documents is to display them on-screen simultaneously. You may want to display them to view different portions of two or more copies of the same document. If you're comparing two different documents or moving text from one to the other, it also can be useful to have them both on-screen at the same time.

Tiling places each open document in its own framed window. To tile a document, press Ctrl-F3, W, T or select the Tile command from the Window menu.

- Tiling is also important when you're remodeling your bathroom. It can be beautiful.
- Each window can be maximized by clicking the up arrow on the right end of the title bar.
- If you're mouseless, you can maximize a window by pressing Ctrl-F3, W, A.
- Don't tile your documents until you've opened all the documents you're going to open. If you do open more documents after tiling, just retile.
- You can only work in one document — the active document — at a time. The active document's title bar is a different color or shade from the other documents' title bars. To make another window the active document, press Home and then the number of the document you want to switch to or just click the other document with the mouse.
- The problem with tiling — especially with several documents open at once — is each window is so small that you can't see much of the document's contents. The solution is to cascade the windows, which is covered in the next section.

Cascading Document Windows

Cascaded windows are organized so that each document appears in its own li'l window but each one occupies the same amount of screen real estate. The documents overlap, obscuring most of the documents except the front one, which is the active document. Just the title bar and a small portion of the left edge of each inactive document are visible. Some people find this effect much better for dealing with multiple documents than the tiling option discussed in the preceding section.

To cascade the open documents, press Ctrl-F3, W, C or choose Window⇨Cascade.

- To bring one of the obscured windows to the foreground and make it the active window, press Home and then the number of the document or just click any visible portion of the document with the mouse.
- Switching to other windows or opening other documents messes up the cascading. Just recascade, Ctrl-F3, W, C, to put things back in proper order.
- It's easier to work with maximized documents than tiled or cascaded document windows. Unless you really need to see two or more documents at once, avoid tiling and cascading.
- If you must work with several document windows on-screen at once, you can change the zoom percentage on some or all of the windows to allow you to see more in a smaller space. Press Alt-V, Z and then use the up- and down-arrow keys to highlight the zoom percentage you want. For example, 75 percent lets you see a bit more text in the window (although it's tiny text). Please don't send your optometrist bills to me if you grow fond of this trick.

Moving and Sizing Windows

You can go nuts trying to work in the cramped spaces created by tiled or cascaded windows. Fortunately, you can move the windows around and resize them to make working in all this clutter a bit less burdensome.

There are two ways to resize windows: the easy mouse method and the painful keyboard method.

1. **Position the mouse pointer over any of the four corners or the left, right, or bottom edge of the active window (so that the pointer assumes the shape of a double-headed arrow) and drag the corner or edge to reshape the window.**
2. **To resize the active window with the keyboard, press Ctrl-F3, W, S. Use the arrow keys to change the size of the window's outline and then press Enter.**

If you want a different location for your window, you can slide it around the screen by using either the intuitive mouse or the clumsy keyboard.

1. **To move a window with the mouse, position the mouse pointer over the title bar so the pointer turns into a four-headed arrow and then drag it to a new location.**
2. **To move a window with the keyboard, press Ctrl-F3, W, M. Use the arrow keys to move the window's outline to its new position and then press Enter.**

- You can't increase the size or change the position of a window that is taking up the entire document area.
- You can only change the size of framed windows. If you want to reduce the size of an unframed document window, first frame it by pressing Alt-W, F.
- TIP: If your windows get too messed up, you can always tile or cascade them again and start all over. Refer to "Tiling Document Windows" and "Cascading Document Windows" earlier in this chapter for the lowdown.

The 5th Wave By Rich Tennant

"YOU KNOW THE RULES, COMRADE. SMUGGLED AMERICAN COMPUTERS CAN NOT BE EXAMINED UNTIL KGB REMOVES ALL 'ESCAPE' BUTTONS."

Chapter 4

More on — shh! — Secret Document Stuff

In This Chapter

- Revealing Reveal Codes
- Auto Code Placement
- Changing the Reveal Codes window size
- Suppressing codes
- Hidden text
- Comments
- Hyphenation

There are some things WordPerfect wants to keep under wraps. Secret stuff. Forbidden. Taboo. I'm talking about hidden text and stealthy codes. Fortunately, none of this stuff is illegal and most of it can be exported from the country (just keep it out of the hands of the KGB). This chapter blows the lid off the web of secrecy surrounding some obscure and baffling — but still mostly handy — features.

By the way, if you are discovered using any of these features, I will disavow any knowledge of your activities, and this book will self-destruct. Please save your document now. Thank you.

Revealing Reveal Codes

WordPerfect's codes are a lot like automotive repair, but without the grease. Essentially, you don't need to know about either WordPerfect's codes or fixing your car until one or the other breaks down. For your car, call the AAA. With a WordPerfect document, you can rely on your PC guru to troubleshoot your document. But with a little knowledge of what's under WordPerfect's hood, you can diagnose and solve many of your own WordPerfect problems all by yourself.

- By the way, WordPerfect's codes are much easier to comprehend than the internal combustion engine.
- Think of the money you'll save on M&Ms and Doritos when you no longer have to bribe your WordPerfect guru!

How it all works

As you type, edit, and format your documents, you leave a trail of hidden codes that tell WordPerfect what to do. Press the Tab key, and WordPerfect sticks a tab code into your document. Center a paragraph, and a center paragraph code is inserted. Of course, these codes don't affect what's on-screen because everything looks and prints correctly. So, most of the time, you never need to bother with the hidden codes.

One day, however, suppose that you create a big mess. A paragraph is all jiggly, and you just can't nail it down. Something is awry, and it's probably a whole ugly hoard of hidden codes messing things up. You may actually need to look at these codes to figure out what the heck you've done.

To see the hidden codes, press the F11 key, the Reveal Codes command. You see your document split into two portions on-screen, as shown in Figure 4-1. The top portion doesn't change much. The bottom portion, however, shows secret, hidden codes that you can't otherwise see in your document.

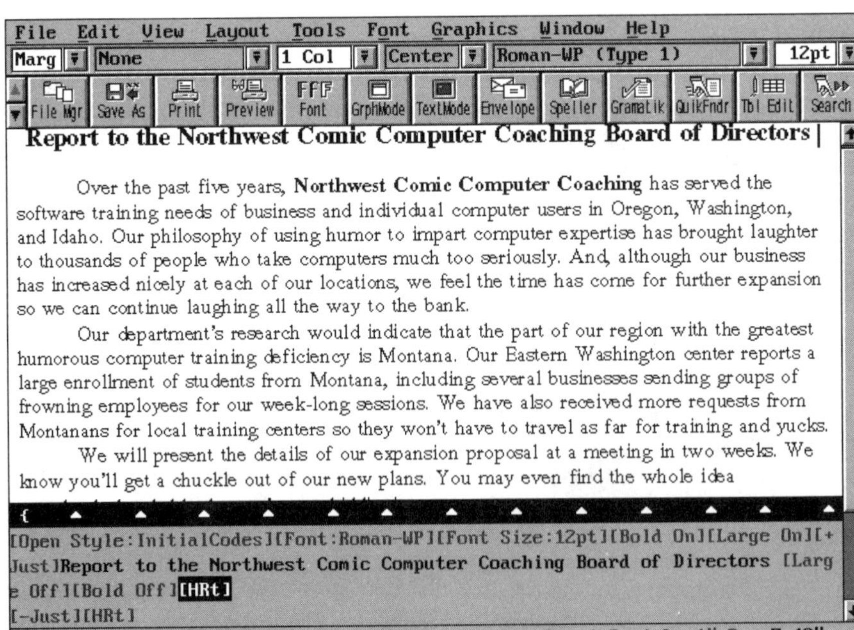

Figure 4-1: A document with Reveal Codes turned on.

- If your keyboard doesn't have an F11 key, you can use the Alt-F3 key combination for the Reveal Codes command.
- The divider line that separates the top and bottom parts of the screen contains some almost-useful information. The triangles represent each tab stop. The left and right brackets represent the left and right margins.
- Table 4-1 lists some of the codes you may see and what they do.
- Some codes just seem to appear for no reason. An example is the *[SRt]* code that appears at the end of each line of text within paragraphs. It represents a soft return. A soft return jiggles around as you edit your text, but it always stays at the end of a line. The *[HRt]* code, the symbol for a hard return, appears when you press the Enter key. This code doesn't move because you don't want it to. You definitely want your paragraph to end right there.
- If you encounter a code that you don't understand in the Reveal Codes window, you can look it up in Appendix B of the *WordPerfect Reference* manual. I don't normally recommend turning to this dreaded manual, but I must make an exception in this case because there's no way I'm going to retype all that information here.
- Some codes come in pairs, and they affect the text between them. For example, bold text starts with a *[Bold On]* code and ends with a *[Bold Off]* code.
- *Open codes*, such as line spacing and justification, affect the entire document from the code's location until either the end of the document or until another code specifies some other kind of formatting.
- At the beginning of every document is an *[Open Style:Initial Codes]* code. This code contains formatting you've added to the Initial Codes style. For more information about how this style works, and styles in general, see Chapter 11.

Examining the codes

When the Reveal Codes window is visible, you can see the codes lurking in your document just as plain as day. Move the cursor about, and you can even highlight some of the codes to read more information about them.

For example, a *[Bold On]* code contains font and size information. If you position the cursor on the *[Bold On]* code, it expands to reveal its hidden information, such as *[Bold On:Dutch 001 Bold; 12pt]*.

You can move the cursor to any code by clicking the code with the mouse.

Deleting excess secret codage

Codes, and the formatting they represent, can be deleted just like ordinary text. To delete a code, position the cursor on the code and press the Delete key. Zap! It's gone.

- You can't delete codes with Reveal Codes turned off. If you try, the cursor just moves past the code without deleting it.
- You can delete a pair of codes by deleting either the on or the off code. For example, deleting the *[Bold On]* or the *[Bold Off]* code zaps the whole pair and returns the text betwixt them to nonbold.
- If you accidentally delete a paired code, you can instantly reverse the damage by pressing Ctrl-Z, the **U**ndo command. Don't use the **Un**delete command to restore paired codes. It won't work.

Auto Code Placement

WordPerfect's formatting codes generally affect text from their location in the document to the end of the document, or until another code changes the formatting. It stands to reason that it's extremely important where the codes are placed in your document, and it explains why formatting can get so unexplainably screwy at times.

A good way to avoid the screwiness of secret code placement (which shouldn't be your concern in the first place because it's all so secret) is to take advantage of WordPerfect's Auto Code Placement feature. With this feature, you never have to worry about where your cursor is or bother with secret codes when you make formatting changes.

With Auto Code Placement, WordPerfect tries to put certain codes in their most logical position. WordPerfect isn't always correct, but at least it tries. Some codes get moved to the beginning of the paragraph that the cursor is in; others are moved to the beginning of the page; and some codes don't get moved at all.

Using Auto Code Placement makes sense. Heck, it's automatic. You don't need to do anything to use it, unless you accidentally turn it off. If Auto Code Placement isn't working and you notice that your formatting is getting screwy, press Shift-F1, E to summon the Environment dialog box. Look at item number T, Auto Code Placement. Be sure that there is an X in the check box. If there isn't, press T. Press Home, F7 to close the dialog boxes.

- Table 4-1 lists some of the more common codes you encounter in your travels through Reveal Codes. An X in one of the Auto Code Placement columns indicates how Auto Code Placement affects that code, if at all.

Table 4-1 Some Common WordPerfect Codes

Auto Code Placement			
How It Looks	***What It Does***	***Start of Paragraph***	***Start of Page***
[Bold On][Bold Off]	Bolds text		
[Und On][Und Off]	Underlines text		
[Ln Spacing]	Sets amount of space between lines	X	
[Lft Mar]	Sets left margin	X	
[Rgt Mar]	Sets right margin	X	
[Bot Mar]	Sets bottom margin		X
[Top Mar]	Sets top margin		X
[Suppress]	Suppresses codes		X
[Just]	Sets justification	X	
[Cntr Cur Pg:On]	Centers contents of the current page vertically		
[Small On][Small Off]	Changes relative font size		
[Ext Large On][Ext Large Off]	Changes relative font size		
[Tab Set]	Sets tab stop positions	X	
[Bookmark]	Sets a location to move to		

- Why turn off Auto Code Placement? Say you want to insert a code at a specific location. I don't know why. But suppose that you do. First, turn off Auto Code Placement (switch off the X in the Environment dialog box) and then turn it back on after you're done with your formatting.
- You must be in the correct paragraph or page for Auto Code Placement to work correctly. For example, you would generally want to be on the first page of the document before changing the top and bottom margins. Thanks to Auto Code Placement, it doesn't matter *where* you are on that page, but it does help to be *on* that page.
- Auto Code Placement sticks formatting codes where they should logically go. So if you press F11 and turn on Reveal Codes, you may not see the code for the formatting you just did. Look at the beginning of the page or paragraph. Auto Code Placement may have placed it there for you.

Changing the Reveal Codes window size

When you turn on Reveal Codes, you see only a small portion of the actual document in the Reveal Codes window. If you want to see a bigger portion of your document shown in this "naked code" manner, you can change the Reveal Codes window percentage by following these steps:

1. **Press Ctrl-F3.**

   The Screen dialog box appears.

2. **Press C (Reveal Codes Window Percentage).**
3. **Type a number from 5 to 95.**

   For example, type **50** to have the Reveal Codes window take up 50 percent or half the screen.

4. **Press Home, F7.**

   The Reveal Codes window size changes. Of course, you can't see the effect until you turn on Reveal Codes, F11.

- You may want to change the Reveal Codes window percentage for different types of documents. For example, if you're creating complex desktop-publishing-type documents, such as brochures or newsletters, you may want to see a larger Reveal Codes window.
- If you like having the Reveal Codes divider line on-screen with its tab and margin markers, consider setting the Reveal Codes window percentage to 5 and leaving Reveal Codes on all the time.

Suppressing codes

Some formatting codes, such as headers, footers, and page numbering, cause information to be placed on every page. Every page! Even that first page, your nifty title page, which looks so utterly dorky with a page number and heading. Yuck. Time to start suppressing.

Suppressing is the art of telling WordPerfect to ignore certain secret codes and remove their effects from the current page. To suppress a code, follow these steps:

1. **Press Shift-F8, P.**

   Or choose Layout⇨Page.

   The Page Format dialog box appears.

2. Press U (Suppress).

The Suppress (This Page Only) dialog box appears, as shown in Figure 4-2.

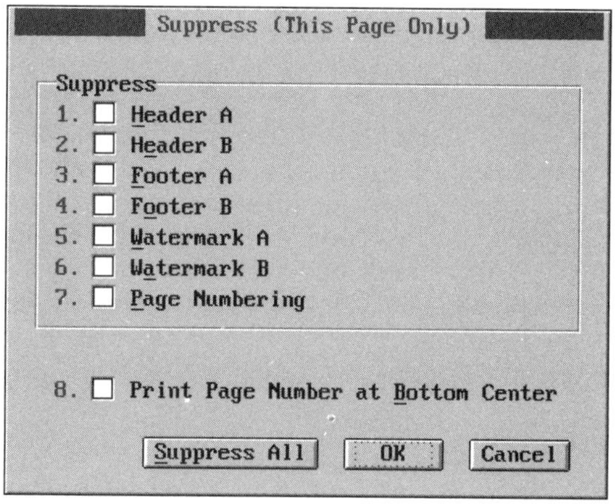

Figure 4-2: The Suppress (This Page Only) dialog box.

3. Press the letter next to each feature you don't want to appear on the current page.

For example, press 1 for Header A and 3 for Footer A, if it's your title page. Or you can press S (Suppress All) if you don't want any of the listed features to appear on the current page.

4. Press Home, F7 to close the dialog boxes.

The features you suppressed won't appear on the current page. They will, however, appear on the preceding and following pages.

REMEMBER

- If you dare to look, a *[Suppress]* code appears in the Reveal Codes window at the top of the current page. See "How it all works" earlier in this chapter.
- You can place the cursor on the *[Suppress]* code to see which features you are suppressing. For example, *[Suppress:PgNum]* means that the page number won't appear on this page.
- If you change your mind and want the page number or header or whatever to appear on the page where you inserted a *[Suppress]* code, just turn on Reveal Codes (F11), use the arrow keys to highlight the *[Suppress]* code, and press the Delete key.

The Secret Joys of Hidden Text

The most modest of WordPerfect's text-formatting attributes is invisible. It's just too shy to show its face. The hidden-text attribute causes your text to show up as nothing on-screen. You can't see it. And it won't print. Sounds next to useless, but there is a point here. Somewhere.

There are some practical uses for hiding text. Suppose that you're writing a report for general distribution in your company, and you'd like to include some information that should only be seen by top management. WordPerfect lets you create the confidential information as hidden text and keep it hidden on the copies you print for general distribution but display it on the top management's copies — or vice versa, depending on how long you plan to work there.

To hide text, follow these steps:

1. **Block the text you want to hide.**

   Refer to Chapter 6 in *WordPerfect 6 For Dummies* for information on marking blocks of text.

2. **Press Alt-F5.**

   The Mark Text dialog box appears.

3. **Press N for Hidden Text.**

   The Hidden Text dialog box appears, as shown in Figure 4-3.

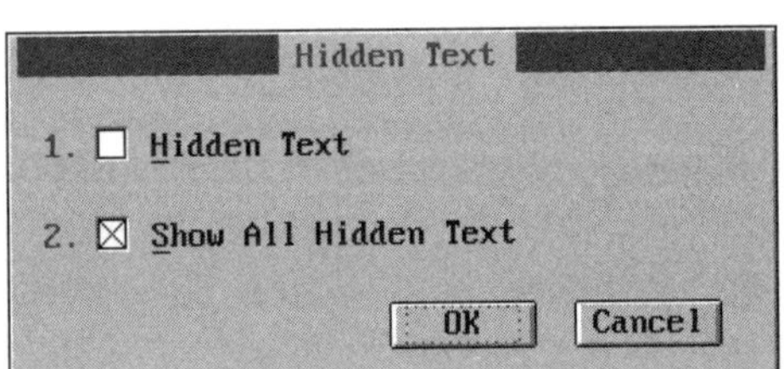

Figure 4-3: The Hidden Text dialog box.

4. **Press H to put an X in the Hidden Text check box.**
5. **Press S to remove the X from the Show All Hidden Text box.**
6. **Press Home, F7 to close the dialog boxes.**

   The text vanishes.

- If you press F11 and take a look at where the text was in the Reveal Codes window, you'll see a *[Hidden]* code. If you highlight the code, it expands to show you as much of the hidden text as will fit in the Reveal Codes window.

- You can display the hidden text at any time by pressing Alt-F5, N, S, Home, F7. The text reappears, just as if it had never been hidden. It is still marked as hidden text, however. Press F11 to turn on Reveal Codes, and you see the text surrounded by *[Hidden On]* and *[Hidden Off]* codes.
- Even though the feature is called Hidden Text, you can hide anything — graphics, tables, fine jewelry, "real" numbers from your tax return, you name it.
- If you want to set the hidden text apart from the unhidden text in the document, consider using another font or appearance attribute. Refer to Chapter 9 for more information about fonts.
- When the text is hidden, it doesn't take up any space in the document.
- When you print a document with hidden text that isn't displayed, the hidden text doesn't print.
- Be careful when editing a document that has undisplayed hidden text. You can accidentally delete the *[Hidden]* code and nuke a bunch of text. If you do make such a disastrous mistake and realize the error of your ways right after you've done it, press Ctrl-Z to undo the damage.

Adding Comments and Suggestions

Comments are notes and suggestions you can write in a document, but unlike Hidden Text, comments never print and can never embarrass you. Basically, a comment is like a sticky note you put in your document to remind you of something or to tell a co-author which way is up. Comments even appear in your text in a nice little frame (and they don't fall off the monitor like sticky notes usually end up doing).

To create a comment, follow these steps:

1. **Press Ctrl-F7.**

   The Notes dialog box appears.

2. **Press C for Comment.**
3. **Press C again for Create.**

   . . . and it looks like it didn't work. But you're really in "Comment mode." You can tell by looking at the left side of the status bar on the bottom of the screen. It says *Comment: Press F7 when done.*

4. **Type your comment text.**

   Dear Ralph, this next section really hurts. Were you drunk?

5. **Press F7.**

   The text you typed appears, surrounded by a double-line border, as shown in Figure 4-4.

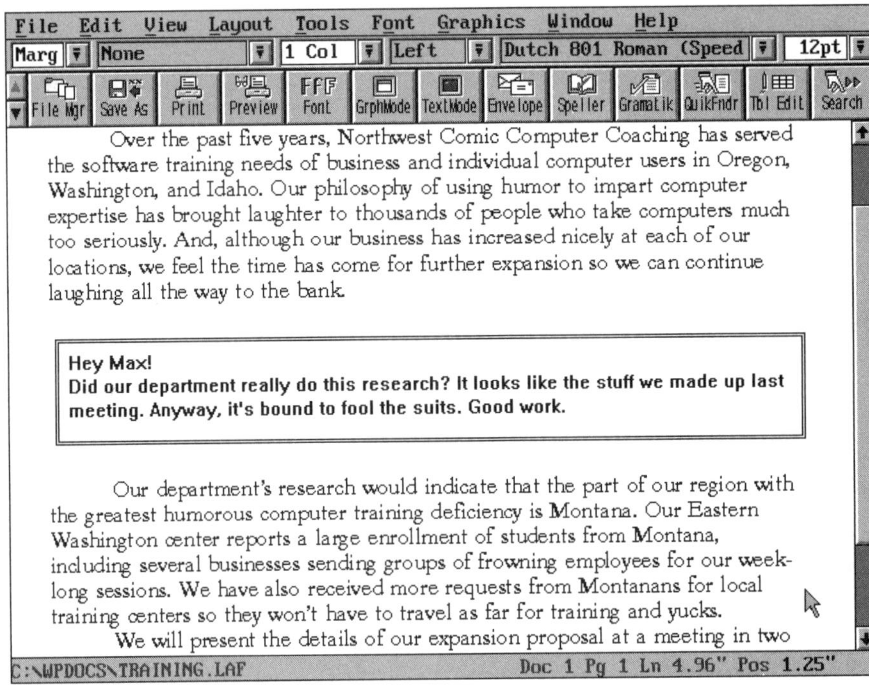

Figure 4-4: A comment within a document.

- Comments can include any elements that are found in normal documents, such as fancy formatting, graphics, and tables. Don't waste too much time, though, because they don't print.
- Because the comment is always there on-screen, the *[Comment]* code in the Reveal Codes window doesn't expand when the cursor is on it. You just have to look at the screen.
- You can hide the display of comments. To hide them, press Alt-V, N, W, D. Be sure that there is no X in the Display Comments box. Then press Home, F7. Repeat the steps to redisplay the comments.
- If you can't see your comments on-screen and you followed the steps in the preceding tip to be sure that Display Comments is turned on, you are probably viewing your document in Page mode. Page mode displays the document the way it looks when it prints. Because comments don't print, you don't see the comment on-screen in this mode. Press Alt-V, G to switch to Graphics mode.
- You can convert a comment to text so that it always appears in the document and prints by pressing Ctrl-F7, C, T.
- Unless you convert a comment to text, it never affects the cursor position in the document.
- You can convert existing text to a comment by blocking the text and pressing Ctrl-F7, C, C.

Hyphenation

You want your documents to look as professional as possible. You want your boss or clients to think you paid big bucks to have every inconsequential memo professionally desktop published. If this is true, you either have to learn a little about hyphenation or spend the big bucks and actually have your documents professionally desktop published.

For most informal business documents that are *left-justified* (meaning the left margin is lined up and the right one isn't) and are not in several narrow columns, you probably don't need to deal with hyphenation. But narrow columns and full justification create big ugly gaps between words on some of your lines. Horrid!

WordPerfect provides several ways to put hyphens in words so that they can be split between lines. The good news is that they're all pretty painless.

Most word processing pros will tell you not to bother with hyphenation. The reason they usually give is that "automatic hyphenation slows down the computer." That's true. But what's more important is that automatic hyphenation looks ugly on standard text.

Automatic hyphenation

The easiest way to hyphenate is, of course, the automatic way. You just tell WordPerfect to hyphenate automatically and let 'er rip. Almost.

To turn on automatic hyphenation, follow these steps:

1. **Move the cursor to the paragraph where you want to start hyphenating.**
2. **Press Shift-F8.**

   The Format dialog box appears.
3. **Press L.**

   The Line Format dialog box appears.
4. **Press Y to put an X in the Hyphenation check box.**
5. **Press Home, F7 to close the dialog boxes and return to your document.**

   Now hyphens are inserted to split words that extend beyond the right margin. This happens automatically as you type. It may even drive you nuts.

Hyphen position is determined by the Speller dictionary. If a hyphen is inserted automatically, you can rest assured that it is inserted in the right place.

The annoying Position Hyphen dialog box

If a word that extends into the right margin isn't in the Speller dictionary, WordPerfect freaks out, and a Position Hyphen dialog box pops up, as shown in Figure 4-5.

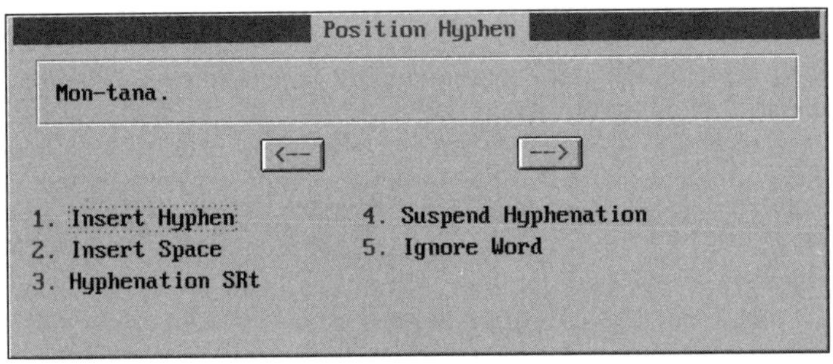

Figure 4-5: The Position Hyphen dialog box.

To insert a hyphen at the suggested location, press the Enter key. To change the position of the hyphen, press the left- or right-arrow keys until the hyphen is correctly positioned, and then press the Enter key. If you don't want the word hyphenated at all, press 5 for Ignore Word, and the entire word is moved to the next line.

- You can choose to split the word with a space instead of a dash by pressing 2 for Insert Space.
- You can split the word without a dash or a space by pressing 3 for Hyphenation SRt. You may choose to use this option to split a word containing slashes, such as and/or.

To prompt or not to prompt

That annoying Position Hyphen dialog box. Who needs it? If it's bugging you, you do have options. You can have WordPerfect hyphenate without bothering you at all. Or, if you're a real masochist or perfectionist, you can choose to be bothered more often. The choice is yours.

To determine when WordPerfect prompts you for hyphenation position, press Shift-F1, E, P. Use the up- and down-arrow keys to select your choice (Never, When Required, or Always), press the Enter key, and then press Home, F7.

- The When Required option is the standard setting and usually the correct one. With this setting, you are prompted only when words that aren't in WordPerfect's dictionary need to be hyphenated.
- The Never option gets rid of the annoying Position Hyphen dialog box altogether, but it doesn't hyphenate any words that aren't in the dictionary. It just wraps them to the next line. Bummer. You can always go back and hyphenate those words manually. See the next section for details on manual hyphenation.
- The Always option is the most annoying of all. With Always set, the Position Hyphen dialog box pops up every time a word is about to be hyphenated, even if the word is in the dictionary. This can be a good option if you always want to determine if and where hyphens are inserted or if you just love dialog boxes and eternal editing.

Manual hyphenation

Instead of letting WordPerfect put hyphens where it thinks they should go, you can do the job manually. There are some good reasons for manual hyphenation. For one thing, it can be fairly unattractive to have too many hyphens in a paragraph. By manually hyphenating, you choose how many hyphens to use and where they go.

To tell WordPerfect that it should hyphenate a word, and where, if the word ever ends up extending into the right margin, position the cursor where you want the hyphen to appear in the word and press Ctrl - -.

Okay, that was confusing. Ctrl - - means to press and hold down the Ctrl key and then press the - (dash) key. Ctrl - - inserts a "maybe" hyphen into the word. WordPerfect hyphenates the word only if it lands at the end of a line, near the right margin. Otherwise, the word is not hyphenated, and the hyphen inserted by Ctrl - - doesn't show up on-screen or when printed.

TIP

- You can spy out the Ctrl - - hyphen by checking out the Reveal Codes window. Press the F11 key and scan for the *[Soft Hyphen]* code.
- If you use automatic hyphenation, you can even use these soft hyphen codes to tell WordPerfect where to hyphenate words that are in the dictionary.
- You can delete the soft hyphen by positioning the cursor on the code and pressing the Delete key.

You've entered the hyphenation zone . . .

WordPerfect decides which words to hyphenate based on an invisible space, called the *hyphenation zone*, on either side of the right margin. The size of the hyphenation zone determines how many words are hyphenated during automatic hyphenation.

Think of the hyphenation zone as a bumpy line on a freeway. Like lazy drivers, words that cross over the bumpy line are ripe candidates for being hyphenated. "Wake up!" Words on either side of the bumpy-line hyphenation zone are on the current line or the next, without being drawn and quartered by a hyphen. There are some other convoluted rules, but the bottom line is the narrower the hyphenation zone, the more hyphens you get; the wider the zone, the fewer hyphens.

To change the hyphenation zone, follow these steps:

1. **Press Shift-F8, L.**

   The Line Format dialog box appears.

2. **Press Z to highlight the number in the Left hyphenation zone box.**
3. **Type a number for the left portion of the hyphenation zone and press the Enter key.**
4. **Type a number for the right portion of the hyphenation zone and press the Enter key.**
5. **Press Home, F7 to accept the changes and return to your document.**

TIP

- The standard hyphenation zone settings are a good compromise. They allow for reasonably tight text without overdoing the hyphens.
- The larger the hyphenation zone values you enter, the fewer hyphens you'll have in your documents, but you may end up with ugly text.
- If you change hyphenation zones in a document that is using automatic hyphenation, you may be prompted to reposition the hyphen for some words.
- The hyphenation zone has nothing to do with the old television series with Rod Serling.

Chapter 5

More on Lists, Indexes, Notes, and Cross-References

In This Chapter

- Using WordPerfect's list features
- Listening to Franz Liszt
- Creating a table of contents
- Creating lists and indexes
- Doing cross-references
- Stumbling over footnotes and endnotes

Who can resist the list? Especially Franz Liszt. But when it comes to WordPerfect, pretty much everyone avoids the overly techy and somewhat focused subject of lists. This isn't a problem for most folk. What is a problem is when you find yourself manually doing what WordPerfect can do automatically. In a few instances, this includes making a list — the secrets of which this chapter divulges in scrutinizing detail.

Using WordPerfect's List-Making Features

Lists are collections of things that appear in your document. For example, you may have several tables or figures — and a desire to have a list of each, along with their page numbers. That's a basic list, something WordPerfect can whip out in no time.

Another type of list is the table of contents. Basically, that's a list of your document's headings along with their page numbers. In the same vein, there are indexes that point to various topics in a book, plus footnotes and endnotes and the ubiquitous cross-references (the see-this-or-that-on-page-24 type stuff).

The problem: To create these lists, you often work manually, referring to page numbers as "page XX" and remembering to replace the XX with a real page number later.

The solution: WordPerfect can create, or *generate*, your lists automagically. You tell it the type of list and what to include in the list, and WordPerfect fills in the page numbers no matter what. Edit your document? No problem. WordPerfect updates the page numbers and regenerates the list in two snaps.

Here are the basic list-making steps:

1. **Tell WordPerfect what type of list you want.**
2. **Mark various bits of text for inclusion in the list.**
3. **Generate the list (done by WordPerfect).**

   No problem.

- WordPerfect lets you create several types of reference lists for your documents, including tables of contents, indexes, and lists of figures and tables. There's even a special list type, called a table of authorities, for lawyerly folks. I think I've hidden under that table a few times in school.
- Though WordPerfect has several types of lists, they're all created the same way. After you know how to create any one of the lists, you'll understand the basic steps for creating the others.
- REMEMBER: Always *generate* your lists before you print your document. Then if you've done any editing of your document, the page numbers are updated on the printed copy. WordPerfect reminds you if you try to print a document that needs to be generated.
- The greatest pianist ever, Franz Liszt, was educated by Mozart-rival Antonio Salieri.

Creating a Table of Contents

A table of contents is basic, simple, and familiar. Though most documents don't need one, WordPerfect can whip it up in a matter of microseconds with the three basic steps for creating any list: Tell WordPerfect what type of list you're creating, mark items to include in the list, and then generate the list. These three steps are outlined in the following sections.

Telling WordPerfect about the table of contents

To create a place for a table of contents in your document, follow these steps:

1. **Move the cursor to the location in your document where you want the table of contents to appear.**

   Normally, this is up front, right after the title page, the copyright information, a Library of Congress information page, about the author information, about IDG Books Worldwide information, the page thanking Pat McGovern, and the page rah-rahing other books in the series.

2. **Put the table of contents on its own private page.**

   Press Ctrl-Enter (Hard Page Break) and then press the up-arrow key once and press Ctrl-Enter again. This puts the table of contents in its own space so that it won't interfere with the rest of the document.

3. **Press Alt-F5, D, C.**

   The Define Table of Contents dialog box appears, as shown in Figure 5-1.

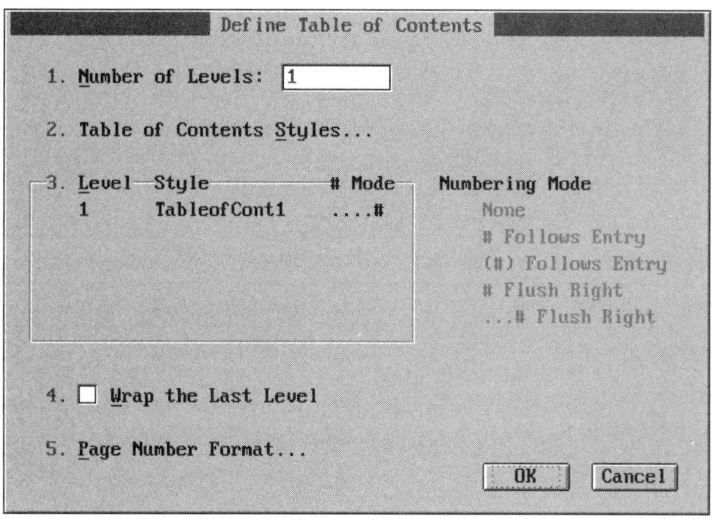

Figure 5-1: The Define Table of Contents dialog box.

4. **Press N and enter the Number of Levels.**

   For example, in a book such as this, the chapter title is the first level, and then there's a main section heading and a subsection heading. So this book needs a table of contents three levels deep. WordPerfect lets you have up to five levels.

5. **Press Enter to lock in the number of levels.**

6. **Press Home, F7.**

   This returns you to your document. It's not very impressive so far, but WordPerfect knows what you're creating (a table of contents) and where to put it.

- Want to be cool? Call the table of contents the TOC (tee-oh-see). That's what publishing people call it.
- You may want to enter a title for the table of contents on the line above the table of contents definition code. Perhaps something off-the-wall, like *Table of Contents*.
- You can have more than one table of contents in a document, each with a different level of detail. For example, this book has a "Contents at a Glance" with just one level and a "Table of Contents" with several levels. Just create the two Table of Contents definitions where you want the tables of contents to appear.
- You can change everything about the way tables of contents are formatted by using the Table of Contents Styles option in the Define Table of Contents dialog box. You change table of contents styles the same way you edit any styles. Refer to Chapter 11 for information on using WordPerfect's Style feature.
- WordPerfect can be told exactly how to set up your table of contents in the Define Table of Contents dialog box (see Step 3). Area number 3 in the dialog box lists styles and formats for the various levels in your TOC. Highlight that area by pressing the 3 key and then use the up- and down-arrow keys to highlight the level you want to change. The numbers to the right of that area and how they format each level are shown in Table 5-1.

Table 5-1 Examples of Numbering Modes

Numbering Mode	*How it formats the TOC*
None	Chapter One, The Beginning
# Follows Entry	Chapter One, The Beginning 1
(#) Number Follows Entry	Chapter One, The Beginning (1)
# Flush Right	Chapter One, The Beginning 1
...# Flush Right	Chapter One, The Beginning....1

Sticking things into the table of contents list

A table of contents contains headings and titles from elsewhere in your document. To put those items in your table of contents, you need to seek them out in your document and mark them by using WordPerfect's unknown marking command. Follow these steps to use the marking command:

1. **Block the text you want included in the table of contents.**

   Highlight the heading, chapter title, or section title as a block. Refer to Chapter 6 in *WordPerfect 6 For Dummies* for specific block-marking instructions.

2. **Press Alt-F5.**

   The Mark Text dialog box appears, as shown in Figure 5-2.

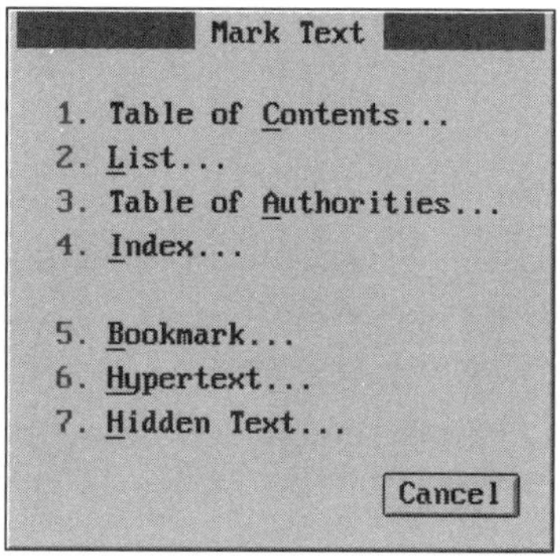

Figure 5-2: The Mark Text dialog box.

3. **Press C (Table of Contents).**

   The Mark Table of Contents dialog box appears.

4. **Type a number for the level of this entry and press the Enter key.**

   For example, a chapter heading would be level 1; sections in the chapter would be level 2; subsections would be level 3; and so on.

5. **Repeat these steps and mark the other entries for your table of contents.**

- If the Mark Text dialog box doesn't appear, you don't have any text marked as a block on-screen.
- When blocking the text for the table of contents, don't include any formatting codes, such as font or attribute codes. If you do, the formatting will be included in the table of contents.
- If you're curious about how WordPerfect knows what text to include in your table of contents (and *I* wouldn't bother), you can use the Reveal Codes command to see some secrets. Press the F11 key and notice the *[Mrk Txt ToC Begin]* and *[Mrk Txt ToC End]* secret codes surrounding the marked text. Refer to Chapter 4 for more information on secret codes and the Reveal Codes command.

Generating the table of contents in your document

After defining the table of contents and marking text to include in it, the final step is to *generate* the table of contents. This is the automatic stuff WordPerfect is famous for. If you're not used to saving time, stand back for a change.

To generate the table of contents list, follow these steps:

1. **Press Alt-F5, G.**

   The Generate dialog box appears.

2. **Press the Enter key.**

   This generates the table of contents, along with any other lists in the document.

   The table of contents appears in your document right where you told WordPerfect to put it. A sample of how this may look is shown in Figure 5-3.

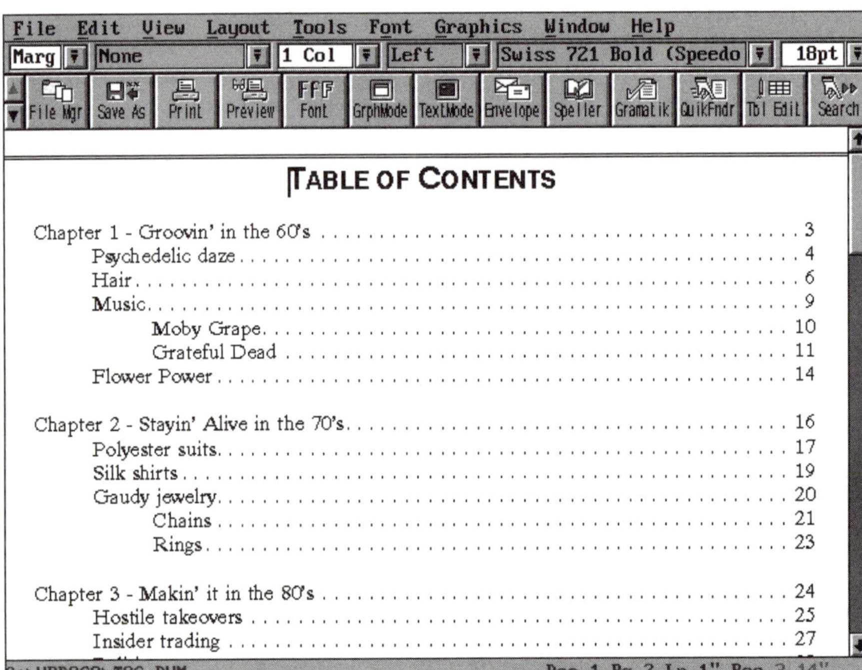

Figure 5-3: A typical table of contents.

- The table of contents is made up of ordinary text. It can be edited and formatted just like any other text in the document.
- You can always add new items to your table of contents. Just seek them out in your document and mark them as described in the preceding section.
- If the table of contents contains a blank, you've probably marked something that wasn't there or some text that was deleted. You need to use the Reveal Codes command, as discussed in Chapter 4, to seek out and delete the extra TOC codes.
- A warning message may appear before the table of contents is generated. That's WordPerfect's way of letting you know that all the lists in your document are about to be updated and replaced. Press the Enter key to continue.
- *Hungarian Rhapsody No. 2 in D Minor* was written by Franz Liszt. Donald Duck and Daffy Duck played it on dueling pianos in the movie *Who Framed Roger Rabbit?*

Creating Lists of Lists

There are other lists besides a table of contents that WordPerfect can deal with. For example, there's the list list, which is just a list. The entries you mark for the list list appear in the list in the order they appear in the document. The only difference is that a list list can have only one level, not multiple levels like a table of contents.

List lists are well-suited for listing things such as captions, tables, figures, graphics, and other unofficial items. Aunt Mary's limericks could be a list, allowing your reader to hurry off and find only them in your document.

As with the table of contents, WordPerfect slaps together a list list in three steps. Please refer to the section "Creating a Table of Contents" earlier in this chapter for the full details. The following steps are brief because, well, I don't like typing out the same stuff twice in one chapter.

To create a list, follow these steps:

1. **Move the cursor to the location in your document where you want the list to appear.**

   Up front is usually best, although the list can be at the end of the document or in the middle. Oh, I should keep my mouth shut.

2. **Press Ctrl-Enter (Hard Page Break) and then press the up-arrow key once and press Ctrl-Enter again.**

   This sets the list off by itself, away from the rest of the document.

3. **Press Alt-F5, D, L.**

   The Define List dialog box appears.

4. **Press C (Create).**

   The Create List dialog box pops up.

5. **Type a name for your list and press the Enter key.**

   The name is just for your reference and doesn't appear in the list. For example, if you're making a list of figures and later a list of tables, call one *figures* and the other *tables*.

   - If you want to include captions from graphics, press I (Include Graphics) and use the up- and down-arrow keys to highlight the graphics box type whose captions you want to include. Refer to Chapter 13 for information on inserting graphics and captions into your documents.
   - You can also select a numbering mode from the dialog box. Refer to Table 5-1 for a description of how the numbering modes work and look.

6. **Press Enter and then S (Select) to complete the list definition.**

   The first part is done. The list is defined in your document. The next phase is to seek out and mark items to include in the list.

7. **Mark items you want to include in your list list.**

   Mark the text in your document that you want included in the list. Then press Alt-F5 to display the Mark Text dialog box. Press L to select the List item. The Mark Text for List dialog box appears. If the correct list name appears in the List Name text box, press the Enter key. If not, press F5 and select the correct name from the List Definitions dialog box.

   - Don't mark any text at all if you want the list to contain only the captions from your graphics. Just tell WordPerfect to include the graphics box type.

8. **Keep marking the items you want included in your list.**

9. **Generate the list.**

After marking the items, press Alt-F5. The Generate dialog box appears. Press G and the Enter key to generate the table of contents, along with any other lists in the document.

Don't forget to generate the document before printing if you've made any editing changes so that the page references are accurate. Press Alt-F5, G and press the Enter key to generate.

Creating an Index

Next to the table of contents, indexes are the most popular type of lists to put in documents. But unlike the table of contents, the index references specific words or portions of text, not just headings and chapter titles. Also, indexes appear at the end of a document and in alphabetical order.

In WordPerfect, an index is created in the same three steps as creating any other list. Full details are provided in the first section of this chapter. Otherwise, to create an index, heed the following steps:

1. **Move the cursor to the location in your document where you want the index to appear.**

   Near the end.

2. **Set aside a page for the index.**

   Press Ctrl-Enter (Hard Page Break) and then press the up-arrow key once and press Ctrl-Enter again. This keeps the index from interfering with the rest of the document.

3. **Press Alt-F5, D, I.**

   The Define Index dialog box appears, as shown in Figure 5-4.

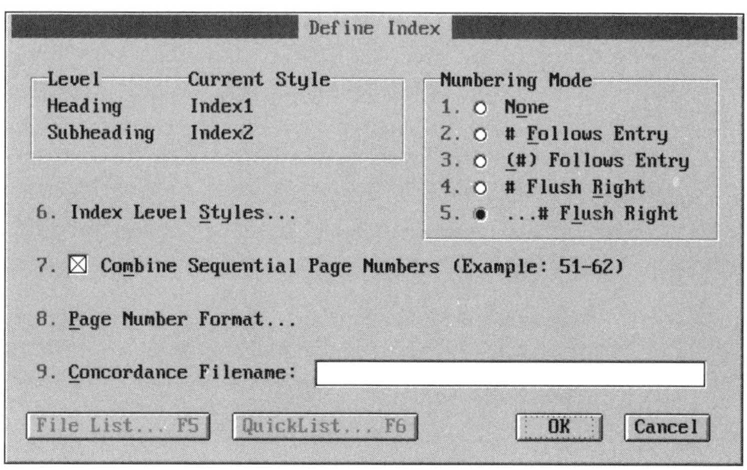

Figure 5-4: The Define Index dialog box.

4. **Press Home, F7 to complete the index definition.**

5. **Mark text in your document to include in the index.**

   Scour your document for index-worthy text. When you find something, mark that text as a block: Press Alt-F4 and use the cursor keys to highlight the text. For example, if you want Franz Liszt in your index, highlight his whole name. With the block marked, press Alt-F5. The Mark Text dialog box appears. Press I to select Index. The Mark Index dialog box appears, as shown in Figure 5-5.

Figure 5-5: The Mark Index dialog box.

   If you want the marked text to appear as an index heading, just press Home, F7 and you're done.

   If you want to add a subheading, press the Tab key, type in the subheading, and press Home, F7.

   If you want the marked text to appear as a subheading, type a heading in the Heading text box, press the Tab key, and then press Home, F7.

   The index entry doesn't have to be the same as the marked text in the document. For example, you can mark the phrase *disk operating system* in the document, but have it appear in the index as *DOS*. Just type **DOS** in the heading or subheading text box in the Mark Index dialog box.

6. **Repeat Step 5 to mark the other entries for your index.**

7. **After you're done, generate the index.**

   WordPerfect seeks out your indexed words and builds an index for you in the spot you specified in Step 1. To activate the Generate command, press Alt-F5, G. The Generate dialog box appears. Press the Enter key to generate the index, along with any other lists in the document.

- Generating your index also generates any other lists you may have in your document (table of contents, list list, and so on). A warning dialog box may alert you to this fact. Just press Enter to continue.
- If you want your index to appear as two or three columns, block the entire index and press Alt-F7, C, N. Enter the number of columns you want and press Home, F7. Refer to Chapter 14 for more information on columns.

- It took the computer industry years before word processing software contained commands to generate indexes and a table of contents. This oversight was primarily due to the fact that the computer manuals lacked those two items until just a few months ago.
- Don't forget to generate the document before printing if you've made any editing changes since you last generated. To generate, press Alt-F5, G and then press the Enter key. If a warning dialog box appears, just press the Enter key again.
- German composer Richard Wagner's father-in-law was none other than Franz Liszt.

Doing Cross-References

Cross-referencing is necessary — see page 51 (an example of a cross-reference). Unfortunately, as you edit a document, the page numbers may change, which means that the cross-references will be wrong, and you'll have to look them up again. What a bother! Fortunately, WordPerfect lets you cross-reference without having to know the exact page numbers.

Easy indexing with the concordance file

Face it, seeking out words and marking them for your index can be a pain. You can use WordPerfect's Search command (F2) and then mess with blocking — Alt-F5 and all that. But what a chore! Aren't computers supposed to make life easier? The answer is, well, they try.

To avoid going through this rigmarole and to have WordPerfect automatically include all occurrences of a word or phrase in the index, you can create a *concordance file* on disk. Just start a new document and type your list of words — the stuff you want included in your index. Type each word, name, or text tidbit on a line by itself and press Enter at the end of each line. If you want a subheading index item, just press the Tab key at the start of the line. Save the concordance file to disk when you're done.

When it comes time to define your index, set it up as described in Steps 1 through 3 in the section "Creating an Index" in this chapter. But in the Define Index dialog box, press C to activate the Concordance Filename text box. In that text box, type the name of your concordance file. Press Home, F7 and you're done. The only additional step you need to take is to generate the index, which is covered in Step 7 of the same section.

There is only one minor drawback to this trick: overindexing. You can end up with so many references for a common word or phrase that the index becomes useless. My advice is to consider using the concordance file for just words or phrases where you're sure that you want to refer to every occurrence in the document. Other stuff you can mark manually.

In WordPerfect, you can cross-reference almost anything: a page number, chapter, footnote, or a graphic's caption number. To create a cross-reference, you need to mark both the reference and the target (the thing being referenced), one after the other. Follow these steps:

1. **Position the cursor where you want the reference to appear.**
2. **Type any introductory text.**

   Such as **See page** or **Refer to**, followed by a space.
3. **Press Alt-F5, M (Mark Text), B (Both Reference and Target).**

   The Mark Cross-Reference and Target dialog box appears, as shown in Figure 5-6.

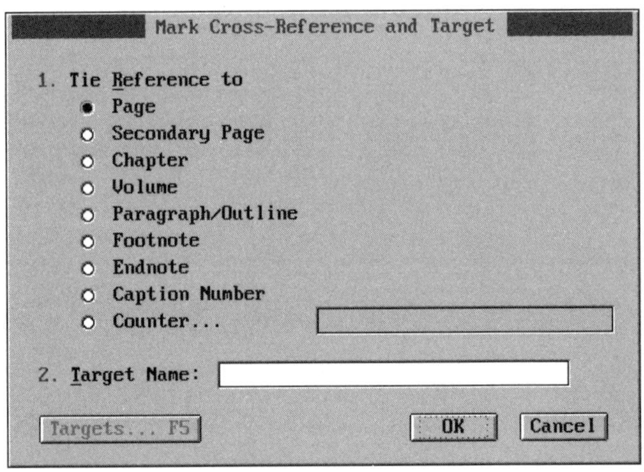

Figure 5-6: The Mark Cross-Reference and Target dialog box.

4. **Press R to select Tie Reference to.**

   Numbers appear on the left side of the list. Press 1 through 9, depending on what you're referencing. For example, if you want to do *Refer to page X*, press 1 for Page. If you're using *See Chapter X*, press 3 for Chapter. Most of the time, you'll press 1 for Page.
5. **Press T to select the name of the Target.**

   Type the name of the target you want to tie the reference to. The name is simply used as something that the reference and target have in common, so any name will do. The name you give it will not appear in the text.
6. **Press the Enter key twice.**

   A special dialog box opens up to reveal a view of your document.
7. **Position the cursor just after the target element.**

   Move the cursor to just after the blank space you typed after *Refer to.*

8. **Press the Enter key.**

   The reference is inserted into your document just as if you typed it. The major difference is that it's a WordPerfect page number reference, not plain old text. Now as you edit and rework your document, the page number will always reflect the location of your cross-reference.

- The target number appears immediately at the reference position only if you follow the preceding steps. If you mark the references and targets separately, the numbers don't appear until you generate the document (press Alt-F5, G, Enter to generate).
- After editing a document containing cross-references, you should generate it before printing to ensure accurate reference numbers. To generate, press Alt-F5, G and press the Enter key. A warning box will remind you of what you are doing.
- You can refer to a target as many times as necessary. Just use the same target name for each reference.

Notes on Footnotes and Endnotes

You can create footnotes or endnotes to more fully explain portions of your document. For example, if your document refers to some fact, a footnote or endnote can give the reference for that fact.[1]

The only difference between footnotes and endnotes is where they appear in the document. Footnotes appear at the bottom of the page containing the text the note refers to. Endnotes are simply a bunch of footnotes that are gathered together and placed at the end of the document.[2]

Creating Footnotes

When you create footnotes, they generally appear at the bottom of the page, separated from the rest of the page by a horizontal line. Although footnotes are usually numbered, you can choose to have them indicated by letters or characters.

[1] Franz Liszt was born in Hungary on October 22, 1811. Another fine Libra.

To create a footnote, follow these steps:

1. **Position the cursor in the document where you want the indicator for the footnote to appear.**

   The indicator means the little 1 or 2 or * or whatever that tells the reader, "Hey! Break that train of thought and jump down to the bottom of the page for an aside." (Even though that's not what the footnote is supposed to do.)

2. **Press Ctrl-F7.**

   The Notes dialog box appears.

3. **Press F (Footnote), C (Create).**

   The status bar lets you know you are creating a footnote by displaying *Footnote: Press F7 when done.* on the left side.

4. **Type whatever text you want for the footnote.**

   All formatting options are available for notes, including graphics and other fun junk.

5. **Press F7 when you're done typing the footnote.**

   The footnote number (or letter or character) appears where you placed your cursor when creating the footnote.

- The footnote itself can be seen only in Print Preview or Page mode view, or after you print (like, duh).
- You may want to press the spacebar to create a bit of space between the footnote text and its number (Step 4).
- To change the footnote numbering scheme, press Ctrl-F7, F, N. In the Set Footnote Number dialog box, press 2 to select a new numbering style. Press Home, F7 after you're done.
- You can edit a footnote by pressing Ctrl-F7, F, E. Then enter the number or letter of the footnote you want to edit and press the Enter key. Edit the footnote text as you would any document text and press F7 after you're finished.
- To delete a footnote, turn on Reveal Codes (F11) and delete the *[Footnote]* code for the footnote you want to delete. Any other footnotes in the document are automatically renumbered. Refer to Chapter 4 for more information on Reveal Codes.
- If you're writing lengthy footnotes, you may want WordPerfect to put a *continued* message at the end of the footnote to let the reader know the footnote is continued on the next page. To do this, move your cursor to the top of the document and press Ctrl-F7, F, O, C. Then press Home, F7.

- You can change the separator line between the footnote and the text by pressing Ctrl-F7, F, O, L and choosing one of the line options in the Footnote Separator Line dialog box.

Creating Endnotes

Creating endnotes works exactly like creating footnotes, as described in the preceding section. The only difference is that you specify you want endnotes in the Notes dialog box.

To create endnotes, follow these steps:

1. **Position the cursor in the document where you want the indicator for the endnote to appear.**
2. **Press Ctrl-F7, E (Endnote), C (Create).**

   You see before you the endnote editing screen. The status bar lets you know you are creating an endnote by displaying *Endnote: Press F7 when done.* on the left side.
3. **Type whatever text you want for the endnote.**
4. **Press F7 after you're done.**

   The endnote number (or letter or character) appears where you placed the cursor when creating the endnote.

TIP

- If you're using both footnotes and endnotes, it's a very good idea to change the numbering method between them. For example, number your footnotes and use letters for the endnotes. Press Ctrl-F7, E, N, 2 to reset the endnote numbering scheme.
- Franz Liszt was a pupil of Carl Czerny, who himself was once a pupil of Ludwig van Beethoven.

[2] Franz Liszt died in Germany on July 31, 1886.

Chapter 6

More on the (Ugh!) Keyboard

In This Chapter

- Making the keyboard your own
- Working the included keyboards
- Creating your own custom keyboard layouts

What more can be said about the keyboard? Especially the way WordPerfect abuses it. I'm certain that on planet Multidigitus, where everyone has 18 fingers on each hand and each one is 9 inches long with 7 joints, they find WordPerfect's keyboard commands a joy to use. "Extremely pleasurable," a Multidigitusian would say, slime dripping from its rubbery mouth. Yech!

The horrid truth is that WordPerfect's keyboard is a completely flexible thing. I have this theory that the fabric of the universe will some day unravel instantly, leaving each of us in a cosmic lurch — so does WordPerfect, which lets you do just about anything to the keyboard: Change it! Reassign keys! Make up your own commands! It can be a mess, which is why most people (including the Multidigitusians) put up with what they're given and never venture to try the exotic things you can do with your keyboard.

Making the Keyboard Your Own

The keyboard is the most personal and intimate of your computer's appendages. It's the part of your computer that you touch and caress as you try to cajole it to do your bidding. You tickle the keyboard. You peck at it. You pound it. Like most loved ones, keyboards take both love and abuse in stride.

The keyboard is such an everyday connection to your computer that there's no complex tutorial required on how to use it. You press the 2 key, and a 2 appears on-screen. Press the Enter key, and the cursor jumps to the beginning of the next line. So who but the most jealous types would want to make the keyboard their own?

Well, it's not really making it your own as much as finding that even-more perfect keyboard just for you. You can take advantage of one of the zillions of secret keyboard shortcuts for performing WordPerfect tasks or for navigating through and between documents. If that bores you, you may choose to use one of the other keyboard layouts included with WordPerfect or to customize the layout to do exactly what you want. Changing and customizing keyboard layouts is easily done and is covered throughout this chapter.

All Them Key Combinations

WordPerfect displays lists of all the available keystroke combinations and shortcut keys in its cuddly Help system. To display the shortcut keys, follow these steps:

1. **Press F1.**

   This displays the Help Contents screen.

2. **Highlight the Keystrokes or Shortcut Keys item.**

   Press the down-arrow key to move the highlight.

3. **Press the Enter key.**

   The Help dialog box listing the keystroke combinations or shortcut keys appears.

4. **Scroll up and down the list to see 'em all.**

   Use the up- and down-arrow keys or the scroll bar to move up and down the lists.

5. **Press the Esc key to clear the Help dialog box.**

TIP

TIP

- The function key shortcuts are listed on the plastic template thingy that should be near your keyboard's function keys. If you've lost yours, you can quickly display a reasonable facsimile by pressing the F1 key twice.
- You can print any Help screen, including the function key template, by pressing Shift-F7.
- If some of the shortcut keys or keystroke combinations don't work as advertised, you have probably switched to a keyboard layout other than the original. For more information, see "Working with the Strange Included Keyboards," later in this chapter. Way down there. Somewhere else. Just keep flipping pages until you find the "Working with the Strange Included Keyboards" section. Trust me. It's here somewhere.

Working with the Strange Included Keyboards

If you're dissatisfied with the way WordPerfect misuses your keyboard, be happy in the knowledge that the key commands are not etched in silicon. In fact, they're etched in Jell-O. An interesting Jell-O that you can change if you don't like it.

The fun-loving folks at WordPerfect have actually included *four* different keyboard command layouts, and each one causes various key combinations to yield different results. This is serious mass confusion!

- Don't get overwrought. There is a purpose for these different keyboard layouts (beyond adding confusion). The idea is to make certain tasks easier.
- The keyboard command layout you normally use, and the one described in this and every other book on WordPerfect, is called the ORIGINAL layout. How original.

To switch from one keyboard layout to another, follow these steps:

1. **Press Shift-F1.**

   The Setup dialog box appears.

2. **Press K (Keyboard Layout).**

   The Keyboard Layout dialog box appears, as shown in Figure 6-1.

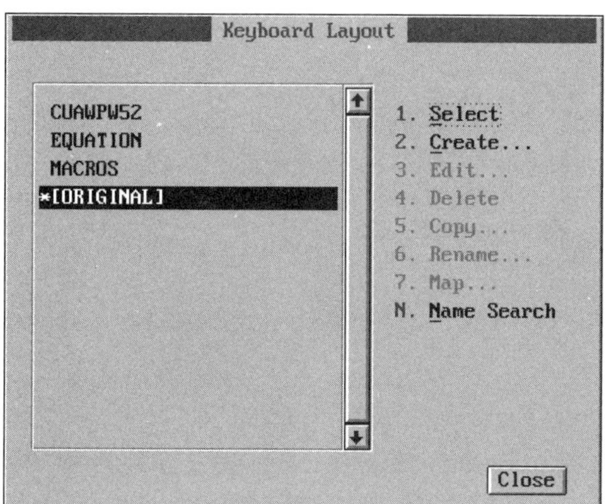

Figure 6-1: The Keyboard Layout dialog box.

3. **Highlight the keyboard you want.**

   Use the up- or down-arrow keys to highlight the keyboard layout name. I discuss each keyboard in the checked list that follows the steps.

4. **Press the S (Select) key when your special keyboard is highlighted.**

5. **Press the F7 key.**

   This closes the Setup dialog box and returns you to your document, with a new and funky keyboard layout that will doubtless aggravate you if you assume nothing has changed.

- You can tell which keyboard layout you are using by pressing Shift-F1. The name of the current keyboard layout is displayed next to the Keyboard Layout option in the Setup dialog box. If nothing is in the box, you are using the ORIGINAL keyboard layout.
- The CUAWPW52 keyboard layout makes navigating in WordPerfect more like navigating in a Windows program, such as WordPerfect for Windows. However . . .
- Avoid the CUAWPW52 keyboard layout if possible, even if you are familiar with Windows keystrokes. It's time to get used to the WordPerfect 6 for DOS method. You'll be less confused in the long run.
- The EQUATION layout facilitates creating equations with the Equation Editor. Refer to Chapter 22 for information on the Equation Editor.
- The MACROS keyboard layout makes using the included macros easier. See Chapter 17 for information on the included macros.
- To see how various keys and key combinations are assigned, refer to the next section.

Rolling Your Own Keyboard

If the included alternative keyboard layouts don't perform all the miracles you dreamed of, you can selfishly create your own keyboard layout. In this mode of operation, you — yes, you — actually tell WordPerfect what to do when you press a particular key or key combination. Such power! Don't let it go to your head.

You can assign one of the following three types of actions to a key or key combination:

1. Text, as in press a key and text is displayed.
2. A command, any command, such as displaying or hiding the Button Bar.
3. A macro, such as a macro for expediting the creation of memos, letters, and fax covers.

- For each keyboard layout, you can change the actions for as many keys and key combinations as you like.
- You can create as many keyboard layouts as you like.
- Refer to the preceding section, "Working with the Strange Included Keyboards," for information on switching between the various keyboard layouts.

To create your own keyboard layout, follow these steps:

1. **Press Shift-F1, K.**

   The Keyboard Layout dialog box appears (see Figure 6-1).

2. **Press C (Create).**

   The Keyboard Name dialog box pops up.

3. **Type a name for your new keyboard layout in the Keyboard Name text box.**

   Keyboard names follow the same rules as other DOS filenames, including WordPerfect document names. Type from one to eight characters using letters or numbers, but try, in the process, to make something intelligent-sounding. Do not specify a filename extension.

4. **Press the Enter key.**

   The Edit Keyboard dialog box appears, as shown in Figure 6-2. This will contain a list of the keys and their associated commands (or text or macros). Right now, the dialog box is blank because you're building a new keyboard layout.

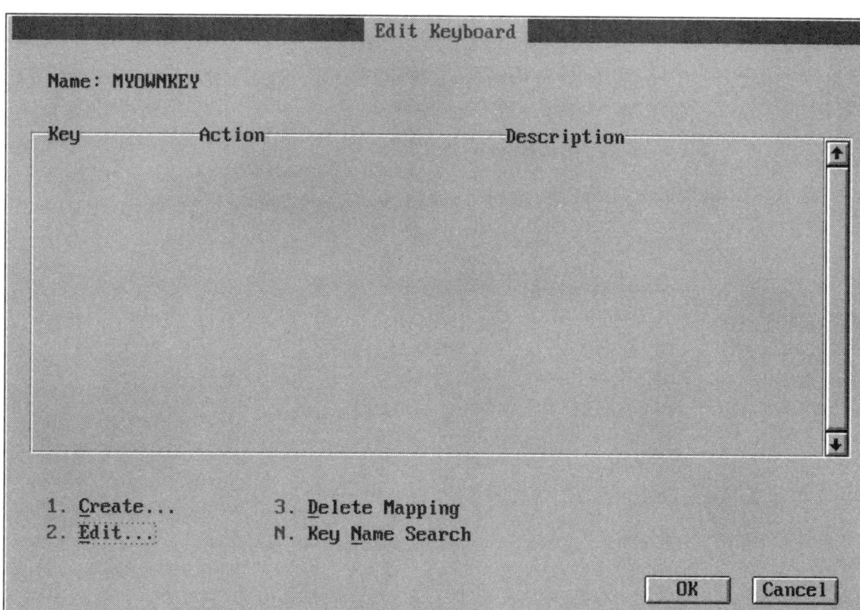

Figure 6-2: The Edit Keyboard dialog box.

5. **Press C (Create).**

   The Create Key dialog box appears, as shown in Figure 6-3, where you become the dictator over WordPerfect's keyboard. Rub your hands together and grin evilly.

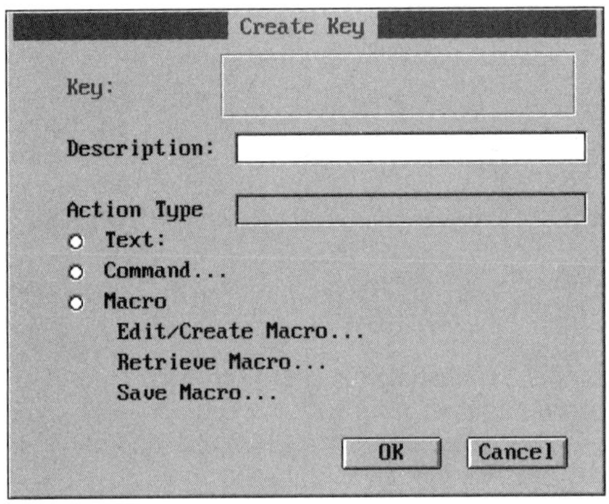

Figure 6-3: The Create Key dialog box.

6. **Press the key or key combination you want to change.**

   If the key already has an action assigned to it, the action is displayed in the Action Type text box. For example, if you press the F7 key, you see *ExitDlg*, which is the "compressed, we don't need any vowels" computer speak for the Exit Dialog command, whatever that is.

7. **Press D (Description).**

   Type in a description of the action you are about to assign in the Description text box.

8. **Press the Enter key.**

9a. **Press T for Text or**

9b. **Press C for Command or**

   The Keyboard Commands dialog box appears, as shown in Figure 6-4. It contains a scrolling list of all WordPerfect's commands, each of which is compressed into a barely readable format. Most of them you can guess at. Others require dragging out the manual for a complete description.

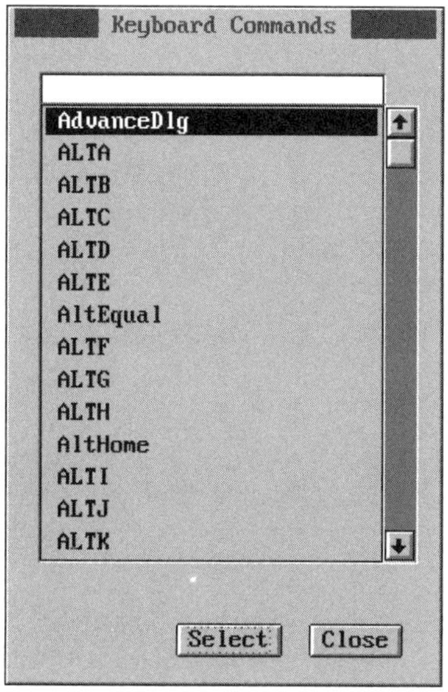

Figure 6-4: The Keyboard Commands dialog box.

9c. Press M for Macro.

Then choose either Edit/Create Macro, Retrieve Macro, or Save Macro. Techy stuff. Refer to Part II of this book for more information on macros if you dare to venture in this option. My advice is to press E to enter the macro editor if you're familiar with it. Press R to retrieve a macro from disk.

10a. Type the text you want to assign to that key or

For example, if you want the word *spumoni* to appear each time you press Alt-F10, type it in the box.

10b. Select the command you want assigned to that key or

Scroll up and down the list to highlight the command. Press Enter to select it or Esc to cancel.

10c. Do nothing — the macro has been assigned in Step 9c.

11. To assign more keys, press K and then repeat Steps 6 through 10 until you've assigned all the keys and key combinations you want. Otherwise . . .

12. Press F7.

This returns you to the Keyboard Layout dialog box.

13. Select your keyboard.

Use the arrow keys to highlight your new keyboard name and then press the Enter key twice to return to your document.

- There's no need to assign *every* key a command when you create a new keyboard layout from scratch. All new keyboard layouts start life with all the key definitions of the ORIGINAL keyboard plus whatever new keys you've created. Whew!
- In addition to normal text, you can assign any of the special WordPerfect characters to a key. When your cursor is in the text box (Step 10a), press Ctrl-W and choose the character you want. Refer to Chapter 9 for information about WordPerfect's special characters.
- You can't change the layout of the ORIGINAL keyboard layout. If you want to assign an action to a key in the ORIGINAL keyboard but leave the rest as they are, create a new keyboard layout.
- You can base a new keyboard layout on an existing layout, other than ORIGINAL, by highlighting the existing layout in the Keyboard Layout dialog box and choosing Copy before typing the name of the new keyboard layout.
- Although you can reassign most keys and key combinations, there are some you can't mess with. For example, you can't assign actions to Ctrl-1 through Ctrl-9. These are secret keys, and who knows what mysteries they unlock?
- Before changing a key assignment, be sure that it doesn't already have an action assigned to it. If an action is already assigned to a key or key combination, it is displayed in the Action Type text box in the Create Key dialog box.
- You can edit an existing keyboard layout by highlighting it in the Keyboard Layout dialog box and choosing Edit.
- The keyboard layouts you create, as well as the included keyboards, are located in the same directory as macros and Button Bars. To find out what directory that is, press Shift-F1, L (Location of Files) and check out the entry for the second item in the list, Macros/Keyboards/Button Bar. The keyboards have an extension (ending filename) of WPK.
- You can see all the key assignments for an existing keyboard layout, except ORIGINAL, by highlighting the layout in the Keyboard Layout dialog box and choosing Map to display the Keyboard Map dialog box. The letter *C* under a key indicates that a command is assigned to it. An *M* means a macro is assigned to it. *T* means that text is assigned to the key.
- Some key assignments aren't really key assignments. The key combinations you press to drop down the menus (for example, Alt-F to open the File menu) and macros that you assign to Alt key combinations aren't actually keyboard layout assignments. However, they can be overridden as you create or edit keyboard layouts, so BE CAREFUL!

Chapter 7

More on the File Manager

In This Chapter

- More on organizing files and directories
- Creating your own directory
- Using the QuickList
- Viewing document summary information
- Viewing long filenames in File Manager
- Specifying conditions for finding files
- Quick-like-a-bunny file location with QuickFinder

One of the *Jeopardy!* categories last night was DOS filenames. This guy from Indiana ran them all. LTRMOM11.DOC: "What is the eleventh letter to Mom, Alex?" Ding! All of them. The guy was a DOS genius. Given only an eight-letter filename, he could figure out the contents of any other file. Typically, that's the kind of knowledge you take to the grave with you. For the rest of us, we just have to guess . . . unless you can work WordPerfect's File Manager.

The File Manager can really be a dreadful place. A few years ago, this feature would have been considered a full-fledged program all by itself. No longer the case, the monster lives inside WordPerfect. This chapter tells you some of the more delicate nuances of using the File Manager, along with its buddies the QuickList and the QuickFinder.

Everything in Its Place and a Place for Everything

Oh, what a tangled web we weave when directories on our hard disk we do conceive.

When you save your documents on your computer's hard disk, you save them in directories. Your hard disk is like a file cabinet, and directories are like hanging files. Just as you may have one hanging file labeled for one type of document — letters, for example — and another for proposals, you can create directories on your computer's hard disk for different types of documents.

You can create them, but do you? Fact is, DOS is rather lenient on the subject. It cares not whether you toil or spin. So most lazy WordPerfect users toss their files around like dirty clothes down a laundry chute. Land where they may. "I'll find it later." This is awful, and it can be avoided if you organize your files into DOS's directories. It's really not that hard.

- Put your documents (files) into directories for organization. This chapter shows you how to set all that up and make it work.
- You can create directories within directories, just as you can place file folders within hanging files. These directories within directories are called *subdirectories.*
- Some directories and subdirectories are created automatically when programs, such as WordPerfect, are installed on your hard disk. Unless instructed to do otherwise, WordPerfect creates, among others, WP60 and WPC60DOS directories for its program files, and GRAPHICS, LEARN, and MACROS subdirectories within the WP60 directory for other files. (See, even WordPerfect is being organized.)
- WordPerfect also creates a directory called WPDOCS and specifies that directory as your document directory. When you save documents, unless you tell WordPerfect to send them somewhere else, their location is WPDOCS.
- My favorite directory strategy is to create a separate directory for each project I'm working on and give it a name that makes sense for that project. For this project, I'm using a directory called MOREWP6.

Directory naming rules

Directories are named just like files. You even see them listed just like files, with the exception that they're not files; they're really directories that contain other files. But the important thing to remember is that you name them just like files.

Here is the basic directory naming rule: The directory name can have from one to eight characters: letters and numbers.

- You can create directories by using the File Manager. The convoluted steps for doing so are covered in the next section.
- You can also create directories by using DOS. Refer to *DOS For Dummies,* 2nd Edition, Chapter 18.

Creating a directory in WordPerfect

Use the following steps to create your very own personal, fully organized directory by using WordPerfect's File Manager:

1. **Press the F5 key twice: F5, F5.**

   This brings up the File Manager window, splattered all over the screen.

2. **Press H (Change Default Dir).**

3. **Type the name of the directory you want to create.**

   It's best to type in a *full pathname* for your directory. So if you want to create a PERSONAL directory in the WPDOCS directory, type **\WPDOCS\PERSONAL**.

   TIP

   Refer to *DOS For Dummies,* 2nd Edition, Chapter 18, for more information on full pathnames.

4. **Press Enter.**

5. **A dialog box appears with the message *Create Directory Whatever?***

   If the dialog box doesn't appear, the directory has already been created. Oh, joy. You see the Specify File Manager List dialog box. Press the Esc key and then start over at Step 2 to create your new directory again.

6. **Press Y for Yes.**

   Thucka-thucka. DOS creates the directory. To start using that new directory, follow Steps 2 through 4 again. Press Enter one extra time in the Specify File Manager List dialog box, and you see your new empty directory, ready to be packed full of interesting documents and files.

- Press the Esc key to quit the File Manager and return to your document.
- Or you can just mess around in the File Manager if you find it a joyful and harmonious place.

Using the QuickList

WordPerfect's QuickList feature is one easy way to avoid the entire DOS directory nonsense — assuming, of course, that you have someone else set it all up for you. After that's done, you can organize your WordPerfect documents into simple categories that have *real* names. This feature is a boon to anyone who is downright afraid of DOS. And the numbers are growing.

Creating a QuickList directory entry

Directories are where you store your documents. You should have a separate directory for everything you do or at least enough directories to keep all your stuff organized. It doesn't matter what the directories are called or where they live on the hard drive. As long as you use WordPerfect's QuickList, you can keep them neat, tidy, and organized.

To add a directory to QuickList's list of stuff, follow these steps:

1. **Press F5, F6.**

   This brings up the QuickList dialog box.

2. **Press C (Create).**

   The Create QuickList Entry dialog box appears.

3. **Type a description.**

   For example, type **Here is where my restaurant reviews go**. You don't have to be that detailed, but you're not restricted to being brief, either.

4. **Press the Tab key.**

   You're now in the Filename/Directory box. That's where you enter a DOS directory, the location of your files.

   You can press the F8 key to see a directory tree at this point. Use the up- and down-arrow keys to highlight a directory on your hard drive or just give up and yell for help from a DOS expert. (The expert should be setting this stuff up for you anyway.)

5. **Press the Enter key once or twice until you're back at the QuickList dialog box.**

   You see your new item in that box. Now you can use it to quickly access those files in that directory, all the while keeping DOS at arm's length.

   I admit that some of the directories that WordPerfect precreated for you when it was set up are dorky. You see these directories, such as Printer Files Personal and Style Files Personal, in the QuickList dialog box. Some of them are unnecessary, and if you find yourself never using them, feel free to get rid of them: Highlight the bogus entry and press D (Delete). Press Enter to select Yes, and it's gone.

Using QuickList to find files on disk

Using the QuickList is a snap. Press F5, F6. The F5 key brings up the Specify File Manager List dialog box, and the F6 key summons the QuickList dialog box, as shown in Figure 7-1.

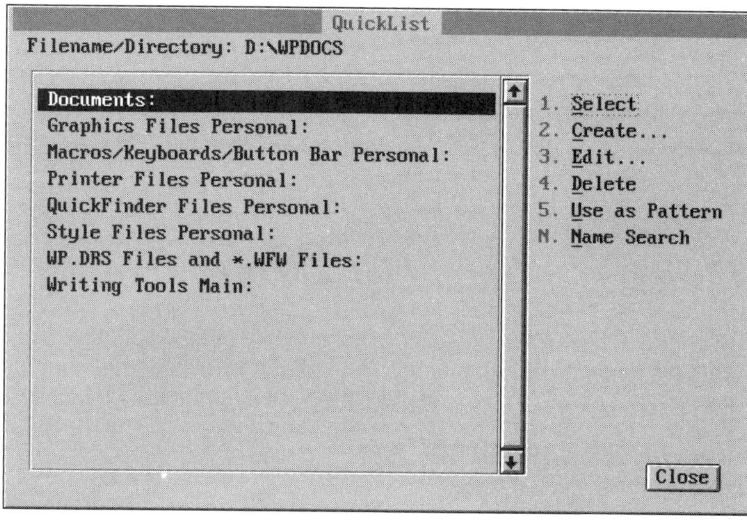

Figure 7-1: The QuickList dialog box.

QuickList shows you a smattering of places where your documents and other interesting things have been placed. For example, the Documents section contains documents (no!). To use it, or any of the other locations listed, follow these cinchy steps:

1. **Highlight the file or location you want.**

   Use the up- or down-arrow keys to move the highlight.

2. **Press S (Select).**

3a. **The File Manager appears, listing the files in that area.**

   Use the commands in the File Manager to open, print, or just look at any of the files.

3b. **The document you selected is loaded into WordPerfect.**

   If what you selected is a document, it is opened and loaded on-screen for you to edit.

- Press the F7 key to quit the File Manager if you're disgusted with the files it displays.
- F5, F6 = QuickList.
- Although the QuickList doesn't entirely free you from dealing with DOS directories, it does help you become a wee bit more organized.

TIP

BUTTONS

- You can also use the QuickList to save a document. Just press the F6 key in the Save Document dialog box and then select a location for your file. You still have to name the file with a DOS filename, but this shortcut dispenses with all the subdirectory and other DOS nonsense.
- Indeed, any dialog box that contains the QuickList F6 button grants you access to WordPerfect's QuickList feature.

Creating a QuickList document entry

Directories are not the only thing that can live in the QuickList. You can also store frequently used documents there. Granted, the document must *really* be used a lot to make this worthwhile. Also, the document is typically used as a reference or *template.* That is, you can't stick a file you work on all the time (like that novel you swear you'll finish) in it, because WordPerfect won't let you save the document back to disk.

Confusing? Yes. That's why I recommend keeping the QuickList reserved for common subdirectories. But if the mood hits you to stick a document or other type of file in there, here is how it's done:

1. **Press F5, F6.**

   This brings up the QuickList dialog box.

2. **Press C (Create).**

   The Create QuickList Entry dialog box splashes on-screen.

3. **Type a description.**

   For example, type **Cuddly Bear story I'll never finish**. You can be brief or very descriptive — it doesn't matter here.

4. **Press the Tab key.**

   You need to enter the filename in the Filename/Directory box. This step gets technical because you must know the full DOS pathname to the document file.

   You can press the F8 key to see the directory tree and use that to find your document's directory, but you still need to manually type in the document filename. For example, you may have to type the following:

   C:\WPDOCS\STORIES\BEAR.DOC

   Yikes!

5. **Press the Enter key once or twice until you're back at the QuickList dialog box.**

   There you see your document highlighted and listed along with other items.

- To load a document listed in the QuickList dialog box, you must obey the instructions in the next section. Alas, this is where QuickList doesn't become so handy any more.
- The best type of documents to stick into the QuickList are common forms or templates you use over and over. For example, maybe put the skeleton of a letter you commonly write in there, or a form for filling in a proposal.
- When you open a document from the QuickList, it is opened as *read-only,* which means that you can edit the document, but you can't save it back to disk unless you give it a new name.

Using QuickList to load a document

QuickList can contain lists of DOS directories, documents, and other goodies. If you want to load a document from the QuickList list, follow these steps:

1. **Press Shift-F10 or choose File⇨Open.**

   The Open dialog box appears.

2. **Press the F6 key.**

   The QuickList dialog box appears.

3. **Highlight your filename in the list.**

   Use the up- or down-arrow keys.

4. **Press Enter.**

   The file opens as read-only, which means that you can edit the document, but you can't save it back to disk unless you give it a new name. Unfortunately, this is the nature of documents put into the QuickList.

REMEMBER

Typically, documents saved in the QuickList are templates or forms that you fill in, edit, print, and then save back to disk with a new filename, if that's your desire.

Viewing Document Summary Info in the File Manager

Does it seem pointless to create those nasty document summaries? After all, most people turn that option off instead of going to the trouble of entering all that boring information. But with the File Manager, document summaries can actually be useful — providing that you bother with them in the first place.

To view the document summary information in the File Manager, you can use its handy Look command, which normally displays the document's contents. But after the document is married to a document summary, you see that information as well. Follow these steps:

1. **Press the F5 key.**

   The Specify File Manager List dialog box appears.

2. **Enter the name of the directory where your documents are located, if it isn't already staring at you in the Directory text box.**

3. **Press the Enter key.**

   The File Manager appears, listing all the files in your chosen directory.

4. **Highlight the file with the document summary information you want to view.**

   Use the up- and down-arrow keys to move the highlight bar thingie.

5. **Press L (Look).**

   The document summary information appears. If the document lacks that information, you see the document's contents displayed instead.

- If you're staring at a document summary and want to look at the text of a document instead, press L (Look at Text). Press L (Look at Summary) again to switch back to the document summary information.
- Looking at a document in the File Manager is not the same as opening the document. You're really just seeing a preview of the document. You can open a document in the File Manager by highlighting it and pressing the Enter key.
- You can print the document summary by pressing I (Print Summary). Be sure that your printer is turned on and ready to print before you do that.
- Just as you can't edit a document while looking at it in the File Manager, you can't edit the document summary while in the File Manager. To edit a document summary, open the document and then press Shift-F8, D, S.
- You can find more information on document summaries in Chapter 2.

Long Filenames for Short Memories

Two innocent items in the document summary can actually help you instantly recognize your documents in the File Manager. The often avoided Descriptive Name and Descriptive Type fields in the document summary can be displayed in the File Manager right next to its ugly and undescriptive filename. These fields are displayed only if you bother with a document summary, as described in Chapter 2 of this book.

To have the File Manager always display the long filenames and types, follow these steps:

1. **Press the F5 key.**
2. **Press the Enter key.**

   The File Manager appears. It doesn't matter what directory is displayed for these steps.
3. **Press Shift-F1.**

   The File Manager Setup dialog box appears.
4. **Press M (Display List Mode).**
5. **Press N (Descriptive Names and Types).**
6. **Press the Enter key.**

   The File Manager displays the descriptive names and types that you entered in the documents' summaries.

- The File Manager displays the normal (DOS) filename for documents that don't have document summaries attached or where you didn't enter a descriptive name or type.
- With descriptive names and types displayed, the File Manager doesn't display the file sizes, dates, and times. However, you can see this information for one file at a time by highlighting the file and looking in the File Information box in the lower-right portion of the File Manager dialog box.
- If you decide you'd rather look at your file lists the normal way, repeat the steps above, but press F (DOS Filenames) in Step 5.

Finding Files in the File Manager

If the prospect of finding the document you're looking for seems as remote as finding the proverbial needle in a haystack, take heart. Just set the File Manager to "Find Needle mode" and let 'er rip.

To have WordPerfect search the entire contents of all the documents in your documents directory to find just the text you're looking for, follow these steps:

1. **Press F5.**

   The Specify File Manager List dialog box appears.
2. **Type in the name of the directory where your documents are located, if it isn't already entered in the Directory text box.**
3. **Press the Enter key.**

4. **Press F (Find).**

   The Find dialog box appears.

5. **Press C (Conditions).**

   The File Manager Find Conditions dialog box throws itself all over your screen.

6. **Press E (Entire Document).**

7. **Type the text you want to search for.**

   Think of some text that is unique to the document you are looking for. For example, enter a name or a key phrase. Something unique.

8. **Press the Enter key twice.**

   A Finding Files box appears and counts the number of files searched. After WordPerfect finishes scouting around, the File Manager displays only those files that contain your textual tidbit.

- Takes a while, doesn't it?
- If no files meet the specifications, a dialog box appears with the terse, unfriendly message *Not found* and an OK button. No, it's not OK. But because there's no other option, press Enter and try again, using another text tidbit.
- If the list is still too long, consider repeating Steps 4 through 7 and entering some additional text that may narrow the list so that you don't have to hunt through so many files to find the one you want.
- In the File Manager Find Conditions dialog box, you can enter multiple conditions. For example, you can search for documents that contain the phrase "so's your mother" in the entire document and the phrase "Mother Goose" in the document summary.
- The Find command can find files only in one directory at a time. If you think the files you're looking for may be in other directories, you need to perform individual searches in each directory. To search for files in multiple directories at one time, use the QuickFinder, which is covered later in this chapter.

Finding Files within a Range of Dates

If you're looking for a date, WordPerfect can't help you. But if you're looking for files that were saved between this and that date, you have a solvable problem.

But first, a reminder: Searching for files in date ranges works only if you are using document summaries with information in the Revision Date field. Otherwise, no dice.

Suppose that you want to find all the files in a directory you created or edited last Tuesday and Wednesday. No problem. Just follow these steps:

1. **Press F5.**
2. **Enter the name of the directory where your documents are located, if it isn't already entered in the Directory text box.**
3. **Press the Enter key.**
4. **Press F (Find).**

   The Find dialog box appears.
5. **Press C (Conditions).**

   The File Manager Find Conditions dialog box appears.
6. **Press O (Show Default Summary Fields Only).**

   This option gets rid of many cluttered fields you don't use.
7. **Press D (Document Summary Fields).**
8. **Highlight the Date box to the right of the Revision Date text box.**

   Press the Tab key until the Date box is highlighted with a dotted box. Press the Enter key. The Find Conditions Date dialog box appears.
9. **Press Shift-Tab.**

   Hold down the Shift key while you press the Tab key. This highlights the Dates prompt to the left of the dialog box.
10. **Press the Enter key.**

    A drop-down list of date options appears.
11. **Highlight the Between option.**

    Use the down-arrow key to highlight the Between option.
12. **Press the Enter key to select Between.**

    My, this is a lot of steps to take for what should be something really simple. Anyway . . .
13. **Enter the range of dates in the text boxes, as shown in Figure 7-2.**

    Type the first date in the first box. Then press the Tab key to move to the next box. Enter the second date.

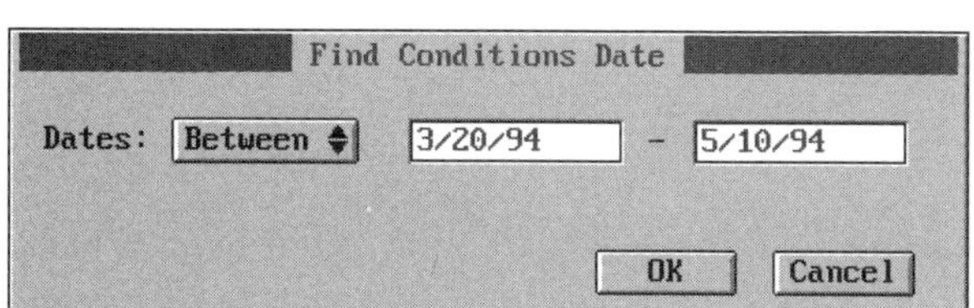

Figure 7-2: The Find Conditions Date dialog box with sample dates entered.

14. **Click OK twice to begin the search.**

    WordPerfect searches through all the files in the current directory. If you have a boatload of large files in the directory, the search can take quite a while. Go get a cup of coffee and relax until the search is completed.

TIP

- If the list of files that meets your search criteria is too long to deal with, narrow down the list by repeating the search with the addition of at least one more search condition. For example, narrow the date range or use another name or phrase that probably wouldn't be in all the files the preceding search found.
- If you want to find files that were revised on, before, or after a certain date, highlight the On, Before, or After options rather than the Between option in Step 11.

Sorting the List of Files

The File Manager sorts its list of files alphabetically (but by which alphabet?). This really isn't a hard and fast rule, however. For example, if you're daring enough to enter descriptive information in a document's document summary, you can direct the File Manager to list your files by their descriptive types — which is another argument for using the document summary (but not one compelling enough to convert yours truly). Otherwise, you can contort the way the File Manager displays files by following these steps:

1. **Press F5 to summon the File Manager.**
2. **Type the name of the directory where your documents are located, if it isn't already entered in the Directory text box.**
3. **Press the Enter key.**
4. **Press S (Sort by).**

   The File Manager Setup dialog box appears, as shown in Figure 7-3.

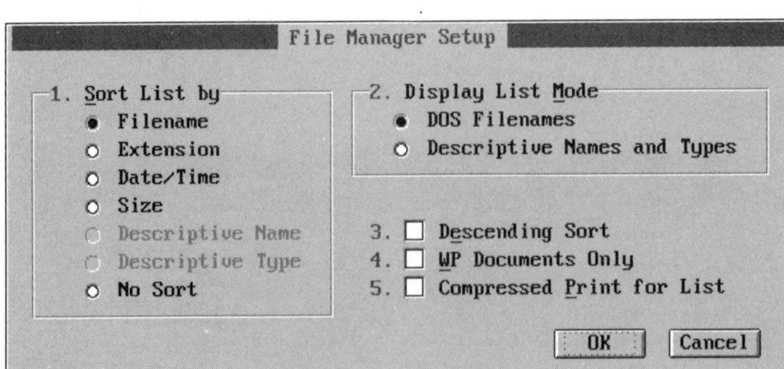

Figure 7-3: The File Manager Setup dialog box.

5. **Press S (Sort List by).**
6. **Choose a new way to sort your files.**

   Press the underlined letter next to the option you want in the Sort List by section of the dialog box. For example, press S (Size) to sort the files by how much space they're hogging on your computer's hard disk.
7. **Press Enter to accept the choice you've made and display the newly sorted file list.**

- Unless you change the option, the files are sorted alphabetically by filename.
- If the Descriptive Names and Types option is chosen in the Display List Mode portion of the File Manager Setup dialog box, only two Sort List by options are available: Descriptive Name and Descriptive Type.
- If you want the files sorted in reverse order (Z to A, for example, or largest to smallest), press 3 (Descending Sort) in the File Manager Setup dialog box.
- Changing the way your files are sorted in WordPerfect doesn't affect the way they are actually sorted on your disk. It just changes the way the files are displayed in the File Manager.
- Unclutter your file lists by displaying only WordPerfect documents. This tip is particularly useful if you store documents from several programs in one directory. To tell WordPerfect to display only WordPerfect documents, press 4 in the File Manager Setup dialog box to put an X in the WP Documents Only box. If there is no X in the box after pressing 4, press 4 again. How does WordPerfect know which files are WordPerfect files? It's smarter than we are.

Using QuickFinder (for Those Who Dare)

Slow and steady wins the race in a children's fairy tale, but when you're looking for documents in WordPerfect, you want all the speed you can get. Watching WordPerfect dawdle through a long list of files is not my idea of a good time. I want speed, speed, speed!

You can use WordPerfect's File Manager and its Find command (as covered in the section "Finding Files in the File Manager" earlier in this chapter) to look for files by plodding through a current directory on your hard drive. In addition to being the slow way to search, however, that current directory thing is one of Find's biggest limitations. The Find command can look only in the current directory. If you want to search several directories, you must perform several searches with the Find command. Personally, I'd rather eat a hot dog with mustard and cat hair dressing.

The incomplete yet correct answer to the problem is to use WordPerfect's QuickFinder thing. It's incomplete because, honestly, people with lots of files to search through usually have a somewhat organized hard drive and generally know where things are. Hopefully. Otherwise, QuickFinder can eliminate those sluggish directory limitations by scanning all the documents in any directory or group of directories you specify and can create special quick-as-a-bunny search-enabling files, called *indexes*, of the contents of all your documents.

The upside to the QuickFinder index is that after it's created, you can find just about any document on disk in a matter of microseconds. The downside is that the QuickFinder index is a cumbersome and time-consuming thing to produce. If you're not mired in files and have a pretty well-organized hard drive, I wouldn't bother.

Creating your very own QuickFinder index

WARNING!

Before creating your very own QuickFinder index, be aware that it can take a very long time, perhaps hours if you have zillions of files and a slow computer. Also, depending on the number and size of the files to be indexed, the index file can take several megabytes of disk space — space you may not have.

To create a QuickFinder index of all the WordPerfect files on your hard disk, follow these steps from your document:

1. **Press F5.**
2. **Press F4 to go to QuickFinder.**

   The QuickFinder File Indexer dialog box appears, as shown in Figure 7-4.

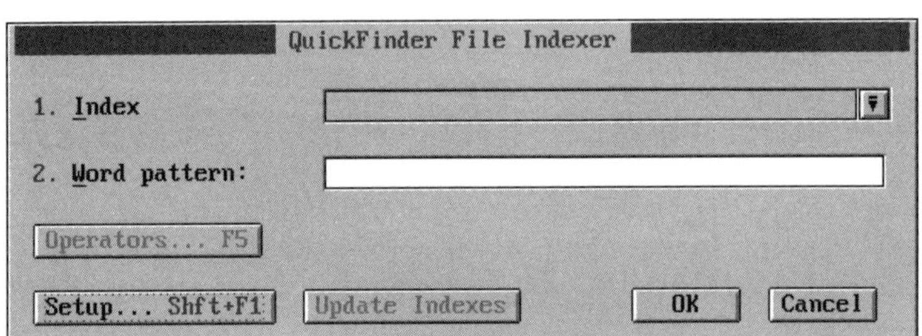

Figure 7-4: The QuickFinder File Indexer dialog box.

3. **Press Shift-F1.**

   The QuickFinder File Indexes Setup dialog box appears, as shown in Figure 7-5.

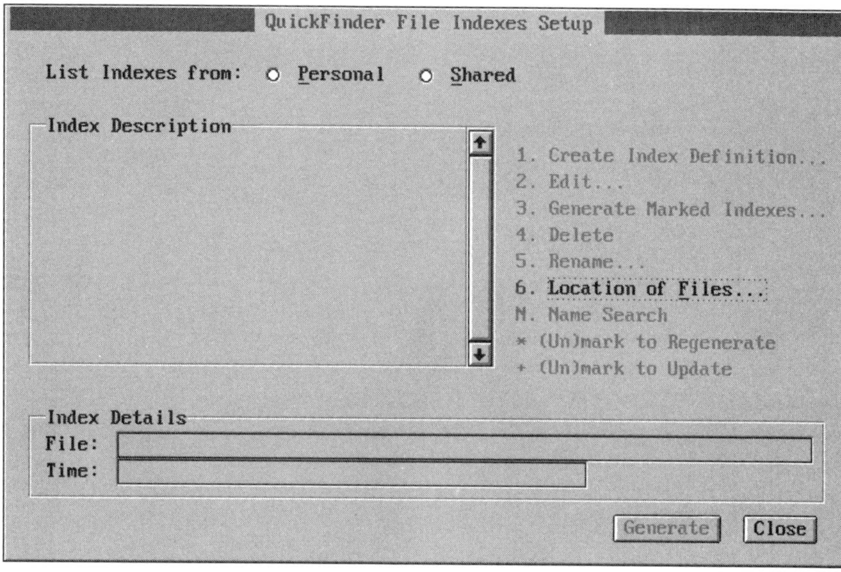

Figure 7-5: The QuickFinder File Indexes Setup dialog box.

4. **Press F (Location of Files).**

   The QuickFinder Index Files dialog box appears, in which you tell WordPerfect where to store the indexes of your files.

5. **Press P (Personal Path).**

6. **Enter the complete path of the directory where you want your index files stored or press F8 to use the Directory Tree to highlight a path.**

   For example, type **C:\WPDOCS** to store the index files in your normal document directory.

7. **Press the Enter key twice.**

8. **Press C (Create Index).**

   The Create Index Definition dialog box appears, as shown in Figure 7-6.

9. **Enter a description for your index in the Index Description dialog box.**

   For example, type **MY FILES**. You can use letters, numbers, and spaces, and, unlike a filename, you can get very expressive if you like.

10. **Press the Enter key.**

11. **Type the filename you want to use for the index.**

    WordPerfect uses the first eight letters of your description for the filename if you don't enter your own filename. Sounds good to me.

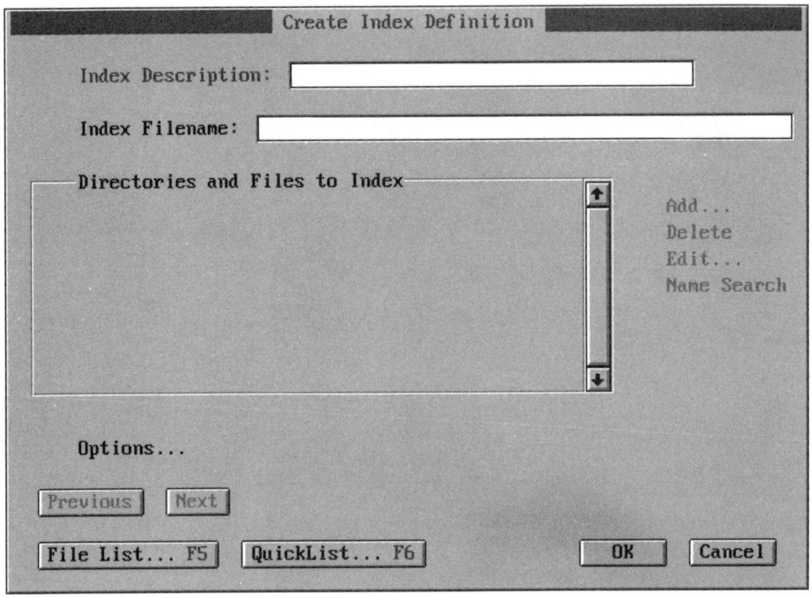

Figure 7-6: The Create Index Definition dialog box.

12. **Press the Enter key after typing the index filename.**
13. **Press A to select the Add option.**

    The Add QuickFinder Index Directory Pattern dialog box appears.
14. **Type C:\ and press the Enter key.**
15. **Press I (Include Subdirectories).**
16. **Press the F7 key twice: F7, F7.**

    You'll find yourself back at the Create Index definition dialog box.
17. **Press O (Options).**

    The QuickFinder Index Options dialog box appears.
18. **Press W (Index WP Documents Only).**

    This tells QuickFinder to index only the words in WordPerfect files.
19. **Press the Enter key twice.**

    You return to the QuickFinder File Indexes dialog box.
20. **Press G (Generate Marked Indexes).**

    The screen goes blank for a few seconds and then starts counting the number of files as they are indexed. This process takes a long, long time. After the files are indexed, they're merged, which takes even more time.

21. **Starbucks coffee.**

    Treat yourself to some fine java, brewed the way only Northwesterners can brew it.

22. **When you see *QuickFinder Index Completed* followed by *Press Any Key* at the bottom of the screen, press the Enter key (your *any key*).**

    You return to the QuickFinder File Indexes Setup dialog box.

23. **Press Home, F7 to return to your document.**

- You don't have to include every directory on your hard disk in the index. You can enter just the directory you want to index in Step 14 and include its subdirectories or not. Press A (Add) to add additional directories to the index.
- You need to update the index as you add and edit files. You may want to do this just before performing a QuickFinder search so that you know the index includes the latest changes and additions. To update an index, press F5, F4 and then press the Tab key and then U (Update Indexes).
- Updating indexes can increase their size, even if the number of files indexed hasn't changed. The way around this problem is to regenerate the indexes every once in a while. To regenerate indexes, press asterisk (*) and then press G (Generate Marked Indexes).

Searching for text with QuickFinder

Creating a nice index of your files, as discussed in the preceding section, means that you can actually search for something by using the index and WordPerfect's QuickFinder. Suppose that you want to find all the files that contain the phrase "buy more Bob Hope videos." With QuickFinder, the process is blindingly fast. Don't blink.

To search for text in your indexed files, follow these steps:

1. **Press F5.**
2. **Press F4.**

    The QuickFinder File Indexer dialog box appears.

3. **Enter the text you want to search for in the Word Pattern text box.**

    Type **Bob Hope**.

4. **Press the Enter key twice.**

    Faster than you can say "What a useful book this is," the File Manager appears with a list of all the files containing your search text. Amazing.

5. **Use the File Manager to open, print, or look at the file(s) found.**

   The commands to perform these functions are listed at the bottom of the dialog box.

- The standard Button Bar has a QuikFndr button that you can click to open the QuickFinder File Indexer dialog box.
- Regardless of how you have instructed the File Manager to display your filenames, QuickFinder lists are displayed in the File Manager with their paths and DOS filenames.

Using operator assistance

Often, searching for text in a file is an either/or type of experience. Maybe you want to find all videos with Bob Hope but not Bing Crosby. If so, or in any of the other numerous circumstances when you're looking for non-Bob Hope text, you can use special *operators* to control the search.

These operators don't work for the phone company; instead, they're choice options or commands, such as And, Or, or Not. Operators help you find text in your indexed documents: for example, "Bob Hope" Not "Bing Crosby." It's techy but sometimes necessary.

To use operators with QuickFinder, follow these steps:

1. **Press F5.**
2. **Press F4.**

   The QuickFinder File Indexer dialog box appears.

3. **Enter the first word or phrase you want to search for.**

   Type **Bob Hope**.

4. **Press the F5 key.**

   The Word Pattern Operators dialog box appears. It lists the *logical operators* — And, Or, Not, or Match Single Character — that help you select documents with one bit of text (what you typed in Step 3). Select the logical operator of your choice. For the Bob Hope example, select Not.

5. **Use the down-arrow key to highlight the operator you want to use.**
6. **Press the Enter key.**

   A special symbol representing the operator is inserted into the Word pattern text box. You'd think the program would insert the English word — but, no, this is WordPerfect, after all.

7. **Enter the other word or phrase you want to search for.**

   Type **Bing Crosby**.

8. **Press the Enter key twice.**

   The File Manager appears with a list of files that meet your search specifications.

- If no matching text is found, the appropriate dialog box appears to disappoint you.
- Some of the operators are actually document summary fields. If you use document summaries and include the document summaries in the Index Options dialog box, you can use these operators to search for text in specific document summary fields. Refer to Chapter 2 for more information on document summaries.
- Don't press the spacebar before adding an operator. A space is added for you.
- The * and ? operators are sometimes called wildcards. The * (asterisk) can take the place of multiple characters, and the ? (question mark) can take the place of a single character. For example, *Bob** finds documents containing the words *Bobby, Bobble, Bobcat, Bobsled, Bobtail,* and so on.

Chapter 8

More on Printing

In This Chapter

- Printing text blocks
- Printing specific pages
- Printing to a file
- Printing the document summary
- Printing booklets
- Saving time printing text and graphics

You spend countless hours wrestling with WordPerfect and the antiquated QWERTY keyboard, specifically designed for maximum inefficiency. Then the great struggle ends and you're faced with the final step, printing your words out. This is the hard copy. The act of "sending to the printer." The final admission that you're completely exhausted and mentally fatigued, and, by golly, it better look good by now because you're entirely sick of it. That's what printing is all about.

To overwhelm you with even more options than you may care to consider, WordPerfect provides plenty of different ways for printing your documents. You can print all or part of your document in color or with graphics. You can bind booklets, if you're clever enough. These advantages more than justify why you spent $1,000 for a decent printer. Your words will truly look nice and pretty, provided you follow the knowledge jewels in this chapter.

Printing Text Blocks

Printing out a 300-page report just to proofread a few paragraphs is a waste of time and trees. You can simply print the page or pages containing the text you want. But I've found it easier to direct WordPerfect to print blocks of text that are highlighted on-screen.

To print a text block, follow these steps:

1. **Highlight the block of text that you want to print.**

   Clever instructions for doing this step can be found in *WordPerfect 6 For Dummies*, Chapter 6.

2. **Press Shift-F7.**

   The Print/Fax dialog box appears. Because you have a block of text marked, the Blocked Text item in the Print area is automatically selected. WordPerfect is ready to print your block.

3. **Make sure that your printer is on and ready to print.**

4. **Press Enter.**

   Zzztt! The block prints.

- WordPerfect doesn't just print your block at the top of a sheet of paper. It calculates where your block should appear if you had printed the entire document. So if the block is in the middle of page 20, the printer spews out a sheet of paper with the block in the middle of the page and with any header or footer or page number labeled "page 20."
- Refer to the sidebar for more information on what prints and what doesn't.

What prints and what doesn't

Contrary to what you may think, WordPerfect doesn't just print your highlighted text block. Instead, it prints all the lines that your highlighted text block covers. For example, suppose that you have the following paragraph in a document:

```
Lots of people are vegetarians because they like animals.
But some people are vegetarians because they hate plants.
```

Suppose that you highlight only a portion of that paragraph to print as a text block (shown as bold underline):

```
Lots of people are vegetarians because they like animals.
But some people are vegetarians because they hate plants.
```

The following lines are what WordPerfect eventually prints out for the text block:

```
Lots of people are vegetarians because they like animals.
But some people are vegetarians because they
```

The moral of the story is that WordPerfect may let you block any old chunk of text, but it always prints one entire line at a time.

Printing Specific Pages

In the old days of word processors, you had a choice of printing the entire document, printing several consecutive pages of a document, or printing individual pages one at a time. If you wanted to print pages 3 through 12 and page 19, you had to tell your word processor to print pages 3 through 12 and then tell it to print page 19. Oh, I'm amazed we survived those halcyon days.

Now, rather than telling WordPerfect to print twice, you can easily tell it just once. WordPerfect lets you print specific pages, no matter where they may be in a document. Now you can print page 4, page 78, and pages 89 through 102 with a single command. Not only does this efficiency save your sanity, but it also saves you time.

Depending on which page or page range you want to print, WordPerfect gives you several options, as shown in Table 8-1.

Table 8-1 Printing Specific Page Ranges

To Print	*Type This in the Page/Label Range in the Print Multiple Pages Dialog Box*
Page 13	13
Pages 1, 4, and 87	1,4,87 (or 1 4 87)
Page 12 to the last page	12–
From the first page up to page 56	–56
Pages 4 through 98	4–98
Pages 4 through 98 and page 198	4–98, 198

To print specific pages, follow these steps:

1. **Press Shift-F7.**

   The Print/Fax dialog box appears.

2. **Press M (Multiple Pages)**

   The Print Multiple Pages dialog box appears.

3. **Press P (Page/Label Range).**

   This step highlights the Page/Label Range text box, where you type in the pages you want WordPerfect to print.

4. **Type the page or page range that you want to print and press Enter.**

   Refer to Table 8-1 or the bulleted list at the end of this section for hints.

5. **Press the Enter key twice.**

You're returned to the main Print/Fax dialog box. From here you can press Enter to print or set other options, if necessary.

- Remember to have your printer on and ready to print before you start printing.
- To print a single page, just type its number in the Page/Label Range text box.
- To print several pages, type in each one, separated by a comma.
- To print a range of pages, stick a hyphen between the first and last page.
- To print from the first page to a specific page, type a hyphen and then that specific page number.
- To print from a specific page to the last page, type that specific page and then a hyphen.
- You can mix and match specific pages with a range of pages, no problem.

Printing to a File

Not every computer in the world has WordPerfect 6 for DOS on its hard disk. Fortunately, that doesn't really matter because WordPerfect actually gives you a way to print WordPerfect files without using WordPerfect 6.

Just use WordPerfect to create your document and then save it in a special printable WordPerfect file. Take this WordPerfect printable file to any computer *without* WordPerfect, and you can print it out by using the DOS COPY command. This is a strange and wonderful feature, and I've actually used it to print on the fancy office printer.

- There are three steps involved here: Setting up the print-to-disk printer, printing to a file on your disk, and finally copying the print file to another printer. These steps are covered in the sections that follow.
- Printing to a file on your disk is great for those times when your printer may be in the shop or when you want to use another printer at another location.

Setting up the print-to-disk printer

To create and print a WordPerfect printable file, follow these steps:

1. **Create your document in WordPerfect.**
2. **Press Shift-F7.**

   The Print/Fax dialog box appears.

3. **Press S (Select).**

   The Select Printer dialog box appears. You see the list of printers you installed when you first set up WordPerfect.

4. **Press A (Add Printer).**

   The Add Printer dialog box appears. Although you may already have this printer attached to your PC, you still need to "define" it in a new way.

5. **Highlight the printer.**

   Use the up- or down-arrow key to locate a printer — but not necessarily your printer! You need to find the printer you'll eventually use to print your file. So if you want to use the office's spiffy Hewlett-Packard HP 9000 printer, you need to select it.

6. **Press S (Select).**

   The Printer Filename dialog box appears.

7. **Press Enter.**

   An Information dialog box appears. Ho hum.

8. **Press Enter.**

   The Edit Printer Setup dialog box appears, where you tell WordPerfect that you are printing to a file on disk rather than to a real printer attached to your computer.

9. **Press P (Port).**

   A *port* is a connection on the back of the PC. The Port dialog box appears.

10. **Press F (Filename).**

    Obviously, you aren't printing to a printer attached to a port — you're printing the information to a "file" on disk. All this means is that the stuff that would normally go to the printer is now saved in a file on disk. (This is *not* the same as using F10 to save a file.)

11. **Type a filename.**

    This filename should be the name of the file on disk that contains your final, printed document. I name my printer file documents PRINTME.PRN.

12. **Press D (Description).**

    The printer already has a name description, one that WordPerfect gives it. But you need to remind yourself that this is a print-to-disk type of printer. So press the End key and type **to disk** at the end of the printer's name so that it looks something like this:

    ```
    HP LaserJet 4 to disk
    ```

13. **Press Home, F7.**

    You're done setting up the print-to-disk printer.

- The print-to-disk printer is just like any other printer you can use in WordPerfect. The difference is that the information that would normally go to the printer is instead saved to a file on disk.
- The printer you select in Step 5 is the printer you'll eventually use, not the printer you currently have. For example, if you have a cruddy little printer from the Stone Age and want to use a fancy laser printer, choose the fancy laser printer in Step 5.
- You can set up as many print-to-disk printers as you have printers.

Printing to disk

To use a printer that you don't have, you must print your document to a disk file. You can then saunter over to another computer with that special printer and magically print your WordPerfect document and truly amaze your friends.

To print a file to disk, follow these steps:

1. **Press Shift-F7.**

   The Print/Fax dialog box appears.

   Take a good look at the Current Printer right at the top of the dialog box. Is it your disk printer? Does it say something like `HP LaserJet 4 to disk`? If so, skip to Step 5. Otherwise, move right along with Step 2.

2. **Press S (Select).**

   The Select Printer dialog box appears.

3. **Highlight your print-to-disk printer.**

   Use the up- or down-arrow key to locate the printer you set up to print to disk in the preceding section. If you followed the steps correctly, it should end with `to disk` in its description.

4. **Press Enter to select the printer.**

   The Print/Fax dialog box reappears.

5. **Press Enter to print to a disk file instead of a printer.**

   WordPerfect creates a special WordPerfect printable file. The file is saved to disk, using the name you specified in Step 11 from the preceding section (possibly PRINTME.PRN).

- When you're done printing to disk, remember to change WordPerfect's printer back to the one you normally use. If you don't make the change, WordPerfect assumes that you still want to use the same print-to-disk printer.
- After the file is on disk, you can copy it to its designated printer to get a hard copy of your document.
- You must set up the print-to-disk printer before you can print to a disk file.
- You can only print-to-disk one document at a time! If you print another document, WordPerfect overwrites the first PRINTME.PRN file with the second document. So, if you want to print another document, copy the new PRINTME.PRN file to a floppy disk or rename it, if you're going to print to disk again.
- The print-to-disk file is not a WordPerfect document, nor is it a text file. It is just a collection of instructions for a specific printer. These instructions print your document when they are "copied" to the proper printer.

Printing the disk file

To print a print-to-disk file, you need to copy it to a printer. Specifically, you must copy it to the same printer that you'd defined when you created the print-to-disk printer. So, if that's an HP 9000 printer, you'd better end up copying the file to that exact type of printer, lest the results look gross.

To print your print-to-disk file, follow these steps:

1. **Take this file to a computer that's connected to the proper printer.**

   Exit WordPerfect and copy the print-to-disk file to a floppy disk. To do this step, you can use this command:

   ```
   C> COPY \WPDOCS\PRINTME.PRN A:
   ```

   You may want to check the size of the file first, to ensure that it will fit on your floppy disk. If the document contains a lot of graphics and fancy fonts, it may be too big to copy.

   After you have the file on a disk, saunter over to the other computer that's happily hooked up to your dream printer.

2. **At the other PC's DOS prompt, type the following:**

   ```
   A> COPY PRINTME.PRN /B LPT1:
   ```

   This is the COPY command, a space, and then your print-to-disk filename, which I'm assuming is PRINTME.PRN here. Then type another space, a slash-**B**, another space, and then **LPT1** (one) and a colon. Double-check your typing.

3. **Make sure that the printer is on and ready to print. Press Enter to print.**

   Lo and behold, out comes your WordPerfect document, formatted exactly as it appeared in WordPerfect. It's miraculous!

If the document doesn't look right, or all you get is a beeping printer and a lot of strange or blank pages, then you're printing on the wrong printer. Be sure to print on the printer you selected in the section "Setting up the print-to-disk printer" earlier in this chapter.

Printing the Document Summary

To help you keep track of when a document was created, last revised, who the typist was, and other information that smacks of Orwellian surveillance and thought control, WordPerfect provides a document summary. This subject is discussed and cussed extensively in Chapter 2.

Normally, the document summary does not print out when you print your document. But if you want to print the document summary — just because you feel like it — WordPerfect gives you the following two choices:

- You can print the document summary all by itself.
- You can print the document summary with the rest of your document.

The following sections tell you about these choices.

- Normally, the document summary is carefully tucked out of sight. But if you want, you can view it at any time by pressing Alt-F, U.
- Okay, I harp a lot on the document summary, but it can be pretty useful — especially if you work with the File Manager. Refer to Chapter 7 for more information on how the document summary can play an important role in managing files.

Printing the document summary by itself

To print the document summary — all by its lonesome self — follow these steps:

1. **Press Alt-F, U.**

   The Document Summary dialog box appears.

2. **Press Shift-F7.**

   A dialog box appears, asking whether you want to print the document summary.

3. **Press Y.**

   The document summary prints.

4. **Press Enter or the F7 key to return to your document.**

The document summary contains a list of all the fields and their contents — the same as you see in the Document Summary dialog box. Blank fields in that dialog box remain blank in the hard copy. In fact, if you ignore the document summary, the only two things you see when you print the document summary are the Revision Date and Creation Date.

Printing the document summary with the rest of your document

To print the document summary along with the other pages in your document, follow these steps:

1. **Press Shift-F7.**

   The Print/Fax dialog box appears.

2. **Press M (Multiple Pages).**

   The Print Multiple Pages dialog box appears.

3. **Press M (Document Summary).**

   X marks the spot.

4. **Press Enter.**

   The Print/Fax dialog box re-appears.

5. **Press R to print your document.**

   Make sure that your printer is on and ready to print before you press R to print.

The document summary page prints first, detailing any information in your document summary.

Printing Booklets

For years, John Kennedy Toole tried to get publishers interested in a novel he wrote in the 60s. Every publisher turned him down. It was only after the author's death that one publisher finally agreed to publish it — and the novel promptly won critical acclaim and the Pulitzer prize in 1981. Perhaps in fitting irony to all the publishers who turned it down, the title of the novel was *A Confederacy of Dunces*.

In today's world of personal computers, laser printers, and (of course) WordPerfect, publishers hold much less power because people can print their own books. To help you become your own publisher, WordPerfect even has a feature specifically designed for laying out pages for printing booklets.

A *booklet* is simply a single page where text appears in two columns. The page is folded in half, stapled, and — voilà! — you have yourself a booklet.

To create and print a document suitable for binding as a booklet, follow these steps:

1. **Press Alt-F, N, Shift-F8.**

   The Format dialog box for a new document appears.

2. **Press P (Page).**

   The Page Format dialog box appears.

3. **Press S (Paper Size/Type).**

   The Paper Size/Type dialog box appears.

4. **Highlight the paper size and type that you want to use.**

   For example, select Letter (Landscape) for doing a booklet.

5. **Press S (Select) to select your new paper size and type.**

   The Page Format dialog box reappears.

6. **Press P (Center Pages) and then A (Subdivide Page).**

   The Subdivide Page dialog box appears.

7. **Press 2.**

   This step tells WordPerfect that you are using two parts of your printed page, two large columns that, in truth, become page 1 and page 2 when you fold the pages over to make a booklet.

8. **Press Home, F7.**

   The screen may look a little strange because you're now typing in a new booklet format. No matter . . .

9. **Type your text.**

   Write that novel! Shame those publishers when your masterpiece is finally selected and they drag their heads low in light of your Pulitzer.

   You can use the Retrieve command to bring in text you've already typed, folding it into your new booklet format.

10. **Press Shift-F7.**

    The Print/Fax dialog box appears.

11. **Press M (Multiple Pages).**

    The Print Multiple Pages dialog box appears.

12. **Press B (Print as Booklet) and press Enter.**

    Make sure that your printer is on and ready to print. If you selected some strange kind of paper format, make sure that you've loaded that paper. For printing Letter (Landscape), you don't need to change a thing.

13. **Press R to print your booklet.**

    If you don't have a printer capable of printing on two sides at once, you have to print half of your pages first, flip them over, and stick them in the printer again. The PC beeps at you when this happens. Follow these steps:

14. **Press Shift-F7, C.**

    The Control Printer dialog box appears. In the Action box, you see the message `Reinsert booklet physical page number X`, where *X* is the first page in your booklet.

    Heed these instructions!

15. **Press G.**

    Your booklet continues printing.

- You may be asked to reinsert specific pages again, repeating Steps 14 and 15 until the entire booklet has finished printing.
- Make sure that you get the pages right. Turning over the stack and reinserting the pages in your printer *does not* work!
- It helps to number the pages in your booklet so that you know which page is which. Remember that the pages asked for in the Control Printer dialog box are *physical* pages.
- When everything is done, you can bind or staple the booklet in the middle, or you can have a copy place duplicate it thousands of times. Think of it — you can become master of your own religion and hire college kids to hand out your booklets at airports and freeway on-ramps.

Saving Time Printing Text and Graphics

Unless you're fanatical about making each document look picture perfect (sounds like the name of a graphics program distributed by WordPerfect, doesn't it?), you probably want your printer to crank out rough drafts quickly. After everything is perfect, you can print the document out slowly and carefully by using the highest quality printing that your printer can provide.

WordPerfect gives you the following four choices for printing quality:

- High
- Medium
- Draft
- Do Not Print

WARNING! Although WordPerfect offers these ranges of draft qualities, not all printers cooperate with WordPerfect in printing drafts of text or graphics. If your printer doesn't cooperate, there's not a whole lot you can do except complain to WordPerfect or your printer manufacturer.

Draft printing text

The higher the print quality, the slower your printing will be. To change the print quality of your text, follow these steps:

1. **Press Shift-F7.**

   The Print/Fax dialog box appears.

2. **Press T (Text Quality).**

   A pop-up list of four text qualities appears.

3. **Highlight the text print quality that you want and press Enter.**

   Use the up- or down-arrow key to select your print quality.

- After selecting a print quality, press R to print your document in that quality.
- Yeah, the Do Not Print setting really causes nothing to print. Don't be shocked when you select it and nothing prints.

Draft printing graphics

Graphics can really slow your printer to a crawl. If you're just editing and proofreading text, it's a good idea to turn graphics printing to the Do Not Print setting. Doing this keeps your printer from wasting time printing the graphic. Instead, your printer just leaves an empty space where the graphic appears.

To change the print quality of graphics, follow these steps:

1. **Press Shift-F7.**

   The Print/Fax dialog box appears.

2. **Press G (Graphics Quality).**

   A list of four graphics qualities appears.

3. **Highlight the graphics print quality that you want and press Enter.**

   Use the up- or down-arrow key to highlight the graphics quality. For example, selecting Do Not Print means that the graphics print "blank," allowing you to paste them in later, but all the text will print.

- When you're ready to print, press R.
- Press Home, F7 to return to your document.
- If you select Draft quality, the image prints, but it may look like a 50th-generation photocopy. This is okay for a quick checkup of your document; however, when you really care, select High quality.

Part II

Formatting for Fun and Profit

In this part . . .

If a word processor were just about putting words on paper, like using a typewriter, life would be so much easier. After all, how the printed page looked wouldn't be an important question. But after computer users discovered that word processors, in conjunction with their printers, can make the printed word look very untypewriterlike, the door opened for all sorts of experimentation. Making the printed page look original is a lofty goal, one that is achieved handily by word processors like WordPerfect. But it is also a goal that exists at the price of transforming us mere word writers into amateur typesetters.

This part of the book discusses the formatting chore in depth. Because this is a *MORE* book, you'll read more about formatting characters, sentences, and paragraphs, as well as get information about WordPerfect's enigmatic Style command and other goodies that you find in the word processing supermarket aisle marked *Formatting*.

Chapter 9

Fun with Fonts and Other Characters

In This Chapter

- Why bother with fonts?
- Printer versus graphics fonts
- Using fonts
- What you see isn't always what you get
- Installing new fonts (dull but necessary)
- Introducing WordPerfect's special characters

Without question, WordPerfect displays and prints your finely crafted text so that it looks like it came out of a manual typewriter. If spending $495 on WordPerfect so that you can turn your $3,000 computer and $1,000 laser printer into a $50 typewriter seems like a backwards use of technology, you're right.

Fortunately, WordPerfect provides a way to spice up your writing so that it looks pretty and expensive, as if a graphics artist designed and printed your work. Besides letting you adjust the size (10 points, 12 points, 14 points, and so on) and appearance (underline, bold, italics, and so on), WordPerfect also lets you use something mysterious called *fonts*.

Why Bother with Fonts?

You never need fonts, especially when you're writing or editing. Just don't mess with 'em; your thoughts on-screen are more important. But when you want to print your prose so that it looks nice, that's when you want to mull over fonts.

You should become somewhat familiar with the following three parts of a font:

- Typeface
- Point size
- Styles

Each of these parts is discussed in the following sections.

Know ye a font by its typeface

What we computer people have come to know as a font (pronounced *phaunt*) is really a *typestyle*, which is actually the typesetter term. A typestyle defines the way the text looks. There are fancy, plain, ornate, and boring font typestyles, and each of them can be put to use for a different purpose.

In WordPerfect, you'll probably use fonts to emphasize certain parts of text, such as headlines, titles, or threats. Here's a quick look at three different fonts:

Courier

Arial

Roman

- Courier is the typewriter style of font, which is what WordPerfect typically starts out using. This font is boring, but every printer can muster it, and people find it easy to read.
- Arial is an example of a *sans serif* font, or a font without curlycues and other ornate doohickeys on the tops and bottoms of the letters. This type of font is used for headings and titles.
- Roman is a font that's well-suited to text. It's called a *serif* font, with serifs being the wee ruffles and flourishes at the ends of the letters. These serifs actually make the text easier to read, which is why this type of font is used for text.
- There are zillions of fonts.
- Fonts should be used sparingly. If you use too many fonts on a single page, it can look as annoying as a roomful of children jumping up and down to get your attention. Ideally, you should stick to one main font for the bulk of your text and one or two other fonts for emphasizing titles, headings, footnotes, and so on.

How big be your font?

The size of a font is measured in points, which are wee little things that must stand 72 high to equal one inch. (For the math heads: There are 72 points in one inch.) So a font that is 36 points big is half an inch tall. A font that is 12 points tall is about 1/6th of an inch in height — which is the typical size of text in most books and newspapers.

- The most popular point size is normally 12. Sometimes 10 is used, but this text tends to get a little tiny. Larger sizes, such as 14, 18, and 24, are used for titles and such.
- Most point sizes are even numbers. You can use odd numbers (11 points is popular), as well.
- In WordPerfect, the size of a font and its typeface are two different things you can set.
- Some fonts come in fixed sizes. That is, you can use the font only at 12, 14, and 18 points. These fonts are known as *nonscalable* fonts. When you can set them to another size, they look ugly. Only at the preset sizes do they look sharp.
- A *scalable* font can be set to any point size.

Special font styles

Most fonts come in different styles, which is more of a traditional typesetter thing. For example, the following are four styles for the Times Roman typeface:

Times Roman Book

Times Roman Bold

Times Roman Italic

Times Roman Bold Italic

The book style is the normal, no-frills style, followed by the special bold, italic, and bold-italic fonts. The text is still in the Times Roman typeface but with different effects.

Unlike typesetters, computers usually apply font styles separately from the typeface. So in WordPerfect, you can select the Times Roman font and then manually make it bold or italic. Even so, some fonts may have different styles listed in WordPerfect's Font menu. For example, you may see a Helvetica Bold or a Bodoni Heavy font, which is merely Helvetica or Bodoni with a special style spray painted over it.

- Some styles use the term *Heavy* to mean *very bold.*
- Sometimes the word *Light* appears instead of *Book*; both terms mean *regular text.*

Printer versus graphics fonts

Forgetting all the typesetter blab-blab for a moment, WordPerfect classifies fonts in the following two categories:

- Printer fonts (also called nonscalable fonts)
- Graphics fonts (also called scalable fonts)

Printer fonts are those fonts your printer uses — the fonts you see in the printer's manual or on a demo sheet of paper at the store. Your printer does these fonts innately, just as the crow flies south. And it does them well. Unfortunately, it may do them only in a fixed set of sizes, such as 10 points, 12 points, 16 points, and so on. Because the fonts cannot be changed to any other size — they cannot be *scaled* — they're known as nonscalable, stupid old printer fonts by WordPerfect.

Graphics fonts can appear in any size you want: They can be *scaled* to any point size, from wee small to bigger than your printer can print. They're called graphics fonts because your printer produces them by using individual dots and not a set of patterns, which is the case with printer fonts. The graphics fonts are actually built inside the computer and then beamed over to the printer when it comes time to print.

There are advantages and disadvantages to each type of font. Printer fonts print faster, but they're limited to a certain set of sizes. Graphics fonts can appear in any size, but they print slower because the computer has to figure them out each time you print.

- Most laser and inkjet printers have built-in printer fonts. The exact number and type depends on your printer. For most purposes, your printer's built-in fonts should be enough, but if you're doing desktop publishing or something really weird with WordPerfect, you may need additional fonts.
- Plug-in font cartridges let you plug one or more cartridges (like the old 8-track cartridges) in to your printer, giving it more fonts to play with. Unfortunately, these font cartridges cost extra and still may not offer all the fonts you need.
- You can mix both printer and graphics fonts in the same document. As far as WordPerfect is concerned, a font is a font, no matter what it may be called.

Obtaining other fonts

WordPerfect can use a number of different fonts, not just the ones it comes with or the ones associated with your printer. You can buy fonts, "steal" them from other programs (such as Microsoft Windows), or download them from a BBS or national on-line service, such as CompuServe. Refer to the section "Installing new fonts in WordPerfect" later in this chapter for the details.

Using Fonts

There are two basic ways to use fonts in your text. The first way is to choose a font and then type away. Everything you type appears in the selected font's style and typeface from that point on. The second way is to type your text and worry about fonts later. When you're ready, you mark your text as a block and then select a font for it.

- A potential third way to change your font is to modify the initial font — the font WordPerfect automatically selects for each new document you create. This technique is covered in the next section.
- Another way to apply a font to your text after you type it is to use WordPerfect's Style command. Refer to Chapter 11 for more information.

Changing the initial font

Every WordPerfect document starts out with the Courier 10 font at a size of 12 points. This font is essentially the same one used by manual typewriters, and you all remember how exciting they were. So why not change things? Why not have your initial font be something more useful, maybe something that says "you" on all your documents?

To change this initial font to something more interesting, follow these steps:

1. **Press Ctrl-F8 (or choose Font⇨Font).**

   The Font dialog box appears, splashing itself all over the screen, like some enormous Oriental rug.

2. **Press Shift-F1.**

   The Font Setup dialog box appears.

3. **Press F (Select Initial Font).**

   The Initial Font dialog box appears, where you tell WordPerfect which font you want it to use to start all new documents.

4. **Press F (Font).**

   A list of available fonts appears.

5. **Highlight the font you want and press Enter.**

   Use the up- and down-arrow keys to scroll through the list. For example, if you want all your documents to start out in Bookman, highlight that name from the list and press the Enter key.

6. **Press S (Size).**

   A list of available point sizes appears for that particular font. Some fonts can appear only in one point size; others may have multiple point sizes available.

7. **Highlight the point size you want and press Enter.**

   As you did with the font, select a size for the typeface you want WordPerfect to use each time you start a new document. For example, I like my stuff big, so I select 12 points.

8. **Press N (All New Documents).**

   This selection changes the initial font for all new WordPerfect documents.

9. **Press Home, F7.**

   You're done, back in your document.

- My advice is to select a printer font as the initial font — because printer fonts print faster than other types of fonts — and to choose something pretty.
- Even though you change the initial font, you're not stuck with this font for all your documents. You can change the font in any document at any time by using the instructions offered in the next two sections.
- Be careful! The initial font you choose depends on the type of printer you have selected to use with WordPerfect. If you change printers, your other printer may not recognize your initial font.

Switching to a new font before typing text

Getting the words on paper is important, more important than sitting around fussing over which font works best. So up front, my advice is to write and get your ideas down before you don your typesetter's hat. On the other hand, if you know which font you want to use, it's perfectly okay to change to that font before you start typing your text.

To choose a font before typing, follow these steps:

1. **Move the cursor to the location where you want to start typing.**
2. **Press Ctrl-F8.**

   The Font dialog box appears.
3. **Press F (Font).**

   A list of available fonts drops down like a window shade on a hot August day.
4. **Highlight the font you want to use.**

   The fonts are listed in alphabetical order by name. Use the up- or down-arrow keys to scroll to the font you want. Note that a preview of how it looks is shown in the Font dialog box's Resulting Font window.
5. **Press Enter twice.**

   Your highlighted font has been selected. You can now start typing text in that new font.

- While you're in the Font dialog box, you can also select other text attributes, such as bold, italic, and other goodies, to your heart's desire.
- An easier way to manage all this font nonsense is to use WordPerfect's Style command, as covered in Chapter 11.
- Yes, it's possible to change fonts in the middle of a paragraph, even in the middle of a word. Just follow the preceding instructions and then be sure to switch back to the old font when you're done.
- The current font appears on the ribbon as the second item from the right. The item normally says *Courier* — unless you've been closely following the instructions in this chapter. To show the ribbon, press Alt-V, R (View⇨Ribbon).

Changing the font for existing text

To change the font for text already typed in your document, follow these steps:

1. **Move the cursor to the beginning of the text that you want to change.**
2. **Press Alt-F4.**

   This step activates WordPerfect's block-marking command.
3. **Move the cursor to highlight the text you want to change.**

   Use any of the cursor-movement keys or type a letter on the keyboard to highlight text up to that letter. The highlighted text is a block you can change by using the Font command.

4. **Press Ctrl-F8.**

   The Font dialog box appears.

5. **Press F (Font).**

   A list of available fonts appears. Select your font from the list by using the up- or down-arrow keys. Highlight the font you want to use.

6. **Press the Enter key twice.**

   WordPerfect magically changes the font for your highlighted block to the new font you've selected.

- The fonts are listed in the Font dialog box in alphabetical order.
- You can also change the font by highlighting the text and then selecting a new font from the ribbon. Click the down arrow by the font box (second from the right) and choose your font from the list. You can change the point size in a similar manner.

Using the ribbon to change fonts

If you prefer using a mouse to change fonts, WordPerfect gives you the option of displaying font choices in the Ribbon (the bar of drop-down lists just below the menu bar).

To use the Ribbon to change fonts, follow these steps:

1. **Click the mouse on the displayed font box's drop-down button.**

   It's that li'l button to the right of the font name. A list of available fonts appears.

2. **Click the font that you want to use.**

   For example, use the scroll bar to find the Ugly font and click it with the mouse to change that font.

- If you don't have a mouse, you can't use the Ribbon, so don't bother even trying.
- Press Alt-V, R to make the Ribbon appear on-screen if it's not there already.

What You See Isn't Always What You Get (The Joys of Document Font Mapping)

Fonts are only as good as your printer. Sometimes your printer may not recognize a font in WordPerfect. This problem may happen when you receive a document from someone else that is laced with strange fonts unbeknownst to your printer. Or it may happen if you switch printers (or if the network wonk does it for you). In these cases, many of the fancy fonts may not be available to your printer.

Rather than complain, WordPerfect simply tries to substitute the font most like the one you have chosen for your original document. When WordPerfect substitutes one font for another in a document, the process is called *document font mapping.*

An even more bizarre situation may occur if you view your document in Graphics or Page mode. In these modes, WordPerfect displays all fonts as graphics fonts, even if your document uses printer fonts. Because graphics fonts aren't always the same as printer fonts, WordPerfect tries its hardest to substitute the closest fitting graphics font for every printer font you use. When this situation happens, it is called *screen font mapping.*

- You don't have to memorize the two mapping terms. Just know that they're the reason why your stuff sometimes looks so funky when printed.
- You should be in Graphics mode when you use WordPerfect 6. To ensure that you're there already, press Alt-V to peek at the View menu. You should see a check mark by the second item, Graphics mode. (The same holds true for Page mode, which simply shows more of the page than does Graphics mode.) If you're not in either mode, select one or the other from the menu now. Otherwise, press Esc and keep reading.

How to change document font mapping

Just in case you don't like the stupid fonts that WordPerfect substitutes in your documents, you can change which fonts it uses. Changing the fonts doesn't mean that everything will look nice. It just means that you get to pick which font gets substituted instead of WordPerfect making a haphazard, roll-of-the-die, inane computer guess. To change the font, follow these steps:

1. **Press Ctrl-F8.**

   The Font dialog box appears.

2. **Press Shift-F1.**

   The Font Setup dialog box appears.

3. Press D (Edit Document Font Mapping Table).

The Document Font Mapping Table dialog box appears, as shown in Figure 9-1.

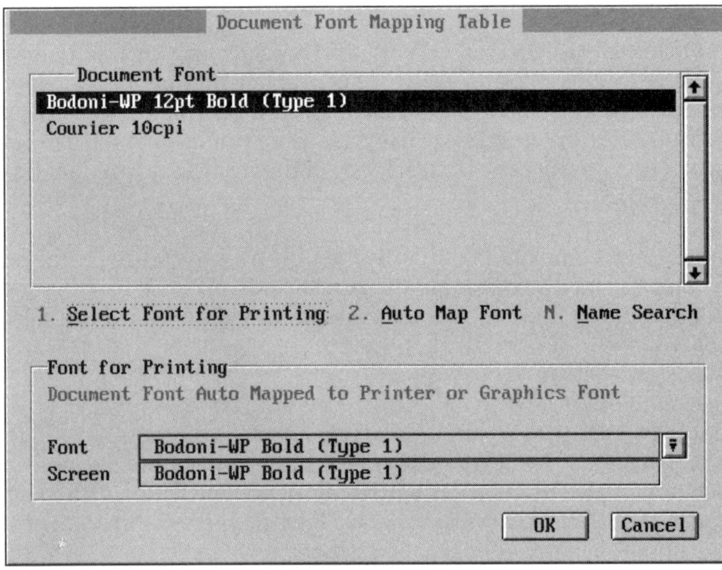

Figure 9-1: The beloved Document Font Mapping Table dialog box.

4. Select a font to change.

Highlight a font to change its document font mapping. For example, the silly Bodoni font looks horrid on your printer. Select it for remapping duty. Use the arrow keys to highlight that font name.

5. Press S (Select Font for Printing).

A list of available printer fonts appears. Suppose that you want to use the Helvetica Bold font when printing Bodoni. Sounds good. Highlight that font from the list.

6. Press Enter.

7. Press Home, F7.

You're back in your document. WordPerfect is now well-aware that when *Bodoni* (or whatever) appears on-screen, your printer takes that to mean *Helvetica Bold* (or whatever).

- The only time you have to worry about document mapping is when you use really bizarre fonts available only on one printer but not another. If you're just using the boring fonts that come with WordPerfect, you don't have to worry about document font mapping. (Of course, the same can be said about every topic in this chapter, if you push it.)

How to change screen font mapping

If you use a lot of printer fonts and you work in Graphics or Page mode (as you should), the fonts that WordPerfect displays on-screen may not be exactly what will actually print out. What a gyp! But it's the price you pay for having a fancy printer with all sorts of goofy fonts and a program like WordPerfect that is just plain dumb about them.

Because WordPerfect isn't always perfect (ha, ha) at guessing the best font to display on-screen, you may want to take control and choose which screen fonts to use in place of printer fonts.

To change the screen font mapping, follow the same steps as outlined in the preceding section. The only difference occurs in Step 3. Instead of pressing D, you should press S for the Edit Screen Font Mapping Table option. Then select the new screen font just as you selected a printer font in the preceding section. It works the same.

- If you never use WordPerfect in Graphics or Page mode or you never use printer fonts, you don't have to worry about screen font mapping.
- Screen fonts aren't as important as printer fonts. No way. The fonts you choose can look just as ugly as they want to on-screen as long as they give you a rough idea of how they will print and look on the page. (Kinda reminds you of the older, text-only days of WordPerfect, eh?)
- I've been bitten by so many mosquitoes recently that I'm thinking of changing my blood type to *snack*.

Installing New Fonts (Dull but Necessary)

Before you can use any new fonts, you have to tell WordPerfect that these fonts exist. Without otherwise being told, WordPerfect already knows how to use the following fonts: Bodoni, CommercialScript-WP, Courier, Dutch, Helve-WP, Line Printer, Roman, and Swiss. If you just want to use these fonts, you don't have to go through the messy process of installing (a fancy term that means copying) fonts because WordPerfect installed them automatically when you went through the messy process of installing WordPerfect.

But if you want to install any additional fonts that may exist as printer, cartridge, soft, or graphics fonts, you have to tell WordPerfect where to find these fonts.

The subject of fonts in WordPerfect is a galaxy of information unto itself. Generally, you can freely ignore this stuff. However, you may enjoy using some of the more esoteric fonts available in WordPerfect — including some Windows fonts. The following sections tell you how.

Types of fonts

When you buy extra fonts on a printer cartridge or on a floppy disk, you may have purchased some of the following six font types, as shown in Table 9-1.

Table 9-1 Font Types

Font Name	*Category*	*DOS Directory*	*File Extensions*
AutoFont	Printer and graphics	\AUTOFONT	.TFM GLUE.TXT
Bitstream Speedo	Graphics	\BTFONTS	.SPD .TDF
CG Intellifont	Printer and graphics	\TD\TYPE\TD\FONTS	.TYP .SFS
Type 1	Printer and graphics	\PSFONTS\AFM \PSFONTS\PFM\PSFONTS	.AFM .PFM .PFB
TrueType (Windows)	Graphics	\TT\WINDOWS\SYSTEM	.TTF
HP LaserJet	Printer	None	Varies

- Autofonts are used by Hewlett-Packard and compatible printers.
- Bitstream Speedo fonts not only have a stupid name, but are also used by only a few programs.
- CG Intellifonts are the native fonts of Hewlett-Packard LaserJet III printers.
- Type 1 fonts are PostScript fonts from Adobe.
- TrueType fonts are used by Windows 3.1.
- HP LaserJet fonts are the native fonts of (what else?) Hewlett-Packard LaserJet printers.
- *Hewlett-Packard* is an ugly thing to type.

Installing new fonts in WordPerfect

Before you can install a font into WordPerfect, you have to know

- The type of font you want to install
- The directory where the fonts are stored

That directory thing means that the fonts have already been copied to your hard drive — an important point. Somehow, some way, you've got the fonts on a disk and have copied them to your hard drive. Therefore, you should know the font type (TrueType, Bitstream Speedo, and so on) and the DOS directory where they're located. Somewhat techy stuff, but important.

To install a font, follow these steps:

1. **Press Ctrl-F8.**

   The Font dialog box appears.

2. **Press Shift-F1.**

   The Font Setup dialog box appears.

3. **Press I (Install Fonts).**

   WordPerfect's Font Installer program runs, which is a Text mode program, so don't let it scare you when it appears on-screen. Eventually, after a few moments of darkness, the Select Font Type dialog box appears.

4. **Highlight the type of font you want to install and press Enter.**

   For example, if you have Microsoft Windows on your system, you can steal some fonts from Windows. Press 5 to select TrueType fonts. (This is sneaky and will doubtless make Bill Gates very angry. But what the hey.)

   The Location of File dialog box appears.

5. **Press 1.**

   You need to tell WordPerfect where to find the files. Type in the DOS directory where your fonts are stored on your hard disk. For Windows TrueType fonts, the directory is C:\WINDOWS\SYSTEM (unless you've put them elsewhere).

6. **Press Enter after typing in the directory name and then press Enter again.**

   The Select Fonts dialog box appears. All the fonts available on your computer are displayed and marked with an asterisk (*).

   At this point, you can pick and choose which fonts you want. The fonts WordPerfect will "steal" are marked with an asterisk. You can use the up- and down-arrow keys to move the highlight bar and select or deselect fonts by pressing the asterisk (*) key when a font is highlighted.

7. **Press I (Install Marked Fonts).**

   The Verify Location of Fonts dialog box appears. Okay.

8. **Press Enter.**

   WordPerfect obediently starts installing your fonts. After it's done, it displays a dialog box saying it's finished, and it annoyingly beeps at you.

9. **Press Enter.**

10. **Press Home, F7 twice.**

    Your fonts are ready to use and you never have to go through this tedious process again (until you get new fonts that you want to use with WordPerfect).

- Installing the fonts takes longer the more of them you install. Expect to wait a bit if you have several dozen fonts to install.
- Aside from stealing fonts from Windows, a great place to get WordPerfect fonts for free is from an on-line service, such as CompuServe. You should refer to the graphic arts or desktop publishing areas, or (on CompuServe) you can go to the WordPerfect forum to scout for fonts.

Introducing WordPerfect's Special Characters

If you want to type letters or numbers, just press the correct key on your keyboard. But if you want to type more unusual characters, such as the cents symbol (¢), copyright symbol (©), trademark symbol (™), mathematical symbols (≥), or foreign currency symbols (₷), what keys do you press?

The answer is simple: none. WordPerfect stores bizarre characters like these in something called *character sets*. Character sets are simply groups of related oddball characters that WordPerfect thinks you may use. WordPerfect provides the following 14 different character sets:

ASCII (character set 0)

Multinational (character set 1)

Phonetic symbols (character set 2)

Box drawing symbols (character set 3)

Typographic symbols (character set 4)

Iconic symbols (character set 5)

Math/Scientific symbols (character set 6)

Math/Scientific extension symbols (character set 7)

Greek (character set 8)

Hebrew (character set 9)

Cyrillic (character set 10)

Japanese (character set 11)

Arabic (character set 12)

Arabic script (character set 13)

- Not all printers can print all these characters. If your printer can print graphics, chances are good that it can also print any strange characters you choose.
- Some of these odd characters, like the Japanese or Arabic characters, appear on-screen as ugly-looking boxes if you're using WordPerfect in Text mode. If you want to see what these characters really look like, switch to Graphics or Page mode or use Print Preview.

Inserting a strange character into a document

To insert one of WordPerfect's strange characters into a document, follow these steps:

1. **Press Ctrl-W.**

   The WordPerfect Characters dialog box appears, which may look something like Figure 9-2.

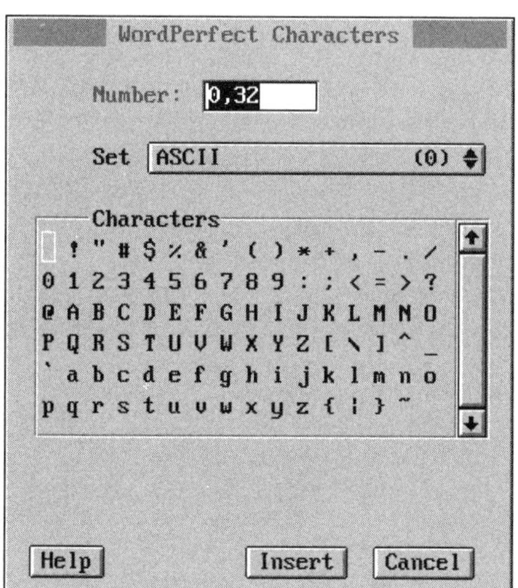

Figure 9-2: The WordPerfect Characters dialog box.

2. **Press Tab and press Enter.**

   WordPerfect displays its list of 14 possible character sets that you can use.

3. **Highlight the character set that you think (hope) contains the character that you want to insert into your document and press Enter.**

4. **Press C (Characters).**

   This step switches focus to the array of characters displayed in the middle of the WordPerfect Characters dialog box. Note that sometimes the list is longer than you can see, so there will be a scroll bar to the right side. Don't neglect those characters you can't see; press the down-arrow key to view them.

5. **Highlight the character you want to insert into your document and press Enter.**

   Use the arrow keys (all four of them) to locate the character you want. Press Enter to insert the character into your document.

- When you get real good (or just weird), you'll memorize the numbers for each character and type them into the Number box in the WordPerfect Characters dialog box. For example, character 4,23 is the copyright symbol, ©.

Inserting an ASCII character into a document

For those impatient souls who find the WordPerfect Characters dialog box too cumbersome to use, there's a shortcut — but it works only with ASCII characters. (ASCII characters are the basic character set your PC uses, which includes a smattering of symbols and foreign language characters.)

To insert an ASCII character into a document, hold down the Alt key and type the number (off the numeric keypad) that represents the ASCII character that you want to display. For example, to type the cents symbol (¢), hold down the Alt key, type **155** from the numeric keypad, and release the Alt key.

Table 9-2 lists several ASCII characters you can insert into your documents by using this Alt-key method.

Table 9-2 Common ASCII Characters You Can Type by Using the Alt Key and the Numeric Keypad

ASCII Character	*Number*
é	130
à	133
ö	148
£	156
Ñ	165
¿	168
½	171

- Press and hold the Alt key and then type the number on the numeric keypad. After you're done, release the Alt key. (It must be held down the entire time you're typing a number.)
- If you need to type these characters regularly, either hang an ASCII chart near your computer or consider using macros to make the whole process less painful.
- Remember, you can type these characters by using only the numbers on the numeric keypad, not the numbers from the top of the keyboard. If you try using the numbers at the top of the keyboard, nothing happens, and then you blame this book for giving you bad instructions.

Quickly inserting any character into a document

If you want to quickly insert non-ASCII characters into your document, WordPerfect gives you a shortcut to do this technique, too. All you need to know are the following two numbers:

- The character set number that the character belongs to
- The number representing the character you want

For those blessed with a photographic memory, this method works quickly. To insert a character into a document by using its numbers, follow these steps:

1. **Press Ctrl-A.**

   The Compose dialog box appears, as shown in Figure 9-3.

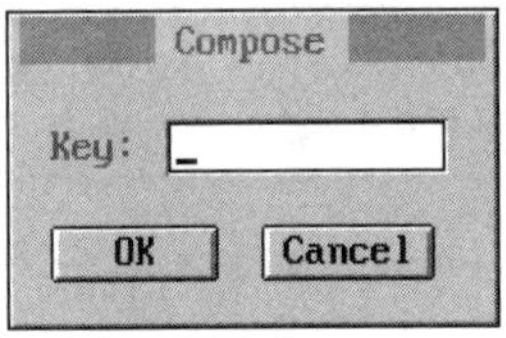

Figure 9-3: The Compose dialog box.

2. **In the Key box, type the number of the character set, a comma, and the number representing the character you want.**

   For example, type **4,23** to represent the copyright (©) symbol. (Yeah, I had to look it up first.)

3. **Press Enter.**

   WordPerfect inserts the special character into the document.

TIP

Appendix A of the WordPerfect manual lists all the character sets available — far more than I'm willing to repeat in this book. Indeed, Appendix A is one thing to convince you that the WordPerfect manual isn't totally useless.

Chapter 10

Formatting Sentences, Paragraphs, and Pages

In This Chapter

- Numbering your pages
- Headers, footers, and watermarks
- Centered pages and page offsets
- Setting document and paragraph margins
- Tabs (not the soft drink)
- Spacing, kerning, and leading

In the business world, people make snap judgments about others within 30 seconds or less. Within those 30 seconds, you had better present yourself well because you don't get a second chance to make a first impression. So if you have a piece of linguini on your lip or a half day's growth of beard covering your face (and you're a woman), you've just blown it.

Likewise, your documents must make a first impression to everyone who reads them, and the first impression people get from your documents is how well your pages are designed.

Even the most finely crafted literary masterpiece looks terrible if the margins are too small or the lines are cramped too close together. If you want people to read what you write, not only do you have to write something worth reading, but you also have to present it in a way that doesn't assault the eyeballs of your readers.

To help you dress up your text so that it's suitable to be seen in public, WordPerfect provides various ways to format your document. Formatting is a fancy term that means "making your text look less ugly."

Not only can WordPerfect format an entire page, but it can get right down to details by formatting paragraphs, lines, and even individual letters, if you want to get fussy about it. With all these wonderful features, there's no excuse for your writing to look less than stellar (unless, of course, you don't have any idea what you're doing in the first place).

Numbering Your Pages

If you print a 300-page document and lose page 209, you won't have any problem putting it back in its right place as long as you have numbered all your pages.

WordPerfect keeps track of your page numbers on-screen but doesn't print your page numbers on your pages unless you tell it these three things:

- Where to print the page numbers
- How to number your pages (with numbers, letters, text and numbers, and so on)
- Where to start and stop printing page numbers

The only way to see your page numbers on-screen is if you switch to Graphics mode or choose the Print Preview command. Otherwise, you just have to trust that WordPerfect is numbering everything okay.

Positioning your page numbers

To help you put page numbers where most people expect to find them, WordPerfect provides eight preset positions for placing page numbers:

- Top Left
- Top Center
- Top Right
- Alternating, Top
- Bottom Left
- Bottom Center
- Bottom Right
- Alternating, Bottom

To position your page numbers, follow these steps:

1. **Press Shift-F8.**

   The Format dialog box appears.

2. **Press P (Page).**

   The Page Format dialog box appears.

3. **Press N (Page Numbering).**

   The Page Numbering dialog box appears.

4. **Press P (Page Number Position).**

   The Page Number Position dialog box appears, with a little diagram that shows you where the page numbers will appear on a page, as shown in Figure 10-1.

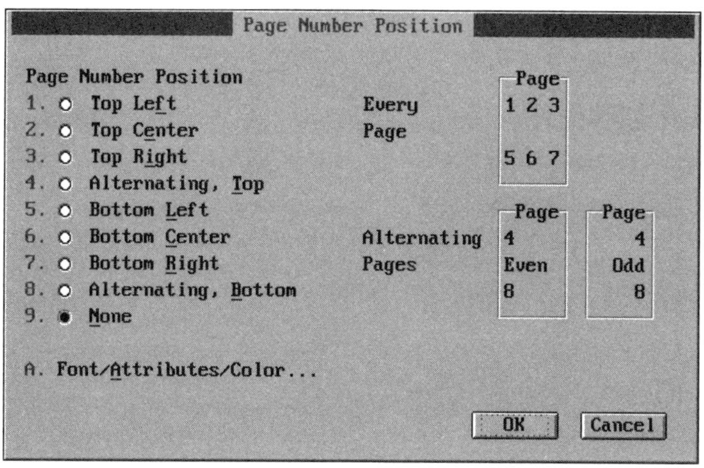

Figure 10-1: The Page Number Position dialog box.

5. **Choose the page number position you want by pressing a number between 1 and 8.**

   Press 6 for Bottom Center, for example; press 5 for Bottom Left (odd pages); press 7 for Bottom Right (even pages).

6. **Press Home, F7.**

   You're back in your document.

You can't see the page numbers unless you go to Print Preview or select Page mode.

- WordPerfect numbers its pages starting with 1 as the first page. To change the page numbering, refer to the section "Starting with a page number other than 1" later in this chapter.
- The following sections describe ways of changing how your page numbers look.

Choosing your numbers

After you've decided to use page numbers and you've decided where you want them to appear on a page, the next step is figuring out what style of numbers you want to use. Normally, you'll use numbers, but just in case you want to be a little silly, WordPerfect provides the following five different numbering styles:

- Numbers (1, 2, 3, and so on)
- Lowercase letters (a, b, c, and so on)
- Uppercase letters (A, B, C, and so on)
- Lowercase Roman numerals (i, ii, iii, and so on)
- Uppercase Roman numerals (I, II, III, and so on)

To choose a numbering style, follow these steps:

1. **Press Shift-F8, P, N.**

   The Page Numbering dialog box appears.
2. **Press N (Page Number).**

   The Set Page Number dialog box appears.
3. **Press M (Number Method).**

   A drop-down list of five different page numbering styles appears. These correspond to the numbering styles listed at the start of this section.
4. **Highlight the page numbering method you want to use and press Enter.**
5. **Press Home, F7.**

Making descriptive page numbers

Unless you tell it otherwise, WordPerfect blandly prints your page numbers with nothing more interesting than a page number. But for you really creative types, WordPerfect lets you create fancier, more descriptive page numbers, such as

- Appendix – 4
- Doe/Dayton/12
- – 34 –

To create descriptive page numbers, follow these steps:

1. **Press Shift-F8, P, N.**

   The Page Numbering dialog box appears.

2. **Press F (Page Number Format).**

   The cursor will blink in the tiny box by Page Number Format.

3. **Type whatever fancy ways you want your page numbers to appear and press Enter when you're done.**

   For example, you can type

   ```
   Page-[page #]
   ```

   or

   ```
   Appendix/[page #]
   ```

4. **Press Home, F7 to return to your document.**

- Another way of creating fancy page numbers is to stick the page number into your document's header or footer. There you can edit it, add graphics, and mess with it just as you can any text in your document.
- You can easily erase the `[page #]` dealie that is found in the Page Number Format text box on the Page Numbering dialog box, if you're not careful. Press Esc and start over, if you accidentally do.

Using fonts with page numbers

To spice up your page numbering even more, WordPerfect lets you change the fonts and attributes of your page numbers. In this way, if you use a really bizarre font in your document and want your page numbers to match, you can accommodate your wishes.

To change the font and attributes of your page numbers, follow these steps:

1. **Press Shift-F8, P, N.**

   The Page Numbering dialog box appears.

2. **Press P (Page Number Position).**

   The Page Number Position dialog box appears.

3. **Press A (Font/Attributes/Color).**

   The Font dialog box appears. This is the same Font dialog box you use to change WordPerfect's text font.

- Refer to Chapter 9 for more information on formatting fonts. Additional information can be found in *WordPerfect 6 For Dummies*, also in Chapter 9. (Coincidence?)
- After selecting your font, press Home, F7 to return to your document.

Starting and stopping page numbering

Not everyone wants page numbers printed on every page. For example, very few people print "page 1" on the front page of their reports. Instead, they print page numbers starting on the second page.

To stop WordPerfect from putting a page number on a certain page, follow these steps:

1. **Move the cursor to the page where you don't want page numbering to appear.**
2. **Press Shift-F8, P.**

   The Page Format dialog box appears.
3. **Press U (Suppress).**

   The Suppress (This Page Only) dialog box appears, where you can temporarily stifle some of WordPerfect's maniacal formatting.
4. **Press P (Page Numbering).**

   X marks the spot, and page numbering is turned off for the current page.
5. **Press Home, F7.**

- Turning off page numbering does not mess up the page count. Only that one page lacks a number. So if you suppress the page numbering for the first page, the next page is still labeled page 2 (or whatever).
- If you want to suppress numbering for the first page and then have the second page be numbered as page 1, refer to the very next section.

Starting with a page number other than 1

Most of the time, you'll want to number your first page as page 1, your second page as page 2, and so on. However, if you're creating a book or other large document for that small minority of people in this world who still read, you may want to start numbering your pages differently.

For example, the second chapter of your book may begin on page 34, not page 1. To tell WordPerfect to start numbering pages other than from page 1, follow these steps:

1. **Press Shift-F8, P, N.**

   The Page Numbering dialog box appears.

2. **Press N (Page Number).**

   The Set Page Number dialog box appears.

3. **Press N (New Number).**

   Type the new number that you want WordPerfect to start using.

4. **Press Enter.**

5. **Press Home, F7.**

Headers, Footers, and Watermarks

Headers are little bits of text that appear at the top of the page, such as "TOP SECRET." Footers are little bits of text that appear at the bottom of the page, such as a book title. Watermarks are graphic images that appear on a page, but they are so faint that you can print text over the marks.

You can have a maximum of two headers, two footers, and two watermarks on each page, although if you have that many headers, footers, and watermarks, you're probably either very competent or completely disorganized.

- The only way to see headers, footers, or watermarks on-screen is if you switch to Graphics mode or choose the Print Preview command.
- When you're creating two headers, two footers, or two watermarks, make sure that their placement doesn't overlap. Otherwise, the text of each header or footer will print on top of one another. Likewise, two watermark images placed in the same location will interfere with one another.
- Watermarks are usually graphic images, but they can also be text displayed in large type size.
- For information on creating headers and footers, refer to *WordPerfect 6 For Dummies*, Chapter 11.
- On whatever page you put the cursor prior to creating a header, footer, or watermark, that's the page on which the header, footer, or watermark begins. All succeeding pages will have the same marks. If you want your header, footer, or watermark to appear on every page in your document, move the cursor to the first page of your document before creating a header, footer, or watermark.

Creating watermarks

To create a watermark, follow these steps:

1. **Press Shift-F8.**

   The Format dialog box appears.

2. **Press H (Header/Footer/Watermark).**

   The Header/Footer/Watermark dialog box appears.

3. **Press W (Watermarks).**

   You now have to choose an A or B watermark. If you plan on having two of them in your document, select A first and then B. If you're only using one, just press A.

4. **Press A or B.**

   The Watermark (A or B) dialog box appears. Now you have to decide on which pages to have your watermark.

   If you're only making one watermark, select All Pages.

   If you're making two watermarks and this is watermark A (your first one), select Even Pages or Odd Pages.

   If you're making two watermarks and this is watermark B, you can select Even Pages or Odd Pages, whichever you *didn't* select the first time around.

5. **Press A (All Pages), V (Even Pages), or O (Odd Pages) to select on which pages you want your watermark.**

6. **Press Enter.**

   You're now looking at a special screen where you create your watermark. The bottom of the screen tells you which watermark you're working with, and it tells you to press the F7 key when you're done.

TIP

- If you want to put graphics in your watermark, press Alt-F9 to bring up the Graphics dialog box. You can create a graphics box, line, boarder, or whatever. Images can also be imported into your watermark by creating a graphics box and then retrieving an image into the box.
- To type text, select a font style, size, and location for your text. Remember that it will appear as a misty gray background on every page of your document.
- Yes, your typing appears misty gray. Don't bother darkening it up — that circumvents the nature of a watermark.
- Use big fonts.
- The only way to see watermarks on-screen is to choose the Print Preview command or waste a sheet of paper and print it out.

Editing watermarks

Each time you create a watermark, WordPerfect identifies it as Watermark A or Watermark B. When you want to edit a watermark, make sure that you remember which is B and which is A. In this way, you avoid loading the wrong watermark and wasting your time.

To edit an existing watermark, follow these steps:

1. **Press Shift-F8, H, W.**

   Press A or B, depending on which watermark you want to edit.

   The Watermark dialog box appears.

2. **Press E (Edit).**

   You're back on Planet Watermark, where you can freely edit any text or graphics you previous slapped down into your watermark.

- Press Alt-F9 to edit any graphics.
- You can edit text on the watermark screen just as you can anywhere else in your document.
- Press the F7 key when you're done.

Turning off watermarks

Sometimes you may not want your watermark to appear on a certain page. To bow to your demands, WordPerfect can selectively turn off the watermark so that it doesn't appear on certain pages, tainting your otherwise virgin white document.

To turn off a watermark, follow these steps:

1. **Move the cursor to the page on which you want to turn off the watermarks.**

2. **Press Shift-F8, H, W.**

   Press A or B, depending on which watermark you want to turn off.

   The Watermark dialog box appears.

3. **Press F (Off).**

   It done be shut down.

4. **Press Home, F7.**

- When you turn headers, footers, or watermarks off, they remain off from the page the cursor is on to the end of your document.
- You need to repeat these steps if you're using two watermarks; you need to shut off both watermark A and B.

Temporarily suppressing watermarks

When you turn off a watermark, you turn it off for good. Sometimes you may want to suppress a watermark just for one page, such as your title page.

To suppress a watermark, follow these steps:

1. **Move the cursor to the page on which you want to suppress a header, footer, or watermark.**
2. **Press Shift-F8, P, U.**

   The Suppress (This Page Only) dialog box appears.
3. **Press 5 or 6.**

   This step depends on which watermark you want to suppress, option 5 for A or option 6 for B.
4. **Press Home, F7.**

   You're returned to your document.

Centered Pages and Page Offsets

For maximum control over your document, WordPerfect lets you format entire pages so they look exactly the way you want. Apparently, WordPerfect's goal was to create the most powerful word processor/desktop publishing combination program possible. The end result is a bunch of powerful formatting commands that hardly anybody knows how to use properly (except for those who read this section).

Centering text within a single page

To center text between the top and bottom margins of a page, follow these steps:

1. **Move the cursor to the page where you want to center text between the top and bottom margins.**
2. **Press Shift-F8, P.**

   The Page Format dialog box appears.
3. **Press C (Center Current Page).**

   This sticks an X in the box, meaning that the current page will be centered.
4. **Press Home, F7.**

   The page is centered.

- Naturally, WordPerfect won't show centered text on-screen unless you switch to Page mode, choose the Print Preview command (Alt-F, V), or print your page out.
- Centering text on a page looks best when you only have a few lines of text, such as a title page.
- Centering a line or paragraph of text is done with the Shift-F6 key. Either press that key command before you start typing, or highlight your text and then press Shift-F6 to center it left to right.

Centering text on multiple pages

To center text between the top and bottom margins of one or more pages, follow these steps:

1. **Move the cursor to the page where you want to start centering text between the top and bottom margins.**
2. **Press Shift-F8, P.**

   The Page Format dialog box appears.
3. **Press P (Center Pages).**

   This puts an X in the Center Pages box.
4. **Press Home, F7.**

- The pages in your document will be centered, top to bottom, from the current page to the last page.
- To turn this page centering command off, move the cursor to the first page where you want the page centering command turned off, and repeat the the preceding steps. (This removes the X from the Center Pages box.)

Binding offsets

A binding offset is a fancy publishing term for something that allows enough space on one side of a page, so you can bind it (punch holes in it, staple it together, and so on) while still making it easy for people to hold open and read.

To define a binding offset for your document, follow these steps:

1. **Press Shift-F8.**

   The Format dialog box appears.

2. **Press O (Other).**

   The Other Format dialog box appears with its array of miscellany.

3. **Press P (Printer Functions).**

   The Printer Functions dialog box appears. You want to concentrate on area number 2, Binding Offset.

4. **Press B (Binding Offset).**

5. **Press 1.**

   This highlights the box by Binding Offset (Add to Margin).

6. **Type the amount of offset you want and then press Enter.**

   This amount is in addition to your left and right page margins. For example, if you want an extra inch for printing on three-holed paper, type in 1. Press Enter after you've typed in an offset value.

7. **Press B (Binding Offset) and then E (From Edge).**

   WordPerfect displays a drop-down list of four options for the binding offset: Left, Right, Top, or Bottom.

8. **Highlight the binding offset you want to use and press Enter.**

9. **Press Home, F7.**

TIP

- Yes, you can buy paper that's already punched with three holes. If you do, follow these steps to give yourself an extra margin for the holes. (I find 1 inch to be okay; 1½ inches is a little too roomy.)
- True to the spirit of WordPerfect, the WordPerfect manual itself suggests that if you're defining the binding offset for a document printed on one side of the page, don't use the above steps. Instead, use the left margin adjustment option. (Press Shift-F8, 2, 5, type the amount of the left margin, press Enter, and press Home, F7.)

Setting Document and Paragraph Margins

For some odd reason, the more white space (the empty part on a page) used, the more inviting the page is to read. (Of course, if you get carried away, you could create a completely empty page, and you'll find that the MTV generation takes to it readily.)

WordPerfect lets you define document and paragraph margins. Document margins define the top, bottom, left, and right margins of a page. Paragraph margins define the white space surrounding a paragraph. (If you set your document and paragraph margins too wide, you won't have any room left to type any text.)

Defining document margins

To define the size of your document margins, follow these steps:

1. **Move the cursor to the first page in a document whose margins you want to define.**
2. **Press Shift-F8.**

   The Format dialog box appears.
3. **Press M (Margins).**

   The Margin Format dialog box appears.
4. **Where is your margin?**

   Press 1, 2, 3, or 4 (depending on whether you want to define the left, right, top, or bottom margin).
5. **Type the size of the margin that you want and press Enter.**

   I like one-inch margins, which WordPerfect automatically gives you. But if you want a little more space on the top, press 3 (for Top) and then type in 1 1/2 or 2 to give yourself a roomier top margin.
6. **Repeat Steps 4 and 5 until you've defined all the document margins you want.**

   Yeah, you have to do each of them individually.
7. **Press Home, F7.**

- WordPerfect automatically allocates space for any headers, footers, or page numbers you may stick on the page; there's no need to artificially compensate for these items using the Margin Format dialog box.
- You can set the left and right margins for an individual paragraph using the bottom part of the Margin Format dialog box. This is covered in the next section.

Defining paragraph margins

To define the size of your paragraph margins, follow these steps:

1. **Move the cursor to the paragraph whose margins you want to define.**
2. **Press Shift-F8, M.**

   The Margin Format dialog box appears.
3. **Set your paragraph margin using the Paragraph Margins area in the bottom half of the dialog box.**

   Type 5, 6, 7, or 8 (depending on if you want to adjust the size of the left or right margins, first line indentation, or paragraph spacing) and press Enter.
4. **Type the size of the margin, indentation, or spacing that you want to use and press Enter.**

   Steps 3 and 4 will need to be repeated if you want to make multiple changes here.
5. **Press Home, F7.**

   WordPerfect magically formats your paragraph right before your eyes, and almost in real time.

Tabs (Not the Soft Drink)

WordPerfect uses tabs to move text a fixed amount of space within your document. As usual, WordPerfect offers several different types of tabs, depending on what you want:

- Left tabs (text appears to the right of the tab position)
- Right tabs (text appears to the left of the tab position)
- Center tabs (text appears centered around the tab position)
- Decimal tabs (text appears aligned around a single character, usually a period or decimal point)

TIP: Always use tabs to line up your text instead of pressing the spacebar. Tabs are accurate, set to certain positions on the page. Pressing the spacebar produces "space characters," which may look all lined up on-screen but will look ugly when printed.

- Most of the time you'll be using Left tabs. The other tabs are for special text effects.
- If you're organizing information in rows and columns, I recommend using WordPerfect's Table commands. Refer to Chapter 12 in *WordPerfect 6 For Dummies*, or take a peek at Chapter 12 in this book. (A coincidence that they're both Chapter 12? Strange. Call Robert Stack.)

Setting tab positions

WordPerfect innately (or inanely) puts left tabs where it thinks most people will use them, spaced approximately every ½ inch across the page. But if you want to change the positions of existing tabs, follow these steps:

1. **Press Shift-F8.**

   The Format dialog box appears.

2. **Press L (Line).**

   The Line Format dialog box appears.

3. **Press T (Tab Set).**

   The Tab Set dialog box appears, as shown in Figure 10-2.

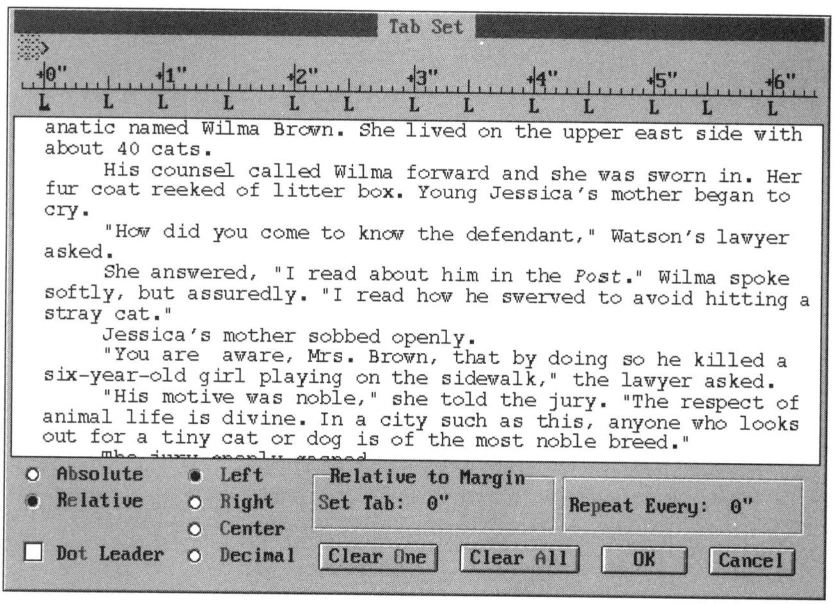

Figure 10-2: The Tab Set dialog box.

4. **Move the cursor underneath the tab you want to move.**

   Use the left- and right-arrow keys. The cursor is there, even if you don't see it right away (it's lurking under the first L on the tab line).

5. **Press Ctrl-left arrow or Ctrl-right arrow to move the tab position to a new location.**

   Holding down the Ctrl key while pressing the left- or right-arrow keys moves the tab.

6. **Press Home, F7 when you're done.**

- An advantage of the Tab Set dialog box's preview window is that you can instantly see how your text is affected by moving tab stops.
- I usually use only one press of the Tab key to separate items. This may not line them up right away, but after following the preceding steps, you can make minor adjustments to line up your lists easily. (One Tab keypress is a lot easier to edit later.)

Deleting single tab positions

WordPerfect gives you two different ways to delete tab positions. If you want to delete one tab position, follow these steps:

1. **Press Shift-F8, L, T.**

   The Tab Set dialog box appears.

2. **Move the cursor underneath the tab you want to delete.**

   Use the left- and right-arrow keys to move the cursor.

3. **Press Delete.**

   The tab mark is gone. You'll see your text jiggle, affected by removing the tab.

4. **Press Home, F7.**

WARNING!

- Deleting a tab affects your entire document, from the cursor's position to the end of text. You might want to scroll around your document after editing the tab line to ensure that things still line up.
- If you do find some oddities after editing the tab stops, there's nothing wrong with editing the tab stops again. Follow the steps in the section "Creating new tabs" later in this chapter.

Deleting all tab positions

If you want to delete all the tab positions in one stroke, follow these steps:

1. **Press Shift-F8, L, T.**

   The Tab Set dialog box appears.

2. **Press A.**

   They're gone.

3. **Press Home, F7.**

Do I need to mention that this really screws up any text you have that contains tabs? Without the tab stops, pressing the Tab key does nothing. Better think this move through before you march forward with it.

Creating new tabs

Most of the time, WordPerfect's naturally selected left tabs and their position (every ½ inch) will be acceptable. But if you need to use right, centered, or decimal tabs, then you'll have to create them yourself.

To create a new tab, follow these steps:

1. **Press Shift-F8, L, T.**

   The Tab Set dialog box appears.

2. **Move the cursor to the location where you want to create a new tab.**

   Use the left- and right-arrow keys.

3. **Choose one of the following:**

   Press L to create a left tab.

   Press R to create a right tab.

   Press C to create a center tab.

   Press D to create a decimal tab.

4. **Press Home, F7.**

- WordPerfect offers a shortcut for creating decimal tabs: Press Ctrl-F6 and Enter.
- A left tab is a standard "press the Tab key and move text over to that spot" tab stop.

- A right tab causes text to be “flush right.” Press the Tab key to a right tab stop and your text will “push left” until you press the Tab key again or press Enter.
- A center tab causes text typed after you press the Tab key to be centered on the tab stop.
- Decimal tabs are used when typing in numbers. The number will push to the left until you type a period (decimal); then the rest of the number will move to the right like normal text. These tabs are ideal for lining up a column of numbers.

Defining tabs with little dots

Look in most books and they’ll have a table of contents that looks something like this:

Chapter 1 1

Chapter 2 23

Chapter 3 49

Although you could create this effect by typing an ant line of periods between the chapter headings and the page numbers, this can get tedious real fast. And you are working with a computer, after all, which is supposed to do all the dirty work for you. Supposedly.

As a shortcut, WordPerfect lets you use dot leaders, which is a fancy term to mean that WordPerfect will automatically display dots (or any other character you wish) in between tabs.

To define a dot leader for any type of tab, follow these steps:

1. **Press Shift-F8, L, T.**

   The Tab Set dialog box appears.

2. **Move the cursor underneath the tab you want to use with dot leaders.**

   What I do in this situation is to delete all the tab stops first (press A). Then I move the cursor over to the right margin and type in an R tab stop. (Type the letter R.) Of course, this setting can only work for the page that contains the dot leaders, like a table of contents. After that, I have to redefine my tab stops or the rest of the document looks severely screwy.

3. **Press T (Dot Leader).**

   This puts an X in the Dot Leader box.

4. **Press Home, F7.**

- From this point on, whenever you press the Tab key, little dots will appear. Then you can type your page numbers (or whatever you want) after these little dots.
- Also refer to Chapter 5 for more information on creating tables of contents and indexes.

Absolute versus relative tabs

WordPerfect makes all tabs relative tabs. Considering that most people don't get along with their relatives, this usually isn't a good assumption to make all the time.

WordPerfect measures relative tabs from the left page margin, which you can define and change any time you want. So a tab of one inch is always one inch from your margin, no matter where your margin lives.

WordPerfect measures absolute tabs from the left edge of a page, which remains fixed. A four-inch tab will be four inches from the left edge of the page, and who cares where the left margin is!

To define a tab as absolute or relative, follow these steps:

1. **Press Shift-F8, L, T.**

   The Tab Set dialog box appears.

2. **Move the cursor underneath the tab you want to change.**

   Use the left- and right-arrow keys to move to the tab stop you want.

3. **Press B to make it an absolute tab or E to make it a relative tab.**

   Either option highlights the circle by `Absolute` or `Relative` in the lower-left corner of the dialog box.

4. **Press Home, F7.**

Spacing, Kerning, and Leading

Occasionally, you may choose a font that grates on your nerves by displaying too much empty space between lines, words, or letters. Fortunately, you can get picky and change all of that.

Adjusting line spacing

To adjust the spacing between lines, follow these steps:

1. **Move the cursor in your document where you want to adjust the line spacing.**

   If you just want to adjust the line spacing of a block of text, highlight that block.

2. **Press Shift-F8.**

   The Format dialog box appears.

3. **Press L (Line).**

   The Line Format dialog box appears.

4. **Press S (Line Spacing).**

   The cursor sits and waits in the wee box by Line Spacing.

5. **Type the amount of spacing you want and press Enter.**

   Type 1 to single-space, 2 to double-space, 1.5 to space-and-a-half, and so on.

6. **Press Home, F7.**

- You can change the line spacing down to a tenth of an inch.
- Changing the line spacing affects all text from the cursor's position to the end of your document.

Adjusting word/letter spacing

To adjust the spacing between words or letters, follow these steps:

1. **Move the cursor in your document where you want to adjust the word or letter spacing.**

2. **Press Shift-F8.**

   The Format dialog box appears.

3. **Press O (Other).**

   The Other Format dialog box appears.

4. **Press P (Printer Functions).**

   The Printer Functions dialog box appears.

5. **Press W (Word Spacing and Letterspacing).**

   The Word Spacing and Letterspacing dialog box appears.

6. **Press W for Word Spacing, or press 2 or L for Letterspacing.**

7. **Choose one of the following:**

   Press 1 for Normal spacing as determined by the font.

   Press 2 for Optimal spacing as determined by WordPerfect.

   Press 3 to define your own spacing value percentage.

   If you press 3, type a value, and press Enter. (A number greater than 100 reduces the spacing; a number less than 100 increases the spacing.)

8. **Press Home, F7.**

Kerning

Kerning means to reduce space between certain letters (such as T or L, which stick out unevenly, or W or V, which slant) so the spacing appears even.

To turn kerning on/off, follow these steps:

1. **Move the cursor in your document where you want to turn on/off kerning.**

2. **Press Shift-F8, O, P.**

   The Printer Functions dialog box appears.

3. **Press K (Kerning).**

   This is an on/off item, so sticking an X in the box switches on kerning, and your documents will print nicely kerned.

4. **Press Home, F7.**

Leading

In the old days before personal computers, printing presses forced some poor, minimally paid worker to insert letters in a cast, which was used to print a page. To adjust the position of these letters, printing presses used thin strips of lead (which probably gave lead poisoning to all of their workers as well).

Nowadays, printing presses don't use strips of lead (although they probably have new ways of poisoning their workers), but everyone still uses the name "leading" for the process of adjusting lines of text.

To turn leading on, follow these steps:

1. **Move the cursor to the beginning of your document.**
2. **Press Shift-F8, O, P.**

   The Printer Functions dialog box appears.
3. **Press L (Leading Adjustment).**
4. **Type the amount of leading to use.**

   Positive numbers increase leading; negative numbers decrease leading.
5. **Press Enter.**
6. **Press Home, F7.**

- The phrase "get the lead out" comes from those ancient, lead-based typesetting machines. It meant removing the empty space between lines of text.
- Another phrase of antiquity, "the die is cast," refers to making a metal die for printing. After the die was cast (prior to printing), it couldn't be changed. This has nothing to do with dice.

Chapter 11

Surviving WordPerfect's Style Commands

In This Chapter

- What the heck are styles anyway?
- Creating your own styles
- Using styles
- Turning off styles
- Editing styles
- Why use style libraries?
- Using style libraries

Part of WordPerfect's greatest strength is its formatting control over practically every aspect of your entire document. Do you want to control kerning, spacing, gutter space, or other topics that only people who do desktop publishing really understand? WordPerfect gives you all this power and more.

With enough patience and technical knowledge, you can format your documents any way you want. Unfortunately, figuring out how to take advantage of WordPerfect's formatting features is enough to drive most people completely batty. In an effort to make formatting easier, WordPerfect offers styles, which is the subject of this chapter (not designed to drive you batty).

What the Heck Are Styles Anyway?

Styles act like cookie cutters for text. With a cookie cutter, you take a handful of dough, flatten it out, shove a cookie cutter over it, and you have a cookie in the shape of a dog, elephant, or boa constrictor.

With a WordPerfect style, you take a block of text, shove a style over it, and you have a block of text in the shape of a script, newspaper heading, or haiku.

- Yes, styles can save a lot of formatting hassle.
- Besides molding text into the shape you want, WordPerfect's styles can also mold graphics boxes, lines, borders, and fills. This chapter doesn't go into the gory details, so just be aware that you can use styles for graphics as well as for text, although probably only three people in the universe actually do so.
- Styles offer three advantages, and when you're stuck using WordPerfect for DOS, you need all the advantages you can get. These three advantages are quick formatting, format consistency, and quick reformatting.

Quick formatting

If you're writing a report and want all the paragraphs to have the same margins, fonts, and typeface (underlining, boldface, and so on), you can scroll through your entire document and change the formatting on each page. For a one-page memo, this procedure isn't too bad, but for a 300-page report, it may drive you insane.

But if you use styles, you can quickly format all or part of your document. Quick formatting means you can format a word, sentence, paragraph, or entire document at the touch of a button, without knowing a single WordPerfect formatting command.

Format consistency

Format consistency means that if you can get everyone in your company to use the same style, all your documents will look the same no matter who writes them. (Styles are extremely popular with software manual writers, which explains why all computer manuals tend to have all the dry, technical appearance of an IRS tax form.)

By storing commonly used styles in something called style libraries, a single WordPerfect guru can create styles that nongurus can use.

Quick reformatting

Quick reformatting means you can reformat an entire document just by changing the style, rather than laboriously changing the formatting of each paragraph in a document.

For example, if you formatted a 120-page screenplay the wrong way, guess what? You have to go back and reformat every single word, line, and paragraph all over again. But if you used styles, you can simply modify your style, reapply the modified style to your 120-page screenplay, and WordPerfect magically reformats the whole thing in seconds.

Open, Paragraph, and Character styles

WordPerfect styles come in the following three varieties:

- Open
- Paragraph
- Character

An Open style contains commands for both character and paragraph formatting. It affects your document from the cursor's position to the end of the document.

A Paragraph style affects (guess what?) paragraphs. It contains paragraph formatting instructions as well as font formatting. Unlike the Open style, you can apply the Paragraph style to individual paragraphs or blocks of paragraphs.

A Character style affects only character formatting (font stuff) and doesn't mess with paragraph or other document formatting. Like the Paragraph style, you can apply Character style to new text that you type or to blocks of text.

- It's entirely possible to apply two or more styles to a single document. For example, you can apply an Open style to the entire document and then apply a Paragraph or Character style to specific parts of that document.
- When you apply two or more styles to a single document, Character styles take precedence over Paragraph styles, which in turn take precedence over Open styles. For example, if your Open style formats your entire document with tiny margins, but your Paragraph style formats everything with wide margins, your paragraphs will have wide margins.
- Besides quickly formatting text, styles can also quickly format graphics, outlines, and borders. Any time you need consistent formatting, use a style.

Creating Your Own Styles

Every WordPerfect document comes with styles that you can examine and play with. These predefined styles let you create outlines faster. Unless you plan to use WordPerfect for outlines all the time, you may want to create additional styles for formatting business reports, essays, poems, screenplays, or nasty letters to your relatives.

When you create a style, WordPerfect gives you the following three choices for where to store it:

- In the current WordPerfect document
- In a personal style library
- In a shared style library

When you create a style, WordPerfect blindly stores it only in the current WordPerfect document unless you tell it otherwise. So if you create a second WordPerfect document, you can't use any styles created and stored in your first WordPerfect document.

- For temporary formatting purposes, storing a style in only one document is acceptable. But if you plan on using your styles over and over again, you'll want to store them in a style library.
- A *style library* lets you store your styles in a single file. In this way, you can use the style in multiple documents.
- For personal use, you can store styles in your own personal style library. If you're willing to share your styles with others, you can store your styles in a shared style library.
- Physically, personal libraries and shared libraries are completely identical. The only difference lies in their names. It's possible to share a personal library and to selfishly hog a shared library. If you're connected to a network, you should store personal libraries where no one else can get to them. Shared libraries should be available to everyone on a network.

Creating a style

To create a style, follow these steps:

1. **Press Alt-F8.**

   The Style List dialog box appears.

2. **Press C (Create).**

   The Create Style dialog box appears.

3. **Type a name for your style and press Enter.**

   Your style name can be up to 12 characters long. Remember to press Enter when you're done typing the name.

4. **Press T (Style Type).**

   A pop-up list appears, letting you choose the type of style you want to create: Paragraph, Character, or Open.

   Open style affects the entire document; Paragraph style formats only a paragraph and its text; Character style changes only font formatting.

5. **Highlight the type of style you want to create and press Enter twice.**

   The Edit Style dialog box appears (see Figure 11-1).

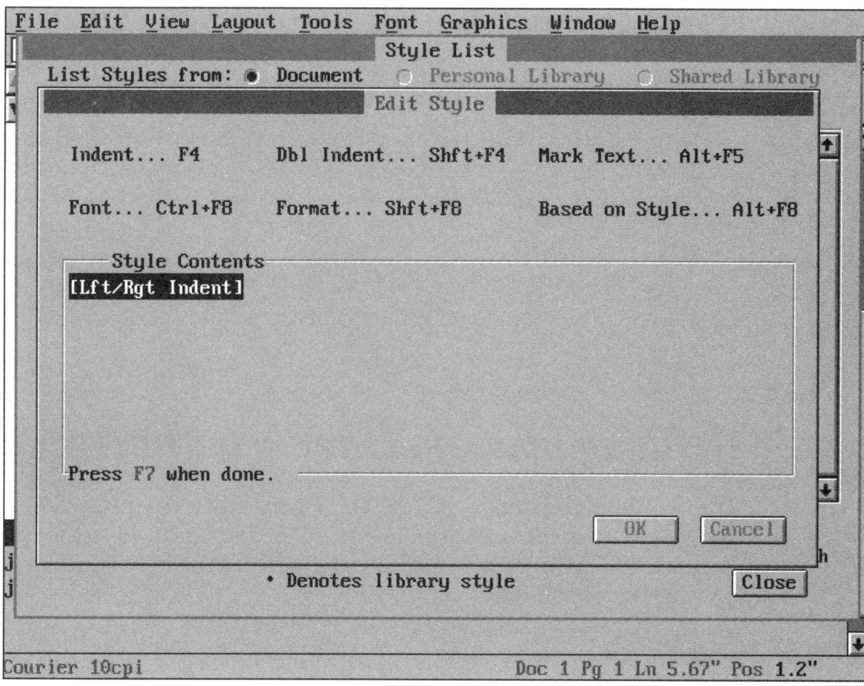

Figure 11-1: The Edit Style dialog box.

6. **Press D (Description).**

7. **Type a brief description of your style and press Enter.**

   Enter a handy description of your formatting style. For example, if you've created a style you want to use for section headings, type **Section Head**. In this book, the format for regular text is a Paragraph style called Body.

8. **Press C (Style Contents).**

   This is where you define your style — where you enter commands that automatically format your text. The chief advantage of styles is that they contain a whole armada of formatting commands that you can apply to text in one fell swoop.

   In Figure 11-1 you see a sample of the Edit Style dialog box set up to define a Paragraph style. Formatting commands are listed at the top of the dialog box. So if you want to create a double indent, press Shift-F4 and the `[Lft/Rgt Indent]` secret code appears in the Style Contents window. To change the line spacing, press Shift-F8, L, S and type in the new spacing.

   All the commands you enter — even text — appear in the Style Contents window.

9. **Press F7 and Enter when you're done defining your style.**

   The Style List dialog box appears with your newly created style displayed inside.

10. **Press Home, F7.**

After creating the style, you can use it. Refer to the section titled "Using Styles" later in this chapter.

Defining how the Enter key affects your style

After you apply a style to text, what happens when you press Enter? Normally, you would think this action would move the cursor down to the next line. Because this is too easy, WordPerfect gives you the following four ways that pressing Enter can affect your style:

- It inserts a hard return.
- It turns off the style.
- It turns off the style, inserts a hard return, and then turns on the style again.
- It turns off the style but then turns on a different style.

To define how the Enter key works with your style, follow these steps:

1. **Press Alt-F8.**

   The Style List dialog box appears.

2. **Highlight the style you want to edit.**

   Use the up- or down-arrow keys.

3. **Press E (Edit).**

   The Edit Style dialog box appears.

4. **Press E (Enter Key Action, Off/On).**

   The Enter Key Action dialog box appears.

5. **Choose one of the following options:**

   Press H and WordPerfect treats your Enter key as a hard return (just like pressing Enter when you're typing).

   Press F and the Enter key turns off the style, allowing you to start a new paragraph without that style. (Pressing Enter means, "I wanna start a new paragraph, no styles.")

   Press O and the Enter key turns the style off and on again. This means that the Enter key ends the paragraph and stops the style but then starts it up again on the next line. Use this option if you are creating a list of items, each on a line, which has to be formatted in the same way.

   Press T and the Enter key turns off the style and then links it to another style. Pressing Enter stops the current style and then activates the next style you specify (which you select from a drop-down list).

6. **Press Home, F7.**

Using Styles

WordPerfect gives you the following two ways to apply styles to your text:

- Apply your style first and then type your text.
- Type your text and then apply a style to it.

Because you can change styles so easily, you're free to experiment with different styles. After all, if you really screw up, you can just remove the styles and start all over again.

Using an Open style

An Open style affects text from the cursor's position to the end of your document (or until you specify another style).

To apply an Open style, follow these steps:

1. **Move the cursor where you want the Open style to start.**
2. **Press Alt-F8.**

   The Styles List dialog box appears.
3. **Highlight the Open style you want to use and press Enter.**

   The remainder of your document is magically altered to fit the specifications of the Open style.

Using a Paragraph style on existing text

To use a Paragraph style to format existing text, follow these steps:

1. **Move the cursor anywhere inside the block of text that you want to format.**
2. **Press Alt-F8.**

   The Style List dialog box appears.
3. **Highlight the Paragraph style you want to use and press Enter.**

- Only the paragraph the cursor lives in is affected by this command.
- To change all or some of the paragraphs in your document, block them first, press Alt-F8, and then select a Paragraph style.

Using a Paragraph style before typing your text

To use a Paragraph style before typing any text, follow these steps:

1. **Press Alt-F8.**

   The Style List dialog box appears.
2. **Highlight the Paragraph style you want to use and press Enter.**
3. **Type your text.**

As you type, WordPerfect automatically adjusts your text to fit within the style's format.

- This command affects all paragraphs you type, from the position of your cursor to the end of your document.
- To remove the Paragraph style, go through the preceding steps a second time after you start a new paragraph but this time select the None style in Step 2.

Using a Character style

To use a Character style, follow these steps:

1. **Mark the text you want to format as a block.**

   Move the cursor to the beginning of the character, word, or sentence that you want to format. Press Alt-F4 to start the block-marking mode. Move the cursor to the end of the character, word, or sentence that you want to format. WordPerfect highlights your block of text.

2. **Press Alt-F8.**

   The Style List dialog box appears.

3. **Highlight the character style you want to use and press Enter.**

   WordPerfect magically formats your blocked text.

- To apply a style to any new text you type, press Alt-F8 and select a character style. Anything you type after that will appear in the selected style.
- Any time you want to see how your styles are affecting your text, press Alt-F3 to see WordPerfect's hidden document codes.

Turning Off Styles

You can turn off a style in the following three ways:

- Change to a different style. By selecting a new Open, Paragraph, or Character style, any new text you type in your document will appear formatted in that style.
- Change to the None style, which effectively disables any styles you've defined so far.
- Delete the secret style code hidden in your document.

Turning off Open styles is the hardest, which is why the next section covers them specifically.

Turning off Open styles

All documents need at least one Open style that formats the entire document. This Open style appears at the very beginning of every document and can never be turned off. However, any Open styles you use to format part of a document can be turned off. To turn off one of these Open styles, follow these steps:

1. **Press Alt-F3.**

   WordPerfect displays the hidden codes for your document.

2. **Move the cursor until the cursor highlights the Open style that you want to turn off.**

   The open style code looks something like this:

   ```
   [Open Style:Dummies]
   ```

   First comes `Open Style`, a colon, and then the style's name. Move the cursor until that secret code is highlighted. When you highlight the code, the code "expands," showing you more information. Don't panic, it's still the same code.

3. **Press Delete.**

   This step deletes the style code, and the formatting for the rest of your document changes instantly (or as close to *instantly* as WordPerfect can muster).

- You can never "turn off" Open styles. The only way to turn off an Open style is to delete the hidden code in your document.

Turning off Paragraph or Character styles

After you've turned on a Paragraph or Character style, that style remains in effect until you turn it off or select another style.

To turn off a Paragraph or Character style, follow these steps:

1. **Move the cursor to the end of the text that you have formatted with a Paragraph or Character style.**

   The text from that point on will lack any Paragraph or Character style.

2. **Press Enter.**

   This step starts a new paragraph, which is a must — Paragraph styles can start or end only on new paragraphs.

3. **Press Alt-F8.**

   The Styles List dialog box appears.

4. **Highlight the None style and press Enter.**

   The Paragraph or Character style has been removed.

- You can also remove the Character style from a block of text by highlighting the block and selecting None as its style.
- If you want to obliterate a Paragraph or Character style, you can always resort to deleting its secret codes in your document. Press Alt-F3 and look for either the `[Char Style On: Name]` or `[Para Style: Name]` secret codes. Delete them to utterly remove that style.

Editing Styles

After you've created and used a few styles, you may need to modify, copy, or completely delete a style from the face of the earth. Modifying a style is often easier than creating one from scratch. You can either modify a style or copy an existing style and modify the copy of the style.

Copying a style

To copy a style, follow these steps:

1. **Press Alt-F8.**

   The Style List dialog box appears.

2. **Highlight the style that you want to copy.**
3. **Press P (Copy).**

   The Copy Styles dialog box appears.

4. **Press D (Document).**

   A Copy Style dialog box appears, where you . . .

5. **Type a name of a style to receive the style that you want to copy.**

   So you copy the old, boring Indent style to the flashy new Pull Quote style by typing **Pull Quote** into the box and pressing Enter.

6. **Press Enter.**

   WordPerfect displays the copy of your style in the Style List dialog box.

7. **Press Home, F7.**

- The idea behind creating copies is that you can subtly modify each one. So after creating your basic style, you can create subtle variations by making copies and then modifying each of the copies just so.
- Editing or modifying a style is covered in the next section.
- If you create too many duplicates, you can always delete a few. This is covered in the section "Deleting a style" later in the chapter.

Modifying a style

To modify a style, follow these steps:

1. **Press Alt-F8.**

   The Style List dialog box appears.

2. **Highlight the style that you want to modify.**
3. **Press E (Edit).**

   The Edit Style dialog box appears. It contains all the information you specified when you created the style.

4. **Press C (Style Contents).**

   This allows you to edit the style's formatting codes shown in the Style Contents window. You can delete codes or add new ones by selecting them from the commands listed at the top of the Edit Style dialog box.

5. **Press the F7 key when you're done editing the style's formatting.**
6. **Press Home, F7.**

Deleting a style

To delete a style — yeah, utterly rub it from existence — follow these steps:

1. **Press Alt-F8.**

   The Style List dialog box appears.

2. **Highlight the style that you want to delete.**
3. **Press D (Delete).**

   The Delete Style dialog box appears.

4. **Press I (Including Codes) to delete the style and remove the style formatting from any text in the document, or press L (Leaving Codes) to delete the style but leave the formatted text in your document alone.**
5. **Press Home, F7.**

When you delete a style, it disappears from your current document's style list. However, deleting a style with this method does not delete it if it is also stored in a style library.

Why Use Style Libraries?

The whole purpose of style libraries is to store styles so that you can use them in more than one document. If you use the same styles over and over again, then all you need to do is "borrow" them from the library — just like you borrow a book from a real library, although without the winos and strange odors.

- WordPerfect stores style libraries in files with the STY file extension.
- To keep your style libraries from mixing with your WordPerfect documents, you should store style libraries in their own separate, isolated, never-to-be-confused directories. Otherwise, some jerk is likely to open your style library, think it's an ordinary WordPerfect document, and mess the whole thing up.
- A single style library can (theoretically) store an unlimited number of styles, although the actual number depends more on the size of your styles and whether you do anything really weird with them.
- Although WordPerfect recommends that you name all your style libraries with the STY file extension, you don't have to. You can actually use any file extension you want. However, for consistency and to keep you from losing your mind, you should stick with the STY file extension.

Creating a new style library

You have to create a style before you can store a style in a style library (duh). To store a style in a style library, follow these steps:

1. **Press Alt-F8.**

   The Style List dialog box appears.
2. **Highlight the style you want to store in a style library.**

3. **Press the * (asterisk) key.**

   This step marks the style with an asterisk, tagging it just as you can tag files for copying or deleting in the File Manager.

4. **Repeat Steps 2 and 3 for as many styles as you want in your library.**
5. **Press V (Save).**

   The Save Styles dialog box appears.

6. **Type the file name (plus the STY file extension) for your style library.**
7. **Press Home, F7.**

   Now the styles have been saved in your own personal style library. To use or retrieve them, refer to the section "Using Style Libraries" later in this chapter.

Storing styles in an existing style library

Most likely, you'll want to store related styles in the same style library. For example, you would put styles for formatting screenplays in one style library and styles for formatting newsletters in another style library. To store a style in an existing style library, follow these steps:

1. **Press Alt-F8.**

   The Styles List dialog box appears.

2. **Press O (Options).**

   The Style Options dialog box appears.

3. **Press L (Libraries Assigned to Document).**
4. **Press the F5 key.**

   The Select List dialog box appears, displaying the directory for your style libraries. (If not, type in the proper directory name.)

5. **Press Enter.**

   The File List dialog box appears.

6. **Highlight the style library file in which you want to store your styles.**

   The directory will end with the STY extension.

7. **After highlighting the file, press Enter a few times until you're back in the Style List dialog box.**
8. **Highlight each style that you want to store and press * (asterisk).**

   This step marks the files. Repeat this step for as many files as you want to include in the library.

9. **Press P (Copy).**

   The Copy Styles dialog box appears.

10. **Press P (Personal Library).**

    If a warning box appears claiming that the `Style already exists`, press N for No. You don't want to replace the style. (Chances are it's the same style, and you're just trying to copy it twice.)

11. **Press Home, F7.**

Using Style Libraries

After you've stored styles in a style library, the next question is how to use those styles in your current document. WordPerfect offers the following two plans of attack:

- Retrieve the style library.
- Assign the style library.

Retrieving a style library simply copies the styles from the style library into your document. If someone changes the style library, the styles in your document remain unaffected.

Assigning a style library links the styles from the style library into your document. If someone modifies the style library, those modifications will change the styles in your document. (If you mess up a style library, you can screw up any documents that are assigned to that style library. Vandals, take note.)

- Retrieving a style is probably your best bet most of the time.
- Reserve assigning a style for those documents whose formatting may need to be changed later. For example, if you're using a certain style for all your corporate memos and the corporate doodyhead in charge wants a new format, you then can change only the style, and all the assigned documents will change their formatting along with it.

Retrieving a style library

To retrieve styles from a style library, follow these steps:

1. **Press Alt-F8.**

   The Style List dialog box appears.

2. **Press R (Retrieve).**

   The Retrieve Styles dialog box appears.

3. **Press F5.**

   The Select List dialog box appears.

4. **Press Enter.**

   The File List dialog box appears.

5. **Highlight the style library file that you want to retrieve and press Enter.**

   WordPerfect copies the styles from the style library into your current document's style list. Now you can use these styles in your current document and enjoy the ease that they provide to help you format your text. If you change the original style library, your document is not affected.

Assigning a style library

To assign styles from a style library, follow these steps:

1. **Press Alt-F8.**

   The Style List dialog box appears.

2. **Press O (Options).**

   The Style Options dialog box appears.

3. **Press L (Libraries Assigned to Document).**

4. **Press F5.**

   The Select List dialog box appears.

5. **Press Enter.**

   The File List dialog box appears.

6. **Highlight the style library file that you want to assign to your current document and press Enter.**

7. **Press Home, F7.**

REMEMBER

This procedure doesn't copy the styles into your document, even though it may seem that way. Instead, your document is borrowing the information from the styles to form a "link." If you or someone else changes the style library, your document will be affected.

Using assigned styles

To view or choose a style library assigned to a document, follow these steps:

1. **Press Alt-F8.**

   The Styles List dialog box appears.

2. **Press L (Personal Library).**

   WordPerfect lists those styles assigned from the style library.

3. **Highlight the style you want to use and press Enter.**

This procedure works just like using a regular style, but you must select Personal Library (at the top of the Styles List dialog box) to see the styles your document has been assigned.

Breaking links to assigned style libraries

An assigned style is defined once (in the style library) but can be used to format multiple documents. If some bozo modifies the style library, the formatting in multiple documents can get all screwed up. You're probably living in fear of this right now.

To prevent this screwup from happening, you can break the link from an assigned style library to your document. A broken link simply acts like a style stored in your document — any changes to its style library won't affect your document at all.

To break the link to an assigned style, follow these steps:

1. **Press Alt-F8.**

   The Style List dialog box appears.

2. **Press O (Options).**

   The Style Options dialog box appears.

3. **Press L (Libraries Assigned to Document).**

4. **Press Delete.**

   This step deletes the link.

5. **Press Home, F7.**

At this point, any formatting done by the style library remains intact in your document. Changes made to the style library elsewhere won't affect your document. (Whew!)

Deleting a style library

Once in a while, you may get a destructive urge to clean useless files off your hard disk. If you find a style library that nobody uses any more, you may as well delete it.

Be careful! If you delete a style library that is assigned to other documents, the formatting within those documents remains intact, but they'll never be able to access those styles again. Heh, heh, heh!

To delete a style library, follow these steps:

1. **Press F5.**

   The Specify File Manager List dialog box appears.

2. **Press F8.**

   The Directory Tree dialog box appears.

3. **Highlight the directory where your style libraries are stored and press Enter.**

   The File Manager dialog box appears.

4. **Highlight the style library that you want to delete.**
5. **Press D (Delete).**

   A dialog box appears, asking if you really want to delete the file.

6. **Press Y (Yes).**
7. **Press Tab twice and press Enter.**

   It's gone!

Chapter 12

Making Tables and Math (Math?)

In This Chapter

- Adding, subtracting, multiplying, and dividing columns of numbers
- Making spreadsheet tables
- Formulas
- Functions

Oddly enough, WordPerfect is more than just a word processor — it's also a simple spreadsheet. Why would you want to use WordPerfect as a spreadsheet when there are perfectly good copies of Lotus 1-2-3, Excel, or Quattro Pro that you can buy? Pain, I suppose.

Besides being expensive, complicated, and hard to use, most spreadsheets are designed for hard-core number-crunchers, such as accountants, mathematicians, and other people who have heated arguments about the number of decimal places one should use for the mathematical constant, *pi.*

For the rest of us who just want to create an invoice form, a sales reporting chart, or an expense report, WordPerfect allows the best of both worlds. By giving you the ability to mix words, numbers, and numeric calculations in one document, WordPerfect makes it easy to write about your numbers and then calculate them accurately so that you don't have to do it yourself.

Adding, Subtracting, Multiplying, and Dividing Columns of Numbers

At its simplest, WordPerfect can add, subtract, divide, and multiply numbers stored in rows or columns. A row is simply a bunch of numbers that appear from left to right. A column is a bunch of numbers that appear one on top of the other.

(Row →)	12	3.45	23.1	903
	45.6	294.45	98	78.35
		(↑ Column)		

To make WordPerfect do math, you have to follow these procedures:

- Create columns to put your numbers in.
- Define columns to display your numbers.
- Type your numbers in your columns.
- Make WordPerfect calculate a result.

Making columns

You can have up to 24 columns across a page when making a WordPerfect spreadsheet. The columns are identified by a letter, so the first column is called column A; the second is column B; and so on.

To make columns, you have to set up your tab stops. To set up tab stops, follow these steps:

1. **Press Alt-L, B.**

   The Tab Set dialog box appears.

2. **Define your tab settings.**

   Press Ctrl-End to delete all current tab stops.

   Press L to set a tab stop.

   Press Delete to remove any one tab stop.

   Press Alt-right/left arrow to move the cursor from one tab stop to the other.

3. **Press Home, F7 when you're done.**

After making the columns, you must define them, which is covered in the next section.

Defining columns

After you've created your columns, the second step is to define whether the column is a Text, Number, or Calculation column. (Remember, this is a spreadsheet-like thing you're building here.)

- A Text column contains text that is used as a label to help you identify what your numbers really mean, such as

Food	34.50	78.30	56.13
Drink	309.87	448.1	209.48

  "Food" and "Drink" are labels. A column defined to hold text can hold both letters and numbers; however, if a Text column holds numbers, WordPerfect *never* uses those numbers for any calculations.

- A Number column contains (what else?) numbers that can represent quantities, amounts, lengths, or whatever else you feel like.

- A Calculation column can add, subtract, multiply, or divide numbers stored in Number columns. Some of the more common signs used in these columns are

+	Add
–	Subtract
/	Divide
*	Multiply

To define columns, follow these steps:

1. **Press Alt-F7.**

   The Columns/Tables dialog box appears.

2. **Press M (Math).**

3. **Press D (Define).**

   The Math dialog box appears.

4. **Press the letter of the column you want to define.**

   To define the first column, press A; to define the second column, press B; and so on.

   After you press a letter, the Define Math Column dialog box appears.

5. **Press T (Column Type).**

6. **Choose the column type, as follows:**

   Press X (Text) to define a Text column.

   Press N (Numeric) to define a column to hold numbers. You need to specify how you want negative numbers displayed (either in parentheses or with a minus sign), and you can set the number of digits after the decimal.

   Press T (Total) to define the column to total the numbers from the column to the left.

   Press C (Calculation) to define the column to hold a formula or calculation. You also need to type a formula, such as:

+	(Adds numbers across a row)
+/	(Calculates the average of numbers across a row)
B – C	(Calculates the result of the numbers in column B subtracted by the numbers in column C)

7. **Press Enter.**

   You return to the Math dialog box, where you can see the changes you've made displayed in the Column Definition area.

8. **Repeat Steps 6 and 7 until you've defined all your columns.**
9. **When you're done, press Home, F7.**

- If you want to add, subtract, multiply, or divide numbers across a row, make your last column a Calculation column to hold a formula.
- You can go back and redo any column — simply repeat Steps 6 and 7 to redefine any one column.

Typing numbers into your columns

After you've created your columns and defined their functions, you're ready to type numbers into those columns. (Of course, by this time you probably could have read the entire 400-page Lotus 1-2-3 manual.)

To type numbers into columns, follow these steps:

1. **Move the cursor to the location in the document where you want to start typing numbers.**
2. **Press Alt-F7.**

   The Columns/Tables dialog box appears.

3. Press M (Math).

4. Press O (Math On).

This puts an X in the Math On box, directing WordPerfect to behave more like a spreadsheet.

5. Press Enter.

WordPerfect displays the word `Math` at the lower-left corner of your screen.

6. Type a number in each column and then press Tab to move the cursor from one column to the other.

- When you move the cursor into a Text or Total column, WordPerfect displays `Math` at the lower-left corner of the screen.
- When you move the cursor into a Number column, WordPerfect displays `Align char = . Math` at the lower-left corner of the screen.
- When you move the cursor into a Calculation column, WordPerfect displays an exclamation mark (!). This mark lets you know that you shouldn't type any numbers here because WordPerfect will calculate a result in this column instead.

Calculating results

WordPerfect doesn't calculate any results unless you've typed in formulas. You can make WordPerfect calculate results across rows or down columns.

- To make WordPerfect calculate a result across a row, you must define your last column as a Calculation column.
- To make WordPerfect calculate a result down a column, you must type a formula at the bottom of a column. For example, if you want to add the numbers in a column, you would set up your columns something like this:

Food	34.50	78.30	56.13
Drink	309.87	448.10	209.48
	+	+	+

The plus sign (+) tells WordPerfect to add up all the numbers in that column.

To calculate a result for a row of numbers, follow these steps:

1. **Press Alt-F7, M.**
2. **Press D (Define).**

   The Math dialog box appears.
3. **Press the letter that represents the last column, closest to the right edge of the screen.**

   The Define Math Column dialog box appears.
4. **Press T (Column Type).**
5. **Press C (Calculation).**
6. **Type a formula, such as**

+	(Adds numbers across a row)
+/	(Calculates the average of numbers across a row)
B – C	(Calculates the result of the number in column B subtracted by the number in column C)
7. **Press Home, F7.**
8. **Move the cursor to the column defined as a Calculation column in Step 6.**

   Use the Tab key to move to that column. WordPerfect displays an exclamation mark (!) where it will calculate a result.
9. **Press Alt-F7, M, C.**

   WordPerfect calculates and displays its results next to all the exclamation marks shown on-screen.

Although you can see the exclamation marks on-screen, they don't print out, *so don't delete them!* The exclamation mark (!) is WordPerfect's way of telling you that the numbers next to it were calculated and not typed in.

To calculate a result from a column of numbers, follow these steps:

1. **Move the cursor to the bottom of the column where you want to calculate a result.**
2. **Type a formula, such as**

+	(Adds numbers in a column)
+/	(Calculates the average of numbers down a column)
B – C	(Calculates the result of the number in column B subtracted by the number in column C)

3. Press Alt-F7, M, C.

WordPerfect calculates and displays its results next to your formulas.

Although you can see your formulas on-screen, they don't print out. The formulas are WordPerfect's way of telling you that the numbers next to them were calculated and not typed in.

Making Spreadsheet Tables

For simple calculations with a few numbers, storing numbers in columns is quick and easy (almost). But if you have lots of numbers, then it's easier to use a WordPerfect table instead.

A table lets WordPerfect mimic a spreadsheet grid, which makes it easy to see your columns and rows. In addition, a table lets you create (and understand) more complicated formulas than simple addition across a row or column of numbers.

Tables consist of one or more cells. A cell can contain text, numbers, or formulas that calculate a result. WordPerfect identifies each cell with a letter and a number, such as A1 or B4.

Cell A1	Cell B1	Cell C1
Cell A2	Cell B2	Cell C2
Cell A3	Cell B3	Cell C3

Creating a spreadsheet table

Before you can store and calculate numbers in a spreadsheet table, you have to create one first (duh). To create a spreadsheet table, follow these steps:

1. Move the cursor where you want the spreadsheet table to appear.

2. Press Alt-F7.

The Columns/Tables dialog box appears.

3. **Press T (Tables).**
4. **Press C (Create).**

   The Create Table dialog box appears.
5. **Type the number of columns you want and press Tab.**
6. **Type the number of rows you want and press Enter twice.**

   WordPerfect draws your table on-screen.
7. **Press Home, F7.**
8. **Type your numbers inside the cells of your spreadsheet table.**

- Use the Tab key to move between the various cells in your table.
- If you press the Tab key in the lower-right cell of the table, WordPerfect automatically adds another row of cells.
- More information can be found on tables in Chapter 12 of *WordPerfect 6 For Dummies*.

Formatting numbers in a spreadsheet table

After you've typed some numbers in a spreadsheet table, you may want to format the table so that it looks nice. WordPerfect gives you the following options for formatting:

- Alignment
- Appearance (bold, underline, italics, and so on)
- Size

To format a single cell, row, column, or entire table, follow these steps:

1. **Move the cursor to the cell that you want to format.**
2. **Press Alt-F7, T, E.**

   The Table Edit dialog box appears.
3. **Choose one of the following:**

   Use the arrow keys to move from cell to cell.

   Press C to format a single cell.

   Press O to format a column of cells.

   Press R to format a row of cells.

Press T to format an entire table.

The Cell Format, Column Format, Row Format, or Table Format dialog box appears, according to which option you press (C, O, R, or T).

6. **Choose the formatting options you want to use.**

   Press Enter to leave the formatting dialog box and return to the table editor.

7. **When you're done, press Home, F7.**

Formulas

After you've created a spreadsheet table and typed in some numbers, you eventually want WordPerfect to start calculating some results from your numbers. To calculate any result, you have to create a formula.

A formula can be as simple as adding (+), subtracting (–), multiplying (*), or dividing (/), such as

- A1 + A2
- C5 – D16
- A4 * D5
- G11 / F45

You can even get fancy and group several formulas together, such as

- (A2 * B3) – (C6 / D8)
- A3 * B4 * 52.12
- B3 * (A2 – (A5 / C10))

TIP

For clarity, always use parentheses so that WordPerfect knows which calculation to perform first. If you don't use parentheses, WordPerfect may calculate your formula differently than the way you expected it to calculate the formula.

Yes, * (asterisk) means multiplication. Don't use the *X*, which WordPerfect understands to be the letter *X*.

Also, the / (forward slash) means division, which isn't as strange as using the asterisk for multiplication. Just avoid using the ÷ character (if you can find it) because it won't work.

To create a simple formula for using addition, subtraction, multiplication, or division, follow these steps:

1. **Move the cursor to the cell where you want to create a formula.**
2. **Press Alt-F7, T, E.**

   The Table Edit dialog box appears.
3. **Press F (Formula).**

   The Table Formula dialog box appears.
4. **Type your formula, such as**

   (A2 – A4) * D4
5. **Press Enter twice.**

   WordPerfect calculates and displays the results of your formula in the cell.
6. **Press Esc.**

Functions

Using WordPerfect's four basic functions (addition, subtraction, division, and multiplication), you can create formulas that can calculate anything from the gross national product of Zimbabwe to the number of hamburgers sold by McDonald's in one month.

However, creating really complicated formulas can be tedious and time-consuming, and you already get enough of that just trying to use WordPerfect. So as a shortcut, WordPerfect offers built-in functions, which are similar to the built-in functions found in all the major spreadsheets of the world.

Some of the more common function are as follows:

- SUM(list) — adds a range of values
- SQRT(number) — calculates the square root
- ROUND(number, precision) — rounds a decimal number
- MAX(list) — returns the largest number from a list of cells
- MIN(list) — returns the smallest number from a list of cells
- AVE(list) — returns the average value from a list of cells

A function is nothing more than a set of formulas that WordPerfect has already created for you to make calculating easier. For example, instead of creating a formula like this one:

```
A1 + A2 + A3 + A4
```

you can simply use a function like this one:

```
SUM(A1:A4)
```

To use a function, follow these steps:

1. **Move the cursor to the cell where you want to create a formula.**
2. **Press Alt-F7, T, E.**

   The Table Edit dialog box appears.
3. **Press F (Formula).**

   The Table Formula dialog box appears.
4. **Press F5.**

   The Table Functions dialog box appears.
5. **Highlight the function that you want and press Enter.**

   WordPerfect types the function in the Table Formula dialog box.
6. **Press F4.**
7. **Move the cursor to the first cell to use in your function.**
8. **Press F4.**

   WordPerfect displays `Block on` in the lower-left corner of the screen.
9. **Move the cursor to the last cell to use in your function and press Enter.**

   WordPerfect automatically fills in the cell references in your function.
10. **Press Enter twice.**

    WordPerfect calculates the results of your function. The Table Edit dialog box appears.
11. **Press Home, F7.**

Now you can glow in the knowledge that WordPerfect makes a mean spreadsheet for you. Why did you even buy Lotus in the first place?

Chapter 13

Graphics and Desktop Publishing Tricks

In This Chapter

- The WPG graphics stuff that came with WordPerfect
- Inserting graphics into a document
- Creating graphics boxes
- Editing graphics
- Adding graphics lines
- Borders around text
- Desktop publishing tricks

Do you mind if I get really graphic? I'm talkin' down-an'-dirty graphics. WordPerfect lets you do more with graphics to add punch, zip, and sparkle to your documents than just about any previous word-processing program.

And what's all this talk about desktop publishing? If you already have a desk, you sure don't need WordPerfect publishing one for you, thank you very much. Not to worry. Desktop publishing isn't about publishing desks. It's about making nifty-looking documents that are fit for publishing.

The WPG Graphics Stuff That Came with WordPerfect

Knowing that a picture is worth a thousand words, WordPerfect comes with about 33,000 words' worth of pictures, sometimes called *clip art*, that can be inserted in your documents. These pictures all use a WPG filename extension and so are called WPG format graphics.

And, for once, the acronym actually stands for something that makes sense. In fact, you can probably figure out what WPG stands for on your own, if you take a minute to think about it. Beep! Time's up. WPG stands for *W*ord*P*erfect *G*raphics.

- The WPG format isn't the only game in town. There is a virtual Tower of Babel of graphics formats. Some of the more common formats have extensions of PCX, TIF, BMP, and EPS. Fortunately, WordPerfect understands and can use these formats and many other popular graphics formats as well.
- The primary advantage to using WPG graphics, versus any of the other formats, is speed. If you use any other format, WordPerfect has to get out its Rosetta stone and go through a tedious translation process. Because WPG graphics are in WordPerfect's native language, no translation is required. *¿Comprende?*
- If you find the selection of graphics included with your WordPerfect program too limited, you can buy more. Surprise, surprise. And guess who'll be more than happy to take your money for additional sets of WPG graphics gems? Why, WordPerfect Corporation, of course. You can also buy sets of clip art images in a variety of formats at your local computer or software store. However, most clip art sets that aren't sold by WordPerfect Corporation are in PCX, TIF, or EPS formats.
- The one file format to watch out for is EPS, which stands for *E*ncapsulated *P*ost*S*cript. All you really need to know about this format is, if your printer isn't set up to print PostScript files (and most aren't), you can't use EPS graphics.

Inserting Graphics into a Document

If you just want a quick fix for a drab document with a bunch of plain old text that just seems to lie there, insert one of WordPerfect's clip art pictures. Instantly, your document has something to grab your reader's attention other than your inspired words.

For the fastest way to insert a graphic into your document, follow these steps:

1. **Position your cursor in the document at the approximate location where you want the graphic to appear.**
2. **Press Alt-F9.**

   The Graphics dialog box appears.
3. **Press Shift-F10.**

   The Retrieve Image File dialog box appears.

4. **Press F5.**

   The Select List dialog box appears.

5. **Press Enter.**

   The File List dialog box appears.

6. **Use the up- and down-arrow keys to highlight the graphic file you want to use and then press Enter.**

   The graphic image appears in your document, as shown in Figure 13-1.

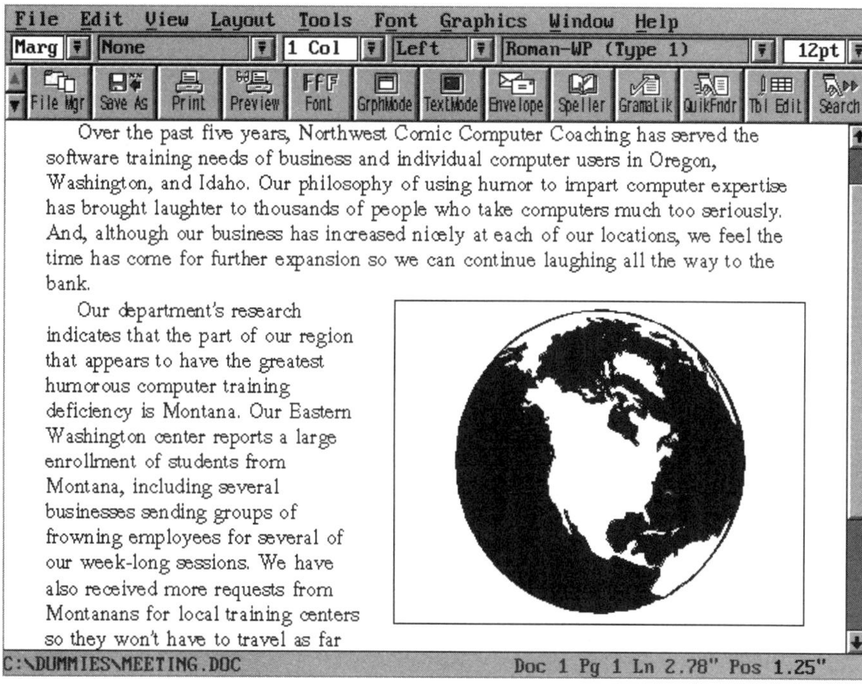

Figure 13-1: A document with a graphic image inserted.

- Any graphic you bring into WordPerfect is placed in a box. The standard box style for a retrieved image includes a single-line border, with the box positioned on the right side of the document, as you can see in Figure 13-1.
- There is an almost infinite variety of box styles. You can change borders, box position, image position within the box, and zillions of other stuff. The next section covers working with boxes.
- If there is another graphic in the document using other graphics box settings, the retrieved image will use the settings from the preceding box.
- Don't stick a graphic into a document just because you think the document needs a picture. The graphic should serve some purpose, or it will detract from, rather than enhance, your message.

Creating Graphics Boxes

You don't have to let WordPerfect box you in when you bring graphics into a document. Just put on your boxing gloves and show WordPerfect who's boss.

Instead of retrieving an image and letting WordPerfect place it in the default box, you can control the process by designating the type of box you want, setting all the box options, and then telling WordPerfect what to put in the box.

Figure 13-2 shows examples of the four most common graphics box types: Table, Figure, Text, and User. As you can see, the contents of graphics boxes aren't necessarily graphics.

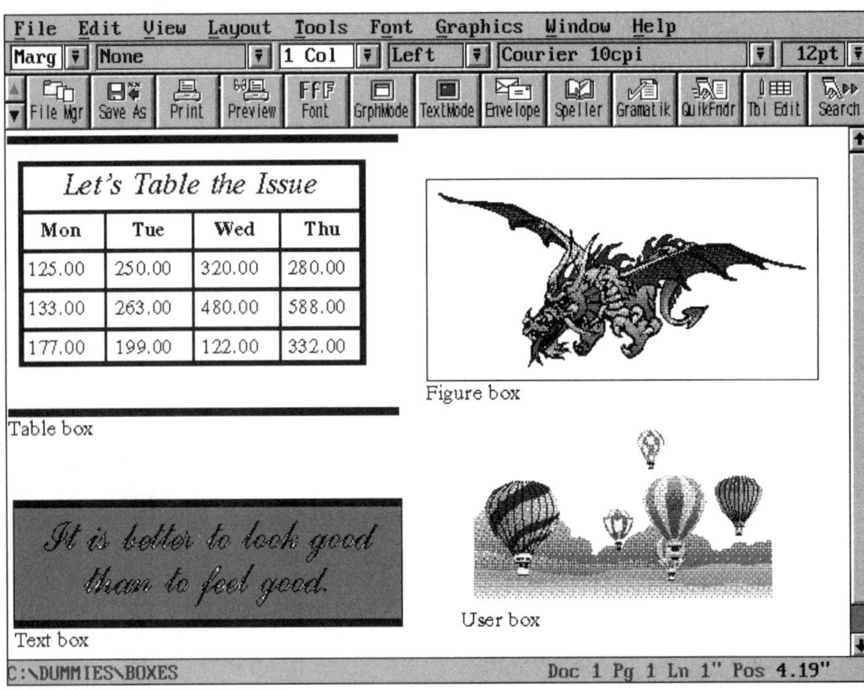

Figure 13-2: Graphics box types.

To create a graphics box, follow these steps:

1. **Position your cursor in the document where you want the graphic to appear.**
2. **Press Alt-F9.**

   The Graphics dialog box appears.

3. **Press B (Graphics Boxes), C (Create).**

   The Create Graphics Box dialog box appears, as shown in Figure 13-3. Notice that the Contents option (just below Filename) is listed as None.

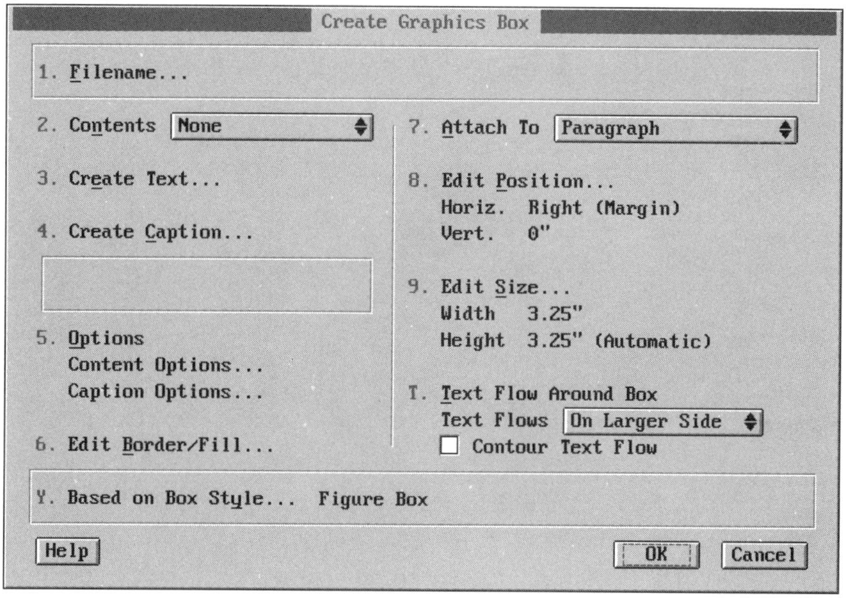

Figure 13-3: The Create Graphics Box dialog box.

4. **Press F (Filename).**

   The Retrieve File dialog box appears.

5. **Press F5.**

   The Select List dialog box appears.

6. **Make a decision, as follows:**

   If the graphic or other file you want is in the directory listed, press Enter. Otherwise, type the complete path of the directory you want, such as **C:\WPDOCS** and then press Enter.

   The File List dialog box appears.

7. **Use the up- and down-arrow keys to highlight the file you want and then press Enter.**

   You are returned to the Create Graphics Box dialog box with the name of the file you selected and its path entered in the Filename portion of the dialog box. Also, notice that the Contents option is now listed as Image.

8. **Press Y (Based on Box Style).**

   The Graphics Box Styles dialog box appears, as shown in Figure 13-4.

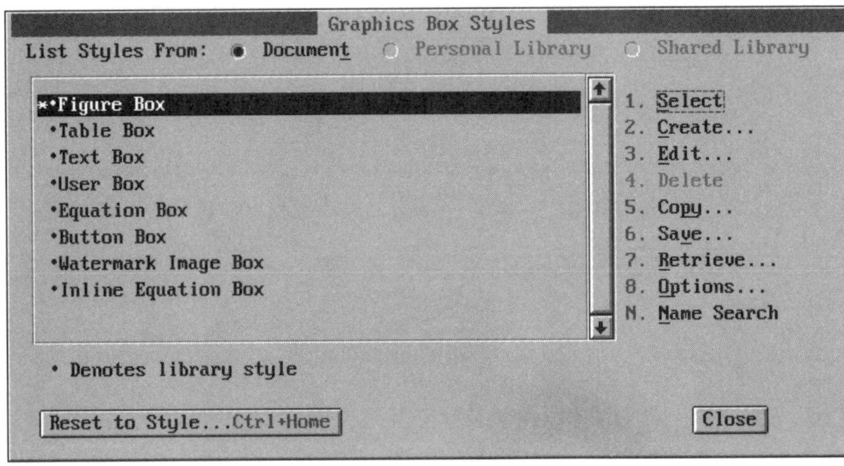

Figure 13-4: The Graphics Box Styles dialog box.

9. **Use the up- and down-arrow keys to highlight the box style you want to use and then press Enter.**

   The Based On Box Style portion of the dialog box now lists the box type you selected.

10. **Press F7.**

    You are returned to your document with the graphics box in place.

- Don't be misled by the names of the graphics box styles. You can put anything in any of them. For example, you can put a table in a Figure box, a graphic image in a Text box, and so on. The box styles simply determine the default border styles and shading.

- TIP: Text boxes have a thick top and bottom border and shading. Figure boxes have single-line borders on all sides and no shading. Table boxes have thick top and bottom borders and no shading. User boxes have no borders and no shading. You can change any of these default settings in the Edit Graphics Box dialog box. Choose Edit Border/Fill in the Create Graphics Box dialog box and change any of the options.

- After reading the last two items, you may be trying to figure out why the idiots in WordPerfect's Department of Naming Things assigned these utterly meaningless names to the various box types. I can save you a lot of time here: There *is* no good reason.
- If you want to type text or create a table or other nongraphic item in a graphics box, don't enter a filename in the Create Graphics Box dialog box. Instead, press E (Create Text). When the blank box screen appears, start typing, creating tables, or adding whatever you like. When you're finished, press F7. You may want to create graphics boxes that contain something other than graphics contents so that you can place the contents anywhere in your document. For example, to place a table between two columns, you have to put it in a box.
- To add a caption to a graphics box, choose Create Caption in the Create Graphics Box dialog box. A blank screen appears with the default caption. The default captions are Text 1, Text 2, or Figure 1, Figure 2, and so on. To replace the default caption, press the Backspace key and type your own caption. You can use any fonts or formatting you want. After you're finished, press F7.
- You can specify the size and position of the box in the Create Graphics Box dialog box by pressing P (Position) or S (Size) and making the changes in the Box Position and Box Size dialog boxes. But for a much easier way, check out the following mouse information.

If you plan to work with graphics more than once in a blue moon, you need a mouse. In fact, if ever there was a reason to run out and buy a mouse (if you don't already have one), graphics is it.

- To move a graphics box, just point to the graphic and drag (hold down the left mouse button while moving the mouse). As soon as you press the mouse button, a dashed outline with small black rectangles, called handles, appears. As you move the mouse, the outline of the box moves. When the outline is in the desired location, release the mouse button.
- To resize a graphics box, click the box and then position the mouse pointer over one of the rectangular handles. The pointer becomes a double-headed arrow, as shown in Figure 13-5. Drag the mouse to resize the box.

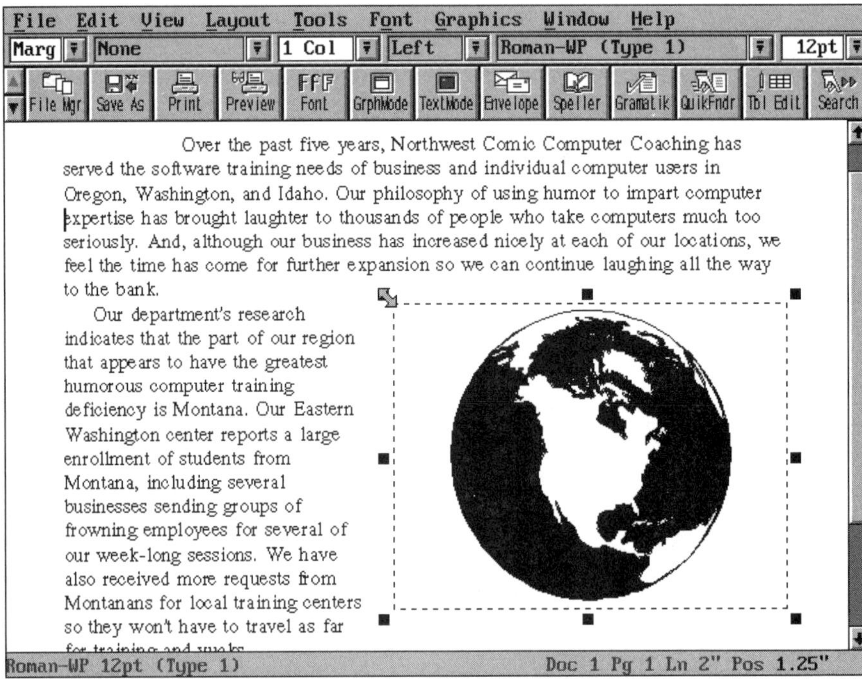

Figure 13-5: A graphic ready to be resized.

Editing Graphics

If you're looking for an outlet for your artistic genius, WordPerfect ain't it. WordPerfect doesn't really let you edit graphics. It doesn't have drawing tools for adding your own touches here and there, and you can't erase small details. However, there are some things you *can* do to edit your graphics. Thank goodness!

To edit a graphic, follow these steps:

1. **Press Alt-F9.**

   The Graphics dialog box appears.

2. **Press B (Graphics Boxes), E (Edit).**

   The Select Box to Edit dialog box appears.

3. **If the box you want to edit isn't listed in the Document Box Number box, press N and enter the number of the box you want to edit.**

   Starting at the top of the document, the first box is number 1; the second box is 2; and so on.

4. **Press Enter.**

   The Edit Graphics Box dialog box appears.

5. **Press E (Image Editor).**

   Your graphic appears in the Image Editor, as shown in Figure 13-6.

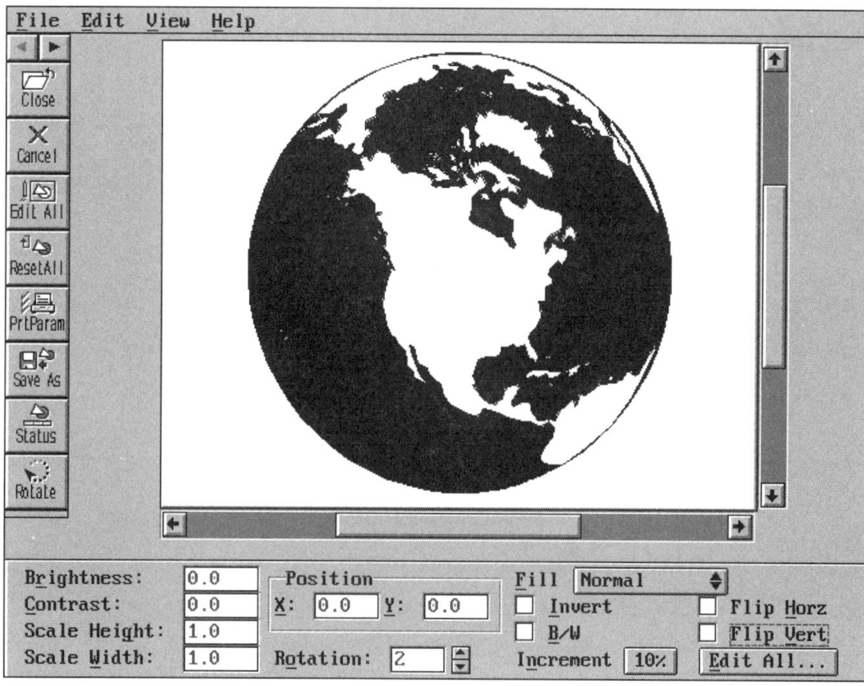

Figure 13-6: A graphic image in the Image Editor.

6. **Make adjustments to any of the options.**

   For example, to rotate the image, press O (Rotation) and enter a number (representing a number of degrees) in the Rotation text box. Or press G (Scale Height) or W (Scale Width).

7. **When you're finished making your adjustments, press F7 twice.**

   You are returned to your document, where you see the results of your edits.

TIP

- To visually rotate your image, press Alt-E, P, R. Lines that look sort of like a T-square appear on the image. Press the + (plus) key to rotate clockwise or the – (minus) key to rotate counterclockwise.

MOUSE

- Using a mouse makes editing graphics much less painful. You can get to the Image Editor by double-clicking the graphic and then clicking Image Editor in the Edit Graphics Box dialog box. Also, you can rotate the graphic by clicking the Rotate button and dragging the right end of the horizontal axis.

- If your image gets too messed up, press Alt-E, R (Reset All) or click the Reset All button on the Button Bar. The image returns to its original state.
- Changing the image's position in the Image Editor changes the image's position within the box but doesn't change the box's position.
- If you want to do more elaborate editing than WordPerfect's Image Editor allows, you need a graphics program, such as WordPerfect Presentations, which, by the way, is one of the best non-Windows graphics programs on the market.

Adding Graphics Lines

Graphics lines? Hmmm. How about something like, "Hey, babe (or stud muffin, as the case may be), want to go back to my place to check out my etchings?" Well, that's not the kind of graphics lines I'm writing about here.

WordPerfect's graphics lines are exactly that — lines that are graphics. Just stick them wherever you need to call attention to a portion of your document or where you need a little extra interest.

To create a graphics line, follow these steps:

1. **Position your cursor where you want to place a line.**
2. **Press Alt-F9.**

   The Graphics dialog box appears.
3. **Press L (Graphics Lines), C (Create).**

   The Create Graphics Line dialog box appears, as shown in Figure 13-7.
4. **If you want a vertical line, press O (Line Orientation) and then press the down-arrow key to highlight the Vertical option and press Enter.**
5. **If you don't want the line extending all the way from margin to margin, press H (Horizontal Position) or V (Vertical Position).**

   A pop-up box with position choices appears with either option.
6. **Use the up- and down-arrow keys to highlight your choice of line position and then press Enter.**
7. **Press Y (Line Style).**

   The Line Styles dialog box appears, as shown in Figure 13-8.

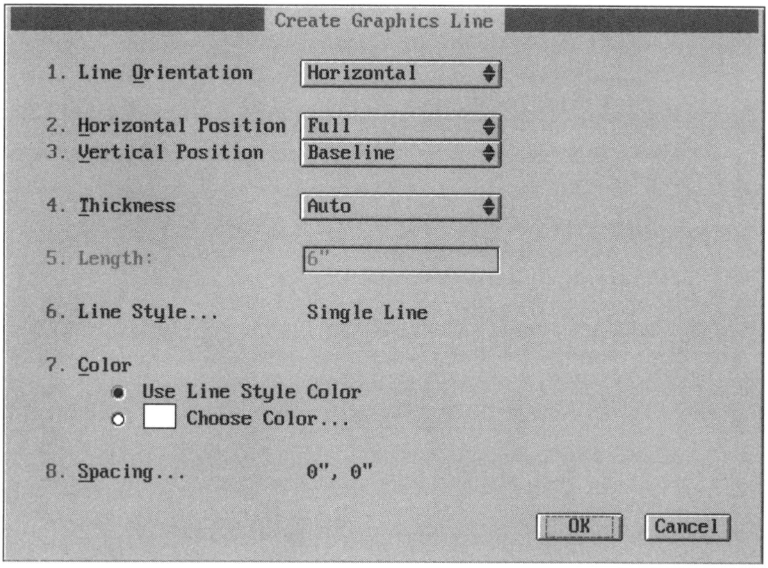

Figure 13-7: The Create Graphics Line dialog box.

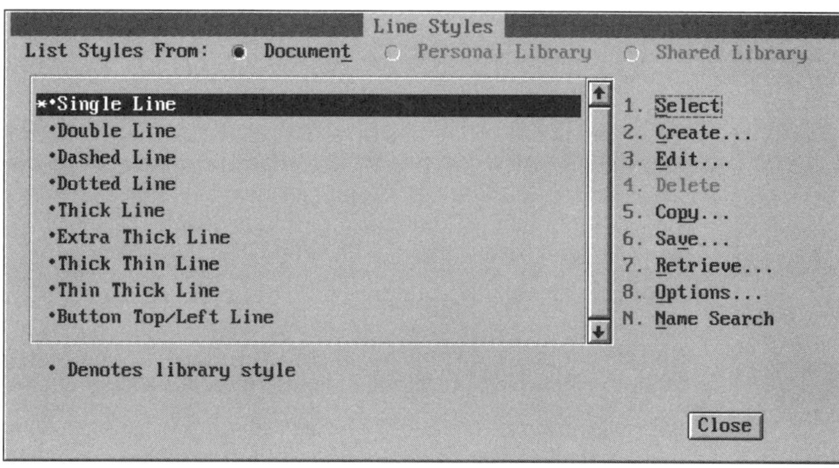

Figure 13-8: The Line Styles dialog box.

8. **Use the up- and down-arrow keys to highlight the line style you want to use and then press Enter.**
9. **After setting any other line options you want, press F7.**

   You are returned to your document, and you can see your new graphics line in all its glory, as shown in Figure 13-9.

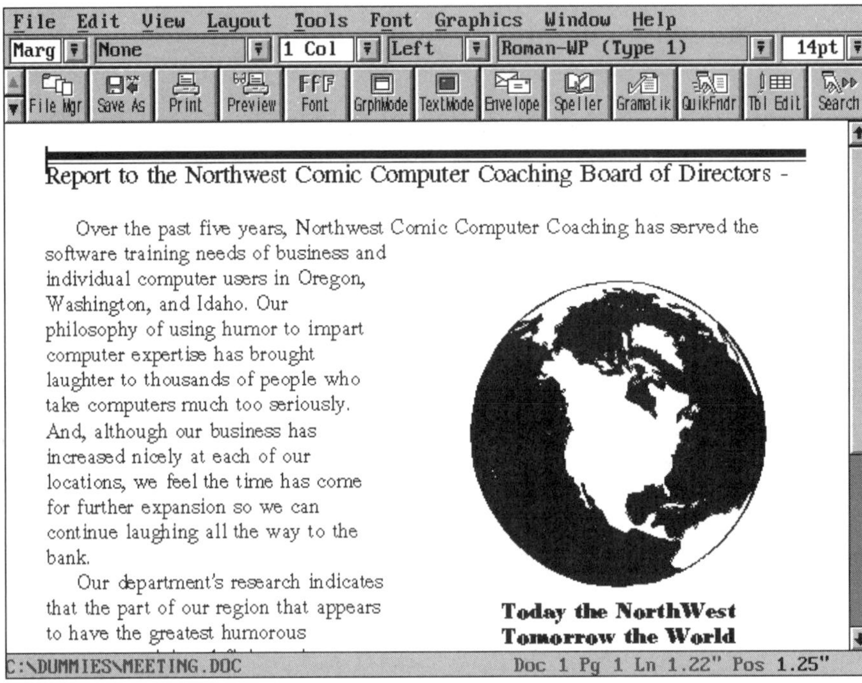

Figure 13-9: A Thin Thick horizontal line above the document's title.

- You can edit a graphics line by pressing Alt-F9, L, E. In the Select Graphics Line to Edit dialog box, press 1 and enter the number of the line to edit and then press Enter. The Edit Graphics Line dialog box appears, with all the same options as the Create Graphics Line dialog box. Make any changes you want and then press F7 when you finish.

- The easy way to edit a graphics line is with the mouse. Click the line. A dashed border (with small rectangles, called handles) surrounds the line. You can move the line by dragging it. You can resize the line by positioning the mouse pointer on one of the handles and dragging.

- It's very important to follow the rules. If you want to be considered hip in the world of graphic design, refer to graphics lines as *rules*. For example, if you were commenting on a graphics line in a Christmas card, you might say, "Hey, that's a cool Yule rule."

- If you're thinking that vertical rules would be great for separating WordPerfect text columns, you're right. However, the easy way to add vertical rules between columns is to specify them by choosing Column Borders in the Text Column dialog box. See Chapter 14 for more information.

Putting Borders Around Text

Does some of your text seem to be getting away from you? Quick — before it slides off the page altogether — corral it by putting a border around it.

To put a border around text, follow these steps:

1. **Block a portion of the paragraphs you want to put a border around.**

   No blocking is necessary to put a border around the entire page.

2. **Press Alt-F9.**

   The Graphics dialog box appears.

3. **Press O (Borders), P (Paragraph).**

4. **Press B (Border Style).**

   The Border Styles dialog box appears.

5. **Use the up- and down-arrow keys to highlight the border style you want and then press Enter.**

   You are returned to the Create Paragraph Border dialog box.

6. **Press Enter.**

   The document reappears with the paragraph nicely bordered, as shown in Figure 13-10.

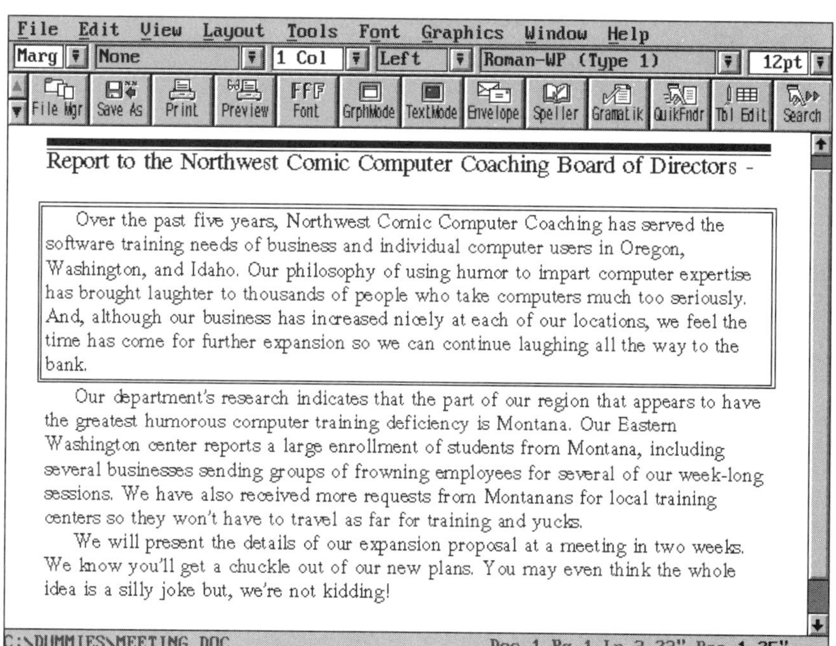

Figure 13-10: A document with a border around a paragraph.

- You can add shading inside the border by choosing Fill Style in the Create Paragraph Border dialog box and then choosing a percent of shaded fill in the Fill Styles dialog box.
- If you use more than 20 percent shaded fill, the background may be too dark to read the text in the foreground easily.
- As with other elements that can add clutter to your document, use borders judiciously.

Desktop Publishing Tricks

I've got a few more tricks up my sleeve to help ensure that your documents don't make your readers puke or fall asleep (or both). Mostly, they aren't tricks, just common sense. Well, here goes.

- If you're having trouble precisely placing some formatting codes because WordPerfect's darned Auto Code Placement keeps putting them where it thinks they should go, you can turn off Auto Code Placement. For example, with Auto Code Placement off, you can place a paragraph border around just a small portion of text within a paragraph. To turn Auto Code Placement off, press Shift-F1, E, T. When the *X* is removed from the Auto Code Placement check box in the Environment dialog box, press Home, F7.
- Unless you're trying to whack your reader over the head with the brilliance of your design work, understated is better than flashy. Keep font usage to a minimum — one or two at most.
- Don't use more than a couple of graphics on a single page — better too few than too many.
- When using rules as graphic accents on your document, don't place them between headings and body text. If you do, the rule acts to separate the heading from the text. Very bad. Instead, place the rule over the heading.
- Allow plenty of space, usually referred to as *white space,* in your document. Use wide margins and allow plenty of room around graphics.

Chapter 14

Columns You Can See Right On-Screen

In This Chapter

- WordPerfect's three types of columns
- Setting up the various columns
- Marking the end of columns
- Moving the cursor around columns
- Making columns look pretty

Throughout WordPerfect's long and illustrious history — when the company was called Satellite Software International, and everyone thought it made programs to control TV satellite dishes — people have used WordPerfect to create everything from memos and letters to business reports and entire newsletters. WordPerfect could handle easy tasks simply and quickly, the hallmark of early WordPerfect. It was the fastest DOS word processor on the planet.

Without question, WordPerfect's blank screen looked perfectly suited for creating letters and reports. But then those wacky guys and gals at old Satellite Software International also gave WordPerfect the capability to create, display, and print documents in separate columns, much like a newspaper or newsletter. Why? Well, it was in demand, and it was a feature that reviewers could rate when reviewing word processing software. Was it necessary? No. Did it slow down the computer? Most definitely.

Fine points aside, this chapter tells you how columns work in WordPerfect and why you'd want to mess with them. But first a word of warning: Working with columns is going to be slow.

WordPerfect's Three Types of Columns

To help you turn your personal computer into your own private printing press (which can get you arrested and shot if you live under a rigid government dictatorship), WordPerfect provides the following three different types of columns to choose from:

- Newspaper columns
- Balanced newspaper columns
- Parallel columns

Yeah, there is no plain old "I just want columns for my church newsletter" stuff here. You must select one of the three types and know the differences between them before you start — which is what the next few sections mull over.

Newspaper columns

The most common columns are called newspaper columns. Newspaper columns work in two ways: When you fill up a newspaper column with text, the text overflows either into the next column on the same page or into a new column on another page, as shown in Figure 14-1.

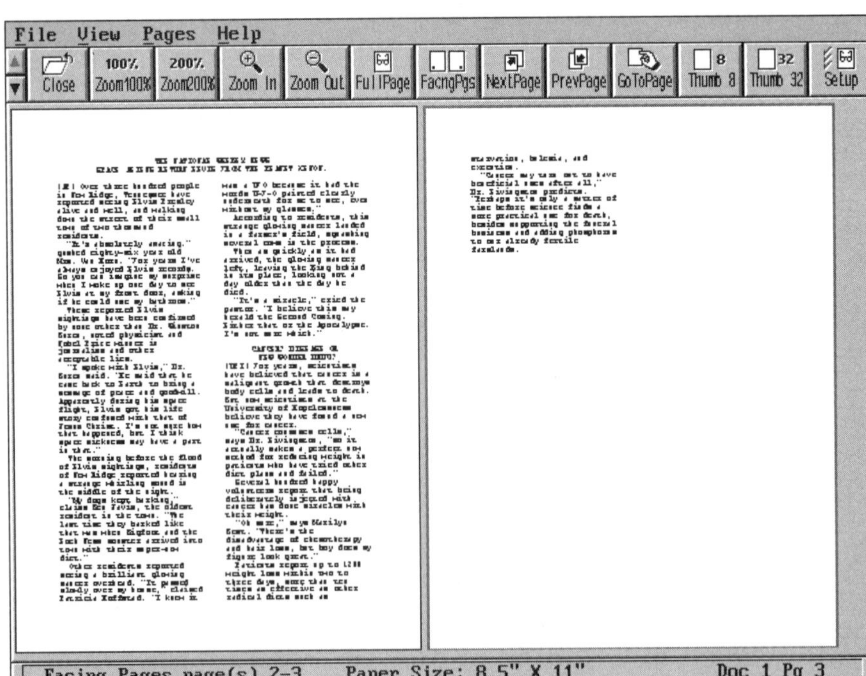

Figure 14-1: How newspaper columns work.

- Figure 14-1 shows a Print Preview look at two pages of a document with newspaper columns.
- With newspaper columns, text pours from one column into the next. This column setup works just as if you were working on separate pages, but WordPerfect slaps down your text in two or more columns on the same page.
- You will probably use regular newspaper columns most of the time when you want to use columns.

Balanced newspaper columns

A balanced newspaper column works exactly like regular newspaper columns except that WordPerfect makes each column end up with the same number of lines (end on the same line). Take a look at Figure 14-2. Normal newspaper columns are shown on the left page, and the same page formatted with balanced newspaper columns appears on the right page.

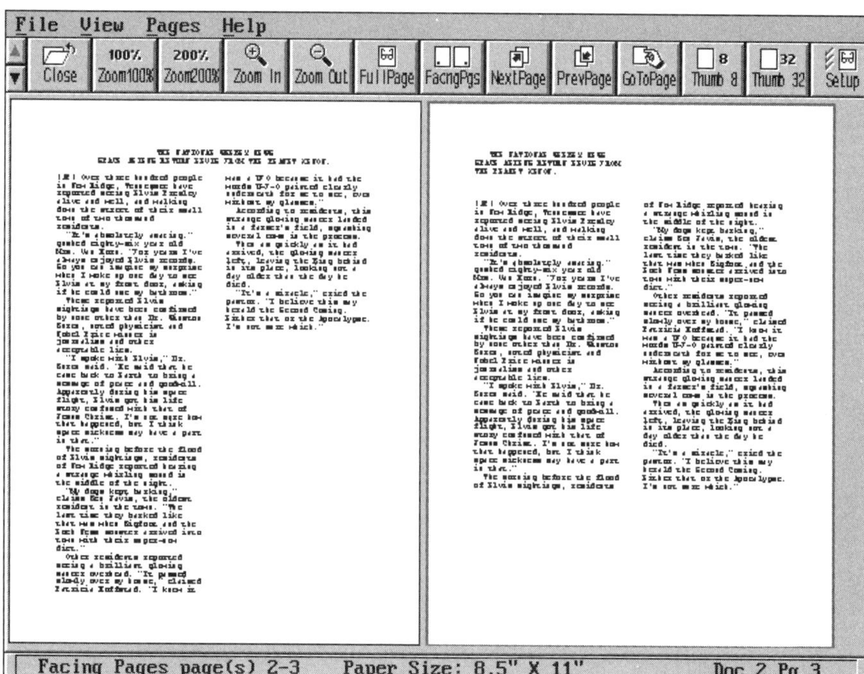

Figure 14-2: Comparison of balanced and regular newspaper columns.

Parallel columns

Sometimes you may not want text to flow from one column to another, like sea water swamping the watertight compartments of the Titanic. If you simply want to display different text side by side in their own columns, you have to use parallel columns instead.

With parallel columns, the text in one column is completely unrelated to the text in any neighboring columns, as shown in Figure 14-3. Common uses for parallel columns may include creating itineraries, scripts, or lists of people you can't stand.

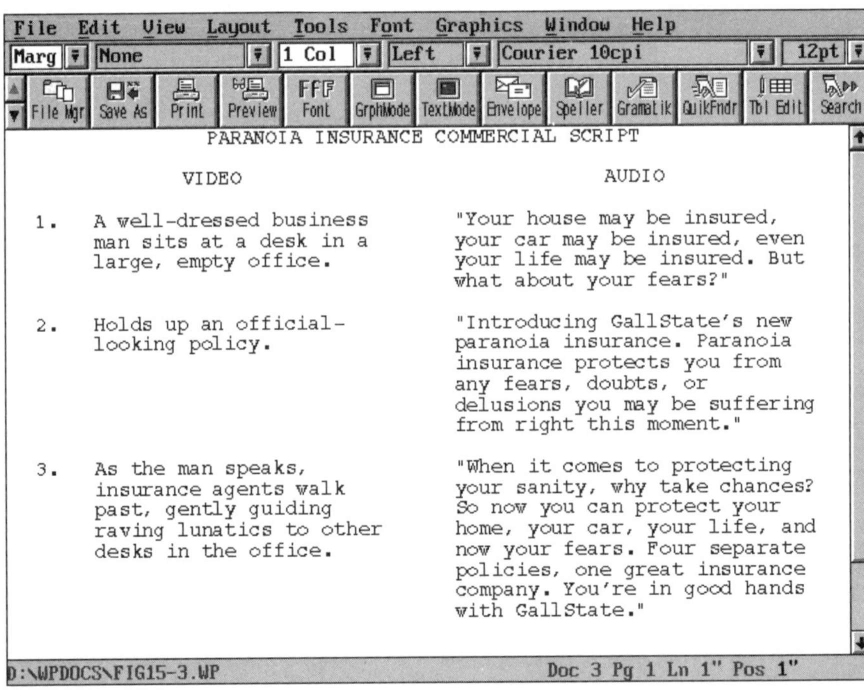

Figure 14-3: What a parallel column looks like.

Columns That Would Impress the Greeks

When you're creating columns, you have two choices: You can either type your text normally in WordPerfect and then have WordPerfect redisplay your whole document in columns, or you can define your columns first and then type in your text. The second process allows you to see exactly how the text appears in the columns as you type.

- Is WordPerfect's general sluggishness getting you down? If so, write your text first and then put it into column format.
- If you move the cursor to the top of the document, you can reformat the entire document to appear in columns. If you move the cursor somewhere in the middle of your document, you can reformat just part of your document in columns.

Creating columns out of existing text

If you have already typed your text and want to change it into newspaper columns, follow these steps:

1. **Move the cursor to the beginning of the text that you want to display in columns.**

   It's best to place the cursor at the start of a paragraph.

2. **Press Alt-F7.**

   The Columns/Tables dialog box appears.

3. **Press C (Columns).**

   The Text Columns dialog box appears. Everything in the dialog box is set up to do newspaper columns two to a page. For information on the various options, refer to the list at the end of this section.

4. **Press Enter.**

   This step selects the newspaper columns, two to a page, and instantly returns you to your document.

- If you want to create another type of column (Balanced Newspaper or Parallel, for example), select that option by pressing T (Column Type) and then selecting the column style from the list, 1 through 4.
- If you want more than two columns to a page, press N (Number of Columns) and type in the new value. The most columns I recommend on a page is three; any more, and the text is too narrow to make reading it fun.
- The Distance Between Columns item sets the space WordPerfect sticks between columns on a page. Make this size wider if you're planning on folding over the paper to make the page read more like a booklet.
- Use your mouse and the Ribbon for a shortcut in selecting the number of columns you want. First, place the cursor where you want the columns to start. Then click the down arrow in the columns box to reveal the choices available to you. Select the number of columns you want by using the mouse. Voilà! You're done.

Creating columns for new text

If you want to create columns for text before you begin writing, follow these steps:

1. **Press Alt-F7.**

   The Columns/Tables dialog box appears.

2. **Press C (Columns).**

   The Text Columns dialog box appears. Everything is set up for newspaper columns, so you can go ahead and press Enter (in Step 3). Otherwise, change any settings that suit you. (Refer to the preceding section for some items you may feel the urge to reset.)

3. **Press Enter.**

   This locks in your column options and you're ready to . . .

4. **Start typing your text.**

   Notice that as you type, WordPerfect automatically word wraps your text within the confines of the columns. This technique may appear funky at first, but remember that you're filling in a column and not an entire page.

   When you reach the bottom of the first column, WordPerfect moves you up to the top of the page at the start of the next column.

Using the cursor keys when you have columns on-screen can be frustrating. My advice is to use the mouse to point-and-click the cursor to a specific spot and save yourself some frustration. Refer to "Moving the Cursor around Columns" later in this chapter for more tips.

Creating block-protected parallel columns

Normally, if a block of text (such as a paragraph) appears in a parallel column near a page break, WordPerfect simply lets the page break bust the text block in half.

If you want to keep page breaks from busting up your text blocks in parallel columns, follow these steps:

1. **Move the cursor to where you want to create the parallel columns.**

2. **Press Alt-F7.**

   The Columns/Tables dialog box appears.

3. **Press C (Columns).**

   The Text Columns dialog box appears.

4. **Press T (Column Type).**

5. **Press B (Parallel with Block Protect).**

   You can set other options here, such as the number of columns or the space between them.

6. **Press Enter.**

   This locks in your block-protected parallel columns and returns you to your document.

7. **Type all the text to appear in the first column.**

   NEW YORK (AP) — In a surprising development, everyone was nice to each other today. . . .

8. **Press Ctrl-Enter.**

   This is the Hard Page command, which tells WordPerfect to start out on a new page. But — aha! — because you're working with columns, WordPerfect moves the cursor to the next parallel column instead.

9. **Type all the text to appear in the next column.**

   Type away. La-la-la.

10. **Repeat Steps 8 and 9 until you've added text to all the parallel columns you want.**

    Each time you press Ctrl-Enter, a new column is born. When you're done, you can end the columns, as described in the next section.

TIP

How to make a three-fold brochure

Here is a common problem: You want to create a snazzy brochure and have it look like a real typesetter tackled the problem. But rather than pay someone else, you can have WordPerfect tackle the problem for you. Follow these steps to make a three-fold brochure:

1. **Start by writing the text for your brochure.**

   Write away. La-la-la. You should edit the text before you start the next step (spell-check and proof your document). Also, be prepared to do some fine-tuning in case the text is too long or too short.

2. **Reorient the page layout to Landscape.**

   This setting is the wide format, which allows you to fold your brochure three times. Press Shift-F8, P, 4. Select Letter (Landscape) from the list (pressing the up arrow once should do it). Press Home, F7 to return to your document.

   Notice that the text runs long on the page — it should. You've just turned everything over on its ear.

3. **Switch on three-column mode.**

   Press Alt-F7, C. Press N and then type in **3** to give yourself three columns across the page. Press Enter. Next, press D to change the distance between the columns to 3/4 inch. Into the box, type **.75** and press Enter. Press Home, F7 to return to your document.

(continued)

(continued)

4. View your document with Print Preview to see whether you have it right.

Press Shift-F7, V. Look to see whether any text slides over the page. If you don't mind that look — great. Otherwise, you need to edit the text so that everything fits on three columns.

Generally speaking, fine-tuning your brochure requires many more steps at this point — mostly futzing with your text to get everything to fit and look right. Consider blocking all your text and making everything full justified (Shift-F8, L, J, F, Home, F7). Also, try messing with the font size and maybe the margins. Eventually you'll get the look you want — but not until after you've printed a few dozen samples.

Marking the End of a Column

If you don't want an entire document to appear in columns, you have to tell WordPerfect when to stop formatting text in columns. At that point, WordPerfect returns the text to one column on a page, which is pretty much what it does normally.

To mark the end of your columns, follow these steps:

1. **Move the cursor to the end of your columns.**

   Position the cursor just after the last paragraph of the last column.

2. **Press Alt-F7.**

   The Columns/Tables dialog box appears.

3. **Press C (Columns).**

   The Text Columns dialog box appears.

4. **Press F (Off) and Enter.**

   Now whatever you type from this point on appears in the normal WordPerfect document mode.

- Another way to shut off columns is to use your mouse to select the column drop-down list from the Ribbon and choose 1 Col from the list.
- Shutting off newspaper columns forces WordPerfect to start your normal text on a new page.

Moving the Cursor around Columns

WordPerfect's normal cursor-movement keys work exactly the same whether or not you have columns on-screen. Pressing Home, Home, ↑ moves the cursor to the top of the document; pressing Home, Home, ↓ moves the cursor to the end of the document. However, WordPerfect offers two ways to move the cursor between columns: Call them the slow way and the fast way.

Moving the cursor (the slow way)

To move the cursor from column to column the slow way, follow these steps:

1. **Move the cursor to the bottom or top of a column by using the up- or down-arrow key.**
2. **Press the left- or right-arrow key.**

   When the cursor reaches the top or bottom of a column, it jumps to the next column when you press the left- or right-arrow key.

   Yes, it takes time to move the cursor to the top or bottom of a column by using the up- or down-arrow key.

Moving the cursor (the fast way)

REMEMBER

To use the fast way of moving the cursor from column to column, do the following: Press Alt-← to move the cursor left one column; press Alt-→ to move the cursor right one column.

Making Columns Look Pretty

With its traditional and persistent lack of imagination, WordPerfect formats your text in two columns. However, you can add more columns, define column widths, adjust the spacing between columns, and even add eye-pleasing borders between your columns. You make all these adjustments in the Text Columns dialog box, shown in Figure 14-4.

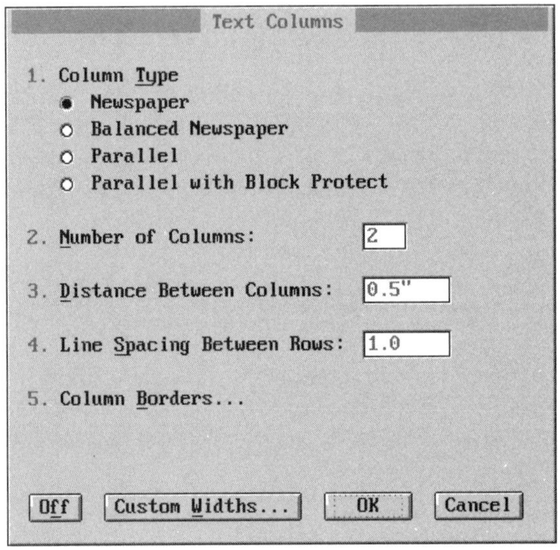

Figure 14-4: The Text Columns dialog box.

Creating three or more columns

To redefine or create your document to display three or more columns, follow these steps:

1. **Move the cursor to the location where you want more columns.**
2. **Press Alt-F7.**

   The Columns/Tables dialog box appears.
3. **Press C (Columns).**
4. **Press N (Number of Columns).**
5. **Type the number of columns you want and press Enter.**

   How about 50? Nah! Keep the number of columns to 2 or 3 — or more, if you're printing on very wide paper.
6. **Press Home, F7.**

   WordPerfect creates your multiple columns like magic, right on-screen.

Defining column widths

Depending on the number of columns you want to display, WordPerfect automatically sticks a certain amount of empty space between them (for example, half an inch between two columns). However, you may want to redefine the width of one or more columns. To change the width, follow these steps:

1. **Press Alt-F7, C.**

   The Text Columns dialog box appears.

2. **Press W (Custom Widths).**

   The Custom Widths dialog box appears (though it's titled Text Columns, which is a mistake), as shown in Figure 14-5. Marvel at this dialog box's impressiveness.

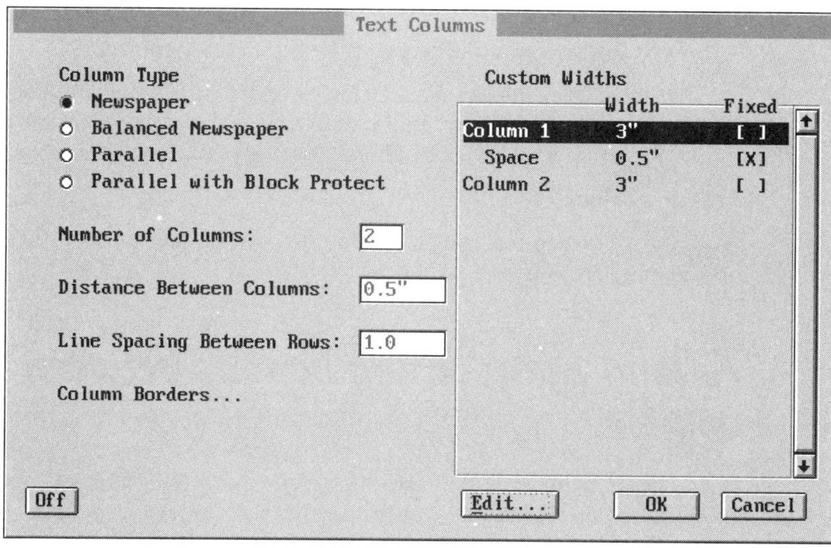

Figure 14-5: The Text Columns dialog box.

3. **In the Custom Widths dialog box, highlight the column whose width you want to change.**

   Use the up- or down-arrow key to highlight the column you want to mess with and press Enter.

   The Column dialog box appears.

4. **Press W (Width).**

5. **Enter the new width of the column in inches and press Enter.**

   WordPerfect adjusts the other column's width to make room (or to fill in the space) as you change the column's size. Don't get too wacky here with unusual numbers; generally you should have a good reason for changing a column's size.

6. **Press Home, F7.**

   You're back in your document. WordPerfect rushes out and adjusts the width of your selected column.

Defining the space between columns

Technically, the space between columns is called the *gutter.* If you want, you can adjust the size of the gutter by following these steps:

1. **Press Alt-F7, C.**

   The Text Columns dialog box appears.

2. **Press D (Distance Between Columns).**

3. **Type the new size of the gutter between your columns.**

   The size WordPerfect normally selects depends on how many columns you have. Keep in mind that numbers less than what WordPerfect suggests will probably make your columns too close together to be readable.

4. **Press Home, F7.**

   Like a Boy Scout aiming to please, WordPerfect automatically adjusts the space between your columns.

Adding eye-pleasing borders between columns

Out of sheer laziness, WordPerfect usually separates columns by empty space. However, if you shrink this empty space or you just want to make sure that some drowsy reader can clearly see the boundaries of your columns, WordPerfect lets you add borders.

To add borders to columns, follow these steps:

1. **Press Alt-F7, C.**

   The Text Columns dialog box appears.

2. **Press B (Column Borders).**

   The Create Column Border dialog box appears.

3. **Press B (Border Style).**

   The Border Styles dialog box appears.

4. **Highlight the border style you want to use and press Enter.**

   Dashed, thick, thin, thick top — it's like selecting a pizza. Use the up- and down-arrow keys to peruse the various styles.

5. **Press Home, F7.**

   Yeah, you're really done at this point. After you return to your document, you can see the border sitting between your columns.

Chapter 15

Learn to Draw

In This Chapter

- How to draw a line
- Drawing different types of lines
- Erasing lines

Even the most competently, finely crafted prose can look intimidating, dreary, and dull if poorly designed. Although paragraph indentations and line spacing can help make text look more inviting, WordPerfect also gives you the chance to draw lines, borders, and boxes in your documents. By underlining or enclosing headings in boxes, you can emphasize certain parts of your document.

In fact, if you ever used an Etch-A-Sketch as a kid, you've already mastered the fundamentals of drawing lines in WordPerfect. And yes, like an Etch-A-Sketch, WordPerfect won't let you draw circles either.

How to Draw a Line

Drawing a line is as simple as pressing the up/down or right/left arrow keys (which explains why you can't draw circles).

If you have a mouse, forget about using it to draw lines in WordPerfect. The only way you can draw lines is by using the cursor keys, so push your mouse aside and forget about it in this chapter.

To draw a line, follow these steps:

1. **Move the cursor to the location where you want to start drawing a line.**
2. **Press Ctrl-F3, L (Line Draw).**

   The Line Draw dialog box appears.

   WARNING! You can only draw lines around text created with a monospaced font, such as Courier. If you attempt to draw around any other text, you'll see a warning box displayed. This warning doesn't apply when you're drawing lines on a blank part of a page.
3. **Draw your lines.**

   Use the up-, down-, left-, or right-arrow keys. WordPerfect draws a line wherever you move the cursor. (Isn't this fun?) Figure 15-1 shows just how fun it is.
4. **Press Esc when you are done.**

Whenever WordPerfect draws lines, it turns on the Typeover feature, which means that if you draw a line through existing text, the line wipes out the text.

TIP: If you're going to be drawing a line around a line of text, put a blank line before and after the text to give yourself room to draw the line. If you're boxing in a paragraph, it's better to use WordPerfect's Border command: Alt-F9, O, P.

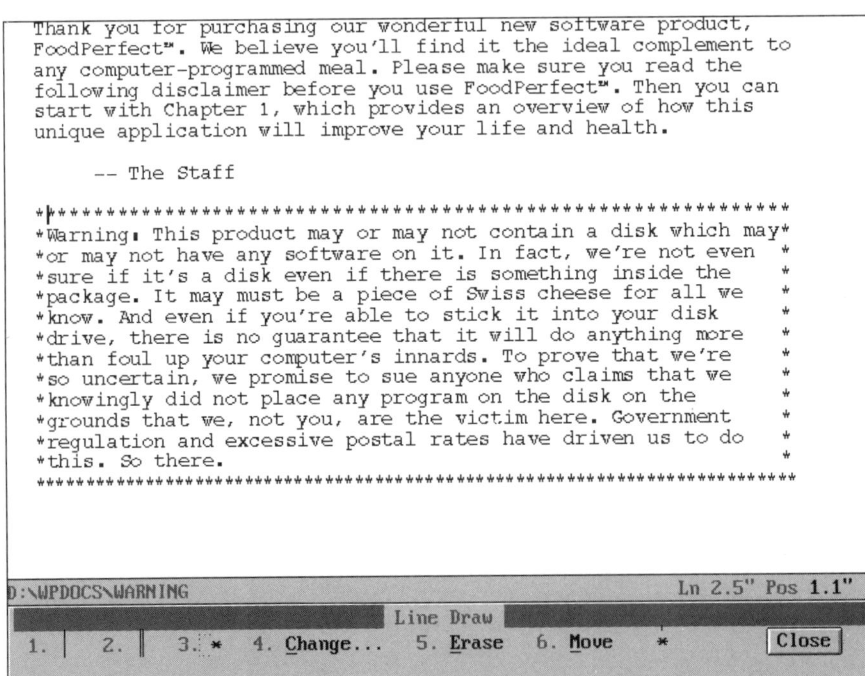

Figure 15-1: Drawing a line.

The remaining sections in this chapter tell you how to draw different types of lines and special stuff like that.

Drawing Different Types of Lines

A line is a line is a line, right? Wrong. Although WordPerfect can draw plain lines, some people may want a little bit more excitement than that. So in addition to a single line, WordPerfect can also draw double lines or lines consisting of any type of ASCII character you want.

To draw with a strange or unusual pen, follow these steps:

1. **Move the cursor to the location where you want to start drawing a line.**
2. **Press Ctrl-F3, L (Line Draw).**

   The Line Draw dialog box appears. Near the bottom of the page you'll see a menu of line drawing options.
3. **Press 1 to draw with a single line.**

   Press 2 to draw with a double line.

   Press 3 to draw with a special character, such as the asterisk.
4. **Press the up/down or right/left arrow keys to draw your lines.**

   WordPerfect draws a line wherever you move the cursor.
5. **Press Esc when you're done.**

- WordPerfect lets you switch between line types any time you want. To do so, press 1, 2, or 3 to switch to that particular line drawing character. The character that you're drawing with appears after the word `Move` on the right side of the Line Draw dialog box.
- If you press C (Change), you can select a new drawing character, something other than the asterisk, for option 3. WordPerfect displays the Change Line Draw Character dialog box (see Figure 15-2) in which you can select eight different types of line characters that you can use in case a single or double line is too boring for you.
- In addition to the eight predefined characters in the Change Line Draw Character dialog box, WordPerfect lets you use any ASCII character as a line drawing character, so you can draw a line of smiley faces or hearts across your document if you want to. Just press U (User-defined) in the Change Line Draw Character dialog box and type the new character that you want to use. (To choose an ASCII character, press Alt followed by the ASCII number representing the character you want. For example, to use the æ character, you would type Alt-145.)

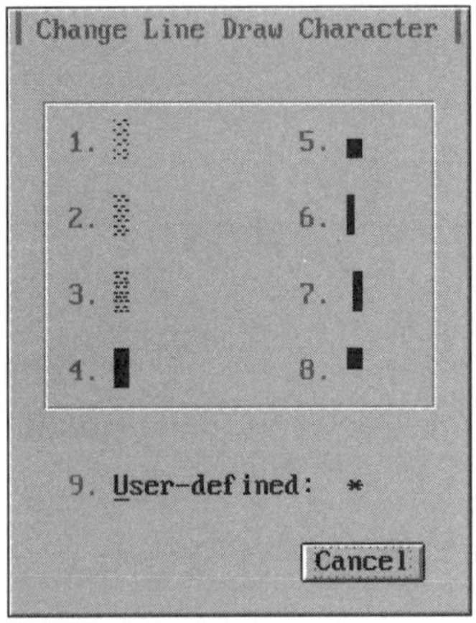

Figure 15-2: The Change Line Draw Character dialog box.

Erasing Lines

If WordPerfect lets you create lines, it's only natural that it would let you erase them as well. Although you can erase a line like any character (press Backspace, Del, Alt-F4 and Del, and so on), WordPerfect also gives you a way to erase a line just as easily as you created it.

To erase a line, follow these steps:

1. **Move the cursor to the location where you want to start erasing a line.**
2. **Press Ctrl-F3, L.**

   The Line Draw dialog box appears.

3. **Press E (Erase).**
4. **Press the up/down or right/left arrow keys to erase your lines.**
5. **Press Esc.**

WARNING!

- When you have WordPerfect's line erase feature turned on, moving the cursor will wipe out existing lines along with any text that gets in the way, so be careful when moving the cursor around.
- There is no way to undo any erasing, so be careful!

Part III

WordPerfect Macroland

The 5th Wave By Rich Tennant

In this part . . .

Run for the hills! It's macro time! Actually, this part of the book provides insight and a brief wade into the waters of WordPerfect's macros. Quite a few examples are presented here, though if you *really* want to go nuts with macros, I recommend that you obtain a book specific to that subject. Using macros is almost like programming the PC, which you'll see an example of in Chapter 17.

Chapter 16

The Whole Deal with Macros

In This Chapter

- Understanding macros
- Using WordPerfect's (secret) macros
- Viewing a macro file
- Printing a macro file

Ideally, WordPerfect should read your mind and automatically do what you want. After all, aren't computers supposed to make your life easier? Mind reading should be one of their most elemental tasks. But until the programming wizards at WordPerfect come up with such a mind-reading feature, the closest alternative is to use macros.

Think of a macro as a shortcut, a quicker way to accomplish some long, boring task. For example, there could be a BABY macro that feeds, burps, changes, and puts baby to bed. In WordPerfect, macros take the burden of typing off your shoulders and put it back on the computer — where it belongs. At the most complex level (which this book only touches upon), macros let you reprogram WordPerfect so completely that even the people at WordPerfect wouldn't recognize their own creation. That sounds devious, but it takes a truly twisted mind to immerse itself that deeply in WordPerfect macroland.

What Are Macros?

So what the heck are macros anyway? Essentially, a *macro* is a way to get WordPerfect to do something at the push of a button — much like launching nuclear missiles, but minus the chilling aftereffects. Essentially, a macro lets you press one key where you may have pressed a dozen or so before. It makes things simple.

For example, think of all the times you had to do finger gymnastics to press all the bizarre keystrokes that WordPerfect demands (Alt-Shift-F1, Shift-F6, Alt-F, and so on). Rather than press two or more of these odd keystroke combinations every time you want to do something, just create a WordPerfect macro. In a way, you're telling WordPerfect to "remember what I'm doing so I won't have to do it again."

To help WordPerfect remember your commands, it stores them in a special file called a *macro file*. You give the macro file a filename — like you would a WordPerfect document — to keep different macros separate and to remember what they do.

The next time you want to accomplish that same task, you say to WordPerfect, "Remember that complicated task I did a while back? Here's the name of the macro file that contains the instructions I want you to follow." And WordPerfect merrily retrieves the macro file that you want to use and flawlessly performs the instructions stored in the file.

Yeah, it works something like that.

- A macro file can be named anything you want, as long as it is limited to the eight-character filename that plagues all computers using DOS.
- After you give your macro file a name, WordPerfect automatically gives it a file extension of WPM, which stands for WordPerfect Macro and not *wampum*.
- Wampum is short for *wampumpaeg*, a Narragansett word meaning money, specifically a string of white shell beads.
- By the way, in WordPerfect there are no such things as micros. *Macro* implies something big, beefy, and important. *Micro* implies something teeny, puny, and insignificant. If you notice all the hard disk space and memory that WordPerfect gobbles up, you'll know that WordPerfect is far from being tiny or small.

Why Use Macros?

Before you get too excited about macros (and I'd never assume that), relax. Macros don't make WordPerfect do anything that it can't already do — like be utterly intuitive and never crash the computer. However, macros can make WordPerfect do things that would normally be too troublesome to do.

Basically, there are five reasons to use a macro:

- Macros save time. Unless you're a masochist who enjoys reading WordPerfect's less-than-perfect manuals, you'll find that learning how to do something once and storing it in a macro is much easier than looking up the right commands every time you need to use them.

- Macros can ensure accuracy. Typing your company's name over and over again, such as Acme Computer Consulting, Psychological Counseling, and Toxic Cleanup, can be cumbersome. But having a macro type this for you ensures that you don't make any spelling mistakes or omit any words, as well.
- Macros enforce consistency. Most large corporations have a specific format for writing memos, letters, and pink slips. To ensure that everyone follows the same format, a macro can automatically create the format so that people don't have to think for themselves.
- Macros make difficult tasks easy. Do you want to load a graphics image into a two-column newsletter? Good luck trying to figure out all the commands you need to use. But using a macro makes complicated tasks as easy as pressing a button (provided, of course, that you press the right button!).
- Macros mystify your coworkers and impress your boss. By learning how to use WordPerfect's macros, you can customize all your company's copies of WordPerfect so that everyone is dependent on your skills. The next time your company tries to fire anyone, you'll be so valuable that they'll have no choice but to keep you.

WordPerfect's (Secret) Macros

If you do a little exploring on your hard disk, you find that WordPerfect has secretly hidden several sample macros on your computer. You can find them in the C:\WP60\MACROS directory on your hard drive. Table 16-1 lists the secret macros and what they do.

Table 16-1 WordPerfect's Secret Macros

Macro Filename	*What It Does*
ALLFONTS.WPM	Displays a list of available fonts for the currently selected printer
BULLET.WPM	Inserts a bullet symbol
CALC.WPM	Displays a calculator on-screen
EDITCODE.WPM	Displays WordPerfect's hidden document codes
EXITALL.WPM	Returns you to the main editing screen when you're currently in another editing screen (headers, footnotes, and so on)
GLOSSARY.WPM	Creates and expands abbreviations, such as CIA, into their full-blown names (Central Intelligence Agency)

(continued)

Table 16-1 *(continued)*

Macro Filename	*What It Does*
INITCAPS.WPM	Capitalizes the first letter of a selected word
LIBRARY.WPM	Contains functions and procedures for other macros to use (By itself, it does nothing.)
MEMO.WPM	Creates a form memo, letter, or fax cover sheet
MOD_ATRB.WPM	Lets you search and replace font attributes used in a document
NOTECVT.WPM	Converts footnotes to endnotes or endnotes to footnotes
PLEADING.WPM	Creates pleadings and other legal work for lawyers
SPACETAB.WPM	Converts spaces into tabs

- Can't find the macros? Then they probably weren't installed when WordPerfect was set up on your computer. That's common. The macro files consume some 1.7MB of disk space.
- The LIBRARY.WPM macro is used only when you're creating your own macros. If you never plan on creating your own macros, you can erase the LIBRARY.WPM macro file and save a whopping 41,851 bytes on your hard disk.

Using the secret macros

Any time you're using WordPerfect, you can invoke these secret macros to perform some action. Let's say you're writing a love letter to your spouse (or a love letter to somebody else's spouse), and you suddenly decide that you need to add two numbers together. Don't add the numbers in your head. Invoke the CALC.WPM macro that pops up a calculator on-screen. Voilà! You've just turned your $3,000.00 computer into a $9.95 pocket calculator!

To use one of WordPerfect's secret macros, such as the CALC.WPM macro, follow these steps:

1. **Press Alt-F10.**

   The Play Macro dialog box appears, as shown in Figure 16-1.

2. **Press the F5 key.**

   The Select List dialog box appears, highlighting the directory C:\WP60\MACROS*.* inside. If you have stored WordPerfect's secret macros in another directory for some odd reason, type the directory where you stored them and then press Enter.

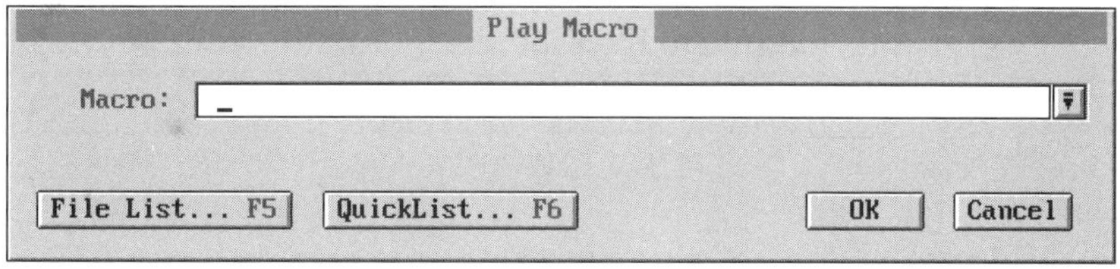

Figure 16-1: The Play Macro dialog box.

3. **Press Enter to choose the highlighted directory.**

   Please wait.

   The File List dialog box appears.

4. **Highlight the macro file you want to use and press Enter.**

   For example, highlight CALC.WPM and press Enter.

   After a few seconds (or a few minutes, depending on how slow your computer may be), the macro does whatever it is that it's supposed to do. If you selected CALC.WPM, you see a calculator dialog box on-screen.

- Yes, that calculator was created by using WordPerfect's macro commands. And you thought this was just a word processor. . . .
- Without macros, getting WordPerfect to pop a calculator on-screen may require wading through multiple menu commands or memorizing a series of confusing keystroke combinations. It could take years.
- After you get the hang of using and eventually creating your own macros, you can use them to turn your $3,000.00 computer into the equivalent of a $1.95 calendar, a 25¢ note card, or a spare piece of scrap paper that you would have thrown out anyway. Macros let you make WordPerfect behave exactly the way you want it to. (Now if only raising children could be this easy. . . .)

Redefining your keyboard to use the secret macros

Pressing Alt-F10 and highlighting the specific macro you want to use (see the preceding section) isn't too bad once in a while. But if you use WordPerfect's secret macros on a regular basis, pressing Alt-F10 and highlighting a macro filename over and over again can be tedious and downright dull, defeating the whole purpose of macros in the first place.

To make WordPerfect's secret macros as easy to use as pushing a button, you have to redefine your keyboard. After you've redefined your keyboard, you can use WordPerfect's secret macros by simply pressing two-button keystrokes, such as Alt-I or Ctrl-G. Table 16-2 lists the shortcut keyboard combinations you can use to redefine your keyboard for using macros.

Table 16-2 Shortcut Keys for Using WordPerfect's Secret Macros

Shortcut Keys	*Macro Filename*	*What It Does*
None	ALLFONTS.WPM	Displays a list of available fonts for the currently selected printer
Alt-B	BULLET.WPM	Inserts a bullet symbol
Alt-C	CALC.WPM	Displays a calculator on-screen
Ctrl-E	EDITCODE.WPM	Displays WordPerfect's hidden document codes
Alt-X	EXITALL.WPM	Returns you to the main editing screen when you're currently in another editing screen (headers, footnotes, and so on)
Ctrl-G	GLOSSARY.WPM	Creates and expands abbreviations, such as CIA, into their full-blown names (Central Intelligence Agency)
Alt-I	INITCAPS.WPM	Capitalizes the first letter of a selected word
None	LIBRARY.WPM	Contains functions and procedures for other macros to use (By itself, it does nothing.)
Alt-M	MEMO.WPM	Creates a form memo, letter, or fax cover sheet
Alt-R	MOD_ATRB.WPM	Lets you search and replace font attributes used in a document
Alt-N	NOTECVT.WPM	Converts footnotes to endnotes or endnotes to footnotes
Alt-P	PLEADING.WPM	Creates pleadings and other legal work for lawyers
Alt-S	SPACETAB.WPM	Converts spaces into tabs

To redefine your keyboard and assign WordPerfect's secret macros to the two-button keystrokes shown in Table 16-2, follow these steps:

1. **Press Shift-F1.**

   The Setup dialog box appears.

2. **Press 4 or K to choose Keyboard Layout.**

   The Keyboard Layout dialog box appears.

3. **Highlight MACROS and press Enter.**
4. **Press Enter to close the Setup dialog box.**

   Congratulations! You've just redefined your keyboard so that most of WordPerfect's secret macros are a two-button keystroke away.

- Refer to Chapter 6 for more details about redefining the keyboard.
- All of WordPerfect's normal keystroke commands will continue to work the same after you select the MACROS keyboard. The only difference is that if you press one of the keystroke combinations shown in Table 16-2, such as Alt-C, you'll run one of WordPerfect's secret macros. Try it now and amaze your family, friends, and loved ones!

Viewing a Macro File

Dissecting a frog in high school biology class helps you understand how the parts of an animal work, or used to work. If you're a chef, dissecting a frog shows you where to find the white meat. Either way, looking at something in a raw fashion gives you a clue as to what's going on. WordPerfect's macros are no different (except that there is no white meat).

WordPerfect macro files are nothing more than ordinary WordPerfect document files. The only difference is that WordPerfect always gives its macro files a file extension of WPM, which still doesn't stand for *wampum*.

If you ever want to see the contents of a macro file, here's how to do it:

1. **Press Shift-F10.**

   The Open Document dialog box appears.

2. **Press F5.**

   The Specify File Manager List dialog box appears.

3. **Press F8.**

   The Directory Tree dialog box appears.

4. **Look for your MACROS directory and select it.**

   Look for the directory named MACROS in the scrolling list. Use the up- and down-arrow keys to find it. (It shouldn't be too far away from the directory already highlighted.) After you highlight the directory, press the Enter key.

   The File Manager dialog box appears.

5. **Highlight the WPM macro file that you want to view.**

   Hey. How about peeking at that awesome CALC.WPM macro and seeing what makes it tick? Or if you want to look at some macro you created, highlight it instead.

6. **Press L (Look).**

   WordPerfect displays the Author and Abstract information about the macro. The Author information shows you who created the macro. The Abstract information briefly explains what the macro is supposed to do.

7. **Press L (Look at text) to see the macro's contents.**

   WordPerfect shows the actual contents of the macro file, something like Figure 16-2. If it looks like a foreign language, you'll know that you did everything correctly.

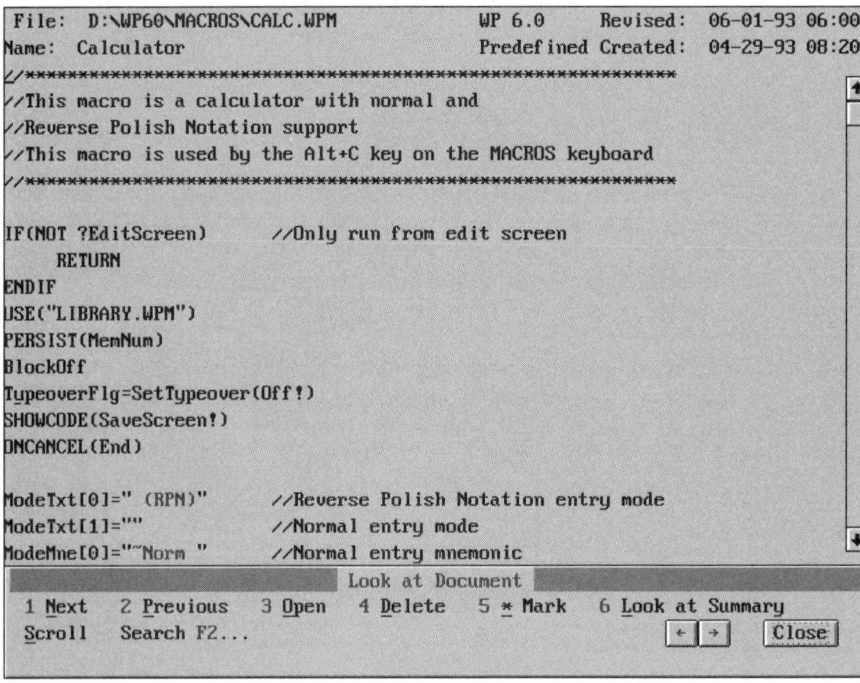

```
File:  D:\WP60\MACROS\CALC.WPM                WP 6.0     Revised:  06-01-93 06:00a
Name:  Calculator                             Predefined Created:  04-29-93 08:20p
//**********************************************************
//This macro is a calculator with normal and
//Reverse Polish Notation support
//This macro is used by the Alt+C key on the MACROS keyboard
//**********************************************************

IF(NOT ?EditScreen)       //Only run from edit screen
    RETURN
ENDIF
USE("LIBRARY.WPM")
PERSIST(MemNum)
BlockOff
TypeoverFlg=SetTypeover(Off!)
SHOWCODE(SaveScreen!)
ONCANCEL(End)

ModeTxt[0]=" (RPN)"       //Reverse Polish Notation entry mode
ModeTxt[1]=""             //Normal entry mode
ModeMne[0]="~Norm "       //Normal entry mnemonic
                         Look at Document
 1 Next   2 Previous   3 Open   4 Delete   5 * Mark   6 Look at Summary
 Scroll   Search F2...                                    ← →   Close
```

Figure 16-2: The CALC.WPM macro file, naked on the screen.

8. **Press Home, F7, F7 when you're bored.**

   This takes you back to your document, where you can do something creative in WordPerfect . . . like *write*!

- Don't be disappointed. It's not like the CALC.WPM macro should make sense or anything. Stuff like this is complex, especially given that it's in a word processor. Some macros and macro programmers really go off the deep end.
- Because WordPerfect macro files are ordinary WordPerfect documents, you can also view WPM macro files by loading them as documents. The only danger is that if you load a macro file as a document, you risk modifying the macro by mistake.
- Chapter 18 contains information on creating your own macro files. Don't assume you can glean any of that knowledge by just looking at WordPerfect's secret macro files on disk.

Printing a Macro File

Sometimes viewing a macro file just isn't satisfying enough. If you really want to see how a macro works (or doesn't work), you need to print it out so that you can study the whole thing.

To print a macro file, follow these steps:

1. **Press Shift-F10.**

   The Open Document dialog box appears.

2. **Press F5.**

   The Specify File Manager List dialog box appears.

3. **Press F8.**

   The Directory Tree dialog box appears.

4. **Highlight the MACROS directory and press Enter.**

   The File Manager dialog box appears.

5. **Highlight the WPM macro file that you want to print.**

   Use the up- or down-arrow keys to highlight the macro file you want to print.

6. **Press P (Print).**

   The Print Multiple Pages dialog box appears. Make sure that your printer is on and ready to print.

7. **Press Enter.**

   WordPerfect cheerfully prints out the macro file that you selected.

- Because WordPerfect macro files are ordinary WordPerfect documents, you can also print WPM macro files by loading them as documents and printing them out by pressing Shift-F7.
- Printing a macro file is one way you can easily pour over its contents and see what makes it tick. But be wary! Some of those files are pretty darn long.

Chapter 17

Making Your Own Macros

In This Chapter

- Creating macros
- Recording a macro
- Pausing macros temporarily
- Stopping a macro recording
- Editing macros
- Storing macros in different directories
- Converting WP 5.1 macros to WP 6 macros

If your favorite toys as a child were Legos, Tinker Toys, and Lincoln Logs, you'll love the idea of creating your own macros. Although you can use the macros provided with WordPerfect, they don't do everything you need. In those cases, you either have to suffer and do things the hard way or take time to create your own macros.

The main reason to create a macro is to simplify a repetitive task. Obviously, if you're only going to do something once, it takes more time to create a macro than to do the actual task. This chapter shows you the rudiments of macroing in a friendly, wholesome, and often useful manner.

The Grand, Deluxe Overview of Creating WordPerfect Macros

Creating a macro can be as easy as recording a television program on your VCR three weeks from now, between 8:00 and 9:30 p.m., on channel 5. It's that simple.

Ha! Just kidding. Actually, creating macros is a lot easier than using a VCR. WordPerfect provides three ways to create a macro:

- You can have WordPerfect "record" your keystrokes as you type them. To create a macro quickly, use this method of recording a macro as you perform a task.
- You can edit an existing macro file, twisting and contorting it so that it types in the commands you want instead of what it does now. To create more complicated macros, use this second method.
- You can wait until somebody else writes the macros you need and then beg, borrow, or steal them for yourself. If you don't want to do anything at all, use the third method.

Recording Macros (the Easy Method)

When you create a macro by recording it, you're telling WordPerfect, "Remember what I'm typing so that I won't have to do it again." That macro then remembers whatever you typed so that it can quickly and flawlessly type it again at your slightest whim.

To record a macro, follow these steps:

1. **Press Ctrl-F10.**

   The Record Macro dialog box appears, as shown in Figure 17-1.

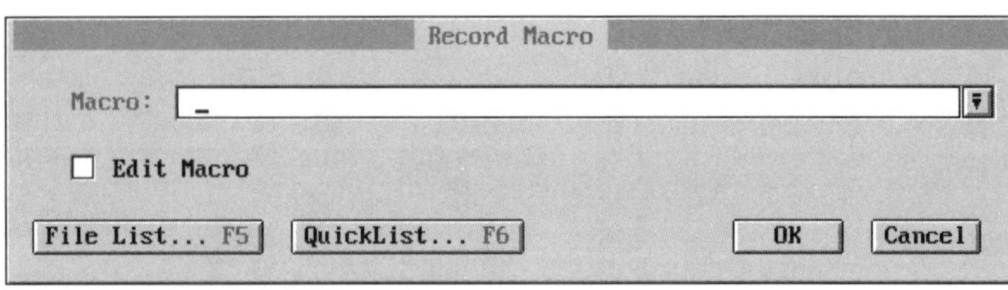

Figure 17-1: The Record Macro dialog box.

2. **Type the name of your macro.**

   Think up something good, but be brief — this is a filename — it can contain only letters and numbers and can be only eight characters long.

   The name that you type is the filename that WordPerfect gives your macro. WordPerfect automatically gives it the WPM file extension and stuffs the macro file in the C:\WP60\MACROS directory, unless you tell it to do otherwise, which I don't recommend.

3. Press Enter.

After a few moments (depending on how slow your computer may be), the Record Macro dialog box disappears and you're back in your document. But, lo, WordPerfect displays the message *Recording Macro* in the lower-left corner of the screen. This message lets you know that WordPerfect is recording any keys you press.

4. Do whatever you want the macro to do.

WordPerfect can record the following three things: any letters, numbers, or symbols that you type; any menu commands that you choose using the keyboard or the mouse; and any key commands you press, such as Shift-F10 to open a document.

5. Press Ctrl-F10 to stop recording your macro.

The *Recording Macro* message vanishes. Your macro has been recorded, saved to disk, and is now ready to use.

TIP

- Before you record a macro, it's a good idea to plan out the commands that you want the macro to do. In this way, you don't fumble around the keyboard and create a macro that mimics your clumsiness.
- It's usually a good idea to record a macro in a new document. Then if you do something wrong, you don't mess up a perfectly good document.
- Macro names are limited by DOS's lame eight-character maximum length. If you type anything longer, WordPerfect rudely truncates it to be a filename.

TIP

- To help you identify your macros later, it's a good idea to use descriptive macro names. A macro named DELLINE is more descriptive than one named MACRO3.
- Besides recording what you want, WordPerfect also records every mistake you make. So if you're recording a macro and you accidentally misspell your name and then correct it, your macro slavishly follows your keystrokes exactly as you entered them — mistakes, corrections, and all.

REMEMBER

- While WordPerfect is recording a macro, you cannot use the mouse to move the cursor or to block text. If you need to move the cursor or block text, you have to use the keyboard. Remember that Alt-F4 is the Start Block-Marking key.
- As soon as you press Ctrl-F10 to stop recording your macro, WordPerfect displays a *Compiling Macro* message box on-screen. After a brief moment, this message goes away by itself.

TIP

Cool macro-naming tips

WordPerfect's macros must be named like DOS filenames, which doesn't leave much room for creativity — something you're already familiar with and moaning about. However, there are some secret names you can give certain macros that make them really cinchy to run. These macros are the Alt-key macros, which run when you press certain Alt-key combinations.

For example, suppose that you want a macro to run every time you press the Alt-Z key combination. If so, name it ALTZ — that's Alt followed by the letter you want to assign the macro. So the ALTZ macro is instantly run when you press the Alt-Z key combination.

This naming technique is the best way to run macros, but there are some limitations. First, you don't want to give your macro the same name as an important WordPerfect key combination. For example, the Alt-F combination activates the File menu. Also, you can't use numbers or other symbols, just letters. That limits you a bit, but it's still the easiest and best way to name macros you use frequently.

Creating Macros from Scratch (the Hard Method)

Grandmothers are famous for making cookies from scratch. Such cookies almost always taste better than mass-produced factory cookies, and they're fun to make — but cleaning up the mess is a pain. The same holds true for making macros from scratch. Such macros may give you more control over WordPerfect, but they're more troublesome to create.

If you insist on making your own macros from scratch, here's how to do it:

1. **Press Ctrl-F10.**

   The Record Macro dialog box appears (see Figure 17-1).

2. **Type the name of your macro.**

   The macro name is a filename WordPerfect uses to save your macro to disk. The same file-naming rules apply here; macro names are limited by DOS's eight-character maximum length. Be descriptive — if it's possible.

3. **Press Enter.**

   After a few moments (depending on how slow your computer may be), WordPerfect displays the message *Recording Macro* in the lower-left corner of the screen.

4. **Press Ctrl-F10 to stop recording your macro.**

   Ha! Fooled them.

5. **Press F5.**

   The Specify File Manager List dialog box appears.

6. **Press F8.**

   The Directory Tree dialog box appears.

7. **Highlight the MACROS directory 'neath the WP60 directory and press Enter.**

   The File Manager dialog box appears.

8. **Highlight the macro file that you named in Step 2 and press Enter.**

   The macro file ends in WPM, so look for only the first part of the filename.

   Pressing 2 and Enter loads the macro as a document you can edit in WordPerfect. You'll lament that it contains only the following:

   ```
   DISPLAY(Off!)
   ```

9. **Underneath this first line, type all the commands that you want the macro to do.**

   See? Isn't it easy? (You were warned.) Chapter 19 contains a list of popular macro language commands for those who are daring. Otherwise, this technique is a bit complex to deal with.

   For the sake of having an honest-to-goodness example, try typing the following:

   Type ("I have no idea what I'm doing.")

   Hard Return.

   Type ("So it's a good thing I'm the boss.")

10. **Save the macro file back to disk.**

    Press Alt-F, C and choose Yes when WordPerfect asks whether you want to save the file. WordPerfect displays its *Compiling Macro* message box on-screen for a moment. Your macro is now ready to use.

- To run your macro, press Alt-F10 and type the macro name into the box. Press Enter and the computer magically types for you!
- WordPerfect's macro language contains over 1,500 commands. Nobody in his or her right mind ever uses them all.
- Because the WordPerfect manuals don't list all 1,500 macro commands, and no other book on WordPerfect does either, you can get a list of all 1,500 macro commands by doing the following: Press Alt-H, M to display the Help window. Choose Macro Commands Index, and there they are.

Getting Macros That Somebody Else Made (the Really Easy Method)

People around the world have been creating WordPerfect macros for their own use, so why bother reinventing a macro when somebody else has already created it?

If you subscribe to an on-line service, such as CompuServe, America Online, or GEnie, you can often find WordPerfect macros available for the taking. Many local bulletin board systems (BBSs) may also have WordPerfect macros that you can copy. Failing that, check if there's a WordPerfect user group in your area. User groups love collecting and handing out stuff like macros for their members.

Finally, you can break down and actually spend money (shudder!) to buy some macros. *WordPerfect Magazine* (published by WordPerfect Corporation) sells 60 macros for WordPerfect for $19.95, including shipping and handling. Just call 800-228-9626 and have your credit card ready. Happy operators are standing by to take your order.

- For those unafraid of long-distance calls, modems, and communications software, you can find many valuable macros available on WordPerfect's own BBS. Call 801-225-4414 at 1200/2400 baud or 801-225-4444 at 9600 baud.
- Don't bother asking me how to use a modem in this book. Get *Modems For Dummies.*

Pausing Macros Temporarily

Whenever you're doing something that requires thought and concentration, inevitably the phone rings, or someone you can't stand shows up.

So what happens if you're in the middle of recording a complicated macro and some jerk — like your boss — interrupts you? Rather than throw your hands up in despair and lose all your hard work, WordPerfect lets you temporarily pause your macro in the middle of recording.

When you get back to your computer, you can start recording your macro at the exact spot where you paused. In this way, you can resume your work until the next jerk interrupts you again.

To pause and unpause a macro in the middle of recording, follow these steps:

1. **Press Ctrl-PgUp to pause your macro.**

   The Macro Control dialog box appears, as shown in Figure 17-2.

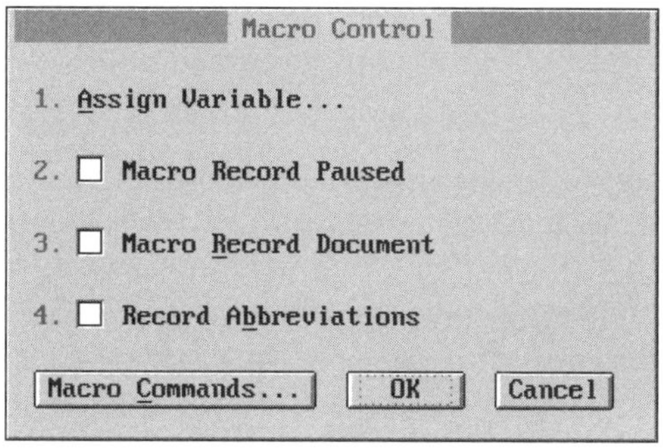

Figure 17-2: The Macro Control dialog box.

2. **Press 2 or P to put an X in the Macro Record Paused check box.**
3. **Press Enter.**

   WordPerfect temporarily pauses the recording of your macro. At this point, you can type anything you want, and it won't get recorded in your macro.

4. **Press Ctrl-PgUp to unpause your macro.**

   The Macro Control dialog box appears again.

5. **Press 2 or P to remove the X in the Macro Record Paused check box.**
6. **Press Enter.**

   At this point, anything you type gets recorded in your macro.

TIP

- Pausing a macro in the middle of recording lets you test a command to make sure that it does what you want before you store it in a macro. After you're sure that you want a certain command in your macro, return to recording your macro again.

WARNING!

- When you pause a macro, WordPerfect still displays the *Recording Macro* message on-screen. Make sure that you remember when you pause a macro recording because WordPerfect doesn't give you any visual clues to help you out.
- You can pause and unpause a macro as many times as you want.

Stopping a Macro Recording

If you're in the middle of recording a macro and suddenly realize you have no idea what you're doing, you can stop recording a macro.

Any time you want to stop recording a macro, press Ctrl-F10, the same key that ends the recording. Regardless, Ctrl-F10 stops the macro, and you can move on from there.

- Even though you may stop recording a macro before you're finished, WordPerfect still creates a macro file and stores it on disk. To completely wipe out a botched macro file, you have to erase it from your hard disk.
- Refer to "Erasing a macro from the face of the earth" later in this chapter for information on erasing macro files from your hard disk.

Editing Macros

Few people do everything perfectly the first time. If they did, we would still be using WordPerfect 1.0. Alas, "improvements" are in the nature of computer things. After you've recorded a macro, you may later decide that you want to edit it to modify, fix, or rewrite it. You can handle these changes in several ways: editing a macro, rerecording it, and utterly destroying it. The following sections mull over the details.

Editing an existing macro

Rather than create a macro from scratch, it's usually much easier to steal an existing macro, modify it, and take all the credit for its creation. In school, this is known as plagiarism. In business, this is a perfectly legitimate practice.

To edit an existing macro, follow these steps:

1. **Press Ctrl-F10.**

   The Record Macro dialog box appears.

2. **Press F5.**

   The Select List dialog box appears. The directory C:\WP60\MACROS*.* appears highlighted. If you've stored your macros in another directory, type the name of the directory.

3. **Press Enter.**

   The File List dialog box appears.

4. **Highlight the macro file that you want to edit and press Enter.**

   A dialog box appears, warning you that the file already exists. So it does.

5. **Press E (Edit).**

   The contents of the macro file appear, like any old document on-screen. Crack your knuckles and . . .

6. **Make the changes you want.**

   Type and edit. Refer to Chapter 19 for macro language commands.

   Okay, that's kind of rude. This step does assume you know something about macro commands (and Chapter 19 helps a great deal). Still, I admit this step is like handing someone a French dictionary and saying, "Here, speak French."

7. **Press Shift-F3.**

   WordPerfect returns you to your document.

8. **Press Ctrl-F10.**

   The *Compiling Macro* message box briefly appears. Your macro is now ready to use.

It's amazing how that works, but it does.

Rerecording an existing macro

Suppose that you have a useless macro named ALTC.WPM, which runs every time you press Alt-C. If you want another macro to run when you press Alt-C, just record a new macro and give it the same name as the macro you want to replace.

To rerecord an existing macro, follow these steps:

1. **Press Ctrl-F10.**

   The Record Macro dialog box appears.

2. **Press F5.**

   The Select List dialog box appears. The directory C:\WP60\MACROS*.* appears highlighted. If you've stored your macros in another directory, type the name of the directory.

3. **Press Enter.**

   The File List dialog box appears.

4. **Highlight the macro file that you want to rerecord and press Enter.**

   A dialog box appears, warning you that the file already exists.

5. **Press R.**

   Type whatever new commands you want the macro to contain.

6. **Press Ctrl-F10.**

   The *Compiling Macro* message box briefly appears. Your macro is now ready to use.

It's a good idea to check what the old macro did before you reassign it like this.

Erasing a macro from the face of the earth

Eventually, you'll find yourself storing on your hard disk many useless macros that you never use any more. Not only do these macros gobble up lots of hard disk space, but they clutter up your macro directory, as well.

To erase macros from the face of the earth, follow these steps:

1. **Press F5.**

   The Specify File Manager List dialog box appears.

2. **Press F8.**

   The Directory Tree dialog box appears.

3. **Highlight the directory where your macros are stored (such as C:\WP60\MACROS) and press Enter.**

   The File Manager dialog box appears.

4. **Highlight the macro file that you want to obliterate and press 6 or D (Delete).**

   A dialog box appears, asking whether you really want to delete the selected macro file.

5. **Press Y.**

   WordPerfect erases the macro file.

- Erasing a file is a sort-of permanent thing in DOS. Don't take this lightly. Although you can undelete macro files, doing so is not a license to go goofy with deleting files.
- *DOS For Dummies,* 2nd Edition, contains information on using the UNDELETE command to recover any files — including macro files — that you may have accidentally deleted.

Storing Macros in Different Directories

WordPerfect stores your macros in the C:\WP60\MACROS directory. Most people are perfectly happy to use this directory, but for those five people on the planet who insist on doing things their own way, WordPerfect lets you store macros in a different directory. I wrote the following sections at great expense for those people who feel like lousing up what WordPerfect has done just fine with up until now.

Creating a new macro directory

To create a new macro directory, follow these steps:

1. **Press F5.**

   The File Manager List dialog box appears.

2. **Press F5 again. Highlight Current <Dir> and press H.**

   The Change Default Directory dialog box appears.

3. **Type the name of a new macro directory, such as C:\MACROS, and press Enter.**

   A dialog box appears, asking whether you really want to create a new directory.

4. **Press Y.**

5. **Press F7 to return to your document.**

REMEMBER

Although you don't see it, WordPerfect creates your new directory.

- There is no reason to create a new macro directory.
- Okay, one reason *may* be if you need a network macro directory because you are hooked up to some network contraption. Even then, I don't know whether the new directory would work, given the strange and dangerous nature of computer networks.
- The directory doesn't need to be named MACROS. You can call it anything — BOB, for example. WordPerfect isn't fussy on the subject.

Telling WordPerfect to use your new macro directory

After you've created a new macro directory, WordPerfect completely ignores it and continues looking for macros in its favorite C:\WP60\MACROS directory.

To tell WordPerfect to use your new macro directory, follow these steps:

1. **Press Shift-F1.**

   The Setup dialog box appears.

2. **Press 5 or L.**

   The Location of Files dialog box appears.

3. **Press 2 or M.**

   The Macros/Keyboards/Button Bar dialog box appears, as shown in Figure 17-3.

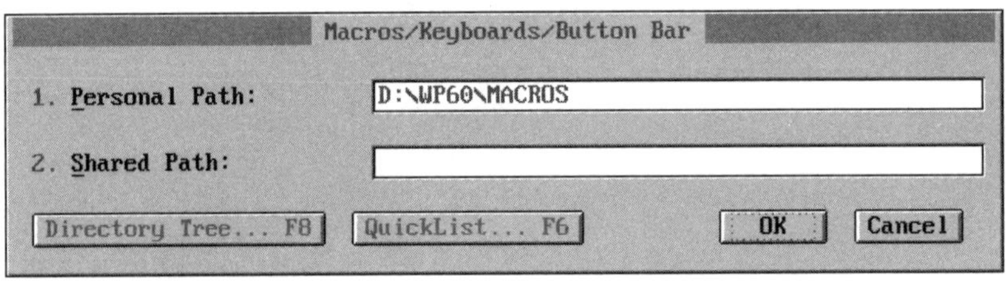

Figure 17-3: The Macros/ Keyboards/ Button Bar dialog box.

4. **Press 1 or P.**

5. **Press F8.**

   The Directory Tree dialog box appears.

6. **Highlight the directory where you want to store your macros and press Enter.**

   WordPerfect is now wise to your new macro directory.

7. **Press Home, F7 to return to your document.**

   I assume that the Shared Path item is for networking macro directories. Go figure. I'm not a network pro, anyhow.

Moving existing macros into your new macro directory

After you've told WordPerfect to use your new macro directory, it completely ignores any existing macros stored in another directory. (Now you know why most people prefer to use the default C:\WP60\MACROS directory instead.)

To move existing macros into your new macro directory, follow these steps:

1. **Press F5.**

   The Specify File Manager List dialog box appears.

2. **Press F8.**

   The Directory Tree dialog box appears.

3. **Highlight the directory where your existing macros are stored and press Enter.**

   The File Manager dialog box appears.

4. **Press F.**

   The Find dialog box appears.

5. **Press 1 or N.**

   The Find Name dialog box appears.

6. **Type *.WPM and press Enter.**

   WordPerfect displays only macro files with the file extension of WPM.

7. **Press Home, Shift-8.**

   WordPerfect marks all the WPM macro files with an asterisk.

8. **Press 5 or M.**

   A dialog box appears, asking whether you want to move all the marked files.

9. **Press Y.**

   A Move/Rename dialog box appears.

10. **Press F8.**

    A Directory Tree dialog box appears.

11. **Highlight the new macro directory you want to store the macros in and press Enter.**

12. **Press Home, F7 to return to your document**

    They're all moved, one by one, to the new directory. There. You've gone to a great deal of work to redo what WordPerfect had done just fine to begin with.

Converting WP 5.1 Macros to WP 6 Macros

Using your old favorite WordPerfect 5.1 macros in WordPerfect 6 is possible, but you must jump through a few hoops first. The old macros don't run as is; you have to convert them first. If you try to run a WordPerfect 5.1 macro in WordPerfect 6, WordPerfect 6 screams and displays an Incorrect Format dialog box.

To convert a WordPerfect 5.1 macro to a WordPerfect 6 macro, follow these steps:

1. **Exit out of WordPerfect.**

   I'm free! I'm free!

2. **At the DOS prompt, type MCV.**

   MCV is the macro conversion program. WordPerfect asks for an Input file or pattern.

3. **Type the WordPerfect 5.1 macro file that you want to convert, including the directory, such as C:\WP51\ALTI.WPM. Then press Enter.**

   WordPerfect asks for the Output file or path.

4. **Type the directory and the macro filename where you want to store the converted macro file.**

   Magically, WordPerfect converts your WordPerfect 5.1 macro into a WordPerfect 6 macro.

- You don't have to type the WPM file extension each time because WordPerfect assumes that anyway.
- For simple macros, WordPerfect's macro conversion program works almost perfectly. For complicated macros, the conversion may not be 100 percent accurate. For such macros, be prepared to do some minor editing so that they work in WordPerfect 6.

The 5th Wave By Rich Tennant

"TECHNICALLY HE'S A WIZARD, BUT AS A MANAGER HE LACKS PEOPLE SKILLS."

Chapter 18

Using Your Own Macros

In This Chapter

- Running macros the generic way
- Making Button Bar macros
- Assigning macros to keyboard layouts
- Stopping macros from running

No matter how wonderful your macros may be, they're worthless if you can't use them. In the spirit of democracy and confusion, WordPerfect provides four ways to run a macro: Press Alt-F10 and choose the macro you want to use; press an Alt-*(letter)* combination; click the mouse on a macro button in the Button Bar; and press an Alt-*(letter)* or Ctrl-*(letter)* combination. I won't bother to mention the "don't bother with macros" option because macros are the subject at hand here.

This chapter is all about your own macros — running them and using them. There are even some clever tricks in here about secretly coding a macro to a special keyboard layout.

Running Macros the Generic Way

Here's a foolproof but somewhat clumsy way to run any macro stored in your macro directory.

To run any macro, follow these steps:

1. **Press Alt-F10.**

   The Play Macro dialog box appears.

2. **Press F5.**

   The Select List dialog box appears. WordPerfect highlights the default macro directory. If you stored your macros in another directory but didn't bother telling WordPerfect, type the directory name now.

3. **Press Enter.**

   The File List dialog box appears.

4. **Highlight the macro you want to run and press Enter.**

   WordPerfect goes off and does whatever.

- If you know the name of the macro, you can type it in Step 1 and press Enter. In this way, you don't have to go through the remaining three steps. You can type just the macro name (such as CALC) or the full macro name (such as CALC.WPM).
- If you press the down-arrow key after Step 1, WordPerfect displays the last four macros you used. Just highlight one of these macro names and press Enter to run it.

Making Button Bar Macros

If pressing an Alt-*(letter)* keystroke combination is still too much work for you, WordPerfect lets you display macros at the top of the screen on a Button Bar. To run a macro, just click the button you want.

- Refer to Chapter 1 for additional, nonmacro information on Button Bars.
- You must have a mouse to use the Button Bar. If you don't have a mouse, skip this section and reward yourself with a cookie or something.

Putting a macro on a Button Bar

To put an existing macro on a Button Bar, follow these steps:

1. **Press Alt-V, S, E.**

   The Edit Button Bar dialog box appears.

2. **Press 3 or C (Add Macro).**

   The Macro Button List dialog box appears. This is a list of all the macros in WordPerfect's macro directory.

3. **Highlight the macro that you want to add to the Button Bar and press Enter.**

4. **Press Home, F7 to return to your document.**

   Your macro is added as the last button on the current Button Bar.

- If your Button Bar displays little icons, your macro button will have a cassette tape as an icon. This is about as creative as WordPerfect can get.
- The name on the Button Bar is the same as the macro filename, which makes for some cryptically named buttons with cassette recorder icons on them.
- Remember that not all the buttons may appear on your Button Bar at once. Use the up and down triangles at the left edge of the Button Bar to display different buttons.

Removing a macro from a Button Bar

Button Bars are best suited for displaying commonly used macros. If you want to remove a useless macro button from a Button Bar displayed on-screen, follow these steps:

1. **Press Alt-V, S, E.**

   The Edit Button Bar dialog box appears.

2. **Highlight the macro you want to remove from the Button Bar.**

   Use the up- and down-arrow keys to move the highlight around.

3. **Press 5 or D (Delete Button).**

   The Delete dialog box appears.

4. **Press Y to zap it to Kingdom Come.**
5. **Press Home, F7 to get back to your document.**

   This removes your macro button from your current Button Bar.

Moving macros on a Button Bar

Every time you add a macro to a Button Bar, WordPerfect puts the macro button dead last. If you want to move a macro button to a new location on a Button Bar displayed on-screen, follow these steps:

1. **Press Alt-V, S, E.**

   The Edit Button Bar dialog box appears.

2. **Highlight the macro you want to move on the Button Bar.**

   Use the up- or down-arrow keys to move the highlight bar.

3. **Press 6 or M (Move).**

   Move the cursor to the location where you want the macro button to appear on the Button Bar (first, second, third, and so on).

4. **Press Enter to paste the button in its new position.**

5. **Press Home, F7 to return to your document.**

   The Button Bar displays the new position of your macro.

There's really no point in getting overly fussy here because all macros look alike. However, you can move the macro buttons around to prevent them from being butt last on the Button Bar, where you have to use the up or down triangles to see them on-screen.

Assigning Macros to Keyboard Layouts

Macros can be directly married to the keys on your keyboard thanks to WordPerfect's fiddle-dee-dee attitude about where the key commands are (see Chapter 6 for more information on the keyboard and WordPerfect's fiddle-dee-dee attitude).

Although there is a macro keyboard layout you can use to access macros easily, you don't have to be that drastic. WordPerfect lets you assign macros to any two-keystroke combinations with the Ctrl key, such as Ctrl-G. The following sections discuss how to do and undo the macro key combinations.

Assigning an existing macro to a keyboard layout

To assign an exciting macro to a key combination on your keyboard, follow these steps:

1. **Press Shift-F1.**

   The Setup dialog box appears.

2. **Press 4 or K (Keyboard Layout).**

   The Keyboard Layout dialog box appears.

3. **Highlight the keyboard layout you want to assign a macro to.**

   Or just keep using the same keyboard you've been using, which should be highlighted already.

You shouldn't mess with the *[ORIGINAL]* layout, which isn't a problem because you can't do the next step unless you're highlighting one of the other keyboard setups.

4. **Press 3 or E (Edit).**

   The Edit Keyboard dialog box appears.

5. **Press 1 or C (Create).**

   The Create Key dialog box appears.

6. **Type the keystroke combination you want to use.**

   For example, **Ctrl-S** for an S-something macro.

7. **Press 5 or M (Macro).**

8. **Press 2 or R (Retrieve Macro).**

   The Retrieve Macro dialog box appears. Here you can type in the name of your macro, if you know it. Or press F5, Enter and highlight the macro you want to use. Press Enter to select it.

   Meanwhile, back in the Create Key dialog box . . .

9. **Press 2 or D (Description).**

   Type a short description of your macro and press Enter twice.

   The Edit Keyboard dialog box appears.

10. **Press Tab and Enter.**

11. **Press Esc twice to return to your document and enjoy using your new keyboard macro.**

- WordPerfect's menus always display the same key combinations for certain commands, regardless of whether you've changed them. For example, the command for saving a file is Ctrl-F12. If you reassign the Ctrl-F12 keystroke combination to do something different, WordPerfect's menus don't reflect this change.

- For a fun practical joke, reassign all of WordPerfect's commands on a friend's computer so that they do the exact opposite of what most people expect. Rather than having Ctrl-F12 save a document, have Ctrl-F12 erase all the files on the hard disk. See how much fun macros can be? And you thought I was kidding when I said that learning macros can make you more valuable in your job.

Removing a macro from a keyboard layout

In case some joker actually follows the preceding steps, or if you want to remove a macro from a keyboard layout, follow these steps:

1. **Press Shift-F1.**

   The Setup dialog box appears.

2. **Press 4 or K (Keyboard Layout).**

   The Keyboard Layout dialog box appears.

3. **Highlight the keyboard layout file containing the macro you want to remove.**

4. **Press 3 or E (Edit).**

   The Edit Keyboard dialog box appears.

5. **Highlight the macro you want to remove.**

6. **Press 3 or D (Delete Mapping).**

   A dialog box appears, asking whether you really want to delete this macro from the keyboard layout.

7. **Press Y.**

8. **Press Tab and then press Enter twice.**

REMEMBER

- Deleting a macro from a keyboard layout does not erase the macro from your hard disk.
- You can always switch back to the ORIGINAL keyboard layout if you tire of the one you created with macros.

Stopping Macros from Running

Macros (like most software) have the potential to run amok. Face it, not everything in a computer does exactly what you think it should do. In case you run a macro that seems to be running amok, here are two magic tricks that stop any macro dead in its tracks:

- Press Esc.

  or

- Press Ctrl-Break.
- Unless you have lightning-quick reflexes, you probably can't stop a macro while it's running — because macros run at the blink of an eye. Still, it's nice that WordPerfect gives you this option, although you'll probably never be able to use it.
- On some keyboards, the Break key is the Pause key. This key may have *Pause* printed on top and *Break* printed on the side. Why do keyboard manufacturers do this? Watch the next episode of *Unsolved Mysteries* for the answer.

Chapter 19
WordPerfect's Macro Language

In This Chapter

- Dissecting a WordPerfect macro
- Keystroke commands
- Cursor-movement commands
- Editing commands
- Screen-display commands
- Text-appearance commands
- Branching commands
- Loop commands
- Subroutine commands
- Debugging macros
- Getting more information

Believe it or not, WordPerfect's macro language is a full-blown programming language like C, BASIC, or Pascal. If you've sworn that you'll never learn any type of programming, skip this chapter. For those who enjoy giving orders to something that will actually listen, this chapter explains many of WordPerfect's macro-language commands.

This chapter isn't meant to give you a comprehensive explanation of macros; just a small taste so that you can see what some of WordPerfect's macros can do. But a fair warning: This is all very technical, and it's slim on how-tos and why's-thats.

Dissecting a WordPerfect Macro

When you record a macro, WordPerfect stores your commands in a macro file. To see how WordPerfect's macro commands work, follow these tutorial steps:

1. **Press Ctrl-F10.**

   The Record Macro dialog box appears.

2. **Type a name for your macro, such as TEST, and press Enter.**

   You're back in your document, but it says *Recording Macro* in the lower-left corner of the status bar.

3. **Type the following:**

   Don't learn WordPerfect.

4. **Press Enter.**
5. **Press Tab.**
6. **Type the following:**

   Make your assistant learn it instead.

7. **Press Ctrl-F10.**

   The macro is done. Now it's time to peek inside and see what makes it tick.

8. **Press F5.**

   The Specify File Manager List dialog box appears.

9. **Press F8.**

   The Directory Tree dialog box appears.

10. **Highlight MACROS and press Enter.**

    The File Manager dialog box appears.

11. **Highlight the macro name you created in Step 2 and press Enter.**

    For example, highlight TEST and press Enter. You see the macro document displayed in WordPerfect, looking a little bit like Figure 19-1.

12. **Press F7, N, N after you're done a-gawkin'.**

```
DISPLAY (OFF!)

Type ("Don't learn WordPerfect.")

HardReturn

Tab

Type ("Make your assistant learn it instead.")
```

Figure 19-1: A sample macro.

- This is an example of a WordPerfect *recorded macro*. Refer to Chapter 17 for more information on recording macros.
- Everything you see is a *macro command*. The TYPE command types text on-screen. So what you see is the command to retype the text you typed when WordPerfect was recording the macro.
- Special characters have their own macro commands: HARDRETURN is the command for pressing the Enter key; TAB is the command for pressing the Tab key.
- Notice that any backspaces you typed are ignored. WordPerfect is wise enough to see the whole picture and not every teeny mistake you type. However, if you were typing commands (Alt-F7 and so on), WordPerfect does record them, no matter what.

How a WordPerfect macro works

A macro file is nothing more than a glorified list of instructions that WordPerfect follows, line by line. The macro in Figure 19-1 contains five lines. Here's what each line does:

> *DISPLAY(Off!)* temporarily freezes the screen until the macro is done. After the macro is done, it displays the result. If the first line were *DISPLAY(On!)*, the macro would update the screen at every command, and it would look junky. For a short macro, this wouldn't be a problem, but for a large macro, you would see menus popping up and letters typing all by themselves as if a ghost were typing at your keyboard. The *DISPLAY(Off!)* command actually makes your macro run faster because it doesn't bother updating the screen after every command.

Type("Don't learn WordPerfect.") tells WordPerfect to type whatever appears between the quotes inside the parentheses.

HardReturn tells WordPerfect to enter a hard return — as if you pressed the Enter key on the keyboard.

Tab tells WordPerfect to enter a tab — as if you pressed the Tab key on the keyboard.

Type("Make your assistant learn it instead.") tells WordPerfect to type whatever appears between the quotes inside the parentheses.

After WordPerfect realizes there are no more commands left in the macro file, it stops, and the macro is finished running. Once again, you have control over your computer.

Types of macro commands

WordPerfect provides over 1,500 macro commands for your amusement, although you have to be out of your mind to think you can ever learn to master more than a fraction of them. Fortunately, the most common macro commands fall into one of the categories in Table 19-1.

Table 19-1 Categories for Macro Commands

Category	*What the Macro Command Does*
Keystroke command	Mimics a user or a poltergeist pressing keys on the keyboard
Cursor-movement command	Moves the cursor around
Editing command	Deletes stuff from a document
Screen-display command	Controls the appearance of your screen
Text-appearance command	Controls formatting, such as margins, line spacing, and fonts
File-management command	Saves, copies, deletes, or somehow manipulates a file
Operator command	Lets your macros add, subtract, multiply, divide, and compare values
Branching command	Gives your macros the capability to make decisions for themselves
Loop command	Gives your macros the capability to repeat a series of macro commands
Subroutine command	Lets you divide a large macro into small parts to make them easier to write and debug

- There is no need to memorize Table 19-1.
- The sections that follow detail some of the more interesting commands in each of these categories. Feel free to watch TV while you scan the commands.
- WordPerfect is not case sensitive, which means it can care less whether you type a macro command in ALL UPPERCASE, all lowercase, or a cOMbiNatiON oF lOWErcaSe aNd uPPercASE. But WordPerfect does scream if you misspell a command.

Keystroke Commands

These commands let a macro use any key on your keyboard. They're useful when you want a macro to type large amounts of text over and over again, such as names, numbers, or alibis.

The TYPE command

The macro command to display text is the TYPE command. It looks like this:

```
Type("Are we having fun yet?")
```

This TYPE command prints the text *Are we having fun yet?* on-screen.

- Text may also be referred to as a *string of text* or just a *string* in WordPerfect macro lingo. Brace yourself for that: string = text.
- Text that the TYPE command displays appears in your document just as if you typed it yourself. If the text flops over the right margin, WordPerfect wraps it back to the start of the next line.
- The TYPE command does not "press Enter" when it's done displaying text. For that, you need a separate command on another line, the HARDRETURN command, covered in the section "Other special key commands" somewhere in this chapter.
- Obviously, anything enclosed in the quotation marks gets typed on-screen, even four-letter words and words that aren't considered politically correct. If the string is long enough, WordPerfect automatically word-wraps it to the next line.

Typing the date

If you want your macro to type today's date and time, the TYPE command is useless. Instead, you have to use one of the following commands:

```
DateText
DateCode
```

- The DATETEXT command prints the date that you ran the macro last. It is equivalent to pressing Shift-F5, T.
- The DATECODE command prints today's date. This date always reflects today's date, which is equivalent to pressing Shift-F5, C.

Other special key commands

There are four other macro commands that represent various keys you press on the keyboard.

For pressing the Enter key, WordPerfect has the ENTERKEY and HARDRETURN commands.

For pressing the Tab key, there are the TAB and BACKTAB commands.

- Both the ENTERKEY and HARDRETURN commands mimic pressing the Enter key. Use whichever boggles your mind less.
- A BACKTAB command is the same as pressing the Shift-Tab keys. It's used in some dialog boxes to get from one area to another. I assume it may do something else fancy in WordPerfect, but I have neither the time nor inclination to look that up right now.
- No, it's BACK*TAB* not BACK*STAB*.

Text-blocking commands

The commands in Table 19-2 mimic the text-blocking techniques that you use with the mouse or Alt-F4. The cursor must be properly positioned before you use any of these commands.

Table 19-2 Text-Blocking Macro Commands

Command	*Size of Text Blocked*
BlockOn(CharMode!)	Character
BlockOn(WordMode!)	Word
BlockOn(SentenceMode!)	Sentence
BlockOn(ParagraphMode!)	Paragraph
BlockOn(PageMode!)	Page
BlockOn(DocMode!)	Entire document

- These commands only *block* the text; they don't do anything with the text. To manipulate the text, you need to use other text-manipulation macro commands.
- To turn off the blocked (highlighted) text, use the BLOCKOFF command.

Getting input from the user

There are a few macro commands that get input from the user — just like WordPerfect does. To ask the user for information, you can use the following command:

```
GetString(Name; "What is your name?"; "Name?")
```

The GETSTRING command displays a dialog box on-screen, as shown in Figure 19-2. *"What is your name?"* becomes the prompt, and *"Name?"* becomes the dialog box's title. Whatever the user types is saved in the *Name* variable.

Figure 19-2: A GETSTRING dialog box.

- The longest string a user can type in a GETSTRING dialog box is 128 characters, including spaces.
- WordPerfect stores — in a variable called *Name* — whatever the user types in the dialog box. To type this string back out again, use the TYPE command, as follows:

```
Type (Name)
```

Giving the user multiple choices

The GETSTRING command retrieves a single string from the user. But if you want to give the user up to nine choices, you need to use this command:

```
MenuList (Choice; {"Option 1"; "Option 2"})
```

This MENULIST command displays a dialog box on-screen, as shown in Figure 19-3.

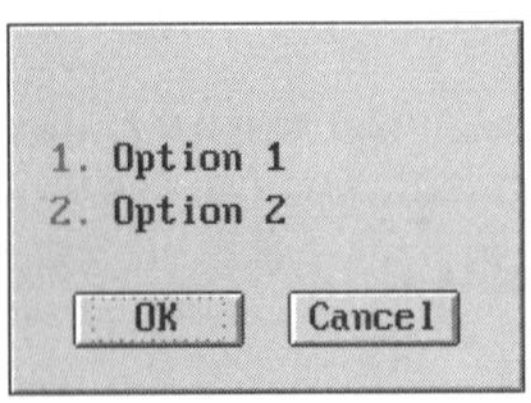

Figure 19-3: A MENULIST dialog box.

To choose an option displayed in the dialog box, the user just needs to type a number between 1 and 9.

- The options are enclosed in curly brackets, not parentheses.
- Whichever option the user selects is saved in the variable *Choice*. The macro somehow examines that option and then does something with it.

Cursor-Movement Commands

This is the scary poltergeist stuff. Sometimes your macro may need to move the cursor to a certain place in a document before doing anything else. If so, there are lots of commands that make this happen. Rather than text all this to death, I listed all the cursor-movement macro commands in handy Table 19-3.

Table 19-3 Cursor-Movement Macro Commands

Command	*Moves the Cursor. . .*
PosDocBottom	To the bottom of the document
PosDocTop	To the top of the document
PosPageBottom	To the bottom of the page
PosPageTop	To the top of the page
PosPageNext	To the next page
PosPagePrevious	To the preceding page
PosWordNext	To the next word
PosWordPrevious	To the previous word
PosLineDown	To the next line (down-arrow key)
PosLineUp	To the previous line (up-arrow key)
PosLineBeg	To the beginning of the line
PosLineEnd	To the end of the line

The cursor-movement macro commands don't require any options, parentheses, or flunkies to work. Just stick them on a line by themselves to make the cursor your slave.

Editing Commands

Stuffed into handy Table 19-4, you'll find the first batch of macro-delete commands. Zap! Whatever the cursor is hovering next to is gone, depending on which command you use. Be careful with these commands; they delete automatically and without mercy.

Table 19-4 Ugly Delete-Stuff Macro Commands

Command	*What It Deletes*
DeleteWord	A word (Ctrl-Backspace)
DeleteToBeginningOfWord	From the cursor to the beginning of a word
DeleteToEndOfWord	From the cursor to the end of a word
DeleteToEndOfLine	From the cursor to the end of the line (Ctrl-End)
DeleteToEndOfPage	To the end of the page (Ctrl-PgDn)
BlockDelete	A block of text

- You must have a block of text marked before you can use the BLOCKDELETE command. Refer to Table 19-2 in the "Text-blocking commands" section in this chapter for a taste of text-blocking commands.
- These are wiseperson-only macros. Because what you delete depends on where the cursor is, using these commands casually can really foul up your text.

Screen-Display Commands

Screen-display commands give your macros a quick way to change the way your screen looks. You can change your screen from Text mode to Graphics mode, Page mode, or any combination. There is really only one command to change your screen — DISPLAYMODE( ). It's what you stick in the parentheses that forces WordPerfect to change its mode.

To change to Text mode, use this command:

```
DisplayMode(Text!)
```

To change to Graphics mode, use this command:

```
DisplayMode(Graphics!)
```

To change to Page mode, use this command:

```
DisplayMode(FullPage!)
```

Yeah, those really are exclamation points in the parentheses. This must be an exciting thing for WordPerfect to do.

Text-Appearance Commands

The TYPE command displays text on-screen. But if you want your text in bold or italics, you have to tell WordPerfect to make the visual adjustment beforehand with the following macro command:

```
AttributeAppearanceOn()
```

The information in the parentheses tells WordPerfect which text attribute to apply to any text the macro types. To turn off the attribute, you need the following command:

```
AttributeAppearanceOff()
```

For example, to turn on italics, use this command:

```
AttributeAppearanceOn(Italics!)
```

Now the TYPE macro command displays text in italics. To turn off italics, use the following command:

```
AttributeAppearanceOff(Italics!)
```

To turn underlining on and off, use these commands:

```
AttributeAppearanceOn(Underline!)
AttributeAppearanceOff(Underline!)
```

To turn bold on and off, use these commands:

```
AttributeAppearanceOn(Bold!)
AttributeAppearanceOff(Bold!)
```

To turn off attributes completely, as if you pressed Ctrl-N, use this command:

```
AttributeNormal
```

In a classic *Twilight Zone* episode, aliens come to Earth with a cookbook called *To Serve Man*. The WordPerfect macro equivalent is TOSERVEMAN (ToServeMan). And you know what was *really* on the menu. . . .

Branching Commands

Deep in the heart of every programming language are commands that make decisions. These are the *branching* commands — commands that do one thing or another, depending on some situation. These commands represent a more technical aspect of WordPerfect's macro language — something that gives the program a near-programming language feel — and stuff definitely worth avoiding if it leaves a bad taste in your mouth.

WordPerfect's macro language lacks a BRANCHDAVIDIAN command.

The IF command

IF commands let your program make decisions between two or more possibilities. If a certain condition is true, the computer follows one set of instructions. If that condition is false, the computer follows a different set of instructions.

The IF command has a companion ENDIF command, which ends the decision part — the part that's followed when the condition is true.

As an example, the following is a WordPerfect macro that uses the IF command to make a decision:

```
DISPLAY(Off!)
GetString(Secret; "What's the password?")
If (Secret = "Open Sesame")
  Type ("That's it!")
Endif
```

The first line temporarily freezes the display until the macro finishes.

The second line displays a dialog box, which asks *What's the password?* After the user types a string and presses Enter, WordPerfect stores this string into the variable called *Secret*.

The third line examines the *Secret* variable. If the user typed **Open Sesame** exactly, the macro would go to the fourth line. If the user did not type it correctly, the macro would stop.

The fourth line types the string *That's it!* on-screen, which is what happens when you type **Open Sesame**.

The fifth line is the end of the IF command.

The IF-ELSE command

When you want the program to examine two possibilities, you will have an ELSE command in the middle of an IF command. For a peek at a real-life example, consider the following macro:

```
DISPLAY(Off!)
GetString(Secret; "What's the password?")
If (Secret = "Open Sesame")
  Type ("That's it!")
Else
  Type ("Sorry, you blew it.")
Endif
```

The first line temporarily freezes the display until the macro finishes.

The second line displays a dialog box, which asks *What's the password?* After the user types a string and presses Enter, WordPerfect stores this string into the variable called *Secret.*

The third line examines the *Secret* variable. If the user types **Open Sesame** exactly, the macro goes to the fourth line. If not, the macro skips to the fifth line.

The fourth line types the string *That's it!* on-screen and skips to the seventh line.

The fifth line divides the two sets of instructions of the IF-ELSE command.

The sixth line types the string *Sorry, you blew it.* on-screen.

The seventh line is the end of the IF-ELSE command.

The SWITCH command

SWITCH commands let your program make multiple decisions. The SWITCH command is often used with the MENULIST command. The following is a macro example of the SWITCH command:

```
DISPLAY(Off!)
MenuList (Choice; {"Open a file";"Save a file"})
Switch (Choice)
  CaseOf 1: FileOpenDlg
  CaseOf 2: FileSaveDlg
EndSwitch
```

This macro displays a dialog box, which gives the user a choice of opening a file or saving a file. If the user presses 1, the File Open dialog box appears. If the user presses 2, the File Save dialog box appears.

Loop Commands

Most of the time, WordPerfect starts at the top of a macro file and follows the instructions one by one until it reaches the end. But if you want to repeat certain instructions over and over again, you can use one of three loop commands: WHILE loops, REPEAT-UNTIL loops, or FOR-NEXT loops.

- Loop commands are for repeating bits of the macro over and over.
- For an example of a loop command in real life, read this sentence twice.
- A loop command generally tells WordPerfect how many times to repeat itself.
- If you don't tell the loop how many times to repeat, it runs amok! Think of a macro that types *AMOK!* on-screen a zillion times, and you have an idea of what programmers call an *endless loop*.

WHILE loops

A WHILE loop repeats one or more instructions as long as a certain condition remains true. Here's the generic template for a WHILE loop:

```
WHILE (Condition)
  Instructions
ENDWHILE
```

And here's an example macro that keeps asking for a password until the user types in the right one:

```
DISPLAY(Off!)
Password = ""
WHILE (Password <> "Open")
  GetString(Password; "What is the password?")
  If (Password <> "Open")
    Prompt ("Wrong password, doofus!")
  EndIf
ENDWHILE
```

This macro displays a dialog box, which asks for a password. If the user types **Open**, the macro stops. If the user types anything else, the macro displays the message *Wrong password, doofus!* at the bottom of the screen and keeps displaying the dialog box until the user types **Open**.

REPEAT-UNTIL loops

The REPEAT-UNTIL loop repeats one or more instructions until a certain condition becomes true. Here's the generic template for a REPEAT-UNTIL loop:

```
REPEAT
  Instructions
UNTIL (Condition)
```

And here's an example macro that keeps asking for a password until the user types in the right one:

```
DISPLAY(Off!)
Password = ""
REPEAT
  GetString(Password; "What is the password?")
  If (Password <> "Open")
    Prompt ("Wrong password, doofus!")
  EndIf
UNTIL (Password = "Open")
```

This macro works exactly like the example for the WHILE loop in the preceding section.

- So what's the reason for bothering with a REPEAT-UNTIL loop versus a WHILE loop? It's techy. Do you really want to know? Well, REPEAT-UNTIL loops always execute once. A WHILE loop has the potential never to work if the condition isn't true to start with.
- See? I told you it was technical.

FOR-NEXT loops

The FOR-NEXT loop repeats one or more instructions a fixed number of times. With both the WHILE and REPEAT-UNTIL loops, you have no idea how many times the loop may repeat itself. With the FOR-NEXT loop, you control exactly how many times it loops.

Here's the generic template for a FOR-NEXT loop:

```
FORNEXT (Variable; Start; End)
  Instructions
ENDFOR
```

The FOR-NEXT loop requires three values: a variable that keeps track of the number of times the FOR-NEXT loop has worked, a starting value, and an ending value.

To make a FOR-NEXT loop repeat three times, the starting value is 1, and the ending value is 3, as follows:

```
DISPLAY(Off!)
Password = ""
FORNEXT(Var; 1; 3)
  GetString(Password; "What is the password?")
  If (Password <> "Open")
    Prompt ("Wrong password, doofus!")
  Else
    QUIT
  EndIf
ENDFOR
Type ("Access denied. Too many tries, doofus!")
```

This macro gives the user exactly three tries to type in the right password. If the user types in **Open** as the password, the macro hits the QUIT command and stops. If the user fails to type in the right password after three tries, the macro prints *Access denied. Too many tries, doofus!* on-screen.

Subroutine Commands

Dive! Dive! The easiest way to tackle a large project is to divide it into smaller ones. For example, any samurai warrior will tell you that bad guys are easier to handle after they've been sliced into little pieces. The same holds true when creating macros.

Rather than torture yourself by writing one huge macro, you can write small parts of a macro and then paste them all together to create one huge Frankensteinian macro.

To help you write macros one tiny piece at a time, WordPerfect provides three solutions:

- You can write and store subroutines within a single macro file.
- You can chain two or more macros together so that the macros run one right after another.
- You can nest macros within one another so that one macro can run another one before its completion.

Again, this is really techy programmer stuff here. A subroutine is a small, bite-sized macro that does one simple task. Other macros may use the subroutine over and over instead of having to do the work themselves.

Actually, the easiest way to tackle a large problem is to make someone else do it.

Subroutine macro commands

The idea of writing subroutines is to break up a large macro into smaller, more (hopefully) manageable parts. To write a subroutine within a macro, you need to use these four commands: LABEL, RETURN, CALL, and QUIT.

The LABEL command identifies the start of a subroutine. The RETURN command identifies the end of a subroutine. The LABEL command looks like this:

```
LABEL (SubroutineName)
```

SubroutineName can be any name up to 30 characters.

The RETURN command looks simply like this:

```
RETURN
```

Here's a sample subroutine:

```
LABEL (Greetings)
  Type ("Greetings!")
  HardReturn
  Type ("This is the subroutine running.")
RETURN
```

This isn't a macro by itself! It's only a small snippet — a subroutine to be used by another macro.

To make a macro use this subroutine, you have to use the CALL command. The CALL command looks like this:

```
CALL (Greetings)
```

A complete macro, using subroutines, may look like the one in Figure 19-4.

```
DISPLAY (OFF!)
Type ("This is the main macro running.")
HardReturn
CALL (Greetings)
Type ("Welcome back from the subroutine.")
HardReturn

//Here's the start of the subroutine
LABEL (Greetings)
  Type ("Greetings!")
  HardReturn
  Type ("This is the subroutine running.")
  HardReturn
RETURN
```

Figure 19-4: A macro that uses a subroutine.

If you run the macro in Figure 19-4, this is what you would see:

```
This is the main macro running.
Greetings!
This is the subroutine running.
Welcome back from the subroutine.
Greetings!
This is the subroutine running.
```

Because WordPerfect blindly follows each instruction listed in a macro file, line by line, it stupidly follows the instructions in the subroutine all over again. To tell a macro when to stop running, you have to use the QUIT command, like this:

```
QUIT
```

To fix the preceding example so that it doesn't run the subroutine twice, just add the QUIT command right before the subroutine. Figure 19-5 shows the fixed macro.

```
DISPLAY (OFF!)
Type ("This is the main macro running.")
HardReturn
CALL (Greetings)
Type ("Welcome back from the subroutine.")
HardReturn
QUIT
//Here's the start of the subroutine
LABEL (Greetings)
  Type ("Greetings!")
  HardReturn
  Type ("This is the subroutine running.")
  HardReturn
RETURN
```

Figure 19-5: The fixed subroutine macro.

Using the CHAIN command

The idea of using the CHAIN command is so that you can run two or more macros one after the other. By using the CHAIN command, you avoid duplicating the commands stored in another macro.

To make a macro end and run another one, just add the following command:

```
CHAIN ("macro name")
```

"macro name" includes the directory and macro file you want to run. (You don't have to add the WPM file extension.)

For example, if you want a macro to load a macro file named CAT.WPM, stored in the C:\HOUSE directory, your CHAIN command would look like this:

```
CHAIN ("C:\HOUSE\CAT")
```

Figure 19-6 shows a real-life example of a macro with the CHAIN command. It displays a menu so that you can choose which macro to use.

```
      DISPLAY (OFF!)
      MenuList (Choice;
{"Calc";"Bullet";"InitCaps"})
      Switch (Choice)
        CaseOf 1: CHAIN ("Calc")
        CaseOf 2: CHAIN ("Bullet")
        CaseOf 3: CHAIN ("InitCaps")
      EndSwitch
```

Figure 19-6: A chained macro sample.

After the user (that means you) presses 1, 2, or 3, this macro stops running and chains to another macro.

Using the NEST command

The idea of using the NEST command is for one macro to run another one. When the second macro is done, the first macro continues on. By using the NEST command, you avoid having to duplicate the commands stored in another macro.

Whenever you want to run another macro within a macro, just use this command:

```
NEST ("macro name")
```

"macro name" includes the directory and macro file you want to run. (You don't have to add the WPM file extension.)

For example, if you want a macro to load a macro file named CAT.WPM, stored in the C:\HOUSE directory, your NEST command would look like this:

```
NEST ("C:\HOUSE\CAT")
```

Figure 19-7 shows a real-life example of a macro with the NEST command. It displays a menu so that you can choose which macro to use.

```
      DISPLAY (OFF!)
      MenuList (Choice;
{"Calc";"Bullet";"InitCaps"})
      Switch (Choice)
        CaseOf 1: NEST ("Calc")
        CaseOf 2: NEST ("Bullet")
        CaseOf 3: NEST ("InitCaps")
      EndSwitch
```

Figure 19-7: A nested macro example.

This macro works almost exactly like the one using the CHAIN command in Figure 19-6. The only difference is that this macro temporarily stops running while it nests to another macro. If there were any more commands in this macro, they would run after the nested macros finish.

Any macros that you run with the NEST command must *not* include the QUIT command. If you do run a macro with the NEST command that includes the all-powerful QUIT command, all your macros immediately stop (QUIT) before finishing.

Debugging Macros

Macros, like most pieces of software, rarely work the first time you write them. Before using (and trusting) a macro with a real document, test it on an empty document or on a document belonging to someone you don't like.

If your macro refuses to work properly, you have three choices:

- *Rerecord it.* If the macro is really messed up, this may be the simplest choice.
- *Edit and debug it.* If the macro almost works, but not quite, this choice is easier than rerecording the whole thing, especially if it's a complicated macro that took you a long time to write in the first place.
- *Cry.* This doesn't help fix your macro, but crying has been medically proven to reduce stress and anxiety, especially among laboratory mice dying of cancer.

Watching your macros screw up

The first step in debugging your macro is finding where it's screwing up. Normally, you see only the results of a macro, but you don't see it work step by step.

To make your macro run step by step, add these two commands to the top of your macro file:

```
DISPLAY(On!)
SPEED(600)
```

DISPLAY(On!) means your macro works right before your eyes.

SPEED(600) slows down your macro so that it doesn't flash by before you can blink. Without otherwise being told, macros run without delay. By using the SPEED command, you can vary the speed that your macro runs by tenths of a second.

- The minimum speed you can use is *SPEED(0)*, which is the normal speed. The maximum speed you can use is *SPEED(600)*, which gives a one-minute delay.
- After you see which part of your macro isn't working, you can (hopefully) edit the macro and fix it.

Commenting your macros

To make your macros easier to read, it's a good idea to use plenty of spaces and blank lines. In addition, good programmers always write comments to themselves that explain what their macros do.

Comments appear in your macro file, but WordPerfect completely ignores them. To make a comment, use the comment command, which is a double slash (//).

```
// This is a comment.
// DISPLAY (Off!)
// The above line is also a comment.
```

The comment command is great for temporarily disabling a macro command that you think is screwing up. By turning a perfectly good command into a comment, you effectively remove the command from the macro file without having to erase it.

Getting More Information

In an effort to conserve paper in a manual that most people never bother to read anyway, WordPerfect does not provide any instruction or reference material on using its macros. The only way to learn about all of WordPerfect's macros is to use the on-line help system.

If you love programming, you'll love digging into detailed, technical explanations about each WordPerfect macro command.

To display help about WordPerfect's macros, follow these steps:

1. **Press Alt-H, M.**

   The Help dialog box appears.

2. **Highlight Macro Command Index and press Enter.**

   The Help dialog box displays a complete, alphabetical listing of all 1,500 WordPerfect macro commands. Just highlight the one you want more information on and press Enter.

REMEMBER

- Fifteen hundred macro commands! It took me six weeks just to teach my dog three commands. Who are they kidding?
- The easiest way to do a macro is to record it, as discussed in Chapter 17. Other advanced stuff is left for those with way too much time on their hands.

Part IV

Advanced, Ugly Tasks Carefully Explained

The 5th Wave **By Rich Tennant**

"THE PHONE COMPANY BLAMES THE MANUFACTURER, WHO SAYS IT'S THE SOFTWARE COMPANY'S FAULT, WHO BLAMES IT ON OUR MOON BEING IN VENUS WITH SCORPIO RISING."

In this part . . .

Advanced Ugly Tasks . . . that pretty much describes about 80 percent of what WordPerfect is up to. Word processing? That's easy. Try outlining, or the equation editor, envelopes, hypertext, or any of a number of features which you know are in there but which a paralyzing fear has prevented you from attempting. Until now.

Chapter 20

Organizing with Outlining

In This Chapter

- Understanding outlines
- Making an outline
- Manipulating outlines
- Working with the Outline Edit mode
- Renumbering outlines
- Doing the Outline Button Bar

Weren't outlines those things you loathed from English class? Incomprehensible and often called "busy work," outlines were a really messy way to dispense with your mom's old 3x5 recipe cards, theoretically forcing you to organize your thoughts so you'll know what you need to write about next. Yeah, like a 15-year-old had need for such a device.

As it usually happens, by the time you start writing, you'll need to change topics around, add new ones, and delete old ones. By the time you finish writing, your final paper bears no resemblance to your original outline. That's fine they told you, which was still a weak justification for doing an outline in the first place: "Here, do this work so that you can ignore it later." It made all those leg lifts in P.E. justified somehow.

To avoid getting bogged down with outlines all over again, WordPerfect offers an outlining feature. It lets you easily create and modify an outline, or create just a series of random thoughts. When your outline is complete, you use WordPerfect to write your final paper. Supposedly, that's how it works. This chapter shows you the nuts and bolts of it all.

Understanding Outlines

Outlines consist of headings and subheadings. A heading represents a main idea and a subheading represents an idea that (hopefully) supports the main idea.

To make outlines easy to read, WordPerfect numbers an outline by using Roman numerals, letters, and ordinary numbers. Figure 20-1 shows how this is supposed to work.

I. The parts of an outline
    A. Headings
    B. Sub-headings
    C. Numbers and letters to identify each
II. Special terms used to describe outlines
    A. Outline topic
    B. Levels
    C. Body text
    D. Family

Figure 20-1: How an outline is supposed to look and feel.

- The keen thing about outlines in WordPerfect (as opposed to those darn 3x5 cards) is that what starts out as your outline can eventually become your document. You just keep editing and adding text and eventually you have a document. Supposedly.
- Four keen terms you should associate with an outline are Topics, Levels, Body text, and Family. These are covered individually in the following sections (and also listed in Figure 20-1).
- As an aside, this book's predecessor, *WordPerfect For Dummies,* was written in only ten days thanks to an outline. Of course, I worked on the outline for about three months. But in the end, it was so tight and clean that creating the final book was merely a matter of fleshing out the outline.

Outline topics

Outline topics represent the basic structure of your outline. Ideally, each topic consists of a single line, although you can get carried away and create a 25-line outline topic if you want. Of course, if you do that, your outline will lose its pristine appearance and look like a typical document.

- The outline for this book (see the table of contents) has topics that consist of the major parts and subtopics that contain all the chapter titles.
- If you're using WordPerfect's outlining capabilities to write a speech, start with all your key points as major topics. Then build down the *levels* from that point.

Levels

A level defines the position of a topic within an outline. There are usually major levels; then sublevels; then sub-sublevels. These levels start with the grand and quickly decay down into the minuscule and obtuse.

The simplest outline might contain one level, making it look like a list:

I. Cover all the exits

II. Take all the Spam

III. Get away

A more complex outline might have two or more levels like this:

I. The joy of talking about making bread

    A. The splendor of the yeast

    B. Breads of the world

        a. From Southern Europe

        b. From Eastern Mongolia

II. The joy of bread with high caloric spreads

- Levels are measured from the left. The major levels are on the left — sublevels are usually indented one tab stop to the right. Additional sublevels are indented even more.
- The higher the level (more to the left), the broader the topic. The more indented the level, the more specific. Ideally, at the furthest indentation is text (*body text*) as opposed to broad ideas.
- Subtopics belonging to a major topic are referred to as *families*. Strange and morbid topics are called *Addams Families*.

- The nifty thing about doing this on a computer is that you can move the ideas around. You can not only change their order, but promote or demote topics to different levels.

Body text

Body text consists of a dollop of text that's attached to an outline topic. Where the outline topic briefly describes an idea, the body text elaborates on it. This is how an outline moves closer to becoming a final report or document.

I. Grandpa loses his teeth.

A. He wakes up in the morning and they're gone.

He's upset and angry, especially because folks can't understand him without his teeth. Sometimes he can get by without his lowers, but without both his lowers and uppers, listening to Grandpa is about the same as trying to recognize a tune Jim Bob is playing on his armpit.

B. He searches the house.

- The beauty of outline topics and body text is that you can structure your ideas using the outline and then flesh out your thoughts one topic at a time with the body text.
- TIP: Just focus on one topic at a time, which is much easier than thinking about the entire outline all at once. When you're done writing body text for each outline topic, WordPerfect lets you make the outline disappear and voilà: Your writing is complete.
- Body text does tend to disrupt the flow of ideas in an outline. This is why WordPerfect will let you hide or *collapse* it. That way you can get a better view of the outline's topics and organization without being distracted.

Family

A family in an outline is nothing more than a heading with one or more subheadings. To make modifying an outline easy, WordPerfect lets you move entire outlines around by families.

I. Plan to take over Europe

A. Create cool army outfits

B. Annoy the French

a. Your food really isn't that great, you know

b. French is a dead language

In the preceding outline, the whole deal under section I is a family. But subsections A and B also are families; section B has two *children* — little a and little b. (This can get awfully sentimental.)

Making an Outline

In WordPerfect you can start off with a new document as an outlines or you can make an outline in the middle of an existing document. The first approach is best for true outlining. The second may have its place — such as when referencing something — but sticking an outline in the middle of another document pretty much defeats the whole purpose of using an outline to organize your thoughts before you start writing.

To create an outline, follow these steps:

1. **Press Ctrl-F5.**

   The Outline dialog box appears.

2. **Press B (Begin New Outline...).**

   The Outline Style List dialog box appears; see Figure 20-2.

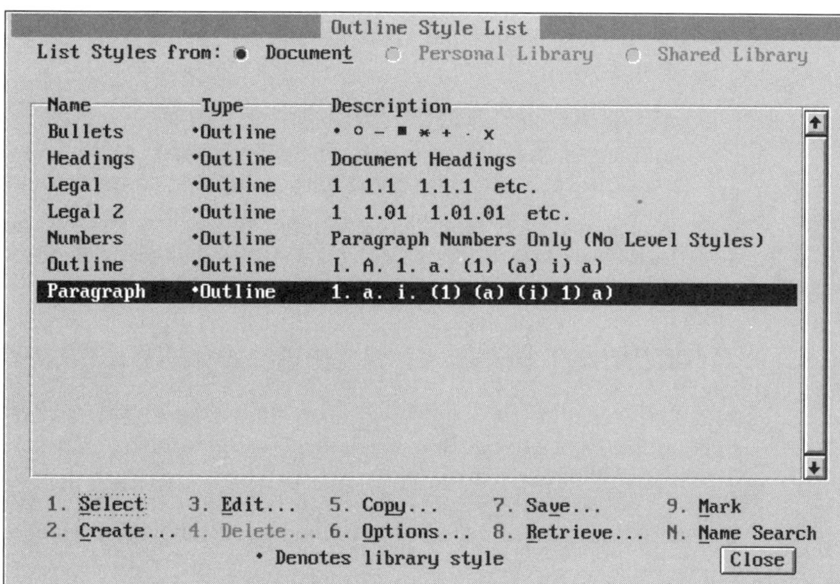

Figure 20-2: The Outline Style List dialog box.

3. Select an outline style.

Use the up- or down-arrow keys to highlight a style.

Highlight the style you want. The Outline Outline type is probably the one you're used to working with. Other strange styles are available.

4. Press S (Select).

You're whisked back to your document where WordPerfect displays a blank, numbered outline topic. For example:

I.

Your job is to now type something to fill in this outline topic.

- You'll notice that paragraph formatting goes a little spooky when you start to outline things. No problem. What you're actually working with here is an outliner, not really a word processor. Forget paragraph formatting for the time being.
- Each time you press Enter to start a new paragraph, WordPerfect automatically inserts a new outline numbering scheme.
- If you edit your document, the paragraphs change their numbering scheme to reflect what you've edited or moved.
- To create a subtopic level idea, start a new line by pressing the Tab key.
- If you change your mind about the subtopic level, press Shift-Tab to promote it up a level (move it to the left one tab position).
- In the Outline mode, paragraph = outline level.
- Outlining is on until you turn it off. So if you want to stop your outline, press Ctrl-F5, E. WordPerfect stops numbering your paragraphs.
- You can manually remove the outlining by deleting the *[Outline]* codes in the Reveal Codes window. Refer to Chapter 4 for more information.

Attaching body text to an outline topic

Although an outline topic can be as many lines as you want, it's a good idea to limit outline topics to one line. If you need to add more text, attach a block of text to an outline topic instead.

To create body text attached to an outline topic, follow these steps:

1. Move the cursor to the outline topic that you want to attach body text to.

2. Press End.

WordPerfect moves the cursor to the end of the outline topic.

3. **Press Enter.**

   WordPerfect displays a new, empty outline topic underneath.

4. **Press Ctrl-T (the Text Toggle command).**

   The outline topic number disappears.

5. **Type your body text and press Enter when you're done.**
6. **Press Ctrl-T to turn text back off.**

   WordPerfect displays a new, empty outline topic.

Moving the cursor around an outline

When you're futzing with an outline, the normal up/down, left/right cursor keys work as they always do. However, WordPerfect provides four additional ways to move the cursor around an outline, as shown in Table 20-1.

Table 20-1 Keys That Move the Cursor Around an Outline

Keystroke	*What It Does*
Alt-left arrow	Moves the cursor to the preceding heading (whether topic or subtopic)
Alt-up arrow	Moves the cursor to the preceding outline topic
Alt-right arrow	Moves the cursor to the next heading (whether topic, subtopic, or sub-subtopic)
Alt-down arrow	Moves the cursor to the next outline topic

The keys in Table 20-1 may seem silly now, but they really can help you scoot around a complex outline a lot quicker than WordPerfect's regular navigation keys.

Manipulating Outlines

Creating outlines is only half the fun. Because nobody puts her or his thoughts in any semblance of organization the first time she or he creates an outline, chances are you'll have to edit, manipulate, and generally mangle your outline until it's in the shape you want.

- Yeah, verily, this is one of the best aspects of outlining — what never comes to you in high school. If you don't like the flow, you can move topics around, up or down or in or out. WordPerfect makes it easy.
- I recommend printing your outline document any time you feel "satisfied" with it. Usually, the first time you feel satisfied isn't the last, so you'll probably mess around with it some more. Then you'll think you had things better before — that's when the printed hard copy helps prove whether you really did.

Editing an outline or body text

Hey: Good news. All of WordPerfect's normal editing commands work just the same when editing an outline topic or outline body text.

Although an outline number appears on-screen, you can't edit or delete it using WordPerfect's normal editing commands. Don't even try.

Deleting an outline topic

Whoops! They cut your speech short by 20 minutes. You'll need to delete some topics. To do so, follow these steps:

1. **Move the cursor to the outline topic you want to delete.**
2. **Press Home, left arrow.**
3. **Press Ctrl-End and then press the Delete key.**

   Essentially, what you're doing is deleting a line of text, but you need that final press of the Delete key to move up the next topic to keep them all numbered properly.

Moving an outline topic up and down

Rearranging topics in an outline is what makes WordPerfect (at $495) much better than working with 3x5 cards (at 35 cents). To move an entire outline topic up or down, follow these incredibly clumsy steps that almost make using a paper outline easier:

1. **Move the cursor to the outline topic you want to move.**
2. **Press Ctrl-F5.**

   The Outline dialog box appears.

3. **Press M (Move/Copy).**
4. **Press M (Move Family).**
5. **Move the cursor where you want the outline topic to appear.**

   If you want to move the topic up earlier in your outline, press the up-arrow key; otherwise, press the down-arrow key. This works like a cut-and-paste operation. The topic is moved to the line the cursor is on, and other topics move down in the outline.

6. **Press Enter.**

   This moves the topic to the line the cursor is on.

- These steps are very clumsy, in my opinion. You should be able to move topics around using special cursor key combinations. But no, that would make too much sense. The program just has to keep reminding you that it's WordPerfect. The crevasse between WordPerfect and making sense is just too great for any one person to cross sanely.
- Refer to the section "The mystery of the Outline Edit mode" for a better way of working with WordPerfect outlines.

Moving an outline topic left and right

Moving a topic left or right is known as promoting or demoting it. For example, if a subtopic seems to take on a life of its own, you should consider moving it up in the pecking order. This happens all the time as outlines develop, the same as major topics tend to slip down as you straighten your thoughts.

Even though moving a topic left or right — promoting or demoting — sounds like a lot of work, it's not. In fact, it's similar to indenting or unindenting a paragraph: With the cursor at the start of the topic's line, use the Tab key to indent (demote) a topic; use Shift-Tab to unindent (promote) a topic.

- To indent the outline topic to the right, press Tab. To unindent the outline topic to the left, press Shift-Tab.

- If you don't move the cursor to the beginning of the outline topic and press Tab or Shift-Tab, WordPerfect may erase part of your outline topic or do something equally unpredictable.

Hiding (and redisplaying) outline families

You'll probably find yourself working on an outline in two modes: The broad, soak-it-all-in mode and the minuscule work-on-details mode. The two modes are different and WordPerfect can help you adjust to each.

For example, if you create a huge outline and want to see the big picture, you can temporarily hide outline families from view. To do so, follow these steps:

1. **Move the cursor to the outline topic whose family you want to hide.**
2. **Press Ctrl-F5.**

   The Outline dialog box appears.
3. **Press H (Hide/Show).**
4. **Press 1 (Hide Family).**

   The outline family disappears from sight, which makes it easier to see other topics.

Because we tend to forget about things when we can't see them, you'll probably want to unhide your hidden families at some point in time. To redisplay a hidden outline family, follow these steps:

1. **Move the cursor to the outline topic whose family you want to redisplay.**
2. **Press Ctrl-F5.**

   The Outline dialog box appears.
3. **Press H (Hide/Show).**
4. **Press 2 (Show Family).**

- Unfortunately, WordPerfect offers no visual feedback that a family has been hidden. You still see the major topic, but no kids! One way around this is to block off your entire outline and then press Ctrl-F5, H, 2. Select All to see your entire outline displayed.
- Another way to deal with hidden families is to read the following section.

The mystery of the Outline Edit mode

When you hide outline families and body text, the screen looks exactly the same as if they had never existed. In case you forget that you've hidden some families or body text, WordPerfect has a way to show hidden families and body text in something called Outline Edit mode.

To view an outline in Outline Edit mode, press Ctrl-O (the letter O). This action shifts your document into Outline Edit mode, and you see the Outline toolbar, as shown in Figure 20-3.

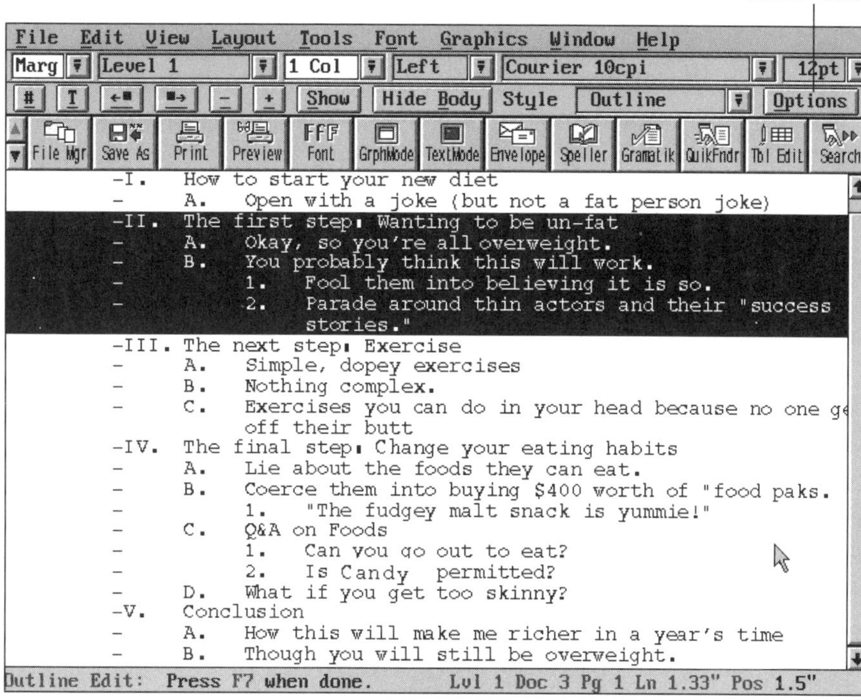

Figure 20-3: The Outline in Outline Edit mode.

- All outline topics appear with a – (minus) sign by them.
- Any outline topic with hidden families or body text appears with a + sign next to it.
- Press Ctrl-O again to return to normal editing mode.
- TIP: It's easy to move topics around in the Outline Edit mode. Use the Ctrl key with the left-, right-, up-, or down-arrow key to promote, demote, or reorder any topic.

Hiding (and redisplaying) entire outlines

After you've created your entire outline and written body text for each outline topic, you can hide the outline so only the body text remains. Doing so leaves you with your finished document, Outline mode be gone!

To get rid of the outline topics in your document, follow these steps:

1. **Press Ctrl-F5.**

   The Outline dialog box appears.

2. **Press H (Hide/Show).**
3. **Press O (Hide Outline).**

- Whoops! Did your whole outline disappear? Then you probably didn't have any body text created. Refer to the section "Attaching body text to an outline topic" earlier in this chapter for information on adding body text.
- WordPerfect gives you two choices: Either hide all body text in an entire outline or display all of it. You can't selectively hide some body text while displaying other body text.

To redisplay a hidden outline, follow these steps:

1. **Press Ctrl-F5.**

   The Outline dialog box appears.

2. **Press H (Hide/Show).**
3. **Press S (Show Levels).**

   A Show dialog box appears, listing the level numbers you can pick from. You want All, so . . .

4. **Press A and then press the Escape key (or click OK).**

   Your outline text reappears.

TIP

- You can use the preceding group of steps (to show a hidden outline) also to view an outline selectively for just one, two, or three levels. For example, if you want quickly to view an outline's major and subtopics, press Ctrl-F5, H, S and then press 2 to view only the first- and second-level topics.

Renumbering an Outline

For purely aesthetic purposes, WordPerfect lets you renumber your outlines. This means it has nothing to do with the order in which your topics are listed. No, you can renumber those topics by moving them as discussed elsewhere in this chapter. This type of renumbering refers to the style of numbers used to illustrate your outline.

For example, if your outline uses numbering like this:

I. Typical outline

A. Using Roman numerals

B. Despite the fact that

C. The Romans could never multiply

D. Large numbers

You can make it look like this:

1. Typical outline

    a. Using Arabic numerals

    b. That allowed us to multiply and

    c. Divide large numbers comfortably

    d. Without writing many bizarre symbols

To change your outline's numbering style, follow these steps:

1. **Press Ctrl-F5.**

   The Outline dialog box appears.

2. **Press O (Outline Style).**

   The Outline Style List dialog box appears.

3. **Highlight the numbering style that you prefer.**

   Use the up- or down-arrow keys to highlight a style that better suits your fancy. For example, you may like the 1.1.1 type of section outlining as opposed to the more traditional I.A.1.a. style.

4. **Press the Enter key.**

   The outline in your document window reflects the new numbering scheme.

The Outline Button Bar

In case you haven't noticed by now, manipulating outlines from the keyboard is incredibly tedious, time-consuming, and annoying—practically destroying the whole purpose of creating and manipulating outlines on a computer in the first place. If WordPerfect tries to tack on any more "advanced outlining features," it might be easier to chisel in stone instead.

But for those with a mouse, Button Bars can come to your rescue. To display the Outline Button Bar, choose View⇨Outline Bar from the menu bar, or press Alt-V, O from the keyboard. The Button Bar appears on-screen, as shown in Figure 20-4.

Figure 20-4: The Outline Button Bar.

The Outline Button Bar contains ten buttons, cussed and discussed in Table 20-2.

Table 20-2 Buttons on the Outline Button Toolbar Thing

Button	*Clicking This Button Does What?*
#	Converts body text into a regular, numbered outline topic
T	Converts a regular, numbered outline topic into body text
←■	Unindents an outline topic. This button has the same effect as pressing Shift-Tab
■→	Indents an outline topic. This button has the same effect as pressing Tab
-	Hides an outline family
+	Redisplays a hidden outline family
Show	Lets you select which levels of an outline you want to display
Hide Body	Hides or redisplays all body text
Style	Lets you renumber your outline using a different outline style
Options	Displays the Outline dialog box (the same as Ctrl-F5)

- The Outline Button Bar automatically appears when you press Ctrl-O to work with the outline in Outline Edit mode.
- You can make the Outline Button Bar a permanent part of WordPerfect's visual display by accessing the Screen Setup command. Press Ctrl-F3, Shift-F1, 1, O to select Outline Bar from the "list of things WordPerfect always tosses up on-screen." Refer to Chapter 1 for more information on screen setup.
- If you don't have a mouse, you can't use the Outline Button Bar. So there.

Chapter 21

Tools for Writers

In This Chapter

- Wringing information out of your document
- Spell-checking (or *i* before *e*)
- Choosing the right word with the Thesaurus
- Watching your language with Grammatik

Most folks are so bowled over by the entire word processing concept that they overlook some of the ways WordPerfect can help them write. This is not just "getting it on paper without eraser smudges or white-out globs" help, but the kind of help that only comes from high-priced editors and those persnickety ladies who man the Shhh! booths in libraries. Yes, WordPerfect can check your spelling, help you find the right word to say exactly what you mean (without resorting to profanity), and examine your writing to make it easier for others to understand.

This chapter concentrates on WordPerfect's tools for writers, which means just about anyone who uses the program. WordPerfect is a complete word-writing package that can turn the most poorly written drivel into finely polished, properly spelled, and grammatically correct garbage. So now you know why WordPerfect is the number one word processor in the legal profession.

Wringing Information Out of Your Document

Whenever you write anything, whether it's a report for a professional journal or a love letter to a professional working girl, WordPerfect dutifully keeps track of how many characters, words, lines, sentences, paragraphs, and pages your document uses. In addition, WordPerfect also calculates the average word length, the average number of words per sentence, the maximum number of words in a sentence, and the size of your document measured in bytes.

Why do people want to know this much detail about their writing? If you're getting paid by the word, it's nice to see how much a publisher should be paying you. If you're writing an article for publication, the editor may ask that you limit your writing to a certain word count. Or if you just want a quick snapshot of your writing style, you can see whether you're writing abnormally long (or short) sentences or using multisyllable words that nobody but an English professor from the University of Cambridge could ever understand.

To display information about your document, follow these steps:

1. **Press Alt-F1.**

   The Writing Tools dialog box appears.

2. **Press D (Document Information).**

   After churning up your hard disk for a moment, the Document Information dialog box appears, as shown in Figure 21-1. Do-dee-do. Ain't it all interesting.

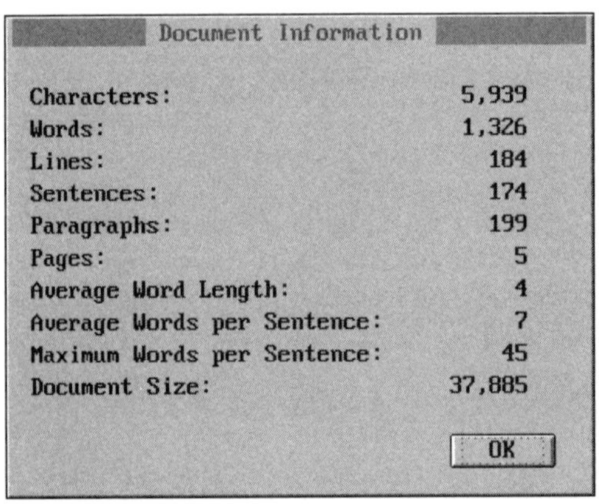

Figure 21-1: The Document Information dialog box.

3. **Press Enter.**

   Back to work.

- When WordPerfect counts words, it only counts the words in your document, not any words in your headers, footers, footnotes, endnotes, and so on.
- If your document contains lots of headings or titles, these additions throw off WordPerfect's word count. Then again, does anyone really care whether a document is 2,398 words long or 2,409 words long?

Spell-Checking (or I before E)

Poor spellers aren't necessarily dumber than good spellers; it just looks that way. After all, a business letter asking for "a business lone two start a gramar skool" won't be taken seriously if you can't spell words printed in your native language.

Rather than burden yourself with a dictionary, let WordPerfect's modern electronic dictionary handle all the dirty work of looking up properly spelled words. In this way, you can focus on converting your thoughts into words and worry about proper spelling afterwards.

Hey, just because WordPerfect has its own dictionary doesn't mean you can dispense with your Webster's. Real dictionaries contain word definitions and explain how words are used in context. WordPerfect can't do that.

Spell-checking one word

Normally, it's a good idea to let WordPerfect spell-check your document before you print it out. However, you may be writing along and suddenly wonder how to spell a particular word correctly.

To check the spelling of a single word, follow these steps:

1. **Move the cursor to anywhere under or in the word that you want to spell-check.**

   If you put the cursor between words (underneath or in a space), WordPerfect spell-checks the first word to the right of the cursor, so be precise.

2. **Press Ctrl-F2.**

   The Speller dialog box appears.

3. **Press W (Word).**

   If the word is spelled correctly, the Speller dialog box reappears. If the word is misspelled, the Word Not Found dialog box appears, and WordPerfect displays a list of alternative words to choose from.

4. **Highlight the correctly spelled word that you want to use and press Enter.**

   Use the up- or down-arrow keys to highlight a word, or you can just press the letter key associated with that word.

   If none of the words matches what you think the proper word should be, press W (Edit Word), which gives you the chance to change the word in the text. Press Enter to spell-check the word again.

5. **Press Home, F7 to return to your document.**

   Press the F7 key to give up.

Spell-checking one page

If you're adding or modifying a single page in a 300-page document, you may want to spell-check only that page. To spell-check one page, follow these steps:

1. **Press Ctrl-F2.**

   The Speller dialog box appears.

2. **Press P (Page).**

   WordPerfect starts spell-checking the entire page. After the whole page has been spell-checked, the Spell Check Completed dialog box appears.

3. **Press Enter.**

   You're done.

Aaron Spelling is a TV producer of such hits as *The Love Boat* and *Beverly Hills 90210*, which also stars his daughter Tori.

Spell-checking an entire document

After you finish writing your masterpiece, it's a good idea to spell-check the entire document for any typos or misspellings. To perform this amazing feat, follow these steps:

1. **Press Ctrl-F2.**

   The Speller dialog box appears.

2. **Press D (Document).**

   WordPerfect starts spell-checking the entire document. After the whole document has been spell-checked, the Spell Check Completed dialog box appears.

3. **Press Enter.**

   Spell-checking your document doesn't make it perfect. You still need to proofread it or run it through a grammar checker. Refer to "Watching Your Language with Grammatik" later in this chapter.

Spell-checking part of a document

Sometimes spell-checking a single page is too little, but spell-checking the entire document is too much. As an alternative, WordPerfect lets you spell-check your document starting from where you position the cursor to the end of the document. To spell-check part of a document, press Ctrl-F2 and press F (From Cursor). WordPerfect starts spell-checking from the cursor position to the end of the document. When done, the Spell Check Completed dialog box appears; press Enter to return to your document.

- Note that WordPerfect ignores any misspelled words that may appear before the cursor, so make sure that the beginning of your document is correctly spelled before using this command.
- You can also mark a chunk of text as a block and spell-check that. This option is helpful when you add text to a document that has already been spell-checked.

Looking Up How a Word Is Spelled

If you want to use a word but aren't quite sure how it's spelled, you have two choices. First, you can type the word the way you think it's spelled and then have WordPerfect check the spelling of that word. This technique is the phonetic stab-in-the-dark approach. Unfortunately, WordPerfect may think you're trying to type an entirely different word than you mean.

Second, you can have WordPerfect look up the correct spelling of a word before you type anything in your document. For your etymological pleasure, WordPerfect offers the following three ways to look up the spelling of a word:

- With the ? wildcard
- With the * wildcard
- Phonetically

A *wildcard* is a fill-in-the-blanks character you can use when you don't know the start, middle, or ending of a word. Or if you know the word has an *i* before *e* — or the other way around, but don't know which — you can use a wildcard and WordPerfect will find the proper match for you.

Looking up a word you almost know how to spell

Suppose that you know how many letters a word contains, but you don't know the exact spelling. (If you did know the exact spelling, you wouldn't be reading this section now, would you?) In this case, look up the word using the ? (question mark) wildcard. Just type the word the way you think it's spelled and type a **?** to represent any single letter that you know must exist but don't know what it is.

For example, if you want to find the correct spelling of *deceit,* but you can't remember whether the rule "*i* before *e* except after *c*" still applies, ask WordPerfect to look up the word by typing the following:

dec??t

This combination of letters and wildcards tells WordPerfect to find all six-letter words that begin with *dec* and end in *t,* such as *decent*, *decant*, and *deceit.* (The rule applies!)

To use the ? wildcard, follow these steps:

1. **Press Ctrl-F2.**

   The Speller dialog box appears.

2. **Press 5 or L.**

   The Look Up Word dialog box appears.

3. **Type the word you want to look up and use the ? wildcard to represent a single letter. Press Enter.**

   For example, type **dec??t**. WordPerfect dutifully displays all the words that match your search.

4. **Highlight the word you want to use and press Enter.**

   A dialog box appears, asking whether you want to add the highlighted word to your document.

5. **Press Y and then Esc.**

   Or if you don't want to use the word, just press Esc.

- The ? wildcard is used to represent only one character. The * wildcard represents a group of characters, from one on up to howevermany.
- This is a great feature to help you solve crossword puzzles when you really should be working. "Let's see, I need a four-letter word that begins with *s* and describes the way I feel when I'm at work. . . ."

Looking up a word you have no idea how to spell

Sometimes you may have no idea how a word is spelled, but you know it begins or ends with a certain letter. For example, what's the word that means "the study and development of word origins?" You may know that the word begins with an *e* and ends with a *gy,* but you have no idea how many or which letters may lie in between. In these tough cases, WordPerfect lets you use the * (asterisk) wildcard.

The * wildcard represents one or more letters. So asking WordPerfect to search for *e*gy* displays lots of possibilities, ranging in different lengths from *energy* and *elegy* to *ecology* and *electrobiology*.

To use the * wildcard, follow these steps:

1. **Press Ctrl-F2.**

   The Speller dialog box appears.

2. **Press 5 or L.**

   The Look Up Word dialog box appears.

3. **Type the word you want to look up and use the * wildcard to represent multiple letters. Press Enter.**

   For example, type **e*gy**. WordPerfect dutifully displays all the words that match your search.

4. **Highlight the word you want to use and press Enter.**

   A dialog box appears, asking whether you want to add the highlighted word to your document.

5. **Press Y and then Esc.**

- This is a great way to get things to rhyme. For kicks, look up all the **ing* words. Or **ology* words are fun to peruse. The **itis* wildcard locates many diseases in WordPerfect's dictionary.
- For you creative types, you can combine the ? and * wildcards together and search for words like *g?l*y*, which returns *galley, galaxy,* and *galactotherapy*.

Looking up a word when you know what it sounds like

Some people don't have the slightest idea how to spell, but they do know what the words sound like. For those people who prefer sounds over spelling, WordPerfect lets you look up the spelling of words phonetically (*fonetiklee*).

To look up a word phonetically, follow these steps:

1. **Press Ctrl-F2.**

   The Speller dialog box appears.

2. **Press 5 or L.**

   The Look Up Word dialog box appears.

3. **Type the word you want to look up — spelling it phonetically — and press Enter.**

   For example, type **fonetikalee**. WordPerfect dutifully displays words, such as *fanatical, fanatically,* and *phonetically*.

4. **Highlight the word you want to use and press Enter.**

   A dialog box appears, asking whether you want to add the highlighted word to your document.

5. **Press Y and then Esc.**

Adding Words to WordPerfect's Dictionary

WordPerfect's dictionary isn't perfect. (Although it recognizes WordPerfect, PlanPerfect, and DataPerfect as proper words, it refuses to recognize Microsoft or Borland as valid.) If you keep spelling perfectly good words, such as names, abbreviations, or words that only people in your profession would ever understand, WordPerfect continues flagging these words as misspelled each time you run the spell-checker.

The solution is to add these words to WordPerfect's dictionary so that it doesn't keep bugging you. WordPerfect provides two ways to add words, which I'll call the simple way and the clumsy way (because it explains both rather accurately).

Adding words to the dictionary (the simple way)

The quick and simple way to add words to WordPerfect's dictionary is to spell-check your document. The Word Not Found dialog box appears. When WordPerfect highlights a correctly spelled word that you want to add to the dictionary, Press T (Add to Dictionary), the third option in the Word Not Found dialog box.

WordPerfect remembers the word, puts it in your personal dictionary, and continues checking the rest of your document. You never have to worry about that word being flagged as misspelled again.

- Only add words that you see over and over again. Otherwise, limit yourself to skipping over words that are particular — and properly spelled — in one document.
- Be careful about adding words to the dictionary! If you're sloppy, you may add a word you didn't want to add. They can be a bear to get out again. (See the section "Removing words you added to the supplemental dictionary by mistake" later in this chapter for the details.)

Adding words to the dictionary (the clumsy way)

The refined but clumsy way to add words to WordPerfect's dictionary is to type the words you want the dictionary to remember. Follow these steps:

1. **Press Ctrl-F2.**

   The Speller dialog box appears.

2. **Press E (Edit Supplemental Dictionary).**

   The Edit Supplemental Dictionary dialog box appears.

3. **Select a dictionary.**

   If you want to keep WordPerfect only from flagging words in the current document, highlight Document Specific and press Enter. This choice means WordPerfect remembers the words you add for this document only.

   If you want to keep WordPerfect from flagging certain words all the time, highlight WP{WP}US.SUP and press Enter. WordPerfect remembers your special words forever and ever. Amen.

4. **Select WP{WP}US.SUP and press Enter — unless you're a masochist.**

   Another Edit Supplemental Dictionary dialog box appears.

5. **Press A (Add), which brings up the Add to Supplemental dialog box, offering you three choices:**

   Word/Phrase to Skip. This option simply skips over your word, and it's the option you should select even though you may read the descriptions of the other two items below.

   Word/Phrase with Replacement. This option lets you type commonly misspelled phrases (like teh or hte) and list the correctly spelled word that you want WordPerfect to replace it with automatically, no questions asked.

Word/Phrase with Alternates. This option lets you type commonly misspelled phrases and lists two or more correctly spelled words for you to choose from.

6. **Press S (Word/Phrase to Skip).**

   The Add Word/Phrase To Skip dialog box appears.

7. **Type the word that you want WordPerfect to ignore.**

   Type your last name, street, city, or whatever WordPerfect commonly accuses you of misspelling.

8. **Press Enter when you're done typing the word.**

   This returns you to the Edit Supplemental Dictionary dialog box.

9. **Repeat Steps 5 through 8 to add more words to the dictionary.**

10. **When you're done, press Home, F7 in the Edit Supplemental Dictionary dialog box.**

Clumsy, clumsy, clumsy. This method works, but it's really slow. That's why I recommend simply using the spell-checker and adding words as you encounter them, as described in the preceding section.

Removing words you added to the supplemental dictionary by mistake

The supplemental dictionary is really a file on disk, one that you can edit should you foolishly add a word you didn't mean to. Editing this dictionary can be a bear to do, which is why you should be careful with adding words in the first place.

To remove a word you mistakenly added to the supplemental dictionary, follow these steps:

1. **Press Ctrl-F2.**

2. **Press E (Edit Supplemental Dictionary).**

3. **Select your dictionary from the list.**

   Use the up- or down-arrow keys and press the Edit button.

   The dictionary you probably want to edit is WP{WP}US.SUP.

   After pressing Enter, you see the Edit Supplemental Dictionary dialog box.

4. **Highlight the word you want to remove from the dictionary.**

   The offending word is probably preceded by the word *SKIP*. Use the up- or down-arrow keys to search for that word. (Everything is in more-or-less alphabetical order.)

5. **Press D (Delete).**

   A confirmation dialog box appears.

6. **Press Y to really, truly zap the word.**

7. **Continue deleting words by repeating Steps 4 through 6 or . . .**

8. **Press Home, F7 when you're done.**

   This step returns you to your document for further editing. You can now rest easy because a spell-check won't include those words you just deleted from the supplemental dictionary.

Choosing the Right Word with the Thesaurus

WordPerfect's built-in Thesaurus lets you choose the right word every time. Face it, only William F. Buckley is William F. Buckley. Everyone else needs help getting the right words. Using big words isn't as important as choosing the right word. All you need to do is type a word that may be the one you want and then summon the Thesaurus. WordPerfect displays a list of words from which you can choose one that better expresses your ideas.

To use the Thesaurus, follow these steps:

1. **Move the cursor to the word you want to look up in the Thesaurus.**

2. **Press Alt-F1.**

   The Writing Tools dialog box appears.

3. **Press T (Thesaurus).**

   The Thesaurus dialog box appears, as shown in Figure 21-2. WordPerfect displays synonyms and antonyms for the word you selected in your document.

4. **Pick a more appropriate word.**

   From the list of displayed words, locate one you want to use and highlight it by using the up- or down-arrow keys. Press R to have that word replace the less appropriate word in your document.

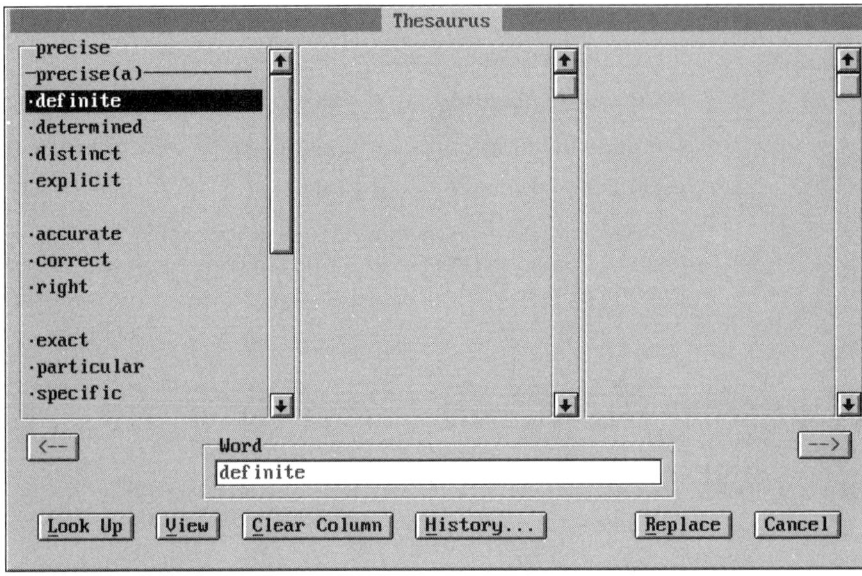

Figure 21-2: The Thesaurus dialog box.

Watching Your Language with Grammatik

After you've finished writing, it's a good idea to wait a few days and then examine your writing all over again. In this way, you have a chance to edit, revise, and strengthen your writing so that it says exactly what you mean (assuming you know what you're trying to say and that you aren't two days behind your deadline).

Because the whole purpose of writing is to communicate a message, the shorter your sentences and words, the easier your writing will be for others to understand. See?

Although the spell-checker catches typos and misspelled words, the grammar checker looks for grammatical, punctuation, and style mistakes. WordPerfect's grammar checker is called Grammatik, which is a separate grammar checker that WordPerfect tacked on to give WordPerfect 6.0 the illusion of technological achievement.

Getting a statistical snapshot of your document

If you want a quick critique of your writing, WordPerfect can bombard you with word, sentence, paragraph, and readability statistics. The word, sentence, and paragraph statistics give more detail than WordPerfect's ordinary Document Information.

The readability statistics give you odd information, such as the stuff shown in Table 21-1. If all this information sounds redundant, you're right, but the more ways WordPerfect analyzes your grammar, the more accurate the overall results will be.

Table 21-1 Stuff WordPerfect Can Tell You about Your Document That You May Not Care to Know

Odd Information	*What It Tells You*
The Fog Index	How difficult it is to understand your writing
Grade Level	How much education someone needs to understand your writing
Reading Ease	How easy it is for someone to read your writing

To view your document's readability statistics, follow these steps:

1. **Press Alt-F1.**

   The Writing Tools dialog box appears.

2. **Press G (Grammatik).**

   Please Wait . . . Then the Grammatik opening screen appears.

3. **Press T (Statistics check).**

   The Grammatik statistics screen appears, similar to what is shown in Figure 21-3. (Although you can't see it, Grammatik is evaluating the first act and scene of *Hamlet.*)

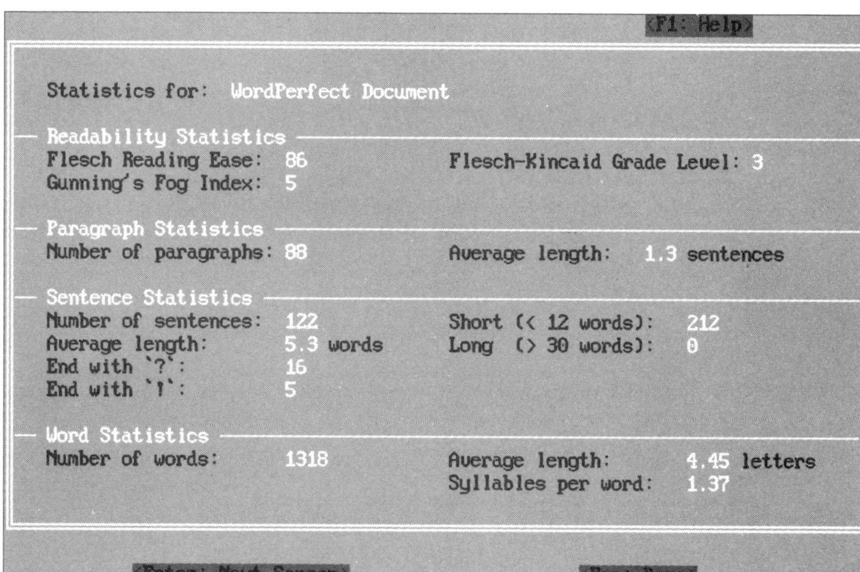

Figure 21-3: *Hamlet* gets rubbed by Grammatik.

4. Press Enter.

Grammatik moves on to display a written interpretation of your document, as shown in Figure 21-4.

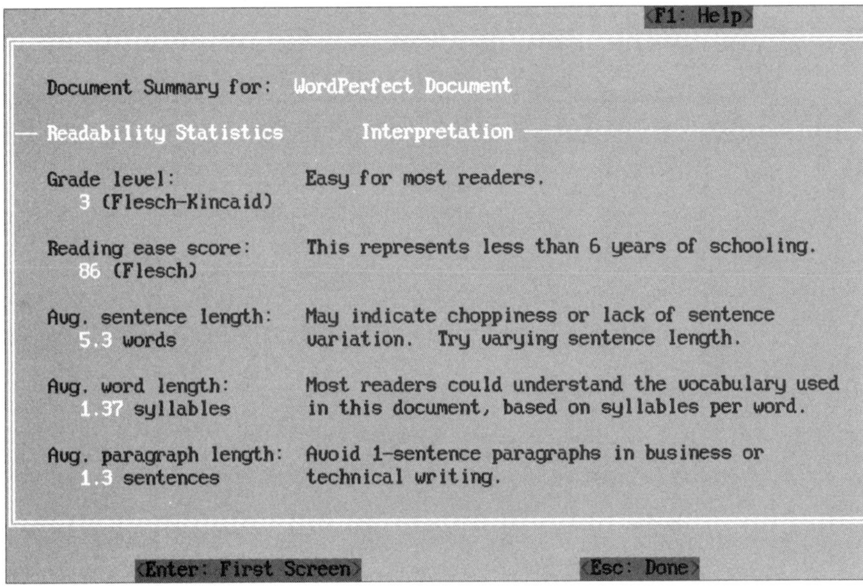

Figure 21-4: Even more ridicule for the Bard.

5. Yawn.

Press Esc and then press Q to return to WordPerfect and your document.

My, but Grammatik sure is slow. Chugga-chugga.

Examining your document interactively

Looking at a screenful of statistics may show you how your overall writing may be, but it does nothing to show you specifically what to correct. (And keep in mind that Grammatik is good at suggesting but is in no way an authority.)

WordPerfect can show you each sentence that you've written and offer a suggestion for improvement. Whenever WordPerfect finds a problem, it gives you three choices:

- Let WordPerfect correct the problem automatically.
- Edit the problem yourself.
- Tell WordPerfect to ignore the problem.

To interactively check your document's grammar, follow these steps:

1. **Press Alt-F1.**

   The Writing Tools dialog box appears.

2. **Press G (Grammatik).**

   The Grammatik opening screen appears.

3. **Press I (Interactive check).**

   WordPerfect splits the screen in half and displays your current sentence in the top half and its suggestions for improvement in the bottom half of the screen, as shown in Figure 21-5.

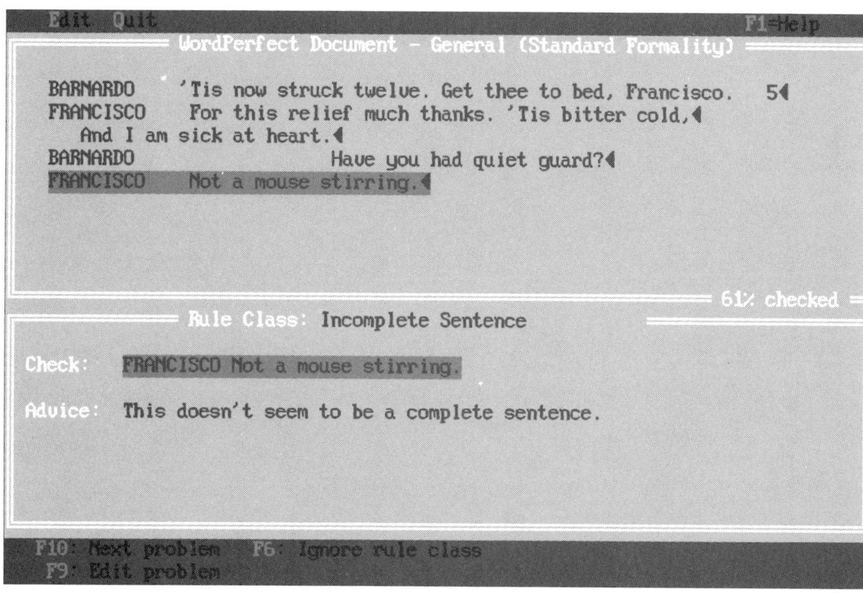

Figure 21-5: Split-screen (and rude) grammar checking.

4. **Press F10 to skip to the next problem or press F9 to edit the current problem.**

   When WordPerfect finishes checking your grammar, you see the Grammatik opening screen again.

5. **Press Q to return to WordPerfect.**

- Press Esc when you tire of Grammatik's suggestions and want to get on with your life.
- Only a complete loser accepts all Grammatik's suggestions. English is a language that barely has rules. If you know how not to use them, you'll be a better writer than if you follow Grammatik's suggestions to a *T*.

Chapter 22

Math and Equations

In This Chapter

- Creating equations
- Using equation commands
- Making equations look pretty
- Saving and retrieving equations

Math teachers, chemists, and mathematicians, rejoice! WordPerfect has finally responded to your demands and now has the capability to create all sorts of scientific symbols and mathematical equations, so you no longer have to resort to using a special scientific word-processing program.

For those of you who will never have to worry about creating an integral sign, square root symbol, or Greek mathematical character, skip this chapter right now before you start having flashbacks about math in high school.

But for those engineers, scientists, or other mathematically inclined people who need to create, edit, and erase equations on a regular basis, this is the chapter you've been waiting for.

- WordPerfect lets you create the most outrageously complicated, bizarre, and even blatantly false equations to your heart's content. Make your document look like a mathematician's doctoral thesis! However . . .
- WordPerfect can't solve any equations you create, nor can it check to see whether they even make sense. If WordPerfect could do all that, what would it need you for?

Creating Equations

When you type letters or numbers, you press a single key on the keyboard, and WordPerfect shows the exact character you typed. Unfortunately, your keyboard doesn't have really complicated mathematical symbols, so you can't press a key to create chemical formulas, calculus derivatives and integrals, or matrices.

Instead, you have to use WordPerfect's equation editor. Just type the proper commands into this equation editor, and the equation editor displays the command's actual image on-screen.

TIP

For example, the command to draw a square root sign on-screen is SQRT; the command to draw a matrix is MATRIX; and the command to draw a long division symbol is LONGDIV. Because you can't type a square root or long division symbol on-screen from the keyboard, WordPerfect has to resort to these long-winded but necessary commands instead.

Opening the Equation Editor

The only place you can create complicated equations is within the equation editor. To open the equation editor, follow these steps:

1. **Move the cursor in your document where you want the equation to appear.**
2. **Press Alt-F9, B (Graphic Boxes), C (Create).**

   The Create Graphics dialog box appears.
3. **Press Y (Based on Box Style).**

   The Graphics Box Styles dialog box appears.
4. **Highlight Equation Box and press Enter.**
5. **Press E (Create Equation).**

   The equation editor appears as shown in Figure 22-1. This is the place where you'll create your equations, which are then slapped into your WordPerfect document just like graphics.

- Press Home, F7 when you're done in the equation editor.
- You'll notice the list of mathematical goobers in the scrolling window on the right side of the equation editor. Here, you'll find the SQRT, MATRIX, and LONGDIV items I mentioned earlier in this chapter.
- The following sections highlight some goofy things that you can do in the equation editor.
- WordPerfect only displays your equations in your document if you are in Graphics or Page mode, or if you choose the Print Preview command.

REMEMBER

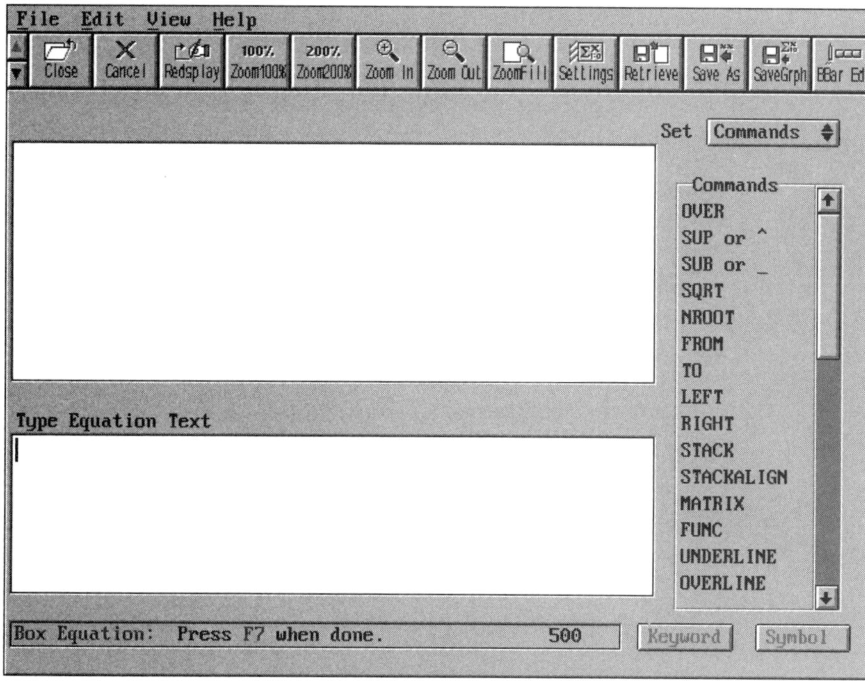

Figure 22-1: The equation editor.

Typing Equations in the Equation Editor

The equation editor consists of two windows (see Figure 22-1). The top window shows what your equation actually looks like, so you can see whether you're messing up or not. The bottom window is where you type your equation, using various commands to create different mathematical symbols.

- You select commands to place in the bottom window by first choosing a command set and then picking commands from the Commands list window. This task is described later in this chapter. Oh, and there are some examples to type in as well.
- Generally, what you type in the bottom window will look like a mish-mash of bizarre commands, symbols, and words. So thank goodness for that top preview window to make sure that you got things right.

Seeing what your equation looks like

When you type something in the bottom window of the equation editor, guess what happens? Nothing! WordPerfect refuses to display what your equation looks like because it takes time to draw a graphic image of your equation in the top window.

To see what your equation looks like, press Ctrl-F3.

After several seconds (depending on how complicated your equation is), WordPerfect displays your equation in the top window so that you can see that it's really what you wanted.

If you made any changes to your equation since the last time you pressed Ctrl-F3, WordPerfect won't show you what your edited equation looks like until you press Ctrl-F3 again.

Using spacing in your equations

Unless you specify otherwise, WordPerfect tries to scrunch your equation in as small a space as possible. If you want to insert spaces within the separate parts of your equation to make it easier to read, pressing the spacebar won't help.

Instead, you have to type the backward accent (`) key or the tilde (~) key. (Hint: They're the same key; use the Shift key to get the tilde.)

Table 22-1 shows the different spacing variations that you can create using the ` and ~ keys:

Table 22-1 Equation Spacing

Spacing	*Equation as Typed*	*Equation as It Appears*
No spacing	X+Y=Z	X+Y=Z
One-quarter spacing	X`+`Y`=`Z	X+Y= Z
Half spacing	X``+``Y``=``Z	X+Y = Z
Three-quarter spacing	X```+```Y```=```Z	X+ Y = Z
Normal spacing	X~+~Y~=~Z	X + Y = Z

Grouping items in an equation

To group items together, surround the grouped items with curly brackets {}. For example, if you typed the following into the equation editor:

```
SQRT X
```

WordPerfect creates the following equation:

$\sqrt{X}$

But if you type

```
SQRT X~--~Y
```

WordPerfect creates the following equation:

$\sqrt{X} - Y$

If you wanted the SQRT command to apply to the entire equation, group the X - Y portion in curly braces like this:

```
SQRT {X~--~Y}
```

This command creates the following equation:

$\sqrt{X - Y}$

Using Equation Commands

WordPerfect comes loaded with globs of different commands for creating all sorts of equations. Fortunately, you don't have to memorize all of the commands. Instead, WordPerfect stores these commands in one of the sets listed in Table 22-2.

Table 22-2 WordPerfect's Sets of Equation Commands

Set	***Description***
Commands	The Command set contains commands for creating common mathematical symbols such as square roots, long division signs, or superscripts.
Large	The Large set contains commands for creating large (hence the name) symbols such as the integral sign, union sign for sets, and other oddball symbols.
Symbols	The Symbols set contains commands for creating equation symbols such as not equal, greater than or equal, or sigma (in case you know what that looks like).
Greek	The Greek set contains all sorts of Greek letters that scientists like to use for variables in mathematical equations.
Arrows	The Arrows set contains arrows pointing up, down, right, and left.

(continued)

Table 22-2 *(continued)*

Set	*Description*
Sets	The Sets set (is that redundant or what?) contains symbols to use for set writing (the mathematical kind).
Other	The Other set contains miscellaneous symbols that WordPerfect couldn't figure out where to put anywhere else.
Functions	The Functions set contains mathematical functions like cosine, arc, and tangent, so you don't have to type these words in yourself.

Switching command sets

Each time you open the equation editor, WordPerfect displays the cursor in the bottom window and displays the contents of the Command set.

To switch to a different set, follow these steps:

1. **Press Tab until WordPerfect highlights the word `Set` in the upper-right corner of the screen.**
2. **Press Enter.**

   The list of eight available sets appears.
3. **Use the up-arrow and down-arrow keys to highlight the set that you want to use and press Enter.**

Choosing a displayed command

The whole purpose of sets is to display the different commands that they contain. To select a command, follow these steps:

1. **Press the Tab key until the Commands list is highlighted (the first word in the list will be highlighted).**
2. **Use the up- or down- arrow keys to highlight the command that you want to use and press Enter.**

WordPerfect automatically types the command in the bottom window of the equation editor.

Using the More Common Equation Commands

Rather than bombard you with a long list of every available command in all eight sets and have your eyes glaze over with boredom, here's a quick list of the more likely equations that you may want to create, unless you're doing something really weird.

Creating fractions with the OVER command

Fractions appear as two numbers or variables stacked one on top of the other with a horizontal bar underneath, as follows:

$$\frac{1}{x}$$

To create the preceding fraction with the OVER command, type the following in the equation editor:

```
1 OVER X
```

Creating superscript with the SUP or ^ commands

Superscript are little numbers or variables often used to designate the exponential power of another number or variable, such as

$$a^2 + b^2 = c^2$$

To create the preceding equation with the SUP or ^ commands, type the following in the equation editor:

```
a^2~+~b^2~=~c^2
```

or

```
a SUP 2~+~b SUP 2~=~c SUP 2
```

Creating subscript with the SUB or _ commands

Subscript are little numbers or variables, often used to identify variables or chemical compositions, such as

$$X_1 + X_2 = N_2O$$

To create the preceding equation with the SUB or _ commands, type the following in the equation editor:

```
X_1~+~X_2~=~N_2 O
```

or

```
X SUB 1~+~X SUB 2~=~N SUB 2 0
```

Creating square root signs with the SQRT command

A square root sign can encompass a single number, a variable, or a group of numbers or variables, as shown in the following:

$$\sqrt{X - Y}$$

If you want the square root sign to encompass a group of numbers or variables, enclose them inside curly brackets. To create the preceding equation with the SQRT command, type the following in the equation editor:

```
SQRT {X~-~Y}
```

Creating the nth root sign with the NROOT command

The nth root sign looks exactly like the square root sign except that it has a little number in front of it that indicates its nth root, as follows:

$$X = \sqrt[3]{3.14}$$

To create the preceding equation with the NROOT command, type the following in the equation editor:

```
X~=~NROOT 3 {3.14}
```

Creating arrows

Arrows are most often used in equations to show that something changes into something else, such as a chemical reaction or a mathematical limit, as shown in the following:

$$NH_4NO_3 \underset{Heat}{\rightarrow} N_2O + 2H_2O$$

You can't type in a command to create an arrow. Instead, you have to choose the arrow symbol from the Arrow set, which requires these steps:

1. **Press Tab until the word** `Set` **is highlighted.**
2. **Select the Arrows set from the list.**
3. **Select the arrow symbol that you want from the Commands list and press Enter.**

   WordPerfect automatically types the arrow symbol in the bottom window of the equation editor.

To create the preceding equation, type the following in the equation editor. Because you can't type an arrow from the keyboard, you have to choose the Arrow set and then choose the right arrow.

```
NH_4NO_3~ FROM {Heat} N_20~+~2H_20
```

Creating upper and lower bounds for integral signs

Integral signs and other mathematical symbols often have numbers or words that appear at the top and bottom of the symbol. For example:

$$\int_{0}^{5} x \, dx$$

To create the preceding equation, type the following in the equation editor:

```
INT FROM 0 TO 5 x~dx
```

Creating the long division sign with the LONGDIVS command

The LONGDIVS command simply draws a long division sign on-screen, such as

$$x - 3 \overline{\smash{)}\, x^2 + 6x - 12}$$

To create the preceding equation, type the following in the equation editor:

```
x~-~3 LONGDIVS {x^2~+~6x~-~12}
```

Making Equations Look Pretty

After you have created your equation, you can modify its font, size, and color to make it look nice. To modify the appearance of an equation, follow these steps:

1. **Press Alt-F9, B, E.**

   The Select Box To Edit dialog box appears.

2. **Press N (Document Box Number).**

3. **Type the box number of the equation that you want to edit and press Enter twice.**

   The last box that you worked on will be specified already. Press Enter if that's the case.

   TIP: You can find out the graphics box number by using Reveal Codes before you start. Press the F11 key and look for the `[Box (Para):1;Equation Box]` code. The "1" will be replaced by the true graphics box number.

   The Edit Graphics dialog box appears.

4. **Press E (Edit Equation).**

   The Equation Editor appears.

5. **Press Shift-F1.**

   The Equation Settings dialog box appears (see Figure 22-2).

6. **Choose one of the following:**

   Press 1 to change the equation's type.

   Press 2 to change the equation's font.

   Press 3 to change the equation's color.

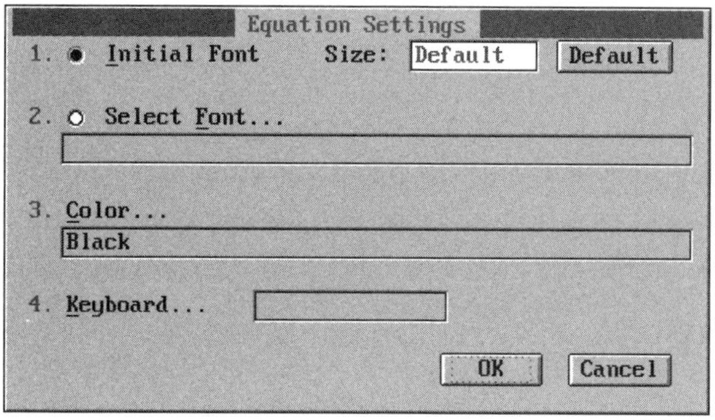

Figure 22-2: The Equation Settings dialog box.

7. **Press Enter.**

   WordPerfect displays your changes in the equation editor.

8. **Press Home, F7.**

Saving and Retrieving Equations

After you create some really complicated equations, the last thing you want to do is type them over and over again when you need them later. Fortunately, WordPerfect lets you save your equations as disk files. That way, when you need your equations, you can just retrieve them off the disk.

TIP

- WordPerfect lets you store equations as either text files or WPG graphic files.
- If you save an equation as a text file, you can edit it later. If you save an equation as a WPG graphic file, you cannot edit it again, ever. To play it safe, save your equations as both text and WPG graphic files.

Saving equations as text files

To save an equation as a text file, follow these steps:

1. **Press Alt-F9, B, E, N.**
2. **Type the box number of the equation that you want to save as a text file and press Enter twice.**

   The Edit Graphics dialog box appears.

3. **Press E (Edit Equation).**

   The equation editor appears.

4. **Press F10.**

   The Save Equation dialog box appears.

5. **Type the filename for your equation and press Enter.**
6. **Press F7.**
7. **Press Home, F7.**

Saving equations as WPG files

A WPG file lets you store an equation's font, size, or color for future use. The main drawback is that you cannot edit an equation stored in a WPG file.

To save an equation as a WPG file, follow these steps:

1. **Press Alt-F9, B, E, N.**
2. **Type the box number of the equation that you want to save as a text file and press Enter twice.**

   The Edit Graphics dialog box appears.

3. **Press E (Edit Equation).**

   The equation editor appears.

4. **Press Alt-F, I.**

   The Save Image dialog box appears.

5. **Type the filename for your equation and press Enter.**

   If you don't specify a file extension, WordPerfect automatically uses the WPG file extension.

6. **Press F7.**
7. **Press Home, F7.**

Retrieving equations stored as text files

To retrieve an equation previously stored as a text file, follow these steps:

1. **Move the cursor to the location in your document where you want the equation to appear.**

2. **Press Alt-F9, B, C (Create).**

   The Create Graphics Box dialog box appears.

3. **Press Y (Based on Box Style).**

   The Graphics Box Styles dialog box appears.

4. **Highlight Equation Box and press Enter.**
5. **Press E (Create Equation).**

   The equation editor appears.

6. **Press Shift-F10.**

   The Retrieve Document dialog box appears.

7. **Type the name of the text file that you want to retrieve and press Enter.**

   The equation appears in the bottom window of the equation editor.

8. **Press Ctrl-F3 to display how the equation will actually appear.**
9. **Press F7.**
10. **Press Home, F7.**

Retrieving equations stored as WPG files

To retrieve an equation previously stored as a WPG graphic file, follow these steps:

1. **Move the cursor to the location in your document where you want the equation to appear.**
2. **Press Alt-F9.**

   The Graphics dialog box appears.

3. **Press Shift-F10.**

   The Retrieve Image dialog box appears.

4. **Type the name of the WPG graphic file that you want to retrieve and press Enter.**

   The equation graphic appears in your document. When a WordPerfect 6 graphic file of an equation is inserted in your document, it cannot be edited with the WordPerfect 6 equation editor because the WordPerfect 6 file is only a kind of photo of the equation and not the actual equation itself.

Chapter 23

Wrestling with the Printer (and Fax)

In This Chapter

- Getting to the source of printer problems
- Printer memory made unforgettable
- What to do when your printer has an identity crisis
- The facts about faxing

If you don't watch out, printers can act pretty uppity. They eat your documents for breakfast and spit out worthless crumpled wads for lunch. They take on other personalities just to confuse you. They print only the portions of your documents they deem worthy. Why does life have to be so difficult? But never mind life, this chapter may help you out a bit with your printer and WordPerfect.

On another, similar score, if you think printer taming sounds about as safe as lion taming, just wait until you try WordPerfect's fax capabilities. The fax facts are at the end of the chapter because I like to save the worst for last. (That gives me time for a root canal before writing about WordPerfect faxing.)

Peter Piper's Pickle Is a Profusion of Printer Problems

According to the folks who keep track of such boring statistics at WordPerfect, more users tear out their hair over printing problems than over any other category. In the old days, WordPerfect had only one tech support line. Today, it has dozens, several of which are dedicated to certain types of printers ("the problem children," they're probably called).

When your documents aren't printing correctly, or at all, there are three places you can look to get at the root of the problem:

- The printer itself
- The computer
- WordPerfect

If nothing comes out of your printer when you tell WordPerfect to print your document, start your Sherlock Holmes routine with these simple, easy-to-correct possibilities:

- I hate to ask, but is the printer properly plugged in and turned on? My most recent printer just didn't print and didn't print. Then I unhooked it and hooked it up again. Sure enough, I must not have made a good connection the first time.
- Is your printer on-line? When the printer is on-line, it's ready to receive data from the computer. Most printers have a button for turning the printer on- or off-line and a light near the on-line button that glows reassuringly when the printer is on-line. If the light isn't glowing, press the on-line button.
- It should go without saying — but, hey, that's never stopped me before — that you have to have paper properly loaded in the printer. No paper, no printing.
- Paper jams are a common problem, no matter what type of printer you are using. I find that I encounter fewer paper jams if I lovingly caress my printer and chant my mantra before printing. Try it, it couldn't hurt.

- It's a good idea to turn off your computer and printer before plugging or unplugging the printer cable at either end. This precaution is a pain, but it can save your printer or your computer from a potentially damaging electrical shock. Laser printers are particularly vulnerable to damage from such shocks.
- Sometimes, simply exiting WordPerfect and then restarting it and trying again to print solves the problem. Don't forget to save your document before exiting WordPerfect.
- Many printers have multiple personalities. For example, you may be able to set up your Dazzelaser laser printer to act like a Hewlett-Packard LaserJet or an Apple LaserWriter. The problem is, if you've told WordPerfect that you're using a Hewlett-Packard LaserJet, but your printer is acting like an Apple LaserWriter, your documents will look like garbage. The solution is to flip a few switches or push a button or two on the printer to make it act like what WordPerfect thinks it is.

Holy Sheet Feeder! Right Document, Wrong Paper

Many printers, especially laser printers, have more than one paper tray or sheet feeder. Other printers allow you to install add-on sheet feeders. Multiple paper trays allow you to load different kinds of paper into the different trays. For example, you may put letterhead in one tray, plain paper in another, and envelopes in a third.

If you're using a printer that has more than one paper source, you need to tell WordPerfect which source to use for your document so that it doesn't just decide for itself. Tell WordPerfect which tray to use by choosing a Paper Size/Type with the correct paper location from the Page Format dialog box. Before you can do this step, however, you must first create Paper Size/Type definitions for your various paper trays.

To define a new Paper Size/Type with a new paper location, follow these steps:

1. **Press Shift-F8.**

   The Format dialog box appears.

2. **Press P (Page).**

   The Page Format dialog box appears.

3. **Press S (Paper Size/Type).**

   The Paper Size/Type dialog box appears, as shown in Figure 23-1.

4. **Use the up- and down-arrow keys to highlight the type of paper you are using.**

   For example, highlight Letter (Portrait) to base your new paper definition on standard 8.5 by 11-inch paper.

5. **Press C (Create).**

   Type a name, such as **My Letterhead**, in the Paper Name text box and press Enter.

   The Create Paper Size/Type dialog box appears, as shown in Figure 23-2.

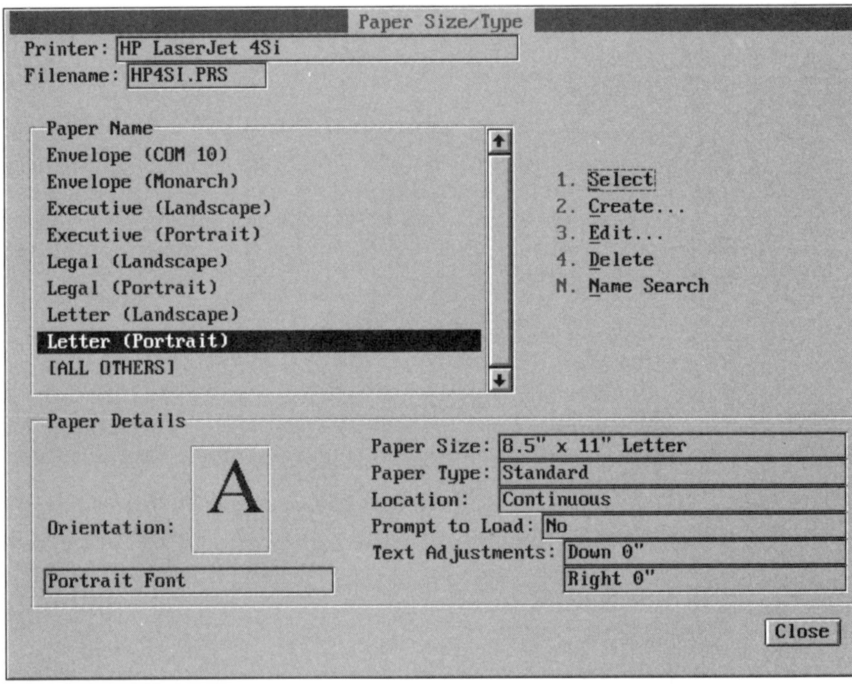

Figure 23-1: The Paper Size/Type dialog box.

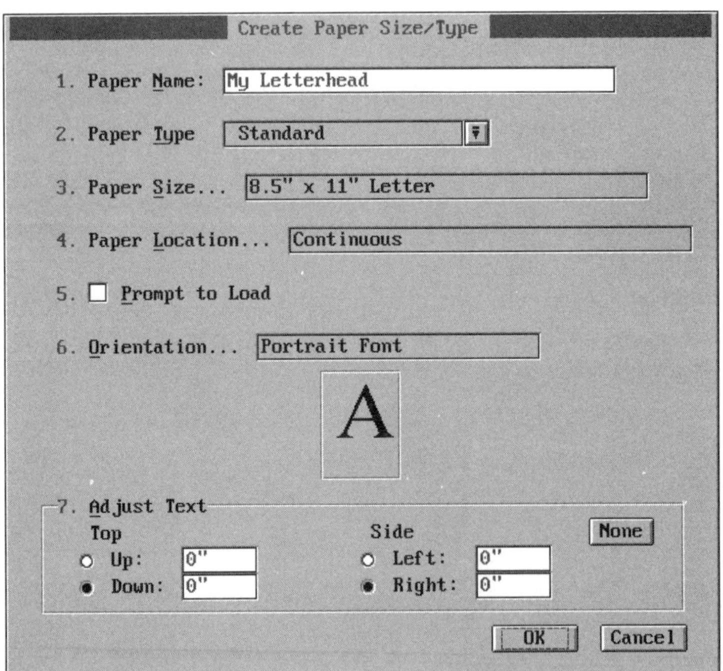

Figure 23-2: The Create Paper Size/Type dialog box.

6. **Press L (Paper Location).**

   The Paper Location dialog box appears, as shown in Figure 23-3.

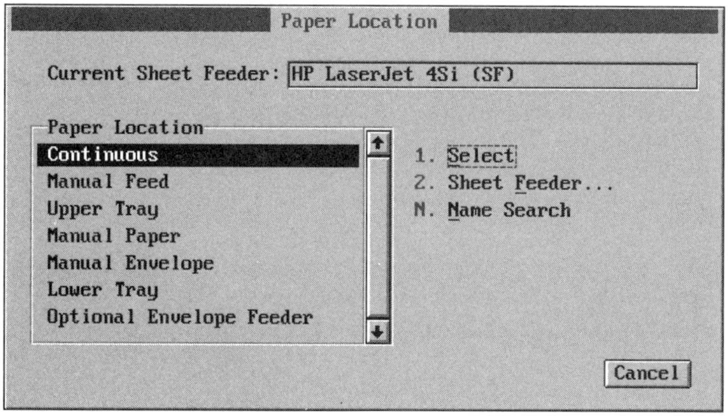

Figure 23-3: The Paper Location dialog box.

7. **Use the up- and down-arrow keys to highlight the location of the paper source you want in the Paper Location list.**

   For example, choose the tray that normally contains your letterhead (perhaps Upper Tray).

8. **Press S (Select).**

   You are returned to the Create Paper Size/Type dialog box with your choice entered in the Paper Location box.

9. **Press F7.**

   The Paper Size/Type dialog box reappears with the new paper definition highlighted in the Paper Name list.

10. **Press S (Select).**

    You are returned to the Page Format dialog box with the new paper definition entered in the Paper Size/Type box.

11. **Press Home, F7.**

    You are returned to your document with the new paper definition specified.

- You can assure yourself that the new paper definition has been inserted in your document by turning on Reveal Codes (F11) and looking at the top of the page your cursor was on when you completed Step 11. Position the cursor on the `[Paper Sz/Typ]` code so that it expands to display the dimensions of the paper and the paper definition name.

- WordPerfect lets you use different Paper Size/Type definitions for each page in your document. If there is only one Paper Size/Type code on the first page of the document, the entire document is sent to that paper tray. You may, however, want to put one Paper Size/Type code on the first page for your letterhead and another code on the second page to send the remainder of the document to the tray containing plain paper.
- If you want to use a Paper Size/Type definition as the default so that it is used for all future documents unless you specify otherwise, press Shift-F8, D, T to display the Initial Codes Setup dialog box. Press Shift-F8, P, S. Highlight the paper name you want to use as a default and press S, Home, F7. Finally, press F7 three times.

Printer Memory Made Unforgettable

Memory isn't something that is found only in your computer (or your head, if you're lucky). Printers need memory, too. When your computer starts blasting data in your printer's direction, the printer can quickly become overwhelmed if it doesn't have enough memory to store some of the backlog of data until it can catch up. Of course, your computer will wait patiently and spoon-feed more data as the printer is ready to accept it.

The good news is that you don't have to wait for the entire document to finish printing before you can get back to work. WordPerfect keeps track of what portion of the document has been sent to the printer and continues sending it — in the *background*, so to speak — so that you can work on another WordPerfect document in the *foreground*.

So how much memory does your printer need? It sounds as though WordPerfect takes care of everything so that your printer doesn't need memory of its own after all. The true answer, however, is that it depends. How much memory your printer needs depends on what kind of printer you are using and what kind of stuff you are printing.

There are primarily two types of printers used with personal computers these days: dot-matrix printers and page printers. Laser printers are page printers. Just about everything else is a dot-matrix printer. Inkjet printers fall into the dot-matrix category for this discussion.

Dot-matrix printers generally don't require extra memory, regardless of what you're printing. Adding extra memory to a dot-matrix printer may let you use more of some kinds of fonts, but other than that, there's no need to add memory to a dot-matrix printer that you use with WordPerfect.

Page printers are another story entirely. A page printer must have enough memory to print an entire page of your document. This is no big deal if you're printing text and not using more than a few fonts. However, when you throw graphics into the mix, things can get dicey. For gobs of graphics, page printers need gobs of memory — often more than they come with out of the box.

TIP

- Typical 300 dot-per-inch laser printers need a minimum of 1MB of available memory to print a full 8.5 by 11-inch page of complex text and graphics at the highest quality. Some of the lasers that print at higher resolution (quality) need even more memory. Because most lasers come with 1MB or less of memory (and some of that is used as soon as you turn on the printer), you may want to add at least an extra megabyte to the printer. You can add an extra megabyte to most lasers for well under $100. Drag your printer into your friendly neighborhood computer store and have the employees install it for you.
- Adding extra memory to a laser printer doesn't make it any faster, no matter what the salesperson selling you the memory tells you. Sorry.

TECHNICAL STUFF

As mentioned earlier, WordPerfect prints in the background while you work on another WordPerfect document. But what if you want to play your cool new computer chess game while WordPerfect prints? Without some extra help, you're out of luck. However, if you add a print spooler or buffer, you can get back to business (or chess) in no time. *Print spoolers* are software programs that let you allocate a portion of your computer's memory specifically for printing. *Buffers* are additional memory added to your printer, either internally or in an external box. In either case, after your document has been sent to the spooler or buffer, you can switch to another program and compute away. Your friendly computer dealer will be happy to sell you the software or hardware you need.

Just the Fax

When your document absolutely, positively has to be there in minutes, don't call Federal Express or United Parcel Service. Instead, call on WordPerfect's Fax Services. WordPerfect turns your computer into a fax machine, allowing you to send and receive documents without even getting up out of your chair. Oh, well, so much for all that aerobic exercise I was getting walking across the room to the fax machine.

All you need to fax with WordPerfect is a *modem* (one of those thingies that lets your computer talk on the phone) with fax capabilities. Most new modems include fax capabilities, so if you have a modem, there's a good chance you have the fax equipment, even if you don't realize it.

- If you don't have a fax/modem, don't despair. All it takes to solve your problem is money — and, fortunately, not too much money. You may decide to spend more to get faster modem speeds or more bells and whistles, but you don't have to.
- You may still need a real fax machine if you need to fax documents that aren't stored as computer files. If you want to fax a photocopy of a newspaper article, for example, WordPerfect just can't help. Okay, I know about scanners for converting documents to computer files, but that's a pretty clunky solution.

Installing Your Fax

Before you can start using WordPerfect fax services, you must inform WordPerfect about the details of your fax/modem, which may have been done when WordPerfect was originally installed on your computer.

To determine if you have to run through the fax installation procedure, press Shift-F7 to display the Print/Fax dialog box. If the Fax Services option is dimmed (grayed out), round up your WordPerfect installation disks and follow these steps:

1. **Exit WordPerfect and get to a DOS prompt, such as**

   ```
   C:\WP60>
   ```

2. **Insert the Install 1 disk in your computer's floppy drive A (or B).**
3. **Type a:install (or b:install if the disk is in drive B) and press Enter.**

   After a few seconds, the opening WordPerfect 6.0 installation screen appears.

4. **If you're using a color monitor, press Y; otherwise, press N.**

   A screen with a list of installation options appears.

5. **Press D (Device Files (Sound, Graphics, Fax, Printer)).**

   The Install files from dialog box appears.

6. **Press Enter.**

   The Location of your WordPerfect Program dialog box appears, listing the drive and directory of your WordPerfect program.

7. **If the drive and directory for your WordPerfect program is correct, press Enter. Otherwise, enter the correct drive and directory before pressing Enter.**

   The Install Device dialog box appears.

8. **Press F (Fax Files).**

   The Fax Device Options dialog box appears, as shown in Figure 23-4.

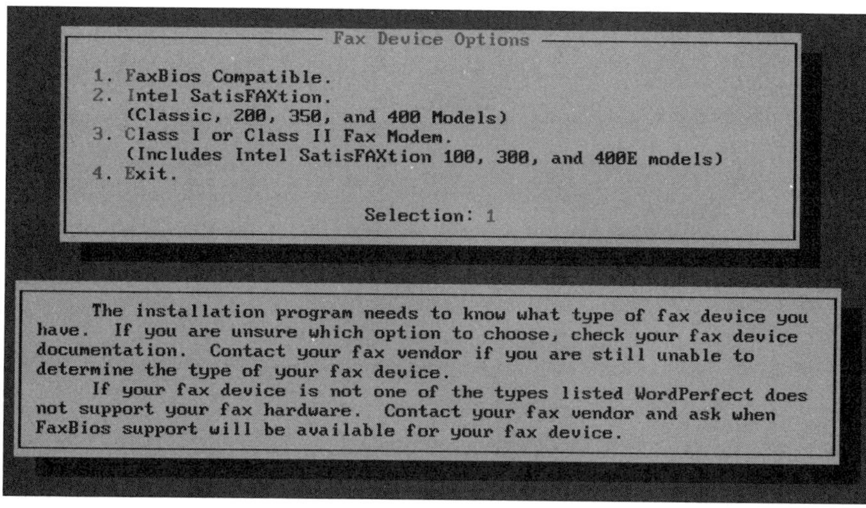

Figure 23-4: The Fax Device Options dialog box.

9. **Press the number that corresponds to the type of fax/modem you are using. If you're not sure what you have, Class I or Class II Fax Modem is the most likely choice.**

   The Install Fax Files To dialog box appears.

10. **Press Enter.**

    A screen appears that tells you to insert one of your installation disks into drive A (or B).

11. **Insert the requested disk into your disk drive and press Enter.**

    If you choose FaxBios Compatible or Intel SatisFAXtion from the Fax Device Options list, your fax information installation will be completed after WordPerfect gets all the information it needs from the disks. If you choose Class I or Class II, a message appears on-screen after a few seconds, asking whether you want to attach FAXDIR and FAXB to the end of your AUTOEXEC.BAT.

12. **Press Y (Yes).**

    If you're short on memory (no, I mean in your computer), you may not want to have your computer automatically load the fax software stuff. It takes up memory that may be put to better use elsewhere.

    Even if you have enough memory, it's usually best to stick the fax software in a portion of memory that doesn't get in the way of WordPerfect and other programs that need as much conventional memory as they can get. To put the fax software in this other location — if you have DOS 6 or later — check out the MEMMAKER section in Chapter 25 of *MORE DOS For Dummies* (IDG Books Worldwide). If you have an earlier version of DOS or are still confused, this is a good time to call on your PC guru.

    The WordPerfect CAS Setup Utility screen appears.

13. **Press Enter.**

    The WordPerfect CAS Hardware Driver Setup screen appears briefly while WordPerfect figures out some essential information about your fax/modem. Then the WordPerfect CAS Setup Utility Main Menu screen appears, as shown in Figure 23-5.

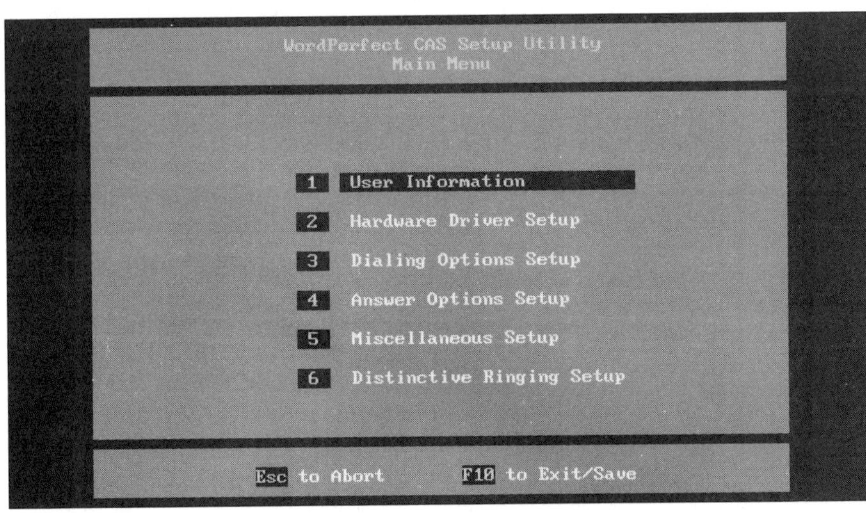

Figure 23-5: The WordPerfect CAS Setup Utility Main Menu screen.

14. **Press Enter to display the User Information screen and enter your name and fax number.**

15. **Press Enter to return to the Main Menu.**

    The user information is optional, but it allows WordPerfect to add your name and fax number to the faxes you send. You shouldn't need to change any other setup details before you're ready to start faxing.

16. **Press the number corresponding to any of the other options you want to set up and fill in the screens.**

    If your computer is connected to a phone line that is shared with a phone and an answering machine, be sure to go to the Answer Options Setup dialog box and set the Answer on Ring number to something higher than your answering machine uses. If you don't do this step, callers get that funny-sounding fax tone and can't leave messages for you.

17. **After filling in the setup options, press F10 to exit the fax setup screens and save your fax setup.**

18. **Press E, E, Y to exit WordPerfect's installation system and get back to a DOS prompt.**

- You need to restart your computer (press Ctrl-Alt-Del all at the same time) before the fax setup information takes effect.
- Most fax/modems come with their own fax software. If you want to use WordPerfect's fax software, don't use the software that comes with your fax/modem. The two programs get into a nasty fight.
- You can change any of the fax parameters later without digging out your WordPerfect disks. Just exit WordPerfect, get to the `C:\WP60` prompt, and type **SETUP**.

Sending Faxes

WordPerfect lets you fax the document that is on-screen or another document that is on your computer's disk. The procedure for faxing is similar to printing your document. In fact, faxing *is* essentially printing your document; however, the printer is a fax machine or fax/modem, and the phone company is required to connect you to the printer.

Here are the steps for quick-and-dirty faxing:

1. **Open the document you want to fax, if it isn't already on-screen.**
2. **Press Shift-F7.**

   The Print/Fax dialog box appears.

3. **Press X (Fax Services).**

   The Fax Services: WordPerfect Corp. dialog box appears, as shown in Figure 23-6. You learn to create phone book entries in the next section.

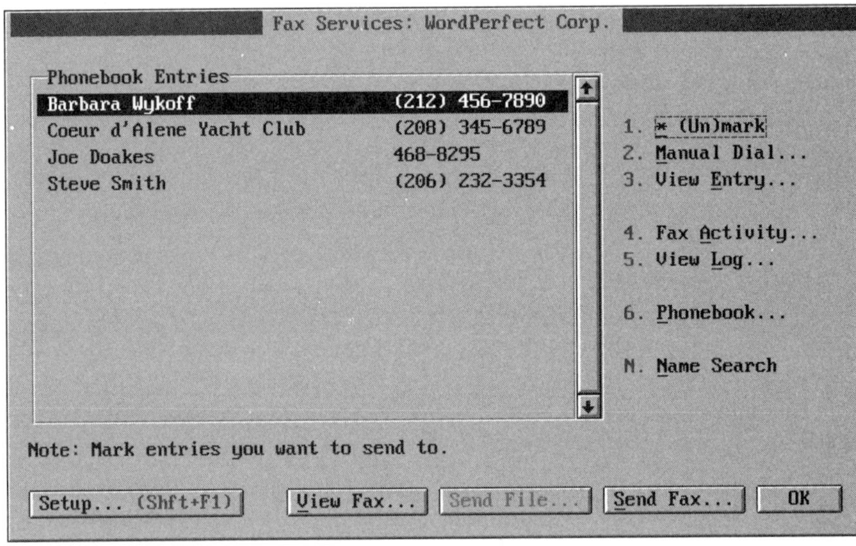

Figure 23-6: The Fax Services: WordPerfect Corp. dialog box.

4. **Use the up- and down-arrow keys to highlight the name you want to fax to in the Phonebook Entries list and then press S (Send Fax).**

   If you're faxing to someone who isn't on your phone book list, press M (Manual Dial) and then enter the recipient's name and fax number in the Manual Dial dialog box. Then press Enter.

   The Send Fax dialog box appears, as shown in Figure 23-7.

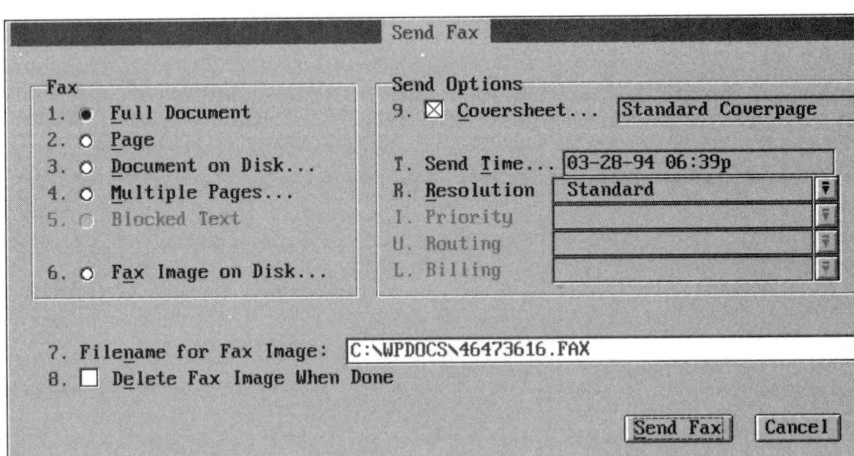

Figure 23-7: The Send Fax dialog box.

5. **Choose the options you want for this fax and then press S (Send Fax).**

   In a few seconds, you start hearing some beeps and hisses from your fax/modem, and the document is sent to its destination.

- In the Send Fax dialog box, you can specify which portion of the document to fax, just as if you were printing it. If you don't specify, the whole document is sent. If a portion of the document is blocked, one of your options is to fax the blocked text.
- If you choose Document on Disk in the Send Fax dialog box, you can enter a name of an unopened document to fax.
- To send a cover sheet with your fax, be sure that the Coversheet check box is checked in the Send Options portion of the Send Fax dialog box. The standard cover sheet includes the sender's and recipient's names and fax numbers, the date, and the number of pages.
- You can add a line of descriptive text to the cover sheet by pressing C, C in the Send Fax dialog box. The Fax Coversheets dialog box appears. Press U (Subject) and enter the subject text. Press Enter and then S (Select) to accept the text and close the dialog box.
- There's usually no need to save the image of the fax as a file on disk after you've sent the fax. After all, you still have the document if you need to refax it. To avoid cluttering your disk with fax files, press E (Delete Fax Image When Done) in the Send Fax dialog box.
- You can send the same fax to multiple destinations by marking each entry in the Phonebook Entries list with an asterisk before choosing Send Fax.
- Use the Fine Resolution setting when faxing anything with graphics or small text. Faxing with this option takes about twice as long to transmit, but it produces much higher quality at the receiving end. The recipients of your fax will thank you. Well, at least they should. To change the resolution, press R (Resolution) in the Send Fax dialog box, highlight Fine in the drop-down list, and press Enter.
- Don't try to fax printed documents by shoving them into your floppy disk drive. I haven't been able to get this technique to work no matter how many times I've tried.

Making Phone Book Entries

If you generally fax to the same people over and over again, it will make your life easier to enter their names in your phone book so that you can fax to them (or groups of them) without going to the trouble of entering their names and fax numbers manually each time.

To make phone book entries, follow these steps:

1. **Press Shift-F7.**

   The Print/Fax dialog box appears.

2. **Press X (Fax Services).**

   The Fax Services: WordPerfect Corp. dialog box appears.

3. **Press P (Phonebook).**

   The Phonebook dialog box appears.

4. **Press C (Create Entry).**

   The Create Entry dialog box appears.

5. **Enter a recipient's name in the Name text box and press Tab.**

6. **Enter the person's fax phone number in the Fax Phone Number text box and press Tab.**

7. **Enter the person's voice number (the normal phone number used for talking) in the Voice Phone Number text box and press Enter.**

   The voice number step is optional and is used just for your reference.

   The Create Entry dialog box now looks something like the one in Figure 23-8.

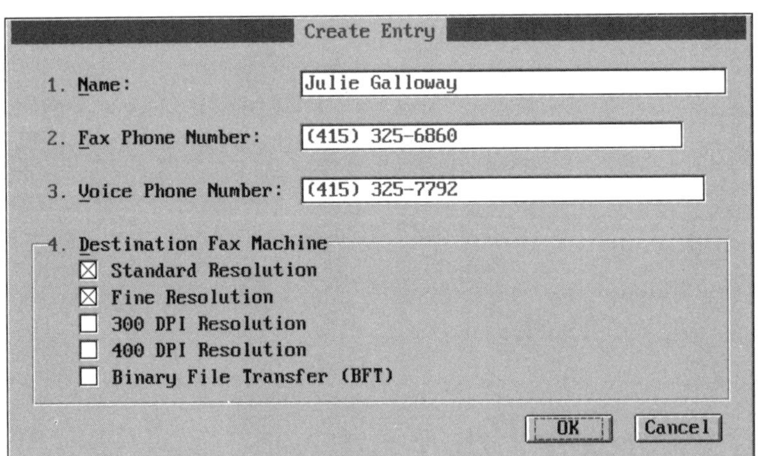

Figure 23-8: The Create Entry dialog box.

8. **Press F7 three times to accept the new entry and return to the Fax Services dialog box.**

- The phone book entries are sorted in alphabetical order by the first word in each entry, so you may want to enter the last name first, followed by the first name.
- To edit a phone book entry, press P from the Fax Services dialog box, highlight the entry you want to edit, and press E. Make any changes you want in the Edit Entry dialog box and then press F7.
- To delete a phone book entry, press P from the Fax Services dialog box, highlight the entry you want to delete, and press D, Y.

Creating Phone Book Groups

You can create groups of phone book entries so that you can fax to the entire group in one fell swoop. Suppose that you regularly send faxes to everyone in the marketing department. By including all the people in a group called, say, *Marketing*, you can send your fax to the marketing group with the assurance that no one is left out.

To create a group, follow these steps:

1. **Press Shift-F7.**

   The Print/Fax dialog box appears.

2. **Press X (Fax Services).**

   The Fax Services: WordPerfect Corp. dialog box appears.

3. **Press P (Phonebook).**

   The Phonebook dialog box appears.

4. **Press G (Create Group).**

   The Create Group dialog box appears.

5. **Enter a name for the group in the Group Name dialog box and press Enter.**
6. **Press N (Name List).**
7. **Use the up- and down-arrow keys to highlight the first person you want to include in the group and then press Enter.**
8. **Repeat Step 7 until all the group members are added.**

   The Create Group dialog box should look something like the one in Figure 23-9.

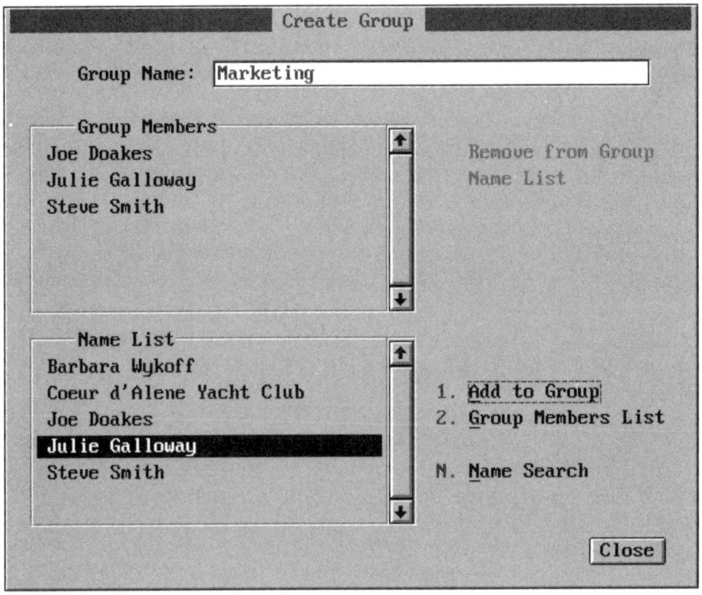

Figure 23-9: The filled-in Create Group dialog box.

9. **Press F7 four times to accept the group entry and return to the Fax Services dialog box.**

- The group name appears in the phone book list, but instead of a fax number in the right column, the word *group* appears.
- To edit a group, press P from the Fax Services dialog box, highlight the group entry you want to edit, and press E. Make any changes you want in the Edit Group dialog box and then press F7.
- To delete a group entry, press P from the Fax Services dialog box, highlight the group you want to delete, and press D, Y.

Chapter 24

Mailing Labels and Envelopes

In This Chapter

- Mailing labels or envelope printing?
- About mailing labels
- Printing labels (the quick way)
- Printing labels (using data files)
- Defining your own labels
- Printing on envelopes

Many people use WordPerfect to create correctly spelled, grammatically correct, desktop-published documents and reports, and then they pop the entire thing in an envelope with the address hastily scribbled in ink that smears the moment you touch it.

If you want to give your correspondence that "professional look" that impresses people with low self-esteem, WordPerfect can neatly print addresses on mailing labels that you can paste onto your envelopes, or WordPerfect can print the addresses directly on the envelopes themselves.

With two choices for addressing envelopes available in WordPerfect, you now have no excuse whatsoever for not producing neat, correctly spelled, addressed envelopes. Unless, of course, you don't feel like reading this chapter.

Mailing Labels or Envelope Printing?

Because WordPerfect can print addresses on mailing labels or directly on envelopes, which method should you choose?

Mailing labels offer the convenience of printing masses of addresses and pasting them on envelopes of all different sizes. If you're in the mass-mailing business, using mailing labels makes more sense than shoving carton loads of envelopes through your printer, especially if you need to print addresses on different-sized envelopes on a regular basis.

Unfortunately, mailing labels are not free, unless you steal them from your company's office supply room. Even worse, pasting mailing labels can be time-consuming and boring, capable of dragging a high-paid executive back down to the world of manual labor and minimum wages.

Printing directly on envelopes is more convenient for occasional use or if you don't feel like wasting your time pasting mailing labels on envelopes all day.

But if you need to use different-sized envelopes or have many envelopes to address, stuffing envelopes one at a time into a printer can be just as bad as pasting mailing labels on them.

Look at how many envelopes you need to address regularly. Some people swear by mailing labels. Others swear by printing directly on the envelopes. Still others just swear at WordPerfect.

About Mailing Labels

Before you can print out mailing labels, you need to buy them (obviously). Walk into any office supply store and you'll find globs of different mailing labels, in different sizes and shapes, made by a variety of manufacturers.

Three crucial features to look for are

- The physical size of the mailing label
- The number of labels on a single page
- The label manufacturer

Why is such information important? The answer is easy: WordPerfect already knows how to use certain brands and sizes of mailing labels. However, if you buy a bizarre mailing label size from a company that WordPerfect has never heard of, good luck trying to get WordPerfect to print your mailing labels correctly.

WARNING!

- Avoid "any old" label. Some labels aren't designed to be run through computer printers. They come off and gum up the works! Use only official computer-compatible labels. (If it doesn't say so on the box, it isn't.)

TIP

- Although you can torture WordPerfect into using your specific mailing labels, buying labels that WordPerfect already knows how to use is *much* easier.
- My advice? Stick with the Avery brand of labels. (No, I don't get a kickback. This is experience talking.)

Using the Mailing Labels

After you've bought your mailing labels, WordPerfect provides you with two choices for creating the addresses to print on them.

First, the quick way enables you to create a new document and type your addresses one at a time. Although this method is simple and fast, it's also a bit time-consuming (translation: *boring*). Even worse, you can't use these addresses for anything else.

The alternative is to type (or import) addresses and store them as a separate WordPerfect data file. Not only does this second method enable you to suck in data stored in other file formats (Quattro Pro, Microsoft Word, and so on), but it enables you to use the addresses on form letters later.

- If you need to use addresses only once, choose the quick and simple method of creating mailing labels.
- If you want to use addresses over and over again, store them in a separate data file first and then print them on mailing labels.

Printing Mailing Labels (The Quick Way)

If you need to print mailing labels with addresses you don't need for form letters later, follow these steps:

1. **Press Alt-F, N to create a new document.**
2. **Press Shift-F8, P (Page), L (Labels).**

   The Labels dialog box appears, as shown in Figure 24-1.
3. **Press L to print labels on a laser printer, or press T to print labels on a tractor-feed printer.**

   WordPerfect displays only those mailing labels for laser printers or tractor-feed printers, depending on which you indicate. (***Note:*** A tractor-feed printer should have some type of automatic will-feed-labels type of contraption on it.)

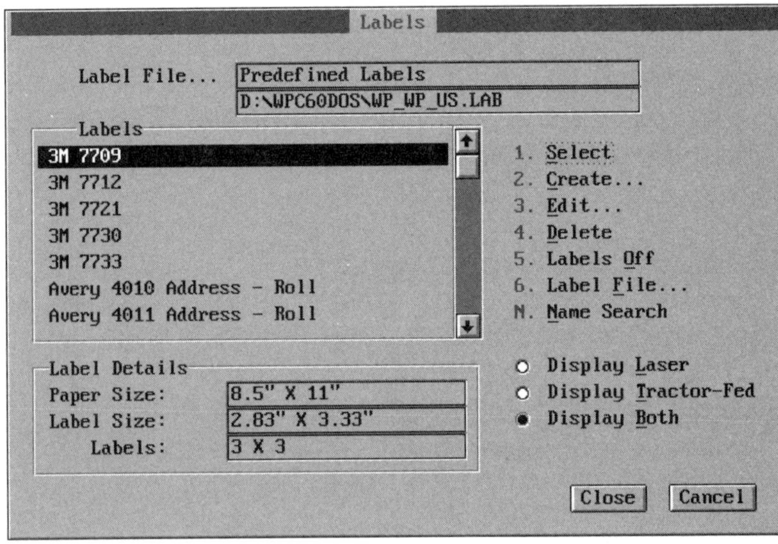

Figure 24-1: The Labels dialog box.

4. **Highlight in the Labels list the brand name that matches the mailing labels you want to use and press Enter.**

   - If you didn't buy 3M or Avery brand mailing labels, check the measurements of your mailing labels anyway. Most mailing labels use the same measurements as 3M or Avery mailing labels, so you can try to match them up with the particular brand name that WordPerfect understands.
   - The label size is displayed in the Label Size box, just below the List o' Labels.
   - The standard mailing address sticky label is Avery number 5160 (Laser).

   After you select a mailing label type and press Enter, the Labels Printer Info dialog box appears. Okay — time to stop the dialog box dive.

5. **Press Home, F7.**

   WordPerfect displays its usual, blank screen. Don't be fooled by this blank screen into thinking that nothing has changed. (Depending on which label size you choose, the screen may look different or it may not.) What's really happened is that WordPerfect has formatted your document to print lots of little labels — like many tiny pages all on one page. WordPerfect word-wraps everything to fit within the confines of your mailing labels, as you can see in Figure 24-2.

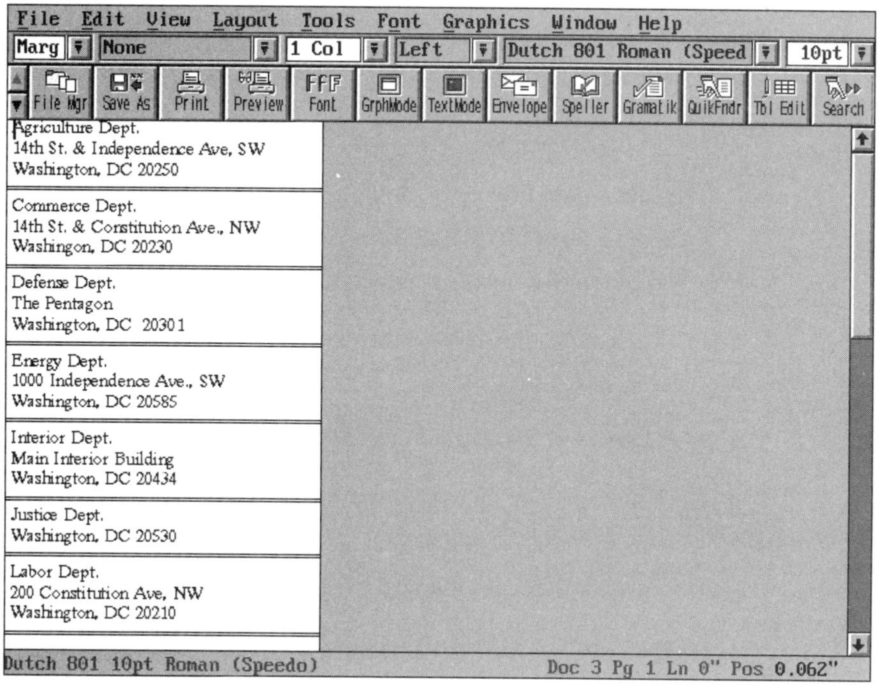

Figure 24-2: Mailing labels displayed on-screen.

To start typing a new address, press Ctrl-Enter (the Hard Page command). If you type too much information for one address, WordPerfect displays a line to show you where the mailing label ends. Oops! Go back and make the address shorter.

While typing addresses, press Enter at the end of each line.

Press PgUp and PgDn to move the cursor from one label to another.

Although WordPerfect displays your addresses on the screen from top to bottom, they actually print from left to right across your mailing labels. (Check this out by choosing Print Preview from the File menu.)

Printing Mailing Labels (Using Data Files)

If you need to keep and reuse addresses for form letters, or if some of your addresses are trapped in another file format, you can save time by using a *data file.*

A data file is nothing more than a separate WordPerfect document that contains names and addresses. After you've created this data file, you need to create a separate *form file* that defines your mailing labels.

Finally, you *merge* the information stored in the data file into the structure defined by the form file, which is much like pouring water (the data file) into an ice cube tray (the form file).

The steps for this process are as follows:

1. **Create a data file containing your names and addresses.**
2. **Create a form file that defines your mailing labels.**
3. **Merge the two together, which makes your printable mailing list.**

Yeah, this smells quite a bit like mail merge, doesn't it?

Creating a data file from scratch

If your addresses don't already exist in another file format, you must type them into the data file yourself.

To create a new data file, follow these steps:

1. **Press Shift-F9, T (Data Table), N (Create a Table with Field Names).**

   The Field Names dialog box appears.

2. **Type `Name` and press Enter.**

   WordPerfect displays `Name` in the Field Name List.

3. **Type `Address` and press Enter.**

   WordPerfect displays `Address` in the Field Name List.

4. **Press Home, F7.**

   Lo and behold! WordPerfect displays a table on-screen, containing a Name and an Address column. Now you need to fill in the table.

5. **Type a name and press Tab to move the cursor to the next address cell.**
6. **Type a street address and press Tab.**
7. **Type a city name, state, and ZIP code and press Tab.**
8. **To add a new name and address, press Tab and repeat steps 5 through 7 above.**

   After you're done or bored, press F7, Y, and then type the filename under which you want WordPerfect to save the document. Press N to remain in WordPerfect.

Creating a form file

After you've created a data file, the next step is to create a form file that tells WordPerfect what to do with all the data stored in the data file.

To create a form file, follow these steps:

1. **Press Alt-F, N to create a new, empty document.**
2. **Press Shift-F8, P (Page), L (Labels).**

   The Labels dialog box appears.
3. **In the Labels list, highlight the brand name that matches the mailing labels you want to use and press Enter.**

   Refer to the section "Printing Mailing Labels (The Quick Way)" earlier in this chapter for help in choosing the labels.
4. **Press Home, F7.**

   You're back in your document again. WordPerfect now knows which labels you plan to use for this document, and it has formatted the document accordingly. The next step is to pull in the names from the data file.
5. **Press Shift-F9, F (Field), F5 (List Field Names).**

   The Select Data File For Field Name dialog box appears.
6. **Type the path and filename of your data file and press Enter.**

   Enter the name of the data file as you saved it to disk — for example: **SUCKERS**.

   The List Field Names dialog box appears, just as it did when you created the names. (They should look familiar here.)
7. **Highlight the NAME field and press Enter.**

   WordPerfect displays `FIELD(NAME)` on-screen. Cool.
8. **Press Enter.**

   Now you can add the Address field.
9. **Press Shift-F9, F, F5.**
10. **Highlight the ADDRESS field and press Enter.**

    WordPerfect displays `FIELD(ADDRESS)` on-screen.
11. **Press F7, Y to save the document.**

    Type the filename under which you want to save the document and then press N to stay in WordPerfect.

Merging data files into form files

After you've created a data file and a form file, the third step is to smash the two together. Because the general public loves euphemisms, this action is commonly called *merging*. (So the next time you drive your car into a fence post, remember — you didn't crash into it; you just "merged" into it.)

To merge a data file into a form file, follow these steps:

1. **Press Shift-F10.**

   The Open Document dialog box appears.

2. **Type the name of your form file and press Enter.**
3. **Press Ctrl-F9, M (Merge).**

   The Run Merge dialog box appears.

4. **Press Enter twice.**

   The phrase `"(Current Document)"` appears in the Form File field.

5. **Type the name of your data file and press Enter twice.**

   Hope you remembered it. If not, press F5 and scour your disk drive to find the file's name.

   If you type the name of a data file that uses a different file format, such as Quattro Pro or Microsoft Word, WordPerfect displays a File Format dialog here and asks that you choose the file format in which the data is trapped.

6. **Type the name of your form file and press Enter twice.**

   WordPerfect displays the result of the successful merge on-screen.

7. **Press Shift-F7 and Enter to print your mailing labels.**

   Or you can press Shift-F7, V to view a print preview of what your mailing labels look like before you print them out.

Defining Your Own Labels

Although WordPerfect recognizes only 3M and Avery mailing labels, nearly every type of mailing label sold today follows the same standards as 3M and Avery. That means that you can buy any brand-name mailing labels and they *should* still work with WordPerfect.

If you do happen to find some bargain mailing labels that have unusual sizes or shapes, however, you may need to define these labels for WordPerfect.

Creating a custom label definition

To create your own custom label definition, you need to look at your box of mailing labels and find the following information for WordPerfect:

- Paper size
- Label size
- The number of labels on a page

To create a custom label definition, follow these steps:

1. **Press Shift-F8, P (Page), L (Labels).**

   The Format dialog box appears.

   The Labels dialog box appears.

2. **Highlight in the Labels list the mailing label name that most closely matches the physical dimensions of your own oddball mailing labels.**

   Refer to the Paper Size (overall size of the sheet) and Label Size (size of each individual sticky label) boxes. Compare those dimensions and find something in the labels list that roughly corresponds to your label sheet. Highlight it by using the up- or down-arrow keys.

3. **Press C (Create).**

   The Create Label dialog box appears.

4. **Type the brand name of your mailing labels and press Enter.**

5. **Make any changes to the label's definition that you need to.**

   These include changing the label size, paper size, and so on. Fill in the various fields as necessary, using information from your labels.

6. **Press Home, F7.**

   The new label definition is added to the list, and you can select it at any time while you work with labels in WordPerfect.

Editing a label definition

Instead of creating a brand-new label definition, sometimes you can more easily just edit an existing one. To edit a label definition, follow these steps:

1. **Press Shift-F8, P (Page), L (Labels).**

   The Labels dialog box appears.

2. **Highlight in the Labels list the mailing label name you want to edit.**
3. **Press E (Edit).**

   The Edit Label dialog box appears.
4. **Make any changes you require to the label definition, such as paper size, label size, and so on.**
5. **Press Home, F7.**

Deleting a label definition

If you stop buying a particular brand of mailing labels, you may want to delete its label definition to free up a whopping few hundred bytes on your hard disk. To delete a label definition, follow these steps:

1. **Press Shift-F8, P (Page), L (Labels).**

   The Labels dialog box appears.
2. **Highlight in the Labels list the mailing label name that you want to destroy utterly.**
3. **Press D (Delete).**

   A dialog box appears, asking if you really want to delete the label definition. You do. Press Y — and it's gone.

Printing on Envelopes

For those moments when you need to print just a few addresses (or just want to look busy and kill time by feeding your printer envelopes one at a time), have WordPerfect print addresses directly on the envelopes. That way, you don't waste a sheet of valuable mailing labels for just one or two addresses.

Defining an envelope for your printer

Before you can print addresses directly on an envelope, you must tell WordPerfect what type of envelopes you intend to use.

To define an envelope type, follow these steps:

1. **Press Alt-F12.**

   WordPerfect displays a dialog box warning that you haven't yet defined an envelope for your printer.

If you don't see this box but instead find yourself in the Envelope dialog box, you're done! Skip ahead to the following section, "Printing an envelope for your printer."

If, instead of seeing this box, you find yourself in the Envelope dialog box, but you know that you still need to create a new envelope size — say, for your sister's wedding — press Shift-F1, E (Envelope Size), C (Create). You're now ready for Step 2.

2. **Press Enter.**

   The Paper Size/Type dialog box appears.

3. **Highlight the envelope type you want to use and press Enter.**

   You'll probably see the word `Envelope` in there somewhere. Highlight it and press Enter. The Create Paper Size/Type dialog box appears.

4. **Type a name for your envelope definition and press Enter.**

   For example, type **My Envelopes**.

5. **Press S (Paper Size).**

   Select an envelope size from the Paper Size list. If you don't see what you want, press O (Other) and manually enter the dimensions. Press Enter to return to the Create Paper/Size Type dialog box.

6. **Press Home, F7.**

   Your new paper size is saved.

To use your envelope, press E (Envelope Size) in the Envelope dialog box and select your envelope from the list.

Creating funky envelope formats is useful but requires patience. My wife actually used WordPerfect to address the envelopes for our wedding invitations. It took a good ten tries before we got the envelope definition and the position of the text right.

Printing an envelope for your printer

After you define an envelope for your printer, you can start printing. To print addresses on an envelope, follow these steps:

1. **Press Alt-F12.**

   The Envelope dialog box appears.

2. **Press R (Return Address).**

   Type the return address and press F7 after you're done.

3. **Press M (Mailing Address).**

   Type the mailing address and press F7 after you're done.

4. **Press B (Bar Code).**

5. **Type the mailing address ZIP code and press Enter twice.**

   WordPerfect displays the mailing address on-screen.

   This step creates *POSTNET bar codes* — those funny little vertical bars that you see on some envelopes. Supposedly, they help the Post Office sort and deliver mail faster (yeah, right). If you don't believe in fairies, or if you don't do many mass mailing (and thus don't need the U.S. Postal discount for using POSTNET codes), you can skip Step 5.

   TIP: If you press Shift-F7, V you can see a print preview of what your envelope will look like before you actually print it.

6. **Insert an envelope in your printer.**

7. **Press Shift-F7 and Enter to print the address on the envelope.**

   Your printer may beg for the envelope. Some printers beep. Some printers flash "Feed me!" messages on-screen.

TIP: The heat of many laser printers unfortunately tends to glue envelopes shut. Believe it or not, however, you can stuff about a dozen envelopes into a microwave oven, spread them out so that the gummed surfaces aren't touching anything, and "nuke" them for one minute. This dries up the glue so that the envelopes don't glue themselves shut going through a laser printer.

Chapter 25

Using Bookmarks and Hypertext

In This Chapter

- Getting around with bookmarks
- Using QuickMarks
- Using the automatic bookmark
- Jumping from here to there with hypertext
- Adding hypertext buttons

Feeling a little lost? Can't get to the part of the document that you want without an inordinate amount of futzing around? WordPerfect's bookmarks to the rescue. They make moving from where you are to where you want to be as easy as, well, using a bookmark to find your place in a printed book.

WordPerfect's bookmarks are even more helpful than your chewing gum wrapper bookmark, because you can have as many bookmarks as your document has points of interest. And if you think bookmarks can help you shuttle around your document quickly, wait until you see what hypertext can do. It's like bookmarks on steroids.

Getting Around with Bookmarks

Before WordPerfect 6 arrived, I used to type `xxx` at each place in my document I thought I might want to get back to later. For example, If I thought a paragraph might need polishing later, I'd end it with `xxx`. When I wanted to find `xxx`, I'd use the search feature (F2) and search for the next occurrence of `xxx`.

The problem was, I had to remember to remove every `xxx` before printing. Also, there was no way to know which particular `xxx` I wanted to get to. Not a perfect system, to say the least.

WordPerfect's bookmarks let you mark all the important parts of your document, assigning each a descriptive name so that you can easily find the one you want. Best of all, because bookmarks don't appear in your document, you don't have to go on a search-and-destroy mission for every nasty little `xxx` before you print.

To add a bookmark to your document, follow these steps:

1. **Move your cursor to the place in your document that you want to mark with a bookmark.**
2. **Press Shift-F12.**

   The Bookmark dialog box appears.
3. **Press C (Create).**

   The Create Bookmark dialog box appears, as shown in Figure 25-1.

Figure 25-1: The Create Bookmark dialog box.

4. **Press Enter to accept the name that appears in the Bookmark Name text box or type the descriptive name of your choice and then press Enter.**

   This returns you to your document. A [Bookmark] code appears in Reveal Codes, which you can see by pressing F11.

- WordPerfect uses the text to the right of the cursor to suggest a bookmark name in the Bookmark Name text box of the Create Bookmark dialog box. Up to 38 characters can be used, or all the text to the end of the line, if that is fewer than 38 characters.
- If you block a word or phrase before creating a bookmark, WordPerfect suggests the blocked text as the bookmark name. You can still, of course, replace the suggested name with one that is more to your liking.
- You can use bookmarks to mark any portion of your document, not just text. A bookmark can mark a graphic, a table, or anything that you've managed to stuff into your document.
- A bookmark that you create for blocked text inserts a bookmark code at both ends of the blocked text. If there is no blocked text, a single bookmark code is inserted at the point of the cursor.
- You can see the name of the bookmark by placing the cursor on the code in Reveal Codes. Refer to Chapter 2.

Finding a bookmark

You don't have to go digging around in Reveal Codes to find the bookmarks that you scattered throughout your document. WordPerfect is quite happy to do the searching for you.

To find the bookmark that you're looking for, follow these steps:

1. **Press Shift-F12.**

   The Bookmark dialog box, listing all the bookmarks in the current document, appears, as shown in Figure 25-2.

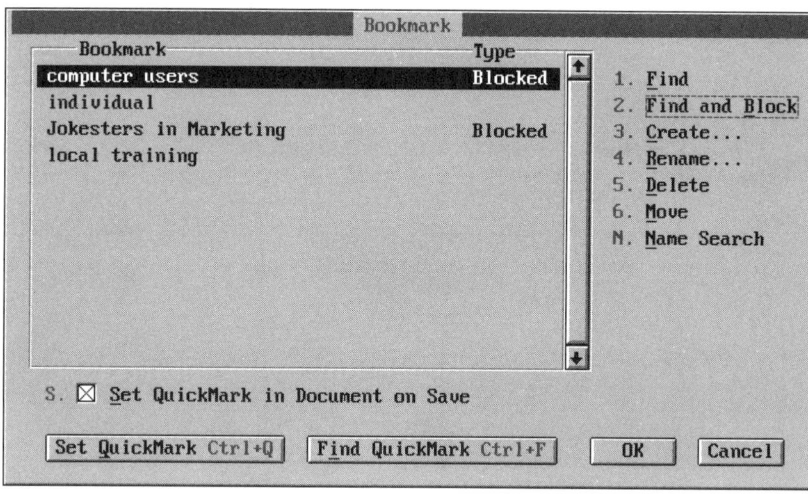

Figure 25-2: The Bookmark dialog box.

2. **Use the up- and down-arrow keys to highlight the bookmark that you want to get to and press Enter.**

   The cursor is now at the point of the bookmark that you highlighted.

- In addition to the names of the bookmarks, the list of bookmarks in the bookmark dialog shows the type of each bookmark, whether it was created from blocked text or from a single cursor location.
- An advantage of creating bookmarks with blocked text is that when you tell WordPerfect to go to that bookmark, the text is blocked.
- If you want to go to the beginning of a blocked-type bookmark without having WordPerfect block it, highlight the bookmark name in the Bookmark dialog box and press F (Find).

- You can rename a bookmark to give a more descriptive name by highlighting its name in the Bookmark dialog box and then pressing R (Rename). Enter a new name in the Rename Bookmark dialog box and press Enter.
- You can delete a bookmark by just deleting the bookmark code in Reveal Codes or by highlighting the bookmark name in the Bookmark dialog box and pressing D (Delete), Y.

Using QuickMarks

If you just need a temporary placeholder — something that you can jump back to and don't need to name — QuickMark fills the bill. You set a QuickMark and later zip to it from another part of the document without messing with dialog boxes, bookmark names, or any of the other normal bookmark nonsense.

To set a QuickMark, follow these steps:

1. **Position your cursor where you want to place a QuickMark.**
2. **Press Ctrl-Q.**

   A bookmark code appears in Reveal Codes. If you highlight the code, you'll see the name of this bookmark is `QuickMark`. To move to your QuickMark, just press Ctrl-F.

- You can have only one QuickMark in a document. If you try to set a second QuickMark, the first QuickMark is deleted.
- You can block text before setting a QuickMark. However, when you press Ctrl-F to move to the QuickMark, the cursor just goes to the beginning of the marked text. If you want the QuickMark text blocked when found, press Shift-F12, highlight QuickMark, and press Enter.
- A QuickMark is automatically set at the cursor location when you save your document. If you want to pick up where you left off the next time that you open a document, press Ctrl-F. The automatic QuickMark feature can be turned off by pressing Shift-F12, S (Set QuickMark in Document on Save) to remove the check in the check box.

Jumping from Here to There with Hypertext

Don't you just hate all the new terms the techno-dweebs come up with to describe technological concepts? *Interactivity*. Whaaaat? *Multimedia*. Huh? *The Information Superhighway*. Oh puh-lease! Well, *hypertext* is just a fancy-schmancy term for linking one part of a document to another so that you can instantly jump from one place to another.

Sounds kinda like bookmarks, doesn't it? Hypertext does have some things in common with bookmarks. In fact, you generally use bookmarks to tell WordPerfect where to jump to from the hypertext. The main difference is that hypertext jumps are set up in advance. You always jump to the same *target* text from a particular piece of hypertext.

So, what good is this hypertext stuff, anyway? It's usually most useful when you're creating documents for other people to use. You can use hypertext as a sort of customized help system.

Suppose that you're creating a document that explains the benefits program for all the new employees in your department. Instead of explaining each new piece of terminology when you come to it in the document, the new guy or gal could use hypertext and simply click the term to automatically jump to a definition.

To create hypertext links that jump to bookmarks in the same document, follow these steps:

1. **Create the bookmarks that you'll want to jump to in your document.**
2. **Block the text that you want to use as a hypertext link.**
3. **Press Alt-F5.**

   The Mark Text dialog box appears.
4. **Press H (Hypertext).**

   The Hypertext dialog box appears, as shown in Figure 25-3.

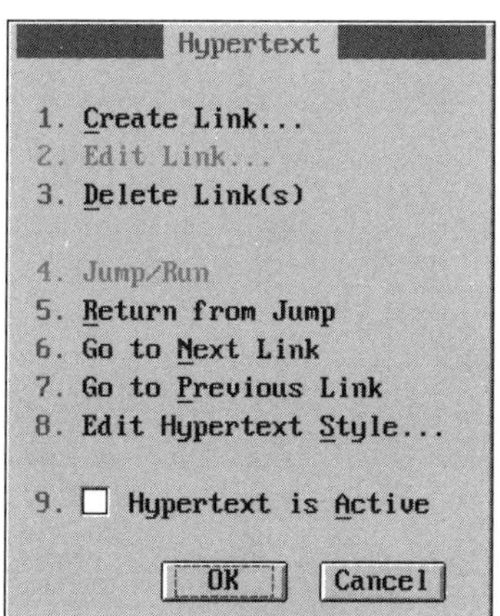

Figure 25-3: The Hypertext dialog box.

5. **Press A (Hypertext is Active).**

   This puts an X in the Hypertext is Active check box so that the Hypertext links will operate.

6. **Press C (Create Link).**

   The Create Hypertext Link dialog box appears, as shown in Figure 25-4.

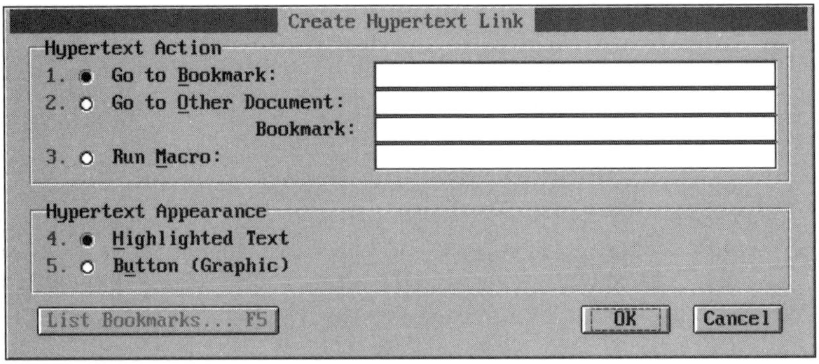

Figure 25-4: The Create Hypertext Link dialog box.

7. **Press B (Go to Bookmark).**
8. **Press F5.**

   The Hypertext Link to Bookmark appears, listing the bookmarks in the current document.

9. **Use the up- and down-arrow keys to highlight the bookmark that you want to link to and press Enter twice.**

   The hypertext link appears in your document as bold and underlined text. Hypertext Begin and Hypertext End codes appear at the beginning and end of the text in Reveal Codes.

   To jump from the hypertext to the target bookmark, click the hypertext with the mouse or position the cursor on the hypertext and press Enter.

MOUSE

- Although you can certainly use hypertext without a mouse, this is one WordPerfect feature that really cries out for rodent power. It's much easier to click hypertext than to position your cursor on it and press Enter.

TIP

- You can make your highlighted text look any way that you want by altering the hypertext style. Press Alt-F5, H (Hypertext), S (Edit Hypertext Style). Edit the codes in the Hypertext Style dialog box as you would any other style. If this style stuff is baffling you, check out Chapter 11.
- Instead of displaying the hypertext in your document as highlighted text (normally bold and underlined), you can display it as a graphical button, as shown in Figure 25-5. To display hypertext as a button, press U (Button Graphic) in the Create Hypertext Link dialog box (Alt-F5, H, C). You can jump to the target by clicking the button or positioning the cursor just to the left of the button and pressing Enter.

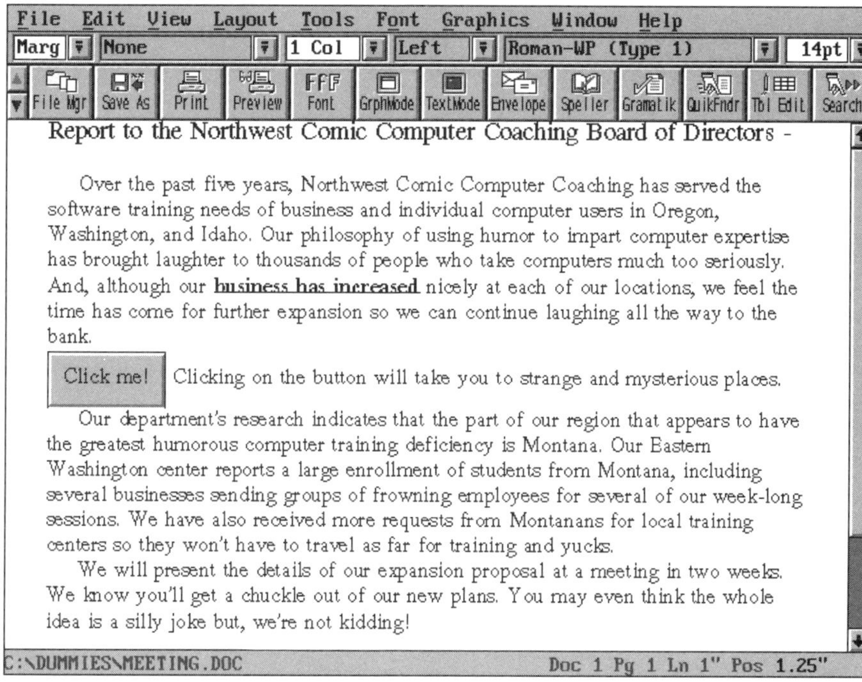

Figure 25-5: This document has highlighted and button hypertext.

- Hypertext buttons appear correctly in only Graphics or Page mode. If you're in Text mode, the hypertext button appears as a single character-sized rectangle with no text. Yuck!
- You can return to the hypertext from the bookmark that you jumped to by pressing Alt-F5, H (Hypertext), R (Return from Jump).
- If you need to edit a hypertext link — for example, to change the bookmark or document the hypertext is linked to — press Alt-F5, H, E (Edit Link) and make the appropriate changes in the Edit Hypertext Link dialog box.
- You don't have to use hypertext for jumping just to text targets. The target can also be a graphic, a table, or just about anything else. As long as your target has a bookmark, you're all set.
- In addition to jumping to bookmarks in the same document, you can jump to bookmarks within other documents, or just jump to another document. To jump to another document, press O (Go to Other Document) in the Create Hypertext Link dialog box. Enter the name of the other document in the text box. If you want to jump to a particular bookmark in the other document, enter the name of the bookmark in the Bookmark text box.
- When you jump to another document, WordPerfect closes the first document. Be sure to save the document if you've made any changes to it, or the changes will be lost. You can return to the document containing the hypertext by pressing Alt-F5, H, R, but that won't bring back unsaved changes.

TECHNICAL STUFF

Hypertext and macros

Instead of using hypertext to jump to a new location, you can really automate things by having your hypertext run a macro. This is useful, for example, if you want to print the definition of the hypertext term and then automatically return the cursor to the original location.

To run a macro from hypertext, press M (Run Macro) in the Create Hypertext Link dialog box (Alt-F5, H, C) and enter the name of the macro in the Run Macro text box. You can get yourself up to speed on what macros are and how to make them do tricks for you by checking out Chapter 16.

Chapter 26

WordPerfect's Grab Bag of Utilities

In This Chapter

- Using that wacky installation program (again)
- Converting macros from WordPerfect 5.1 to WordPerfect 6.0
- Converting alien file formats to WordPerfect
- Using the WordPerfect shell
- Using the WordPerfect editor
- Before you call WordPerfect's technical support

In an effort to give you more value for your money (and justify its $495 retail price tag), WordPerfect didn't just pack a word processor in the latest package of WordPerfect for DOS — they actually loaded it down with a fistful of utility programs.

After you know that these utility programs exist and how to use them, you may find that they make WordPerfect just a little bit easier (or at least more tolerable) to use.

Using That Wacky Installation Program (Again)

The first time that you installed WordPerfect, you had to stick the Master Disk 1 in your computer, type **INSTALL**, and press Enter.

Then the installation guided you through various menu options that you probably didn't care about, prompting you to insert a new disk periodically. Eventually, the installation program ended, and that was the last time that you needed the installation program.

Until now.

You have to run the installation program all over again any time that you add (or remove) an accessory to your computer, such as a sound card or fax board, or if you want to customize WordPerfect to work in another language.

To run the installation program again, follow these steps:

1. **Exit out of WordPerfect if you're using it now.**

   The DOS prompt appears, all ugly and gross.

   If the DOS prompt doesn't appear, and you see a menu system or Microsoft Windows, then quit that environment as well. Okay, you don't really have to quit; you can run a "DOS shell" from within your menu system or Windows. The point is that you shouldn't be running WordPerfect and the Install program at the same time.

2. **Type Install and press Enter.**

   The WordPerfect Installation Screen appears and asks whether you see red, green, and blue boxes.

3. **Press Y if you do or N if you don't see different colored boxes.**

   The WordPerfect 6.0 Installation dialog box appears.

4a. **Press D (Device Files) to install new devices.**

   This is how you set up WordPerfect to work with such goodies as fax boards, graphics cards, or sound boards, or to install a new printer driver.

4b. **Press G (Graphics Fonts) to add more fonts to WordPerfect.**

4c. **Press L (Additional Language) to customize WordPerfect to work in another language.**

   WordPerfect will prompt you to stick one or more of the original master disks into your computer.

5. **Press E (Exit) when you're done.**

   Or if you're not done, you can continue to select more options in Step 4.

6. **Press Y to quit the installation program.**

TIP

- No, selecting another language doesn't mean WordPerfect will teach you French or anything. It just means that special characters for that language will be available to you from your keyboard.
- Option 5 (Update) allows you to quickly update your copy of WordPerfect to a newer version.
- No need to bother with the first three options, which you originally used to set up WordPerfect.

Converting Macros from WordPerfect 5.1 to WordPerfect 6.0

If you have any macros designed for WordPerfect 5.1, guess what? You can't use them in WordPerfect 6.0 until you convert them into WordPerfect 6.0 format. I bemoaned this fact extensively in Part III of this book.

Now before you rail against WordPerfect for this callous disregard toward previous loyal customers, there's a reason for this: WordPerfect 5.1 macros simply recorded actual keystrokes. As a result, when you study a complicated WordPerfect 5.1 macro, you might have no idea what commands all these keystrokes are supposed to do, not to mention the fact that a few keystrokes changed between version 5.1 and 6.0 (Cancel, Repeat, and Help, for example).

So, if you created a WordPerfect 5.1 macro to turn italics on or off by pressing Alt-I, the macro might look like this:

```
{DISPLAY OFF}{FONT}ai
```

This WordPerfect 5.1 macro tells WordPerfect to pull down the Font menu, choose the Appearance command, and choose Italics. Real easy to understand, huh?

In comparison, WordPerfect 6.0 macros are a complete programming language. The same macro to turn italics on or off by pressing Alt-I would look like this:

```
DISPLAY(OFF!) AttributeAppearanceToggle(Italics!)
```

This macro tells WordPerfect to forget about menus and just turn on italics. (It also proves that, in the future, spaces between words will be optional in English.)

To convert WordPerfect 5.1 macros into WordPerfect 6.0 format, you have to run a special utility program called MCV.EXE. To see all the options for using the MCV.EXE program, type the following at a DOS prompt:

```
MCV /H
```

The list will be displayed on-screen. La-di-da.

To run the MCV.EXE program, follow these steps:

1. **Bail out of WordPerfect.**

   Save your documents and get WordPerfect off the screen. The DOS prompt appears like a blazing sunrise.

2. **Type MCV and press Enter.**

   WordPerfect asks for an `Input file or pattern`. (Yikes! Were old DOS programs *always* this ugly?)

3. **Type the complete path and filename of the WordPerfect 5.1 macro that you want to convert.**

   For example, suppose that your old macros were in the C:\WP51\MACROS directory. If you wanted to convert your old Alt-I *italics* macro, you would type the following:

   ```
   C:\WP51\MACROS\ALTI.WPM.
   ```

4. **Press Enter.**

5. **WordPerfect asks for the** `Output file or path`**.**

   Type the directory where you want to store the converted macros, such as **C:\WP60\MACROS**, and press Enter.

   WordPerfect cranks away and then returns you to the DOS prompt when it's done. Inelegant. Ugly. Hey, that's DOS.

- WordPerfect automatically assumes that your macros will have a file extension of WPM, so you don't have to type this if you don't want to.
- Any time that you want to abort the macro conversion program, press Ctrl-Break and Enter.
- When the WordPerfect macro conversion program asks for an input file or pattern, you can use ? and * wildcards to convert batches of WordPerfect 5.1 macros all in one shot.
- Does this macro conversion program work 100 percent correctly? Of course not — this is the world of computers, remember? Although the conversion process is probably 90 percent accurate, complicated macros may not translate correctly. Be prepared to test your translated macros and edit them if necessary.

Converting Alien File Formats to WordPerfect

Some diehards out there insist on using word processors that most people have never heard about. In case you have to share or edit a document created by one of these oddball word processors (with names like OfficeWriter, DisplayWrite, MultiMate, and WordStar), read on to learn how to work with these files in WordPerfect.

Besides word processor files, WordPerfect can also suck in and convert graphics and spreadsheet files created by programs such as AutoCAD, Lotus 1-2-3, Quattro Pro, PC Paintbrush, and WordPerfect Graphics.

For your convenience and confusion, WordPerfect provides two ways to suck in alien file formats and convert them into normal WordPerfect 6.0 files: the slow way and the fast way.

Converting alien files (the slow way)

If you have one or two files stored in an alien format, the simplest solution is to run WordPerfect, load the alien document into WordPerfect, and then save it as an honest-to-goodness WordPerfect 6.0 file.

To load an alien file into WordPerfect, follow these steps:

1. **Press Shift-F10.**

   The Open Document dialog box appears.

2. **Type the path and filename of the alien file, such as B:\LETTER.DOC and press Enter.**

   The File Format dialog box appears. WordPerfect highlights and marks with an asterisk (*) the file format it thinks the alien file is stored in.

3. **Highlight the file format that the alien file is stored in and press Enter.**

   WordPerfect displays the complete contents of the alien file on-screen.

4. **Press F10.**

   The Save Document 1 dialog box appears.

5. **Type the new path and filename that you want to store the document in, such as C:\WP60DOCS\LETTER.WP and press Tab.**

6. **Press Enter.**

WordPerfect displays a list of all possible file formats that you can store the document in. Thus, it's possible to suck a WordStar document into WordPerfect and spit it back out as a DisplayWrite file.

7. **Highlight WordPerfect 6.0 and press Enter twice.**

   The conversion process is complete!

Converting alien files (the fast way)

If you have multiple files that you want to convert from one alien format into WordPerfect 6.0, loading each file and saving it can be tedious. Unless you have an assistant earning minimum wage just for this type of manual labor, you'll probably want a faster way to convert files.

That's why WordPerfect supplies a handy program called ConvertPerfect. To run ConvertPerfect, follow these steps:

1. **Exit WordPerfect.**

   The DOS prompt appears, creeping up like a garbage truck spinning out of control on an icy road.

2. **Type CV and press Enter.**

   The ConvertPerfect screen appears. If this is the first time that you've run the ConvertPerfect program, it asks you to type your license number. (You'll only have to do this once.)

   The ConvertPerfect dialog box appears.

3. **Press L (List Files).**

   The List Files Directory dialog box appears.

4. **Type the directory containing the files that you want to convert, such as B:\, and press Enter.**

   The List Files dialog box appears.

5. **Press Tab and Enter.**

6. **Highlight the file that you want to convert and press *.**

   WordPerfect displays a list of all possible file formats that you can store the document in. Thus, it's possible to suck a WordStar document into WordPerfect and spit it back out as a DisplayWrite file.

7. **Press I (Insert Jobs) when you're done highlighting all the files that you want to convert.**

   A dialog box appears, asking whether you want to add all marked items to the job list.

8. **Press Y (Yes).**

   The Insert List Entries dialog box appears.

9. **Type the path and filename where you want to store the first newly converted file, such as B:\NEW.WP, and press Enter twice.**

   If you're converting a batch of files, just type a different pathname. This will store the newly converted files under the same filename but in a different directory while leaving your original files untouched.

   The List Files dialog box appears again.

10. **Press Home, F7.**

    The ConvertPerfect dialog box appears again.

11. **Press C (Convert).**

    ConvertPerfect displays messages telling you that it's hard at work, converting your files. When it's done, it displays the ConvertPerfect dialog box again.

12. **Press X (Exit).**

Using the WordPerfect Shell

Because MS-DOS is the operating system that helped define the term "user-unfriendly" to most of the world, WordPerfect provides a shell program that displays your DOS programs in a menu. Rather than typing the actual DOS command to run a program, you just choose from the menu.

If you let WordPerfect's installation program install WordPerfect, you'll find the shell program in the C:\WPC60DOS directory.

Setting up the shell program for the first time

The first time that you run the shell program, it doesn't have any idea what types of programs exist on your hard disk. Fortunately, the shell program is smart enough to hunt out common programs on your hard disk and install them in a menu for you.

To set up the shell program for the first time, follow these steps:

1. **Exit WordPerfect and change to the C:\WPC60DOS directory.**

   Press Home, F7 to bail from WordPerfect, saving any files as you leave. Then type the following:

   ```
   CD \WPC60DOS
   ```

This moves you to the \WPC60DOS directory, which is on the same disk drive as WordPerfect. (You may need to change drives if the preceding command somehow doesn't work.)

2. **Type shell and press Enter.**

   The Getting Started dialog box appears.

3. **Press S (Select Programs).**

   The List Programs dialog box appears.

4. **Press F2 (Search).**

   The List Programs dialog box appears again with various programs listed, as shown in Figure 26-1.

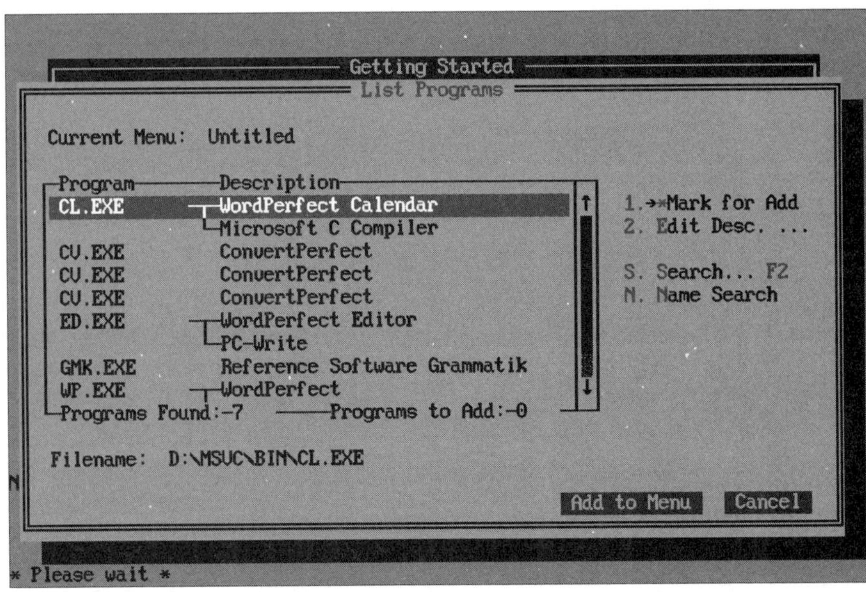

Figure 26-1: The List Programs dialog box.

5. **Highlight each file that you want to add to the shell menu and press Enter.**

6. **Press Tab and Enter.**

   The Menu Description dialog box appears.

7. **Type whatever name you want to describe your menu, such as Bob's Computer or Not Windows, and press Enter.**

   WordPerfect displays your shell menu on-screen.

8. **Highlight a menu choice and press Enter.**

   Your highlighted program appears on-screen.

9. **Press F7.**

   A dialog box appears, asking whether you want to exit.

10. **Press Y.**

The WordPerfect shell is shown in Figure 26-2.

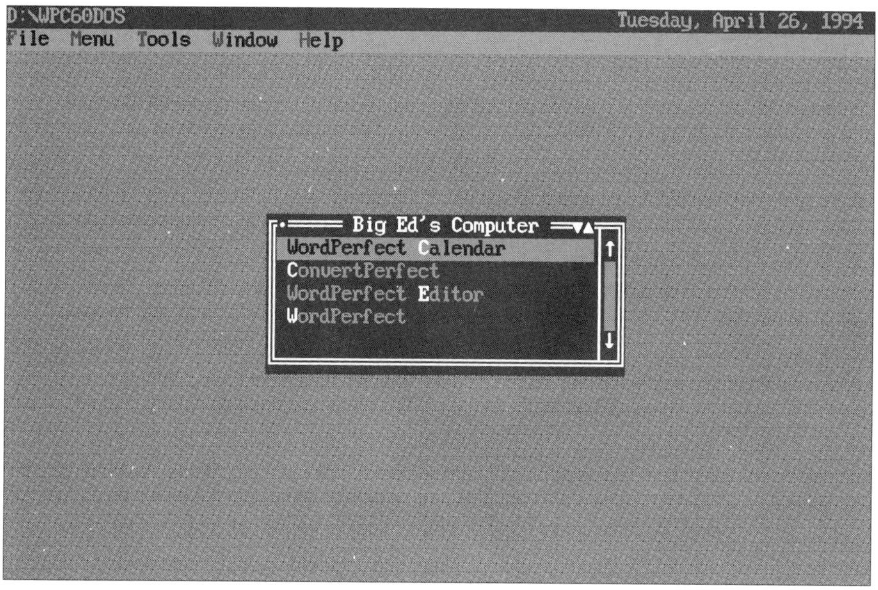

Figure 26-2: The WordPerfect shell in action.

TIP

Instant WP shell on start-up

If you want the shell program to pop up onscreen the moment that you turn on your computer, add the C:\WPC60DOS directory to your path in your AUTOEXEC.BAT file, such as the following:

```
PATH C:\;C:\WP60;C:\WPC60DOS
```

Then add the following line at the end of the AUTOEXEC.BAT file:

```
SHELL
```

Adding an item to the shell menu

The shell menu can list and run any DOS programs. If you have a favorite program that you want to display on the menu, you can add it by following these steps:

1. **Start the shell program.**

   If it doesn't start automatically, change to the \WPC60DOS directory and type **SHELL** at the DOS prompt.

2. **Press Ins (the Insert key).**

   The Add Item(s) dialog box appears.

3. **Press P (Program).**

   The Define Program dialog box appears.

4. **Press D (Description).**

   The Description dialog box appears.

5. **Type the name of the program that you want to add, such as Lotus 1-2-3, ProComm, or Leisure Suit Larry, and press Enter.**
6. **Press I (Directories).**
7. **Type the directory where the program is stored, such as C:\123, C:\COMM, or C:\GAMES and press Enter twice.**
8. **Press F (Filename).**
9. **Type the complete filename of the program, such as 123.EXE, PROCOMM.EXE, or LEISURE.EXE and press Enter.**
10. **Press Enter.**

    Your menu item appears on-screen.

- Repeat Steps 2 through 10 to add more items to the shell's menu.
- To edit an item already on the shell's menu, highlight the item that you want to edit and press F6. Make any changes in the Define Program dialog box and press Home, F7 when you're done.
- To delete an item from the shell's menu, highlight that item and press the Delete key. The Delete Item dialog box appears, where you press D (Delete) to zap the item to kingdom come.
- TIP: The shell program remembers the last item that you wiped out from the menu, allowing you to undo your delete and restore a menu item. To do so, press the Esc key in the shell to see the Undelete Item dialog box. Press U (Undelete) and the menu item reappears.
- To exit from the shell, press F7. In the Exit dialog box, press Y, and you'll be back at the DOS prompt.

Using the WordPerfect Editor

Although WordPerfect can store, retrieve, and edit ASCII files, it can be a nuisance to use WordPerfect to edit simple ASCII files, such as your AUTOEXEC.BAT or CONFIG.SYS files.

For these simple editing jobs, you can use the simpler WordPerfect Editor instead, which is stored in the C:\WPC60DOS directory as the ED.EXE file.

Loading the WordPerfect Editor

To load the WordPerfect Editor, follow these steps:

1. **Change to the C:\WPC60DOS directory.**

   At the DOS prompt, type **CD \WPC60DOS** and press Enter.

2. **Type ED and press Enter.**

   Mr. Ed appears!

   No, seriously — you'll see the Editor program, which I'd show you in a figure, but it's really boring. The only information you'll see is on the bottom line:

   ```
   DOS  File 1 Pg 1 Ln 1     Pos 1
   ```

Something like that. Ho-hum.

- All of WordPerfect's ordinary editing commands work exactly the same in the WordPerfect Editor.
- Don't expect any formatting commands to work. This is plain, boring text that you're working with here. Formatting? Ha!
- The main difference between the WordPerfect and ED is that ED doesn't do word wrapping and doesn't display a menu to choose commands from.
- The program was named ED in honor of all the men and women in the world named Ed.

Getting help within the WordPerfect Editor

To get help from the WordPerfect Editor, press the F3 key. Yes, the same F3 that displayed help for generations of WordPerfect. It also works that way in the Editor.

- Don't expect the help to be too friendly.
- Press F3 twice to see a function key layout.
- Press the spacebar to exit from the help screens.

Exiting the WordPerfect Editor

To exit from the WordPerfect Editor, press F7. Press Y to save your file or N to quit without saving.

If you pressed Y, the Editor asks for the name of the file to save. Type the filename and press Enter. The Editor asks whether you want to exit. Press Y.

Before You Call WordPerfect's Technical Support

What happens when you call WordPerfect's fabulous technical support hotline? Usually, the support technician will ask you a bunch of questions like, "What's in your AUTOEXEC.BAT file?", "How much memory does your computer have?", and "Why are you bothering me during my lunch hour?"

If you can't answer these questions, then you'll waste valuable time (yours, not theirs) trying to find the answer. So, before you call WordPerfect's technical support hotline — or if you just want to know the technical capabilities of your computer — run WordPerfect's system information program first.

This system information program simply lists the internal guts of your computer (processor type, BIOS manufacturer and date, amount of extended memory, and so forth).

To run the WordPerfect system information program, follow these steps:

1. **Exit WordPerfect.**
2. **At the DOS prompt, type WPINFO and press Enter.**

   A listing of your computer's internal guts appears on-screen, as shown in Figure 26-3.
3. **Press Enter.**

   A listing of your AUTOEXEC.BAT file contents appears on-screen.

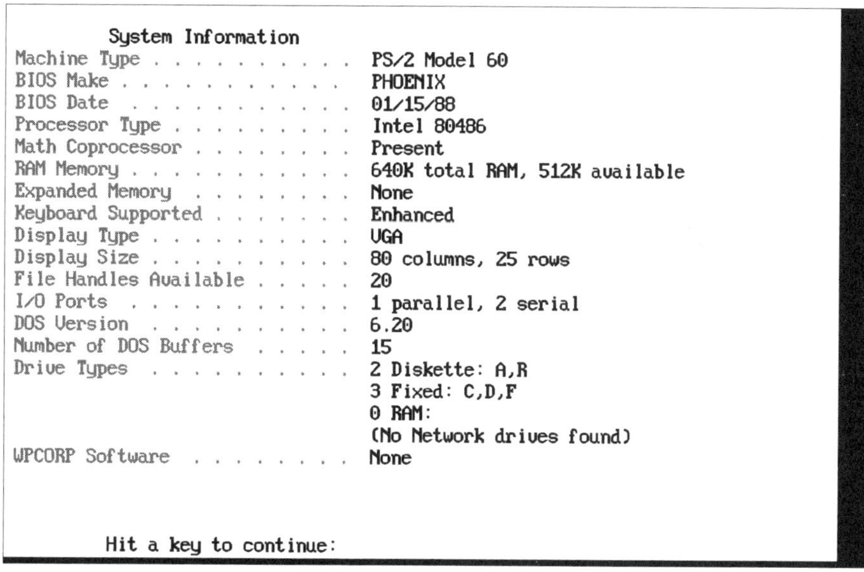

Figure 26-3: The first System Information screen.

4. **Press Enter.**

   A listing of your CONFIG.SYS file contents appears on-screen.

5. **Press Enter.**

   The boring DOS prompt appears again.

- To print out the screen images created by the WordPerfect system information program, turn on your printer and make sure it's ready to print. Press Shift-Print Screen. Zip-zip-zip, it prints.
- The info may not be that accurate. For example, in Figure 26-3 it says that I have an IBM PS/2 Model 60. In fact, I have a Gateway 2000 computer. The rest of the information is, thankfully, correct.

The 5th Wave **By Rich Tennant**

"...AND FOR THE HI-TECH MAN IN YOUR LIFE, WE HAVE THIS LOVELY PC-ON-A-ROPE."

Part V
Shortcuts and Tips Galore

The 5th Wave By Rich Tennant

"HOW'S THAT FOR FAST SCROLLING?"

In this part . . .

This last section provides a fun way to end what's been a mostly technical book. The chapters herein contain tips, warnings, and suggestions for the WordPerfect fancier. Consider this the dessert to your five-course meal. And unlike all those swanky restaurants, here you didn't need to order this soufflé before dinner.

Chapter 27

101 WordPerfect Tips

In This Chapter

- Scores of WordPerfect tips
- In no particular order

Tips galore! If ever a subject deserved a chapter full-o-tips, WordPerfect is it. Overall, I'd say that most people's biggest problem is underusing the program. (And this book proves that WordPerfect is a lot of program to underuse.) So even if you think you're stuffed to the gills by now with WordPerfect this and WordPerfect that, take the time to at least casually skim the 101 tips shown on the next few pages. You may actually pick up some nifty trick that you didn't know before.

- More WordPerfect tips definitely exist than the token 101 listed in this chapter.
- Some are tips; some are warnings; some are merely suggestions.
- He or she who obeys these tips shall be a better WordPerfect user.

1. **If a document refuses to print, try pressing Shift-F7, C.**

   This displays the Control Printer dialog box. The Message line tells you whether WordPerfect knows what's wrong, and the Action line tells you what (if anything) you can do about it.

2. **Rewrite the WordPerfect screen by pressing Ctrl-F3, R.**

   This command eliminates any excess garbage, lines up paragraphs correctly, and puts the screen back into normal WordPerfect order.

3. **Get a little friendly with your mouse.**

   You can do nearly everything in WordPerfect by using only the keyboard, and many things are more efficient and easier to do that way much of the time anyway. Some things, however, are better done by using the mouse — so for those things, use the mouse. I mean, you paid for it, didn't you?

4. **Always, always, *always* exit correctly from WordPerfect before resetting or turning off your PC.**

5. **Number your pages automatically.**

   This way, page numbers don't shift through your document every time you do a little editing.

6. **Pay attention whenever WordPerfect is talking to you.**

   WordPerfect uses many Yes/No prompts. Always read what each prompt is asking you *before* answering. If you sputter off in agreement without thinking about it, you could delete text, delete files, or perform a bad replacement operation without even realizing it. (And, no, this isn't covered under the new health care package.)

7. **Break a page right *there* by pressing Ctrl-Enter.**

   This is a hard page break and much more reliable than those flimsy Enter-Enter-Enter models.

8. **Save your document to disk before quitting.**

   Press F10.

9. **Save your document to disk before printing.**

   Press F10.

10. **Save your document to disk often and at regular intervals while working.**

    Press F10.

11. **Turn the printer on before you try to print.**

12. **Autosave your document.**

    Extra insurance for your precious documents. Press Shift-F1, E, B.

13. **Back up your work.**

    All of it. Even the stuff you don't think is really *that* important, because the moment after you realize it's been lost, it suddenly seems like the most important document you've ever worked on.

14. **Return to your previous position in a document by pressing Ctrl-Home, Ctrl-Home.**

    This is especially handy after a Search or Replace command, after a spell check, or if you're just plain lost.

15. **Go directly to a specific page in your document.**

    Press Ctrl-Home, type the page number, press the Enter key, and you're there!

16. **Customize your Button Bar.**

    If you're going to keep such things around, cluttering up the screen, they may as well be the ones you actually want there. Heck, maybe you can even find some tools that are actually useful!

17. **Wonder-ize your document by adding unique, bizarre characters.**

    Press Ctrl-W (where *W* stands for *Weird*) to insert oddball characters in your text.

18. **Date your text by pressing Shift-F5, T.**

    The date on which you do this is inserted into your document just as though you typed it there yourself.

19. **Date your text by pressing Shift-F5, C.**

    A date *code* is inserted into your document instead of the actual date. This code always displays (or prints) the current date. (Not the date you inserted the code.)

20. ***Don't* date your boss.**

    Or, for that matter, anyone with whom you work. Or have ever worked with. Or lived with. Or lived near . . .

21. **Fortify your hyphen by pressing the Home key and then the hyphen key.**

    This creates a *nonbreaking hyphen* so that words and phone numbers aren't split up at the end of a line.

22. **Press Ctrl-B to make your text bold.**

    This key combination also turns off the bold effect.

23. **Press Ctrl-I to italicize your text.**

    Press it again to turn off the effect.

24. **Press Ctrl-N to return your text to normal.**

    This switches off any and all crazy, mixed-up formatting effects you are currently using.

25. **Repeat a WordPerfect command eight (or any number of) times by pressing Ctrl-R: the Repeat command.**

    Eight is just the default number; you can set it to repeat any number of times you like.

26. **Insert a QuickMark in your document by pressing Ctrl-Q.**

    Flip back to the location of that QuickMark anytime by pressing Ctrl-F.

27. **Instantly beam to the spot in a document where you left the cursor at the close of your last WordPerfect session by pressing Ctrl-F after you open the document.**

    WordPerfect magically marks the cursor's position as you close a document.

28. **Automatically hyphenate words at the end of lines in your document by pressing Shift-F8, L, 6.**

29. **Switch on the Outlining mode by pressing Ctrl-F5, B.**

30. **Calculate math problems by using WordPerfect's math function, Alt-F7, 3.**

    But wait! Before you press those keys, you must set up rows and columns in which to manipulate your numbers. Probably better just to use your desk calculator . . . .

31. **Make a "Comment" in your text by pressing Ctrl-F7, C, C.**

    Type the comment and then press F7. Your comment is surrounded by a box on-screen but does not print.

32. **Hire yourself a coach to help train you through just about any topic.**

    Press Alt-H, O or F1, O.

33. **Dog-ear your text with numerous bookmarks by pressing Alt-F5, B, C.**

    To flip to a marked place, press Alt-F5, B, highlight the bookmark for which you're searching, and press Enter.

34. **Snazz up your document by printing it over a watermark (sorta like a subliminal graphic printed under your text).**

    Press Shift-F8, H, W.

35. **Print labels by pressing Shift-F8, P, L.**

    Hint: Start from a new document.

36. **Switch to another document window by pressing Ctrl-Y: the cycle windows shortcut key.**

    Other documents must be open (and they must be WordPerfect documents); Ctrl-Y then stops to visit each one in sequence.

37. **Cut a block of text by using the shortcut Ctrl-X. You can then paste that block someplace else by using the paste shortcut, Ctrl-V.**

38. **Copy a block of text by using the shortcut Ctrl-C. You can paste that text in another location by using the paste shortcut, Ctrl-V.**

39. **Undo just about anything you've gotten yourself into by pressing Ctrl-Z: the Undo key.**

40. **Begin blocking text by pressing Alt-F4 or F12.**

    Both shortcuts turn on the block-marking mode.

41. **Go directly to File Manager by pressing F5, Enter.**

42. **Bring up the character/font formatting menu by pressing Ctrl-F8.**

43. **Bring up the main line/page/document formatting menu by pressing Shift-F8.**

44. **Open a file by pressing Shift-F10.**

45. **Print the document on which you're currently working by pressing Shift-F7, 1.**

46. **Begin a search-and-replace mission by pressing Alt-F2.**

47. **Save your document the first time by pressing F10.**

    Subsequent times, quicksave the document by pressing Ctrl-F12. Often.

48. **Begin a basic Search mission by pressing F2.**

    Type the text for which you're searching and press F2 to send WordPerfect on its way.

49. **Spell-check your document by pressing Ctrl-F2.**

    I know it's a pain, but do it anyway.

50. **Check out just how horrific your grammar is by pressing Alt-F1, 3.**

    Ouch.

51. **Buy the highest capacity disks your computer can use and format them as soon as you open the box.**

52. **Keep printer paper, toner, and supplies handy.**

53. **Keep your desktop references within easy reach.**

    I particularly recommend Strunk and White's *Elements of Style*, and spell-checking will never replace a trusty dictionary and a thesaurus.

54. **Keep your files organized.**

55. **Label your disks.**

56. **Remember the Esc key.**

    Esc is the *cancel* key. Use it to back out of a series of dialog boxes, stop a search, quit spell-checking, or cancel any other operation about which you've become faint-of-heart.

57. **Quickly start WordPerfect with a document already open.**

    At the DOS prompt, type **WP** followed by a space and the name of the document you want to edit.

58. **Use clever, memorable filenames.**

59. **Write first; *then* edit.**

    WordPerfect tempts you with its countless formatting tools and toys. But the program works best if you write your text first and only then go back and play with it.

60. **Filenames can contain up to eight characters: letters and numbers, but no spaces, punctuation, or symbols.**

61. **You can further set your filename apart by giving it an optional three-character extension, separated from the filename by a period.**

62. **Quit WordPerfect by pressing F7: then press Y to save the document (or N to ditch it), and Y again to exit.**

63. **Use Ctrl with the up- or down-arrow key to move up or down by one paragraph.**

64. **Use Ctrl with the left- or right-arrow keys to move left or right by one word.**

65. **Pressing the minus key on the numeric keypad moves the cursor to the top of the screen. Press it a second time to move back one screenful of text.**

66. **Pressing the plus key on the numeric keypad moves the cursor to the bottom of the page. Press it again to move forward one screenful of text.**

67. **View your document in the margin-to-margin mode.**

    Open the View menu and choose Zoom. Choose Margin Width from the Zoom submenu, and you're there!

68. **Lost in your document? Get back to where you were by pressing Ctrl-Home, Ctrl-Home.**

    No need to click your heels.

69. **Overuse the keyboard.**

70. **If you become helplessly confused doing something in WordPerfect, pressing F1 summons helpful information on whatever it is that you are doing.**

71. **Obliterate an entire word at a time by pressing Ctrl-Delete or Ctrl-Backspace.**

72. **Delete everything from the cursor's position to the end of the page by pressing Ctrl-PgDn.**

    A dialog box double-checks this with you before carrying out the command.

73. **ALWAYS save a document to disk before performing any massive operation.**

    That way, if something goes terribly wrong, you can reload the document in its original form (by pressing F7, N, N) and pretend that nothing ever happened.

74. **If you need to re-mark the same block you just marked, press Alt-F4, Ctrl-Home, Ctrl-Home.**

    This works best if you do it immediately after you issued the first block command that made the block marking disappear.

75. **Use the Select command to mark a block of text.**

    Position the cursor in the middle of what you want to mark as a block; from the Edit menu, choose Select. From the Select submenu, choose to mark the sentence, paragraph, or page in which your cursor is nestled.

76. If you cut and paste a block of text but then decide that you don't want it where you moved it, be aware that the Undo command only unpastes the block — it doesn't return the block to its original position.

To move the text back to its original location, you must position the cursor there and press Ctrl-V to repaste the block.

77. Check to make sure that you've quit all programs before shutting off or resetting your PC.

78. Back up today's work.

79. Don't be too quick to press the Y key.

80. Drive slowly in icy weather.

Chains and snow tires can help get you started, but nothing makes you stop on a sheet of ice. (You wouldn't know this if you live in Southern California.)

81. Always have someone else to blame. (Remember: it's probably *never* your own fault.)

82. If a disk can't be formatted, toss it out!

I'm serious. Keeping a dead disk drawer is a waste of precious space.

83. If you have trouble remembering which is drive A and which is drive B, label them.

84. Draw yourself a picture of how paper, envelopes, or anything else goes into your printer, and tape it to the printer.

85. Keep to a regular backup schedule.

Here is my schedule: Daily, I do a work backup. Weekly, I do a "new files" backup. Monthly, I back up the entire hard drive — all 600MB of it.

86. On a cold day, wear a hat.

Heat escapes from the head, no matter how much hair you have. So if you want to keep warm, wear a hat. And always put a cap on Baby, even in the summer (to shade her eyes).

87. Take the spoon out of your iced tea before you drink it.

It could stab you in the eye.

88. Use a screen dimmer or shutdown on your monitor.

The perils of phosphor burn-in are a bit overstated with today's color monitors. Still, turning off the monitor whenever you aren't going to use it for a bit — or employing a screen-dimmer program — is a good idea.

89. WordPerfect assumes that every word with a number in it is misspelled.

To remedy this, you must get into the Tools menu's Spell command and choose 6. This shuts off number-checking.

90. If spell-check doesn't recognize a word that you know you are spelling correctly, add it to your dictionary.

When spell-check encounters it, choose 3. WordPerfect now recognizes the word in its current spelling as correct.

91. You still must read over and proof your own work, even after you go through the pains of spell- and grammar-checking your document.

Sorry, but, as amazing and advanced as WordPerfect is, your brain is still superior in many ways. Probably. Best to check through your work yourself, just in case.

92. To get a quick word count on your document, press Alt-F1.

From the menu, choose option 4.

93. If you quit WordPerfect before your printing is finished, all printing stops.

94. Weld two keyboard characters together by using the Compose command.

Press Ctrl-A and then type each of the characters you want welded.

95. To quickly change the justification in a document, press the following keys:

For left justification: Shift-F8, L, J, L, F7, F7

For center justification: Shift-F8, L, J, C, F7, F7

For right justification: Shift-F8, L, J, R, F7, F7

For full justification: Shift-F8, L, J, F, F7, F7

96. Change line spacing by pressing Shift-F8, L, S.

Enter a new line-spacing value; press Enter, F7.

97. Put a page number at the bottom center of every page in the document by pressing Home, Home, Home, up arrow. Then press Shift-F8, P, N, P, 6, Enter. Then press Home, F7.

98. Use the Suppress command to keep page numbers, headers, or footers from appearing on the first page.

Move to the first page in your document; press Shift F8, P, U; select what you want to suppress.

99. Press Home, F7 to return to your document quickly from any dialog box.

100. Paste your graphics in last.

Nothing slows WordPerfect down like a few purty pictures on-screen.

101. Read this book!

No one really expects you to learn everything you can possibly know about WordPerfect. You don't even need to know most of the things in this book. But you can make life *so much* easier if you keep it within arm's length and flip through it whenever you have a question.

Chapter 28

Solving Frustrating Formatting Problems

In This Chapter

- Dealing with widows and orphans
- Block protecting
- Conditional end of page

Looks aren't everything, but they sure can help attract attention in a hurry. To make sure your documents get the attention they deserve, it's important that your text appears inviting and easy to read, which comes about only through proper formatting and profound respect for the WordPerfect gods in Utah.

Perhaps the most frustrating problems with formatting occur when WordPerfect blindly inserts page breaks throughout your document. Normally this is fine, but sometimes a page break can chop a paragraph in half, quarters, fifths, or eighths, scattering the remnants of your prose across separate pages.

To keep your text intact across page breaks, WordPerfect gives you several formatting options:

- Eliminating single lines of text (known as widows or orphans) that appear all by themselves on an otherwise blank page.
- Block protecting a paragraph to keep those nasty page breaks from busting them in half.
- Conditional end of page, which specifies the minimum number of lines in a paragraph that can appear at the bottom of a page.

Dealing with Widows and Orphans

Widows are single lines of a paragraph that appear all by themselves at the bottom of a page, while the rest of the paragraph appears at the top of the next page.

Orphans are single lines of a paragraph that appear all by themselves at the top of a page, while the rest of the paragraph appears at the bottom of the previous page.

Like their real-life human counterparts, WordPerfect's widows and orphans evoke a sense of sadness, sympathy, and compassion among outside observers. But unlike real-life, WordPerfect widows and orphans can be ruthlessly eliminated in your document without evoking the ire of even one special-interest group.

To eliminate widows and orphans from your document, follow these steps:

1. **Press Home, Home, up arrow.**

   The cursor magically jumps to the beginning of your document.

2. **Press Shift-F8, O (Other), W (Widow/Orphan Protect).**

   This puts an X in the `Widow/Orphan Protect` box, which starts a huge, endless government program to funnel money toward . . . Wait! No, it causes any potential widow or orphan lines to be moved to the next or previous page, respectively.

3. **Press Home, F7.**

   From this point on, WordPerfect automatically prevents widows or orphans from appearing in your document.

REMEMBER

- Widows are old (typically), which means they'd appear toward the bottom of a page if you think of text as getting older toward the bottom of a page. Orphans, young ones for the most part, sit on the top of the page.
- If you press Alt-F3 to Reveal Codes, you'll see the following code at the top of your document:

```
[Wid/Orph:On]
```

TIP

- You can make Widow/Orphan protection a part of all your WordPerfect documents. Press Shift-F8, D, C. This displays the Document Initial Codes box. Press Shift-F8, O, W to activate Widow/Orphan protection. Press Home, F7 to return to the Document Initial Codes dialog box. Press F7, and then Home, F7 to quit. Now all your documents will have Widow/Orphan protection.

- Widow/Orphan Protection sounds like something an insurance agent would try to sell you.
- Studies show that having children is hereditary. Odds are that if your parents didn't have any children, you won't either.

Block Protecting

Sometimes widows and orphans are not as big a problem as having a page break ruthlessly slice a paragraph in two, placing the separate halves on different pages.

To prevent this problem from occurring, you can highlight a block of text and specifically tell WordPerfect, "Never break this text block for any reason, or I'll erase you from my hard disk and switch to Microsoft Word."

Block protecting can be particularly useful for keeping names and addresses or short lists together.

To block protect text, follow these steps:

1. **Select the paragraph you want to protect.**

   Move the cursor to the front of the text that you want to block protect. Press Alt-F4. Move the cursor to highlight the entire text block that you want to protect.

2. **Press Shift-F8, O (Other), B (Block Protect).**

   This puts an X in the `Block Protect` box, which saves the selected paragraph from any page-splitting peril.

3. **Press Home, F7.**

- You cannot block protect a text block larger than a page.
- If you press Alt-F3 to Reveal Codes, you'll see the following code at the beginning of your text block:

  ```
  [Block Pro On]
  ```

  And the following code appears at the end of your text block:

  ```
  [Block Pro Off]
  ```

Conditional End of Page

Protecting against widows and orphans simply prevents single lines of text from appearing by themselves at the top or bottom of a page. Unfortunately, protecting against widows or orphans does nothing to prevent *two* lines of a paragraph from appearing at the bottom or top of a page. Although two lines don't look as bad as a single line, this can still be ugly.

Block protecting keeps an entire text block together at all times. Unfortunately, this sometimes leaves a huge empty space at the bottom of a page, as WordPerfect slavishly moves an entire text block to the next page to prevent a page break from cutting the text block in half.

As a happy medium, WordPerfect also offers a conditional end of page feature. This feature lets you specify the minimum number of lines that can be broken apart by a page break.

For example, if you have a five-line paragraph, you can specify that at least three of those lines must appear together; otherwise, keep the entire paragraph intact.

To turn on the conditional end of page feature, follow these steps:

1. **Move the cursor to the first line of your text block.**
2. **Press Shift-F8, O (Other), C (Conditional End of Page).**
3. **Type the minimum number of lines that must be kept together and press Enter.**

   For example, press 3 to always keep three lines of a paragraph together.
4. **Press Home, F7.**

- Another trick you can try is to use Page Preview (Shift-F7, V) to see how each page looks. If you don't like having a two-page letter with even three lines of text on the last page, consider one of the following: moving in your margins; selecting a larger font size; 1.5 line spacing; or even adding a few blank lines at the start of your document.
- If you press Alt-F3 to Reveal Codes, you'll see the following code at the beginning of your text block:

```
[Cond1 EOP:x]
```

  where *x* is the minimum number of lines that you specified in Step 3.

"YEAH, MY PEOPLE ARE STILL GETTING HEADACHES – DANG THESE VDT SCREENS!"

Chapter 29

Sprucing It Up and Fooling Them All!

In This Chapter

- Using dot leaders
- Making bulleted lists
- Drawing pretty borders

None of the stuff in this chapter is necessary, but lots of stuff in life isn't necessary (ice cream, cookies, banana splits, and so on) but we like them because they make life more enjoyable.

If you're tired of cranking out the same old, tired-looking WordPerfect documents, here's your chance to spruce them up with fancy effects that won't make your writing any easier to read, but you can at least dazzle your friends with your WordPerfect competence.

Using Dot Leaders

Dot leaders are little dots (obviously) that WordPerfect automatically inserts between your text and the left margin. The main reason to use dot leaders is for aesthetic purposes only — no one really cares if you use them or not.

For example, you could use dot leaders to create items like the following:

The Every Mall in America Directory

Food That's 90% Grease .... 2nd floor

Over-Priced Clothing .... 1st floor

Over-Specialized Store .... 1st floor

Size 7 Clothes Only .... 2nd floor

Rip-Off Shoe Store .... 2nd floor

Toys That Kids Won't Play With .... 3rd floor

Mall Rat Arcade .... Basement

- When using dot leaders, you may choose to have text appear ragged left or flush right.
- Ragged-left text appears in the middle of the screen. As you type, the text moves towards the left.
- Flush-right text appears at the right margin of the screen. As you type, the text moves towards the right.

Creating ragged-left text dot leaders

To create dot leaders with ragged-left text, follow these steps:

1. **Move the cursor to the location in your document where you want to create dot leaders.**
2. **Press Shift-F6 twice.**

   The dot leaders appear.
3. **Type your text.**

Creating flush-right text dot leaders

To create dot leaders with flush-right text, follow these steps:

1. **Move the cursor to the location in your document where you want to create dot leaders.**
2. **Press Alt-F6 twice.**

   The dot leaders appear.
3. **Type your text.**

Making Bulleted Lists

People make lists all the time. Teachers make lists of kids who are absent, housewives or househusbands make grocery or laundry lists, even Santa Claus makes lists to keep track of who has been naughty or nice.

Creating lists can be as simple as creating separate paragraphs for each line. But for that more organized look that businesses and people with low self-esteem crave so desperately, WordPerfect has a simple way of making bulleted lists.

To create a bulleted list, follow these steps:

1. **Move the cursor to where you want to create a bulleted list.**
2. **Press Ctrl-F5, B (Begin New Outline)**

   The Outline Style List dialog box appears.
3. **Highlight** `Bullets` **and press Enter.**

   WordPerfect automatically types a bullet at the beginning of each line.
4. **Type your text and press Enter.**
5. **Repeat Step 4 until you want to quit.**
6. **Press Ctrl-F5, E (End Outline).**

Drawing Pretty Borders

Just as clothes make the man (or at least make the man look like he's not naked), borders make your document look like something special (even when it's not).

WordPerfect lets you draw borders around pages or text blocks. Borders can be in black and white or color and help emphasize the text inside.

- You can see page borders only in Page mode or by choosing the Print Preview command.
- Reserve using borders for material that really needs it. Overusing this trick is tiresome and makes use of it ineffective.

Drawing page borders

To draw a border around one or more pages, follow these steps:

1. **Move the cursor to the first page where you want borders to appear.**
2. **Press Alt-F9, O (Borders), A (Page).**

   The Create Page Border dialog box appears.
3. **Press B (Border Style).**

   The Border Styles dialog box appears.
4. **Highlight the border style you want to use and press Enter.**
5. **Press Home, F7.**

Drawing paragraph borders

To draw a border around a paragraph or text block, follow these steps:

1. **Highlight the text block that you want to surround with a border.**
2. **Press Alt-F9, O (Borders), P (Paragraph).**

   The Create Paragraph Border dialog box appears.
3. **Type B (Border Style).**

   The Border Styles dialog box appears.
4. **Highlight the border style that you want to use and press Enter.**
5. **Press Home, F7.**

Turning off borders

After you turn on page borders, WordPerfect blindly draws borders around every page from that point on. When you want to turn off borders, follow these steps:

1. **Move the cursor to where you want to turn off borders.**
2. **Press Alt-F9, O (Borders).**
3. **Type 1 to turn off paragraph borders; type 2 to turn off page borders.**
4. **Press O (Off).**

   That does it. You are automatically returned to your document without pressing Home, F7.

Editing borders

After you've created borders initially, you can edit them later to choose a new border style, fill style, or color.

Changing border styles

To change border styles, follow these steps:

1. **Move the cursor to the text block that is surrounded by a border that you want to edit.**
2. **Press Alt-F9, O (Borders).**
3. **Type 1 to edit paragraph borders; type 2 to edit page borders.**

   The Edit Paragraph or Page Border dialog box appears.
4. **Type B (Border Style).**

   The Border Styles dialog box appears.
5. **Highlight the border style that you want to use and press Enter.**
6. **Press Home, F7.**

Changing the fill style inside a border

The fill style refers to the shading inside a bordered area. Sometimes, to emphasize text, you may want to draw borders around text and then shade the text area.

To change the fill style inside a border, follow these steps:

1. **Move the cursor on the page or in the text block surrounded by a border that you want to edit.**
2. **Press Alt-F9, O (Borders).**

3a. **Type 1 to edit paragraph borders.**

3b. **Type 2 to edit page borders.**

The Edit Paragraph or Page Border dialog box appears.

4. **Type F (Fill Style).**

   The Fill Styles dialog box appears.
5. **Highlight the fill style that you want to use and press Enter.**
6. **Press Home, F7.**

Changing border colors

To change border colors, follow these steps:

1. **Move the cursor on the page or in the text block surrounded by the border that you want to edit.**
2. **Press Alt-F9, O (Borders).**
3. **Type 1 to edit paragraph borders; type 2 to edit page borders.**

   The Edit Paragraph or Page Border dialog box appears.
4. **Type C (Customize), O (Color).**

   The Border Line Color dialog box appears.
5. **Type C (Choose One Color For All Lines).**

   The Color Selection dialog box appears.
6. **Highlight the color that you want to use for your borders and press Enter.**
7. **Press Home, F7.**

Index

• C •

• E •

• F •

• I •

• K •

• L •

• M •

• Q •

• R •

• T •

• Z •

IDG BOOKS

Order Form

Order Center: (800) 762-2974 (8 a.m.-5 p.m., PST, weekdays) or (415) 312-0650

For Fastest Service: Photocopy This Order Form and FAX it to: (415) 358-1260

Quantity	ISBN	Title	Price	Total

Shipping & Handling Charges

Subtotal	U.S.	Canada & International	International Air Mail
Up to $20.00	Add $3.00	Add $4.00	Add $10.00
$20.01-40.00	$4.00	$5.00	$20.00
$40.01-60.00	$5.00	$6.00	$25.00
$60.01-80.00	$6.00	$8.00	$35.00
Over $80.00	$7.00	$10.00	$50.00

In U.S. and Canada, shipping is UPS ground or equivalent.
For Rush shipping call (800) 762-2974.

Subtotal

CA residents add applicable sales tax

IN and MA residents add 5% sales tax

IL residents add 6.25% sales tax

RI residents add 7% sales tax

Shipping

Total

Ship to:

Name ______________________________

Company ______________________________

Address ______________________________

City/State/Zip ______________________________

Daytime Phone ______________________________

Payment: ❑ Check to IDG Books (US Funds Only) ❑ Visa ❑ Mastercard ❑ American Express

Card# ____________________ Exp. __________ Signature ____________________

Please send this order form to: IDG Books, 155 Bovet Road, Suite 310, San Mateo, CA 94402.

Allow up to 3 weeks for delivery. Thank you!

IDG BOOKS WORLDWIDE REGISTRATION CARD

RETURN THIS REGISTRATION CARD FOR FREE CATALOG

Title of this book: MORE WORDPERFECT 6 FOR DOS FOR DUMMIES

My overall rating of this book: ❑ Very good [1] ❑ Good [2] ❑ Satisfactory [3] ❑ Fair [4] ❑ Poor [5]

How I first heard about this book:

❑ Found in bookstore; name: [6] ❑ Book review: [7]

❑ Advertisement: [8] ❑ Catalog: [9]

❑ Word of mouth; heard about book from friend, co-worker, etc.: [10] ❑ Other: [11]

What I liked most about this book:

What I would change, add, delete, etc., in future editions of this book:

Other comments:

Number of computer books I purchase in a year: ❑ 1 [12] ❑ 2-5 [13] ❑ 6-10 [14] ❑ More than 10 [15]

I would characterize my computer skills as: ❑ Beginner [16] ❑ Intermediate [17] ❑ Advanced [18] ❑ Professional [19]

I use ❑ DOS [20] ❑ Windows [21] ❑ OS/2 [22] ❑ Unix [23] ❑ Macintosh [24] ❑ Other: [25] ______ (please specify)

I would be interested in new books on the following subjects:
(please check all that apply, and use the spaces provided to identify specific software)

❑ Word processing: [26] ❑ Spreadsheets: [27]

❑ Data bases: [28] ❑ Desktop publishing: [29]

❑ File Utilities: [30] ❑ Money management: [31]

❑ Networking: [32] ❑ Programming languages: [33]

❑ Other: [34]

I use a PC at (please check all that apply): ❑ home [35] ❑ work [36] ❑ school [37] ❑ other: [38] ______

The disks I prefer to use are ❑ 5.25 [39] ❑ 3.5 [40] ❑ other: [41] ______

I have a CD ROM: ❑ yes [42] ❑ no [43]

I plan to buy or upgrade computer hardware this year: ❑ yes [44] ❑ no [45]

I plan to buy or upgrade computer software this year: ❑ yes [46] ❑ no [47]

Name: Business title: [48] Type of Business: [49]

Address (❑ home [50] ❑ work [51]/Company name:)

Street/Suite#

City [52]/State [53]/Zipcode [54]: Country [55]

❑ **I liked this book!** You may quote me by name in future IDG Books Worldwide promotional materials.

My daytime phone number is ______

IDG BOOKS

THE WORLD OF COMPUTER KNOWLEDGE

☐ **YES!**

Please keep me informed about IDG's World of Computer Knowledge.
Send me the latest IDG Books catalog.

SECRETS™

...FOR DUMMIES™
COMPUTER BOOK SERIES FROM IDG

MACWORLD MW AUTHORIZED EDITION

AUTHORIZED PC WORLD EDITION

NO POSTAGE NECESSARY IF MAILED IN THE UNITED STATES

BUSINESS REPLY MAIL

FIRST CLASS MAIL PERMIT NO. 2605 SAN MATEO, CALIFORNIA

IDG Books Worldwide
155 Bovet Road
San Mateo, CA 94402-9833